VIZ GRAPHIC

THE ALL-NEW TENCHI MUYŌ!

DOOM TIME

STORY AND ART BY
HITOSHI OKUDA

8/06

D0149898

This volume contains THE ALL-NEW TENCHI MUYÔ!
monthly comic series Part 2 #1 through #5
in their entirety.

STORY AND ART BY HITOSHI OKUDA

English Adaptation/Fred Burke
Translation/Lillian Olsen
Touch-up & Lettering/Dan Nakrosis
Cover Design/Hidemi Sahara
Graphic Design/Carolina Ugalde
Editors/Jason Thompson & Eric Searleman

Managing Editor/Annette Roman
Director of Production/Noboru Watanabe
VP of Publishing/Alvin Lu
Sr. Director of Acquisitions/Rika Inouye
VP of Sales & Marketing/Lisa Coppola
Publisher/Hyoe Narita

Printed in Canada.

Published by VIZ Media, LLC.
P.O. Box 77010
San Francisco, CA 94107

10 9 8 7 6 5 4 3 2
First printing, July 2003
Second printing, June 2005

For advertising rates or media kit,
e-mail advertising@viz.com

store.viz.com

CONTENTS

Chapter 1
DOOM TIME
3

•

Chapter 2
CONFUSION
27

•

Chapter 3
MASS CONFUSION
51

•

Chapter 4
OVERLOAD
75

•

Chapter 5
CLASS BEGINS
101

•

Chapter 6
SOWING THE SEEDS
125

•

Chapter 7
DARK WASHU
149

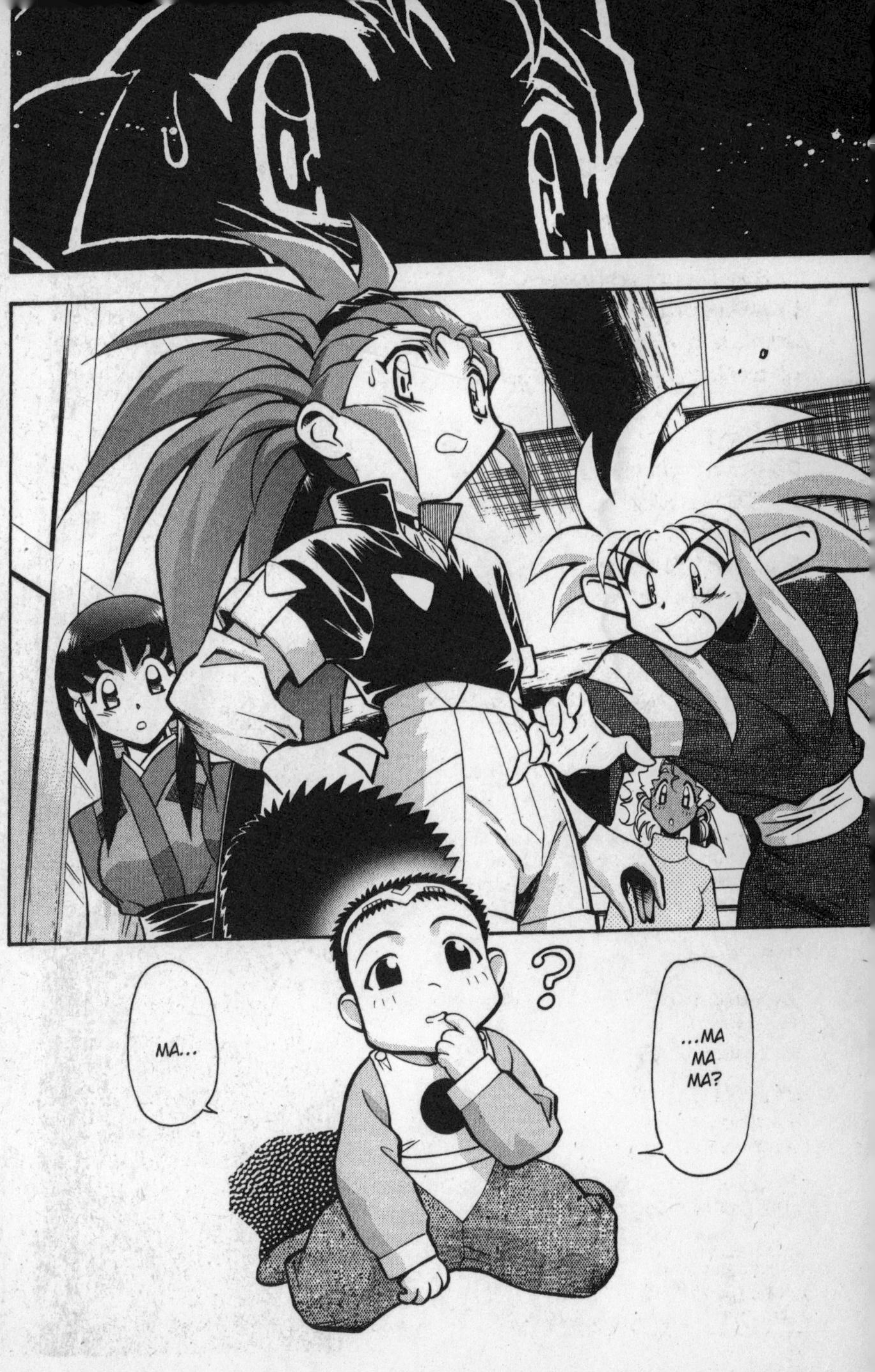
MA...
...MA
MA
MA?

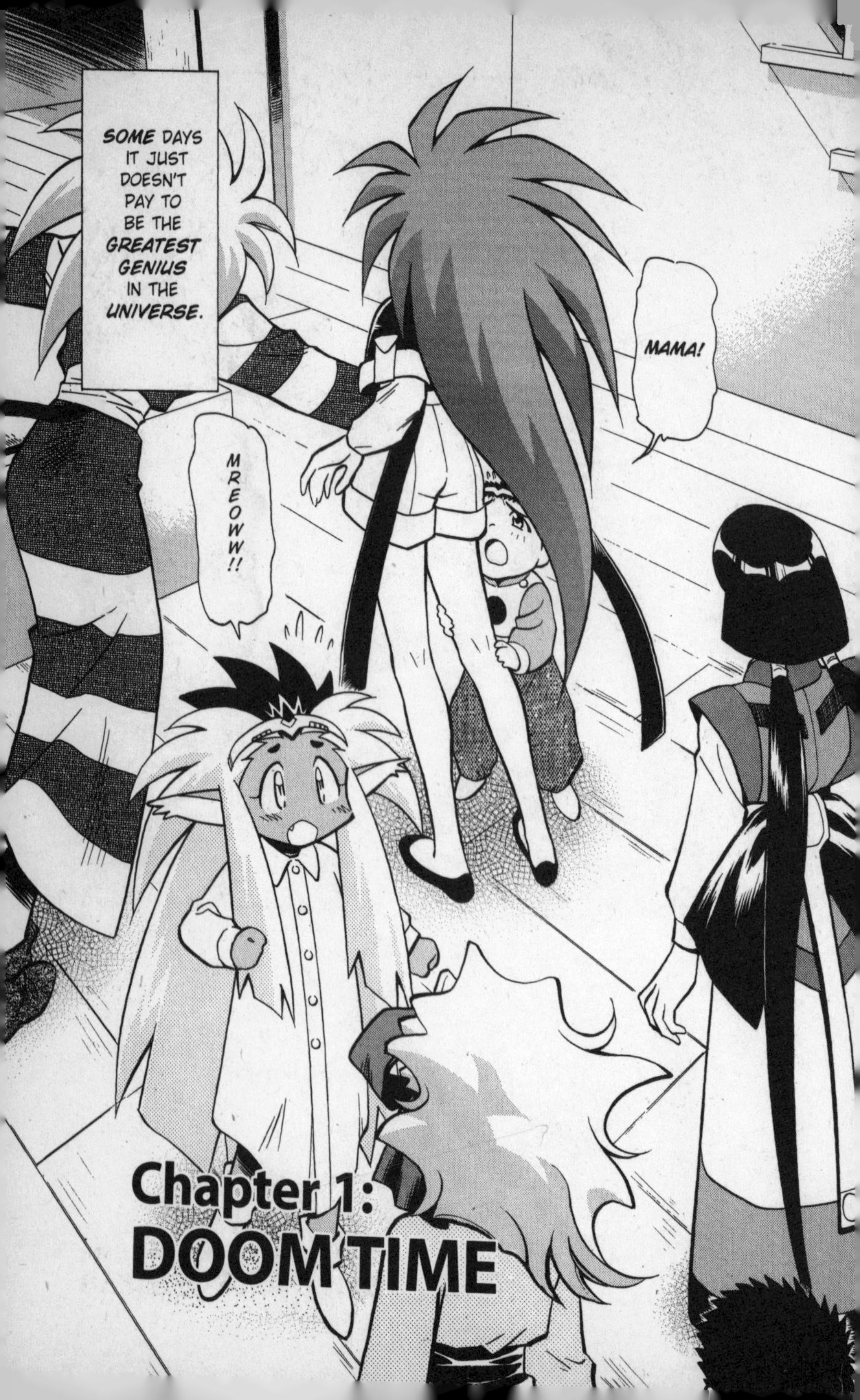
SOME DAYS IT JUST DOESN'T PAY TO BE THE GREATEST GENIUS IN THE UNIVERSE.
MAMA!
MREOWW!!
Chapter 1:
DOOM TIME

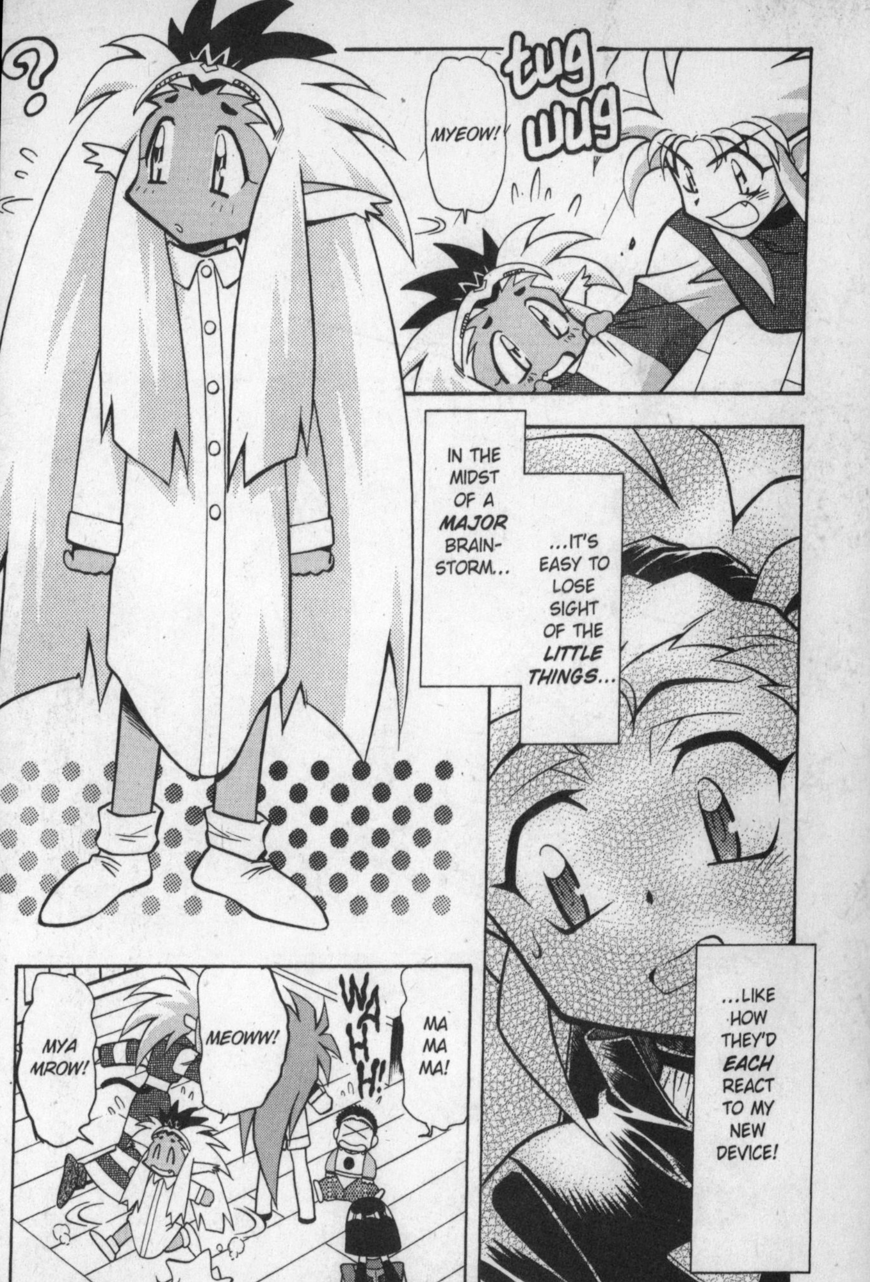
?
MYEOW!
tug wug
IN THE MIDST OF A ***MAJOR*** BRAIN-STORM...
...IT'S EASY TO LOSE SIGHT OF THE ***LITTLE THINGS...***
...LIKE HOW THEY'D ***EACH*** REACT TO MY NEW DEVICE!
MYA MROW!
MEOWW!
WAHH!!
MA MA MA!

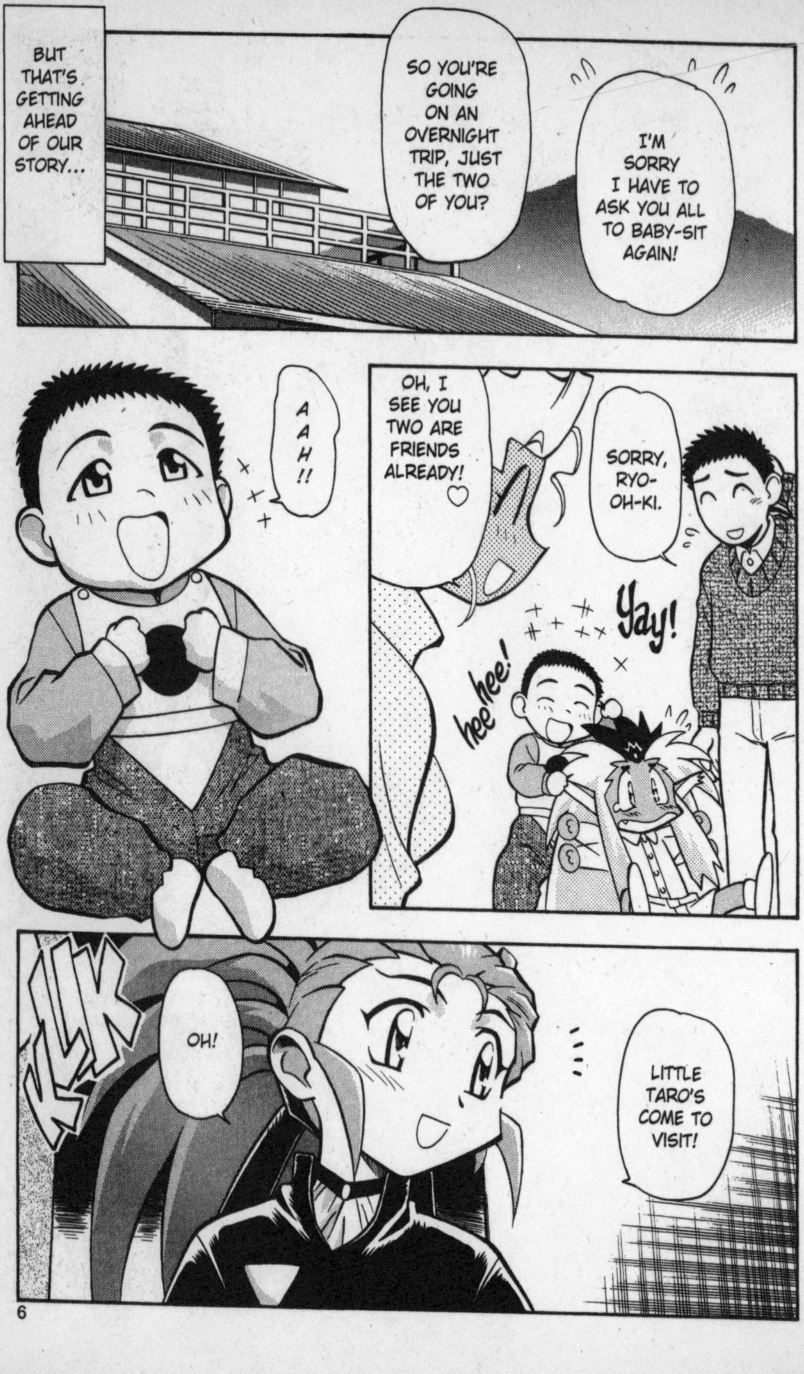
BUT THAT'S GETTING AHEAD OF OUR STORY...
SO YOU'RE GOING ON AN OVERNIGHT TRIP, JUST THE TWO OF YOU?
I'M SORRY I HAVE TO ASK YOU ALL TO BABY-SIT AGAIN!
AAH!!
OH, I SEE YOU TWO ARE FRIENDS ALREADY! ♡
SORRY, RYO-OH-KI.
Yay!
hee hee!
KLIK
OH!
LITTLE TARO'S COME TO VISIT!

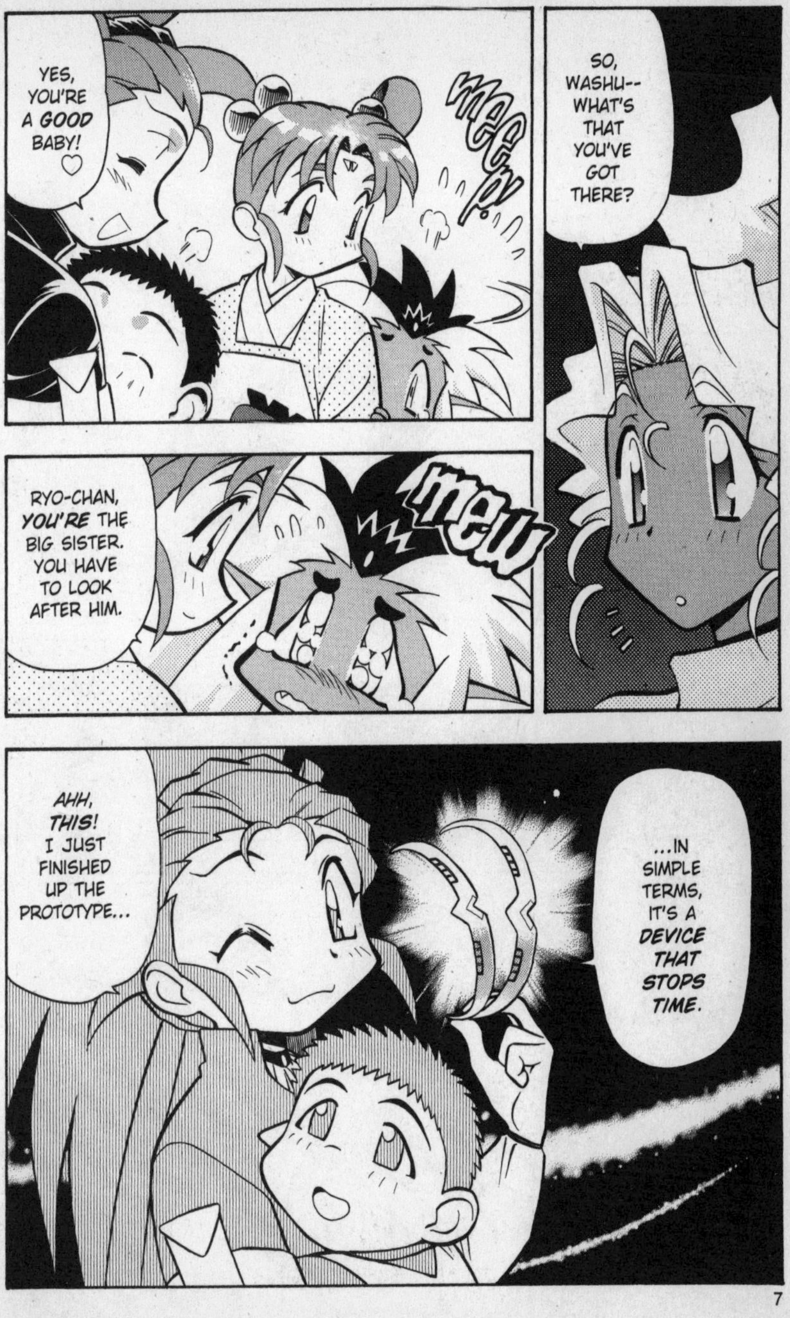
YES, YOU'RE A GOOD BABY! ♡
meep!
RYO-CHAN, YOU'RE THE BIG SISTER. YOU HAVE TO LOOK AFTER HIM.
mew
SO, WASHU--WHAT'S THAT YOU'VE GOT THERE?
AHH, THIS! I JUST FINISHED UP THE PROTOTYPE...
...IN SIMPLE TERMS, IT'S A DEVICE THAT STOPS TIME.

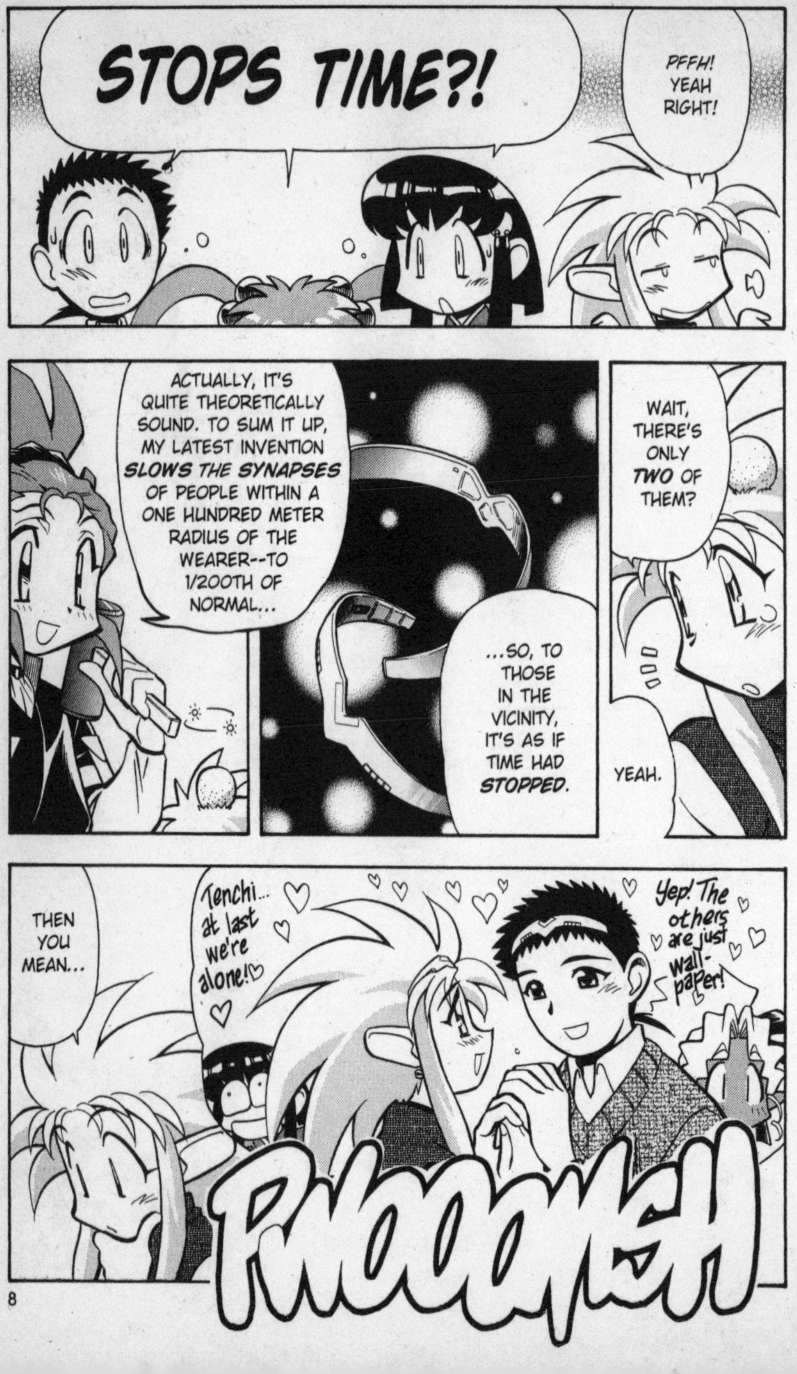
STOPS TIME?!
PFFH! YEAH RIGHT!
ACTUALLY, IT'S QUITE THEORETICALLY SOUND. TO SUM IT UP, MY LATEST INVENTION **SLOWS THE SYNAPSES** OF PEOPLE WITHIN A ONE HUNDRED METER RADIUS OF THE WEARER--TO 1/200TH OF NORMAL...
...SO, TO THOSE IN THE VICINITY, IT'S AS IF TIME HAD **STOPPED**.
WAIT, THERE'S ONLY **TWO** OF THEM?
YEAH.
THEN YOU MEAN...
Tenchi... at last we're alone!♡
Yep! The others are just wall-paper!
PHOOOOOSH

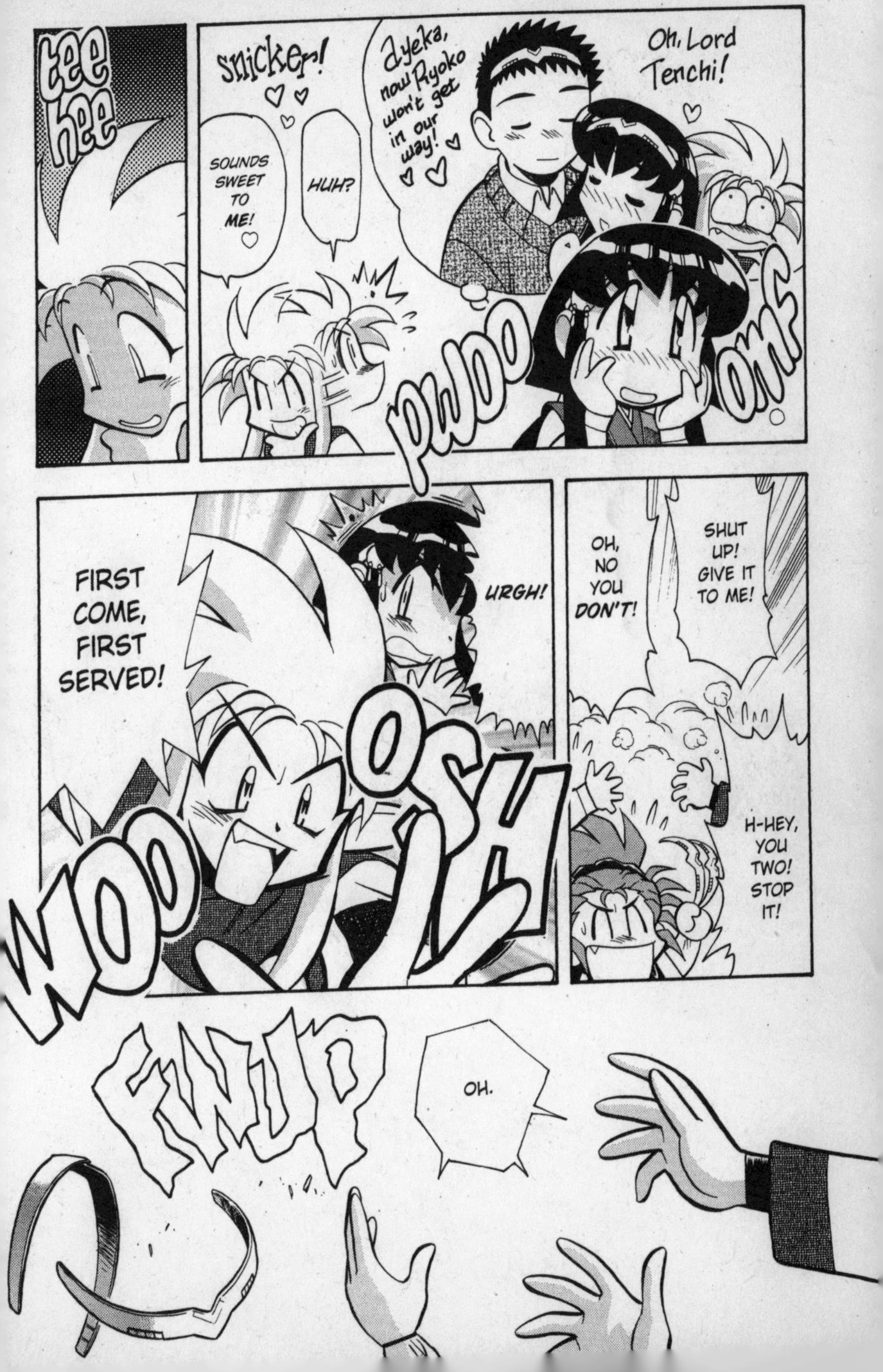

tee hee
snicker!
SOUNDS SWEET TO ME!
HUH?
Ayeka, now Ryoko won't get in our way!
Oh, Lord Tenchi!
PWOOOMF
FIRST COME, FIRST SERVED!
URGH!
WOOOSH
OH, NO YOU DON'T!
SHUT UP! GIVE IT TO ME!
H-HEY, YOU TWO! STOP IT!
FWIP
OH.

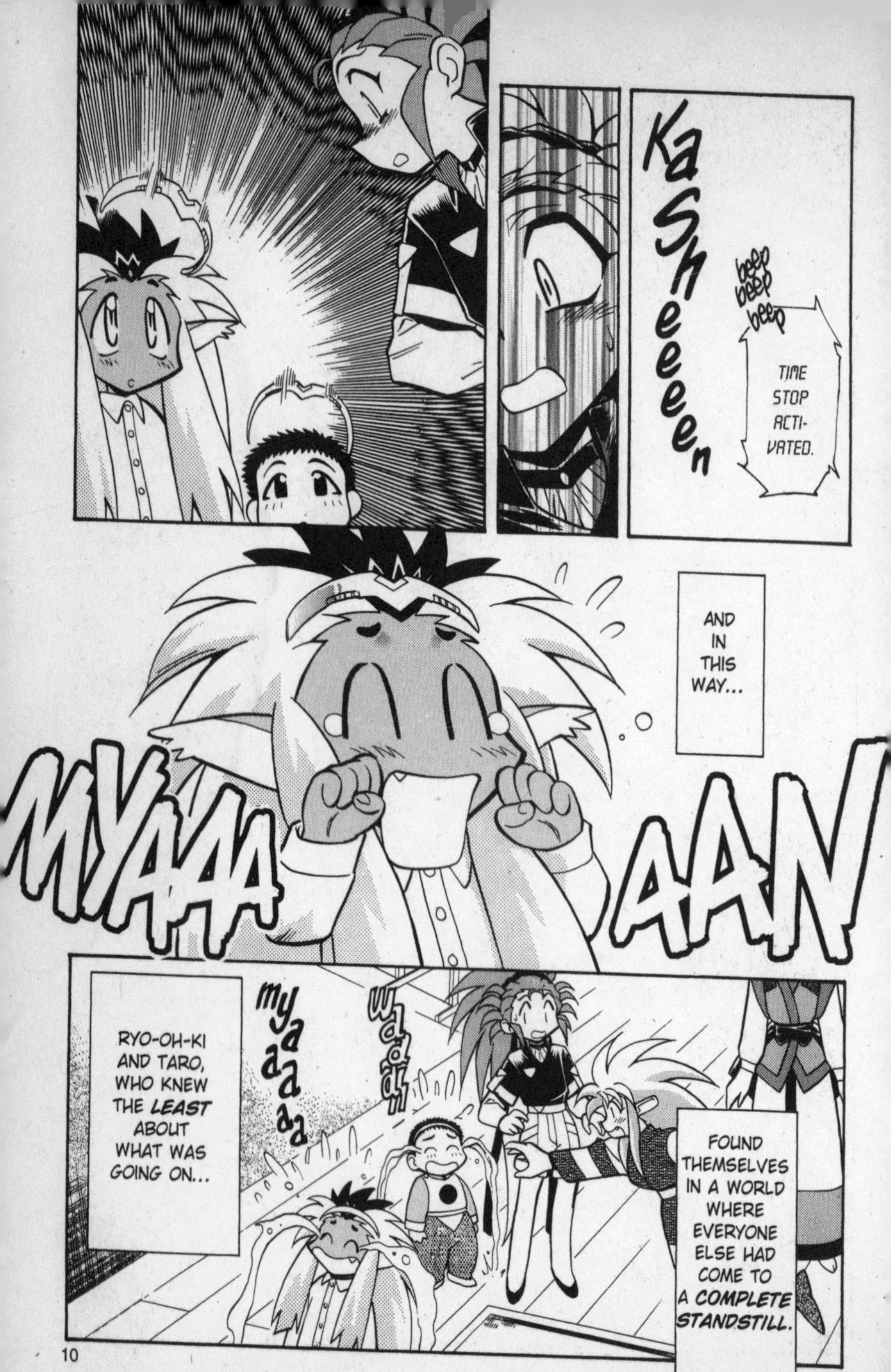
KaSheeeeen
beep beep beep
TIME STOP ACTI-VATED.
AND IN THIS WAY...
MYAAAAAN
RYO-OH-KI AND TARO, WHO KNEW THE *LEAST* ABOUT WHAT WAS GOING ON...
myaaaaaa
waaah
FOUND THEMSELVES IN A WORLD WHERE EVERYONE ELSE HAD COME TO A ***COMPLETE STANDSTILL.***

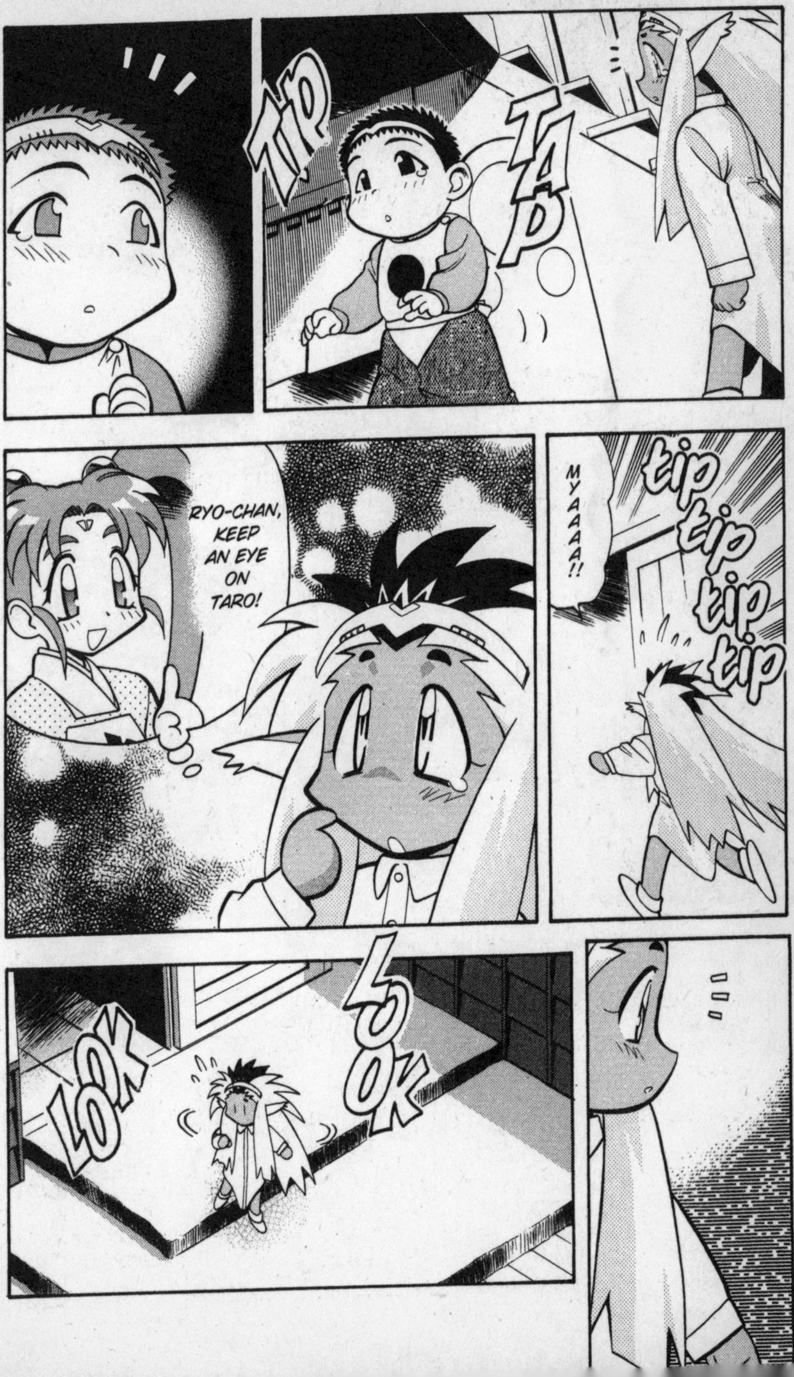
TIP
TAP
RYO-CHAN, KEEP AN EYE ON TARO!
MYAAAAA!!
tip tip tip tip
LOOK
LOOK

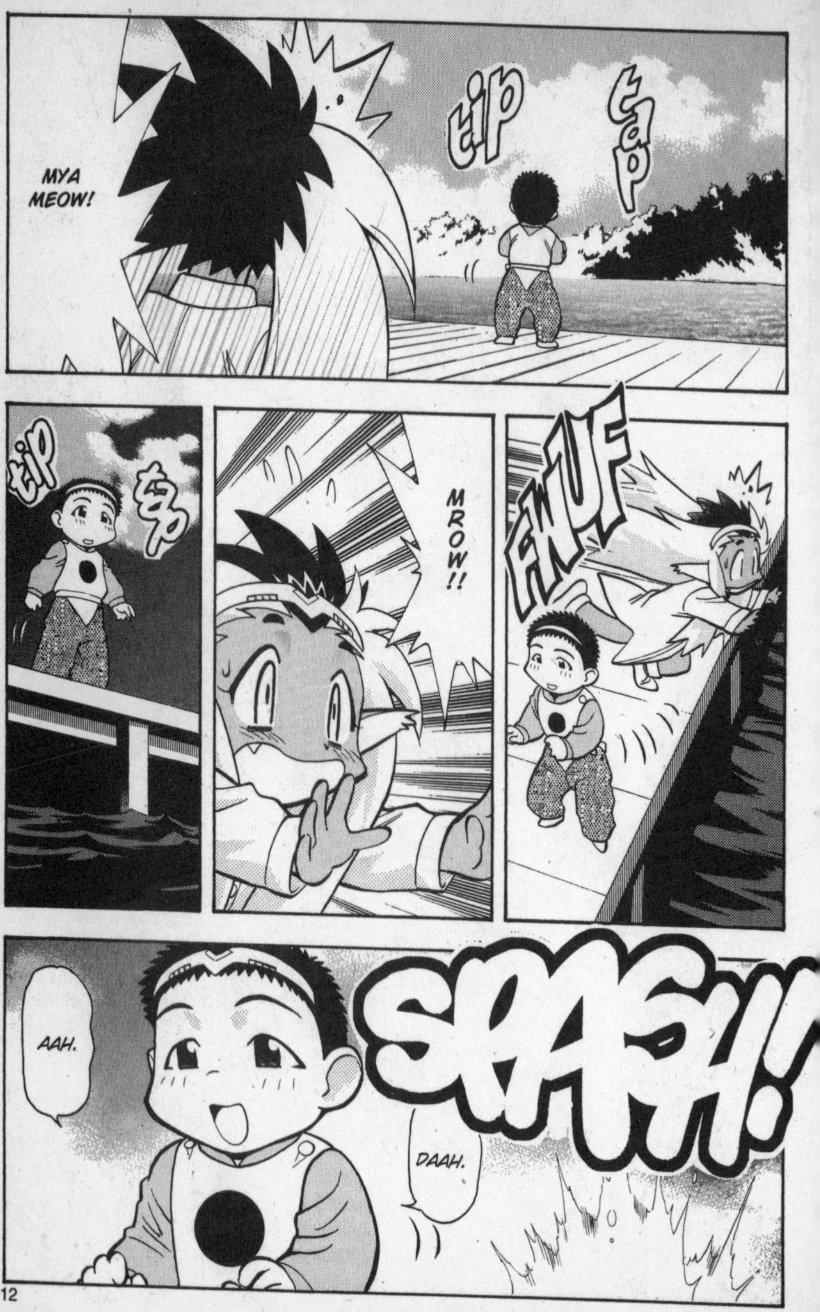
MYA MEOW!
tip
tap
tip
tap
MROW!!
FWUF
AAH.
SPASH!
DAAH.

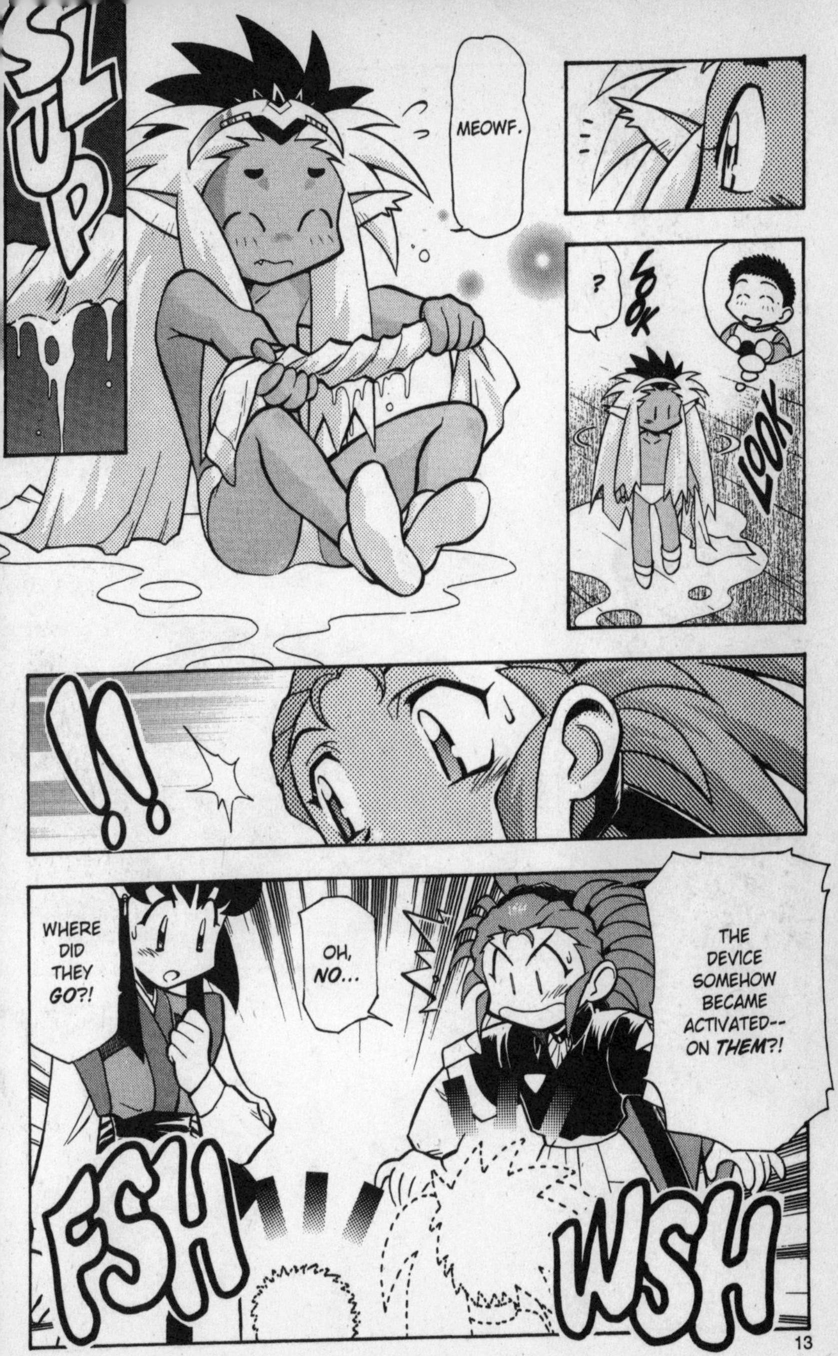
SLURP
MEOWF.
?
LOOK
LOOK
!!
WHERE DID THEY *GO*?!
OH, *NO*...
THE DEVICE SOMEHOW BECAME ACTIVATED-- ON *THEM*?!
FSH
WSH

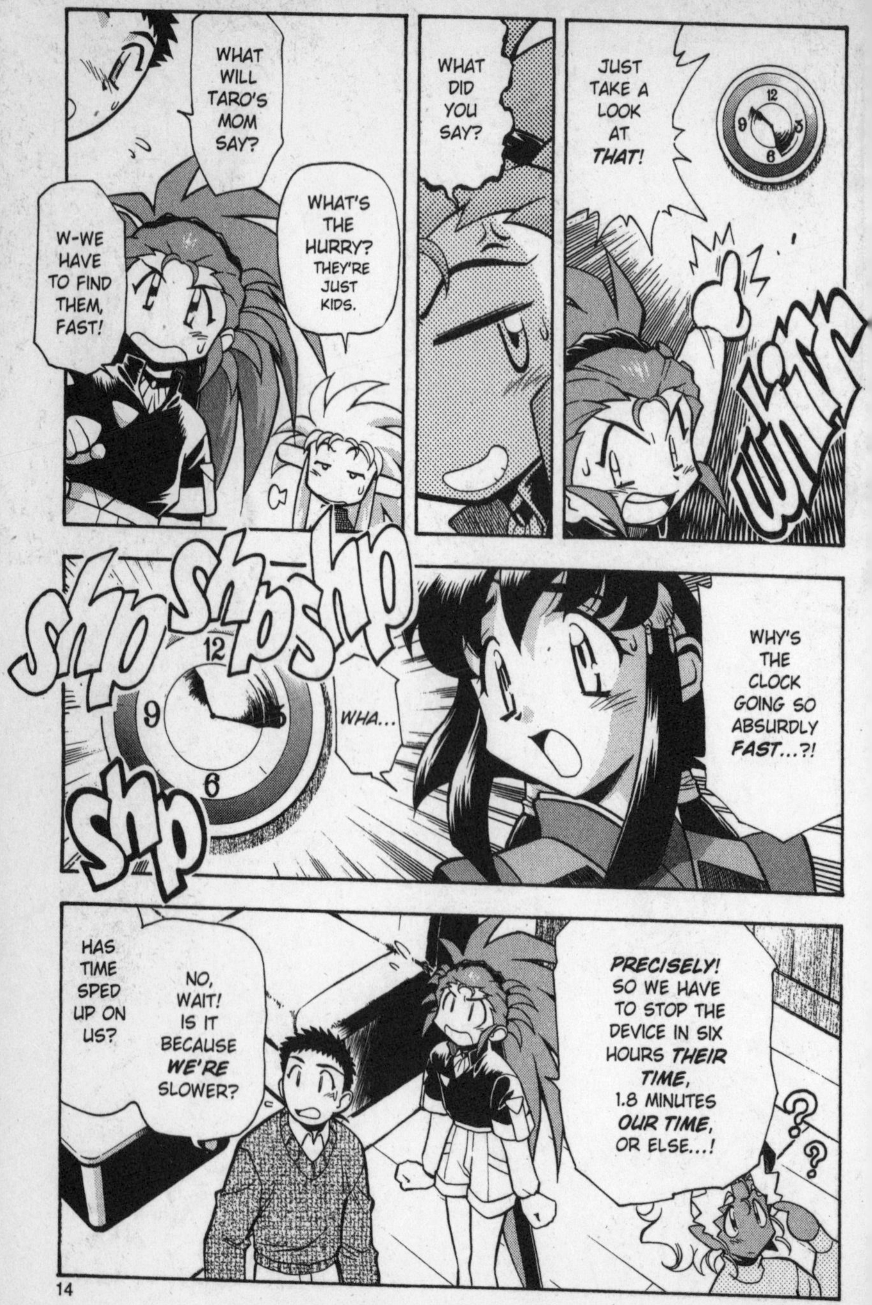
WHAT WILL TARO'S MOM SAY?
W-WE HAVE TO FIND THEM, FAST!
WHAT'S THE HURRY? THEY'RE JUST KIDS.
WHAT DID YOU SAY?
JUST TAKE A LOOK AT THAT!
WHIR
SHP SHP SHP SHP
WHA...
WHY'S THE CLOCK GOING SO ABSURDLY FAST...?!
HAS TIME SPED UP ON US?
NO, WAIT! IS IT BECAUSE WE'RE SLOWER?
PRECISELY! SO WE HAVE TO STOP THE DEVICE IN SIX HOURS THEIR TIME, 1.8 MINUTES OUR TIME, OR ELSE...!
??

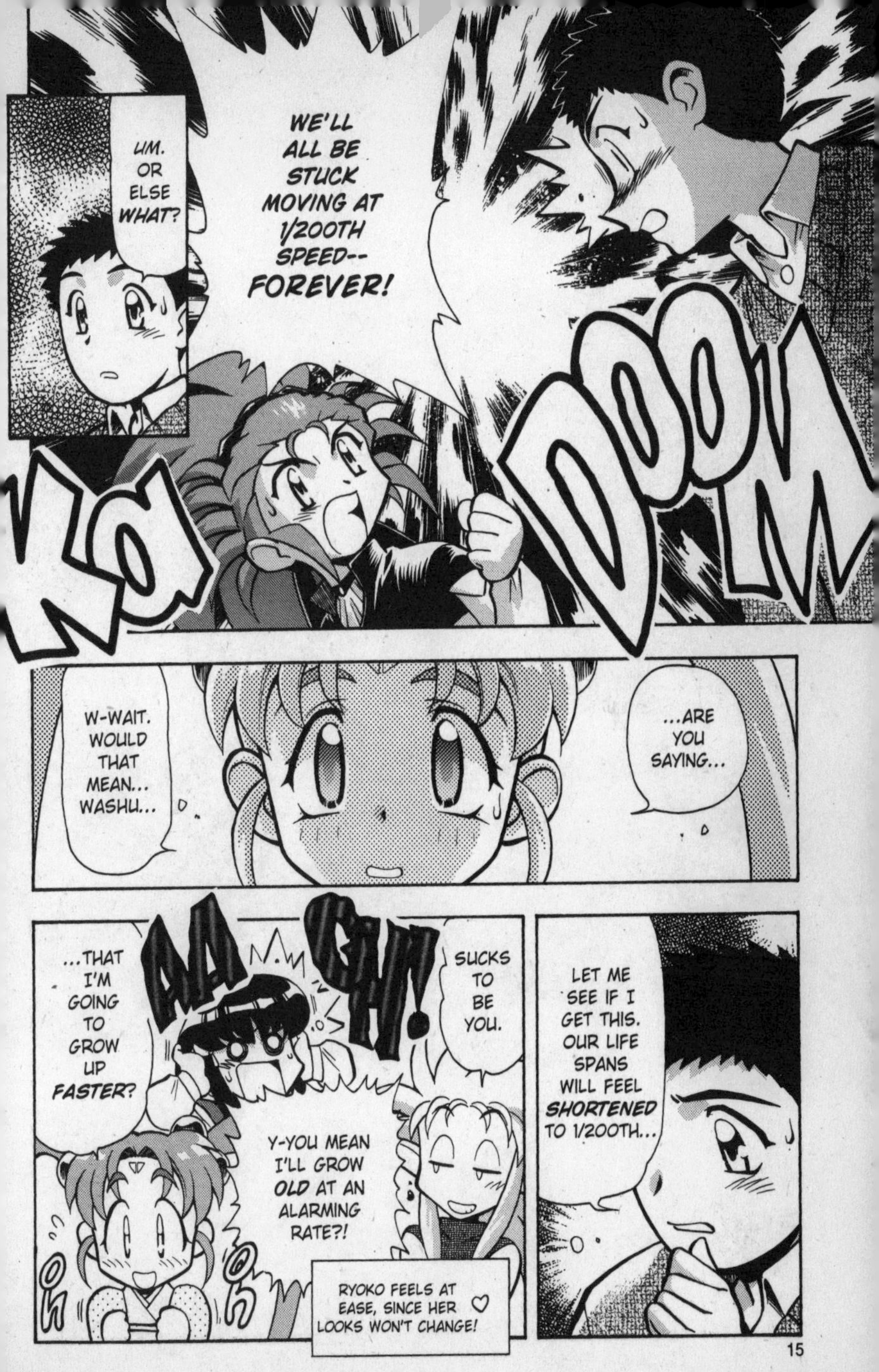
UM. OR ELSE WHAT?
WE'LL ALL BE STUCK MOVING AT 1/200TH SPEED-- FOREVER!
KA
DOOOM
W-WAIT. WOULD THAT MEAN... WASHU...
...ARE YOU SAYING...
...THAT I'M GOING TO GROW UP FASTER?
AAGH!
SUCKS TO BE YOU.
Y-YOU MEAN I'LL GROW OLD AT AN ALARMING RATE?!
RYOKO FEELS AT EASE, SINCE HER LOOKS WON'T CHANGE! ♡
LET ME SEE IF I GET THIS. OUR LIFE SPANS WILL FEEL SHORTENED TO 1/200TH...

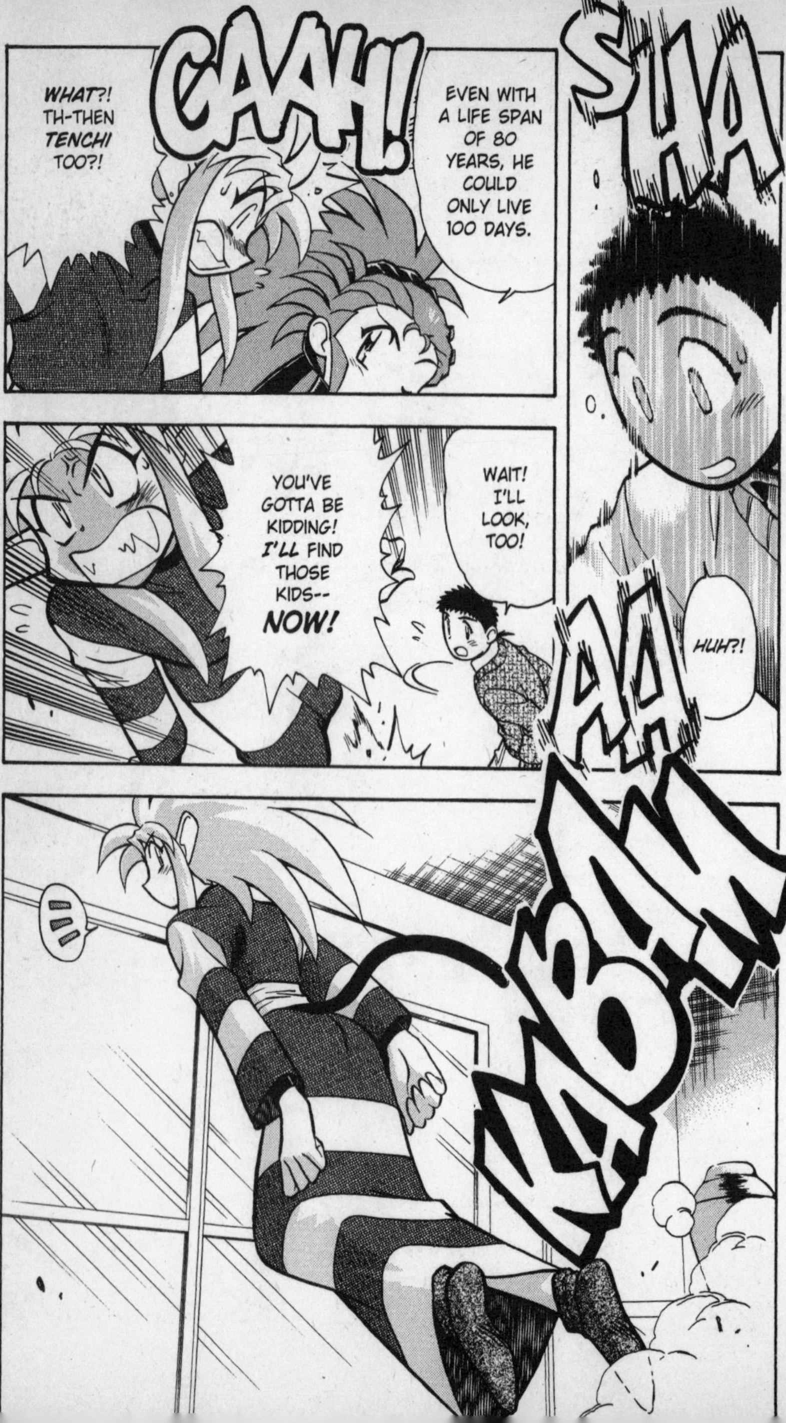

WHAT?! TH-THEN *TENCHI* TOO?!
CAAH!
EVEN WITH A LIFE SPAN OF 80 YEARS, HE COULD ONLY LIVE 100 DAYS.
YOU'VE GOTTA BE KIDDING! ***I'LL*** FIND THOSE KIDS-- ***NOW!***
WAIT! I'LL LOOK, TOO!
SHA
HUH?!
AAA
KABOOM

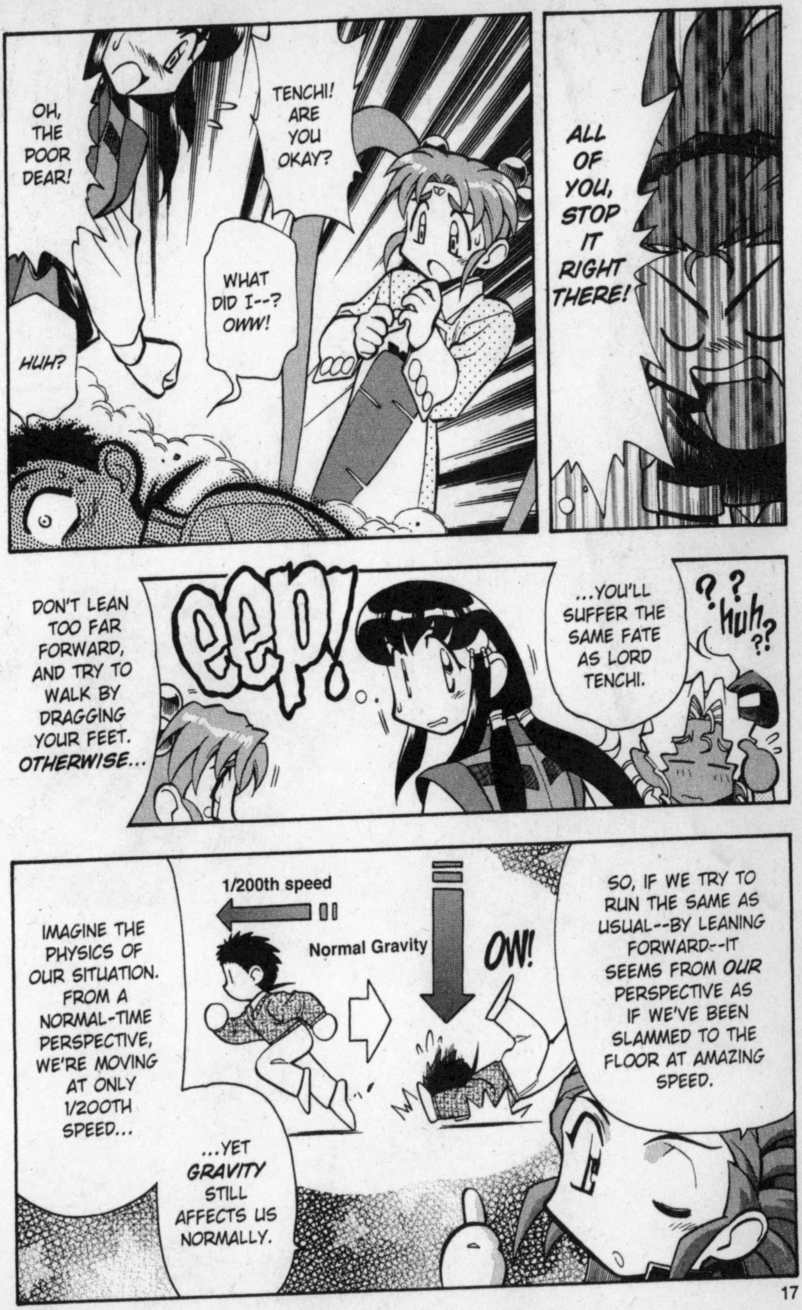
OH, THE POOR DEAR!
TENCHI! ARE YOU OKAY?
HUH?
WHAT DID I--? OWW!
ALL OF YOU, STOP IT RIGHT THERE!
DON'T LEAN TOO FAR FORWARD, AND TRY TO WALK BY DRAGGING YOUR FEET. OTHERWISE...
eep!
...YOU'LL SUFFER THE SAME FATE AS LORD TENCHI.
? ? huh ? ?
IMAGINE THE PHYSICS OF OUR SITUATION. FROM A NORMAL-TIME PERSPECTIVE, WE'RE MOVING AT ONLY 1/200TH SPEED...
1/200th speed
Normal Gravity
OW!
...YET GRAVITY STILL AFFECTS US NORMALLY.
SO, IF WE TRY TO RUN THE SAME AS USUAL--BY LEANING FORWARD--IT SEEMS FROM OUR PERSPECTIVE AS IF WE'VE BEEN SLAMMED TO THE FLOOR AT AMAZING SPEED.

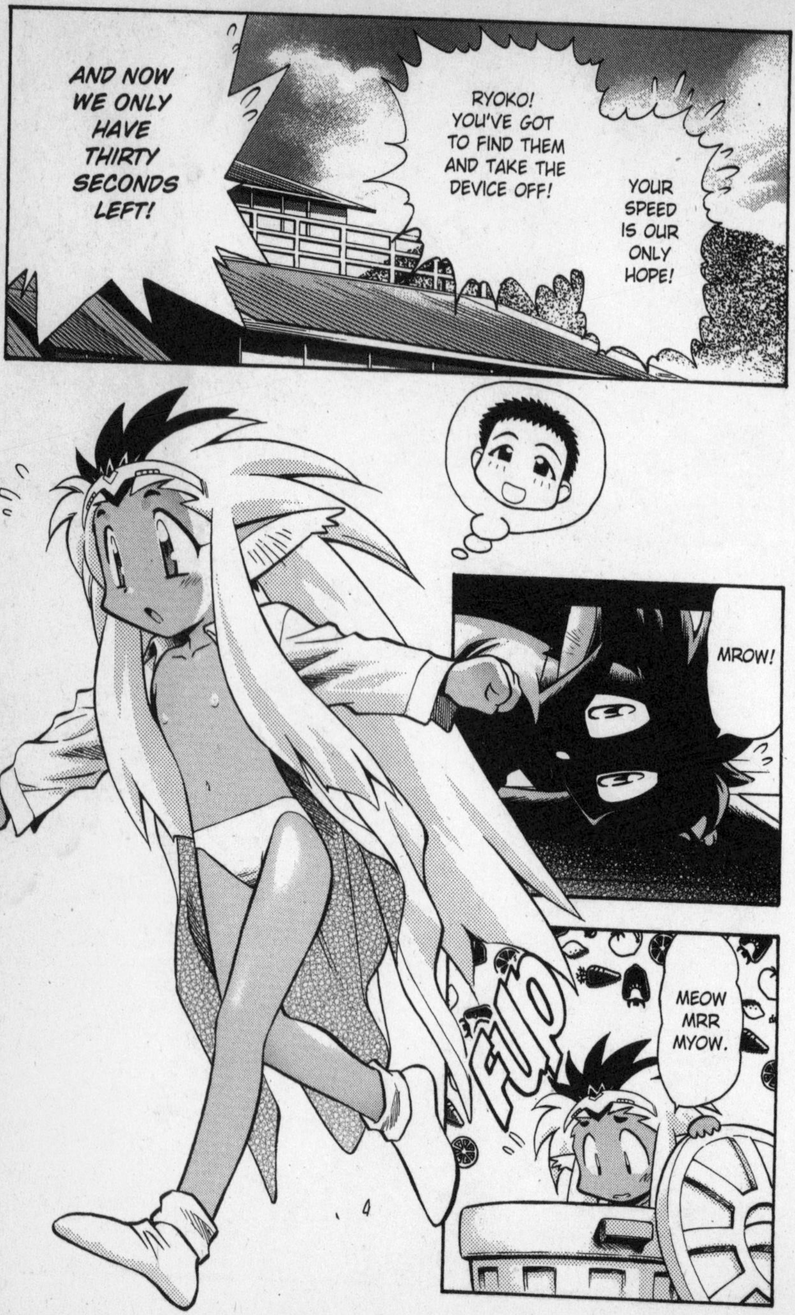
AND NOW WE ONLY HAVE THIRTY SECONDS LEFT!
RYOKO! YOU'VE GOT TO FIND THEM AND TAKE THE DEVICE OFF!
YOUR SPEED IS OUR ONLY HOPE!
MROW!
FUP
MEOW MRR MYOW.

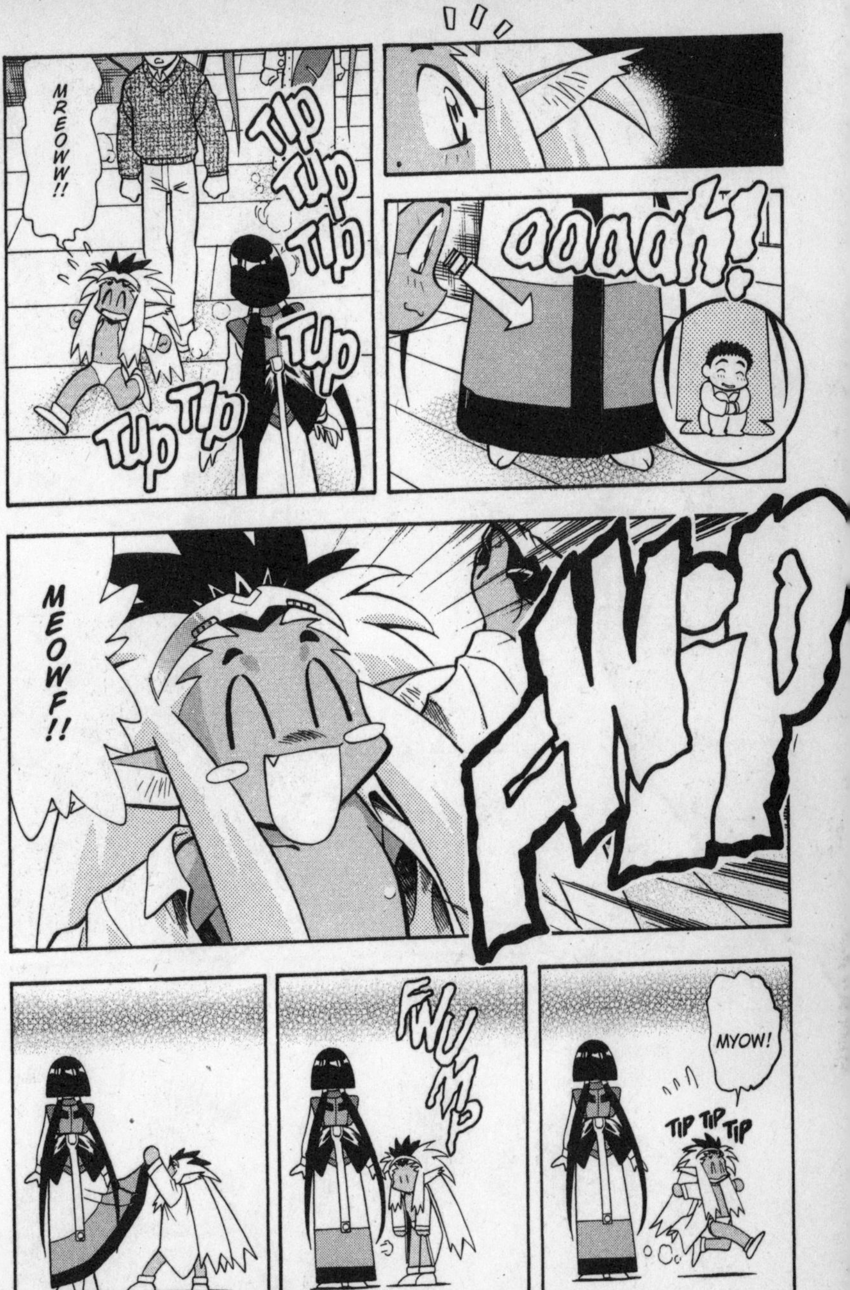

MREOWW!!
TIP
TUP
TIP
TUP
TUP
TIP
aaaah!
MEOWF!!
FWIP
FWUMP
MYOW!
TIP TIP TIP

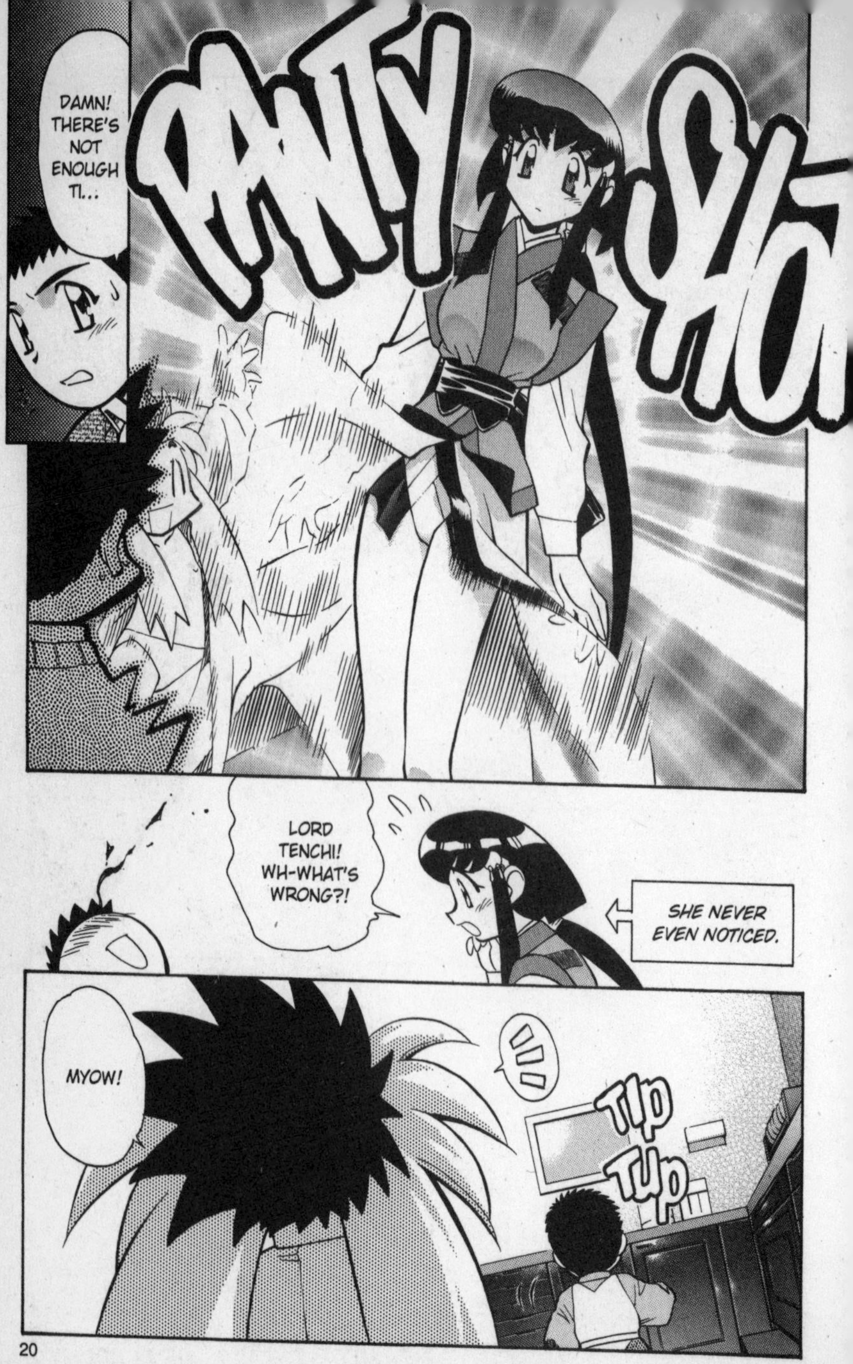
DAMN! THERE'S NOT ENOUGH TI...
PANTY
LORD TENCHI! WH-WHAT'S WRONG?!
SHE NEVER EVEN NOTICED.
MYOW!
!!!
TIP
TUP

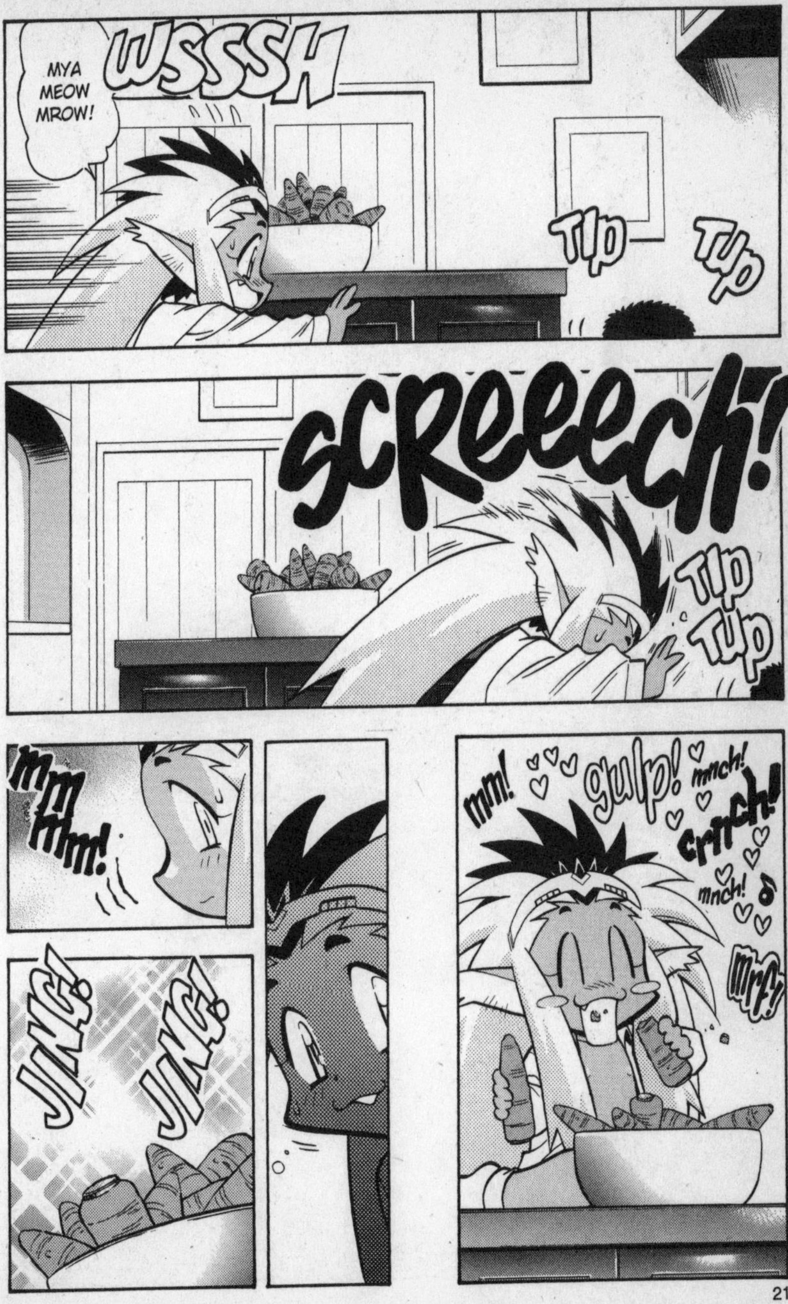
MYA MEOW MROW!
WSSSH
Tip
Tup
SCREEECH!
Tip
Tup
mm hmm!
JING!
JING!
mm!
gulp!
mnch!
crnch!
mnch!
mrf!

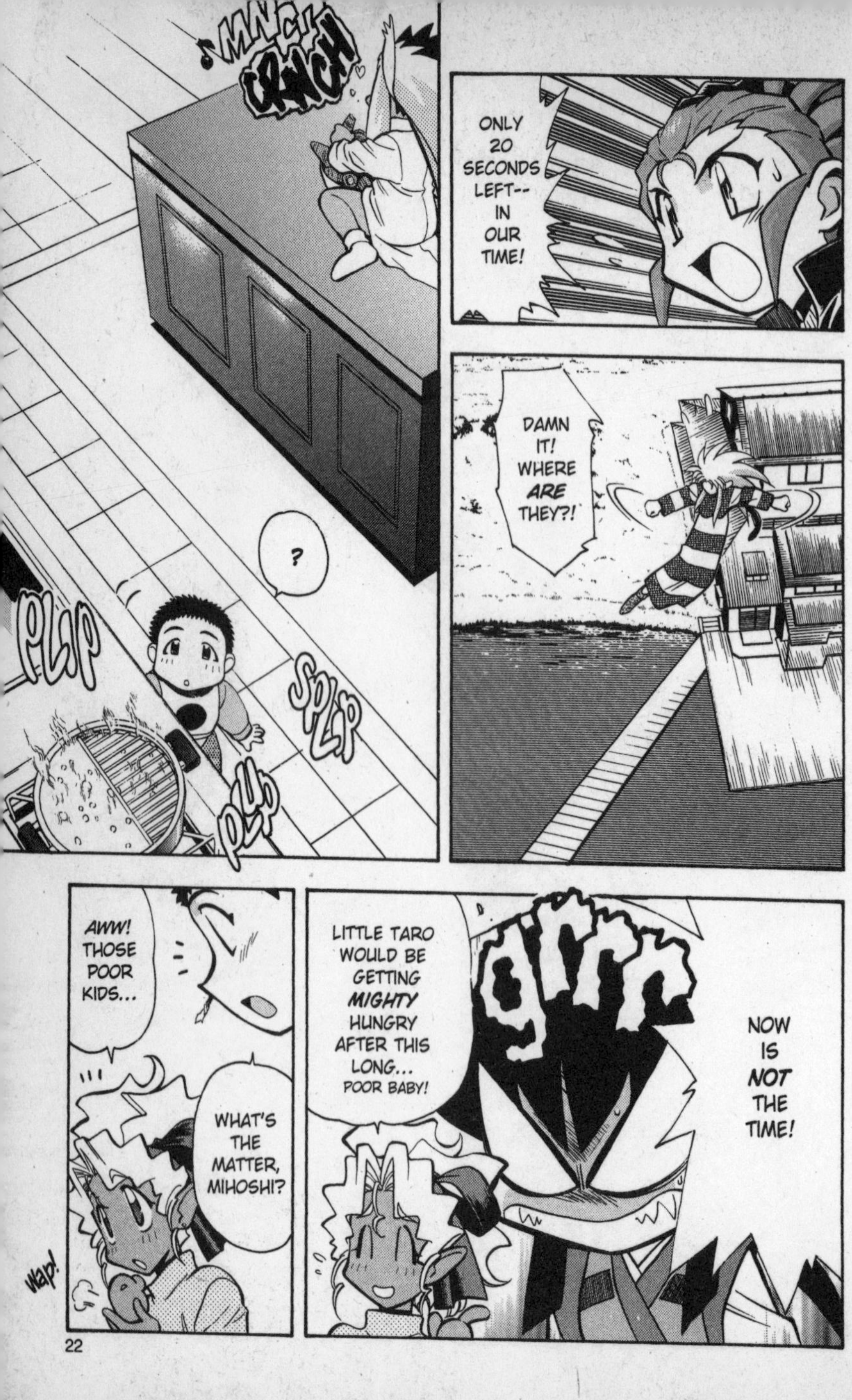

MNCH
CRUNCH
?
PLIP
SPLIP
PLIP
ONLY 20 SECONDS LEFT-- IN OUR TIME!
DAMN IT! WHERE *ARE* THEY?!
AWW! THOSE POOR KIDS...
WHAT'S THE MATTER, MIHOSHI?
wap!
LITTLE TARO WOULD BE GETTING *MIGHTY* HUNGRY AFTER THIS LONG... POOR BABY!
grr
NOW IS *NOT* THE TIME!

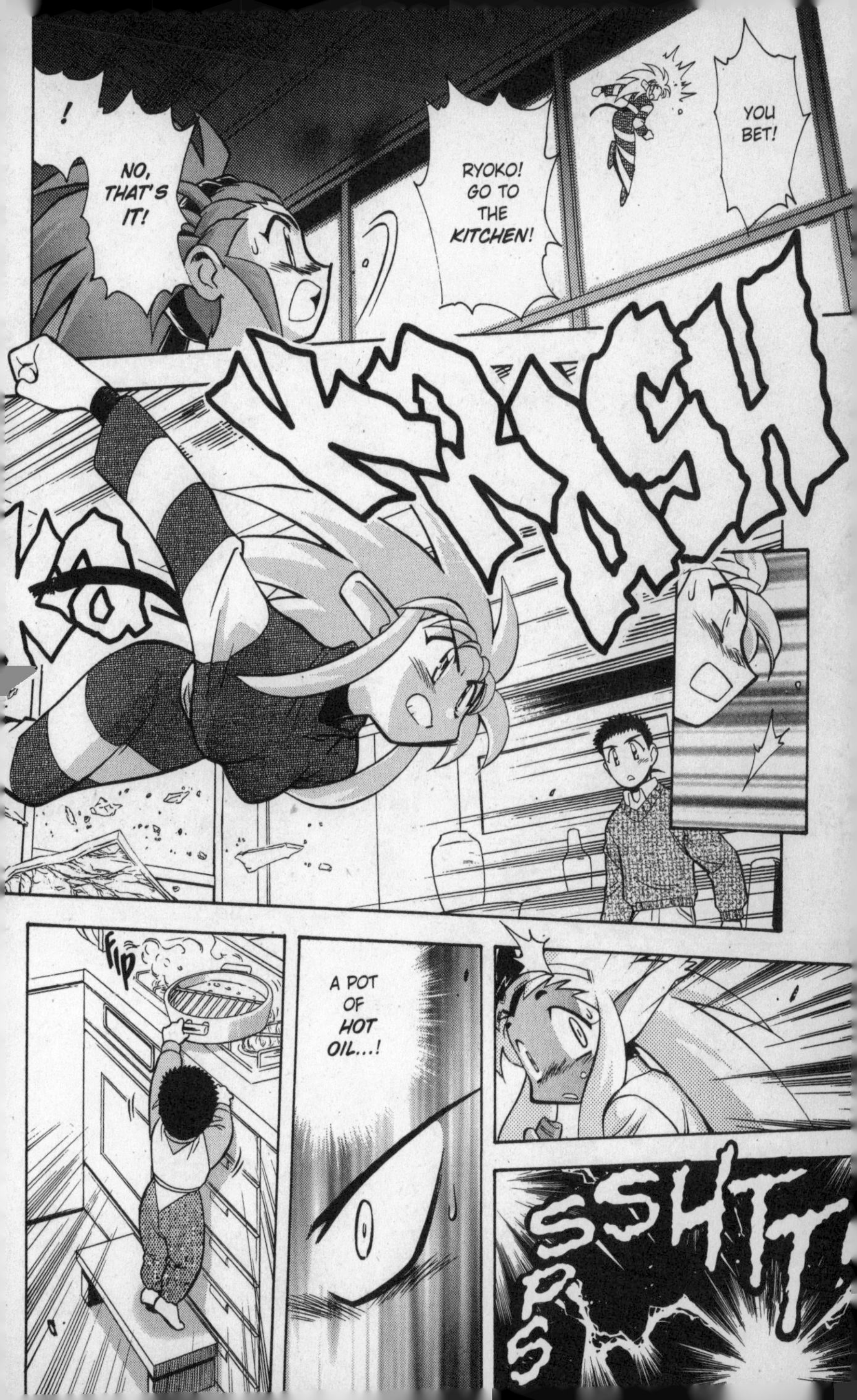
!
NO, THAT'S IT!
RYOKO! GO TO THE KITCHEN!
YOU BET!
Flip
A POT OF HOT OIL...!

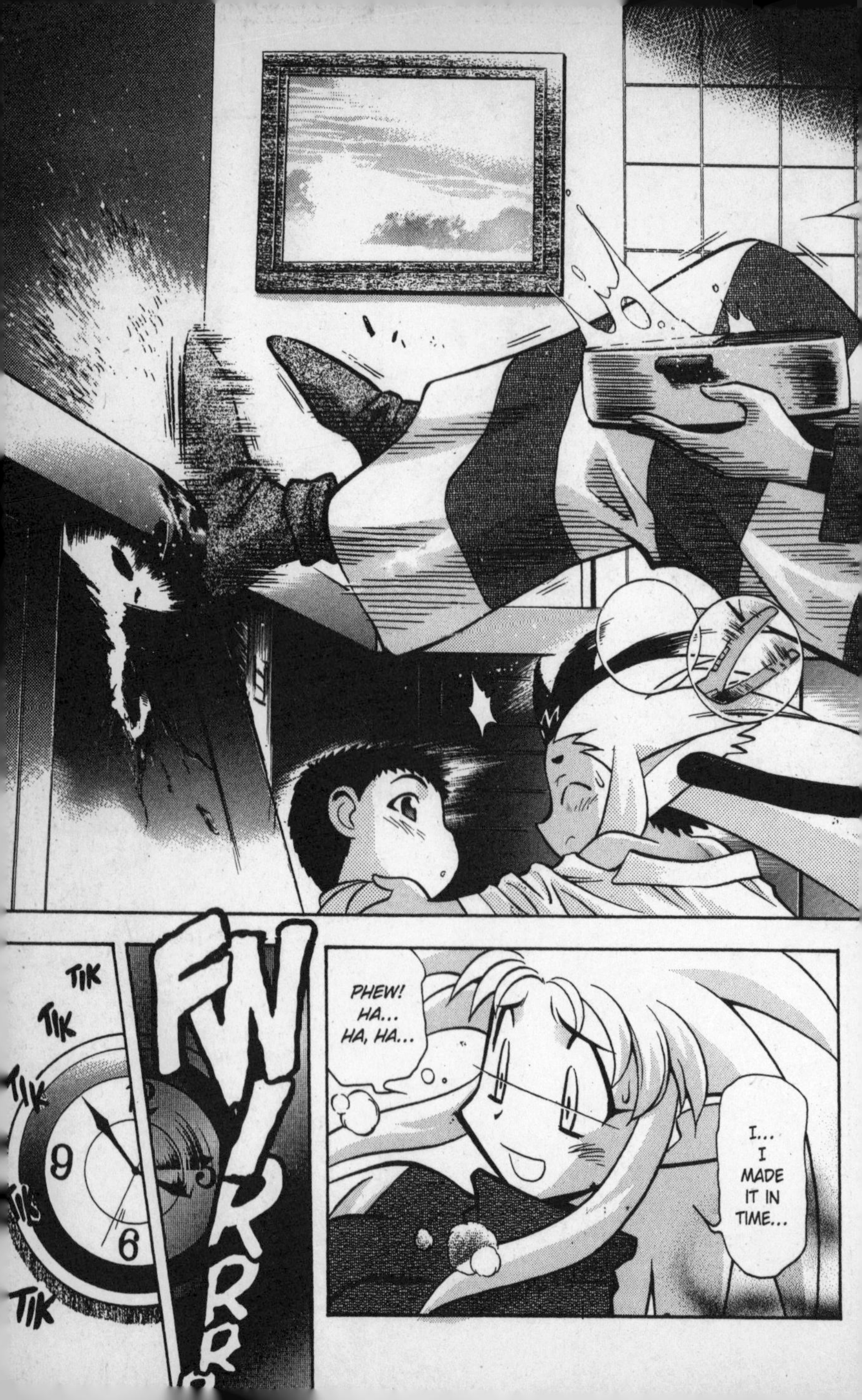
TIK
TIK
TIK
TIK
FWRRR
PHEW! HA... HA, HA...
I... I MADE IT IN TIME...

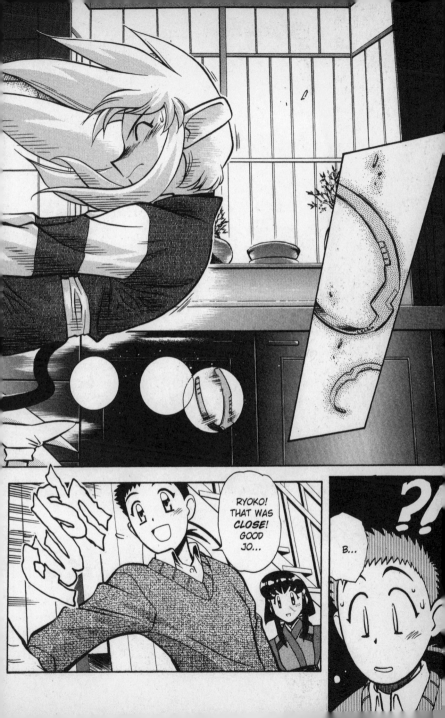

FLUSH!

RYOKO! THAT WAS *CLOSE!* GOOD JO...

?!

B...

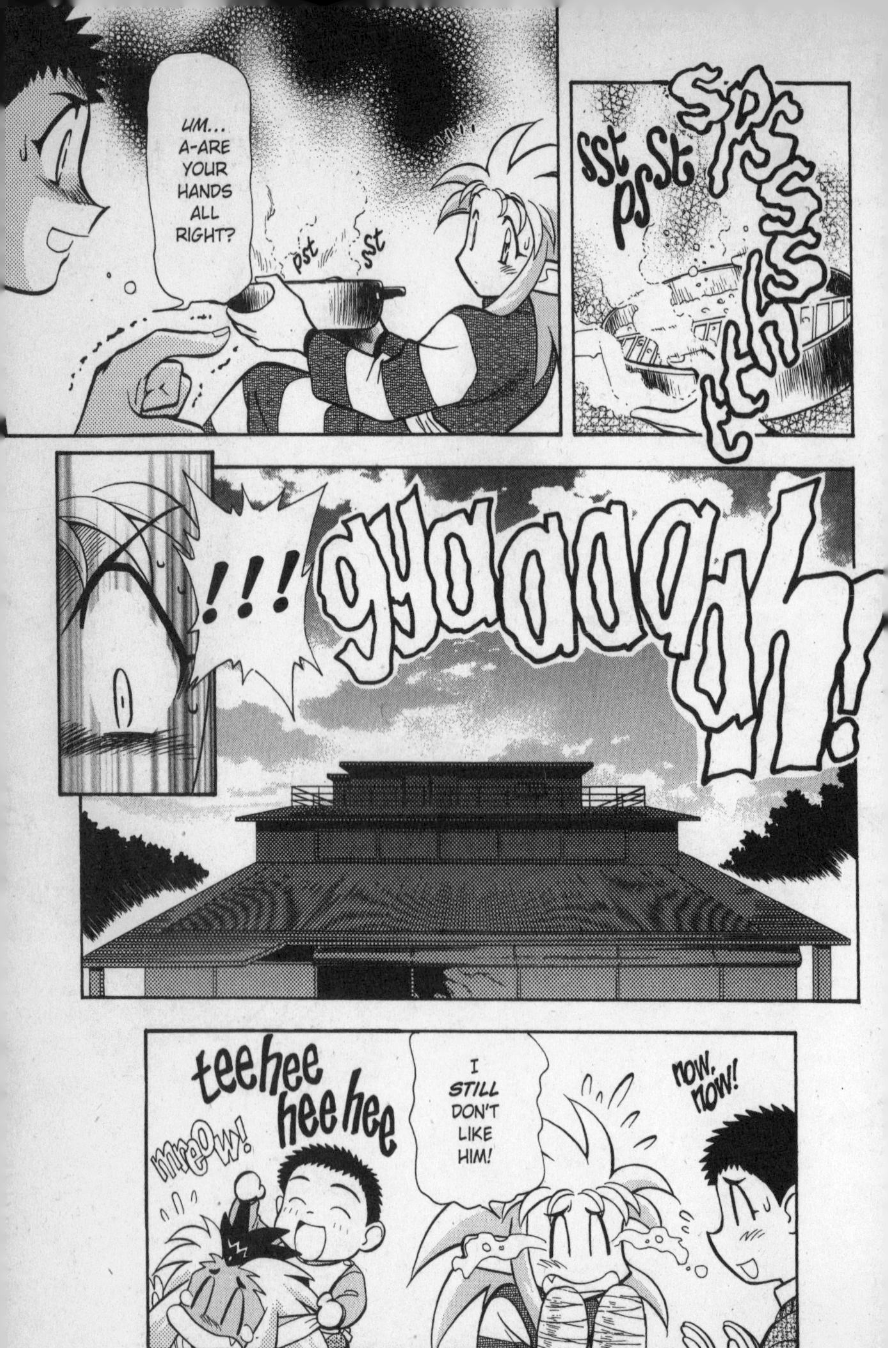

UM... A-ARE YOUR HANDS ALL RIGHT?
pst sst
sst pst psst
SPRSSHTTT
!!!
gyaaaah!
teehee hee hee
mreow!
I STILL DON'T LIKE HIM!
now, now!

Chapter 2: CONFUSION

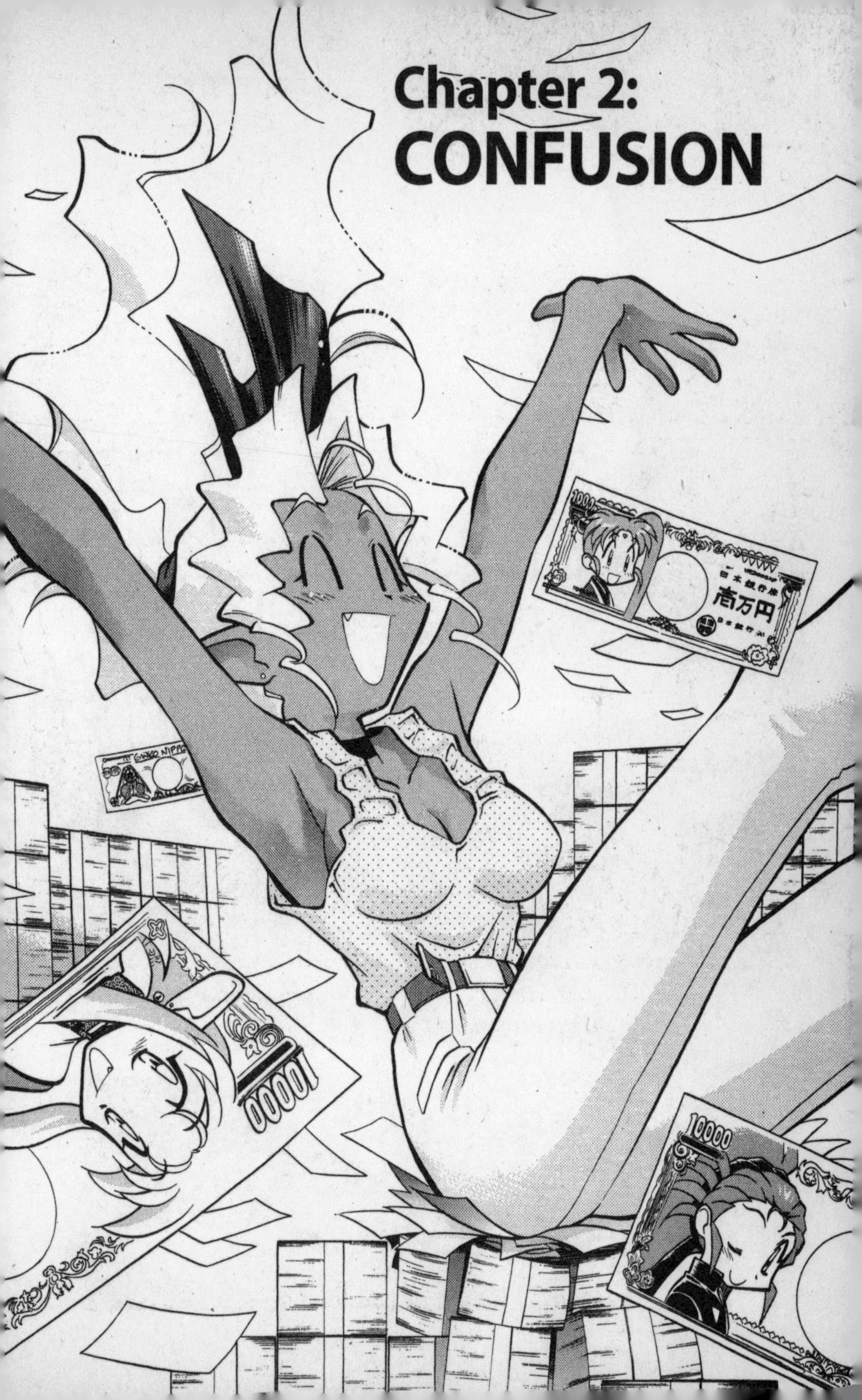
10000
10000

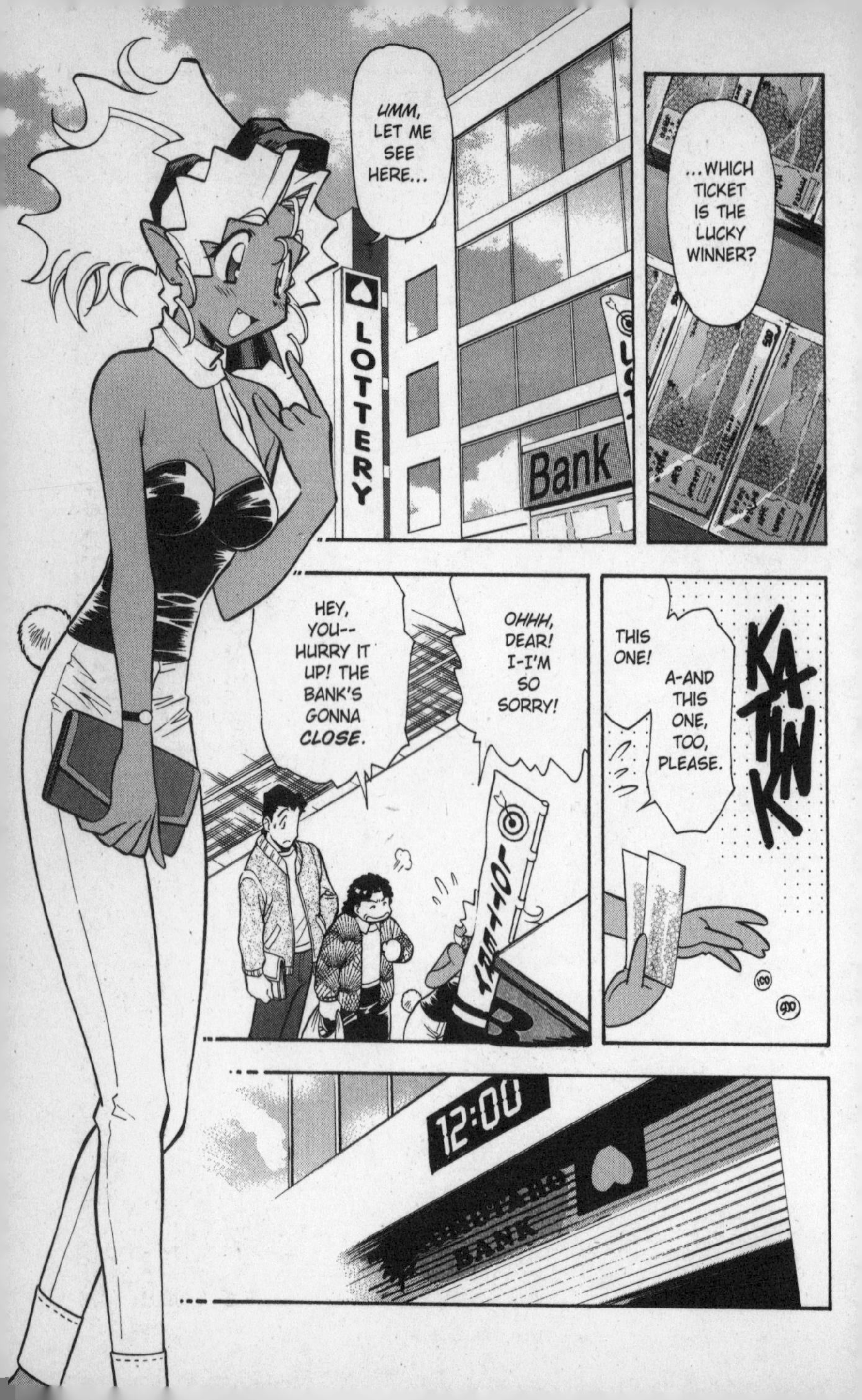
UMM, LET ME SEE HERE...
LOTTERY
Bank
...WHICH TICKET IS THE LUCKY WINNER?
HEY, YOU-- HURRY IT UP! THE BANK'S GONNA *CLOSE*.
OHHH, DEAR! I-I'M SO SORRY!
THIS ONE!
A-AND THIS ONE, TOO, PLEASE.
12:00
BANK

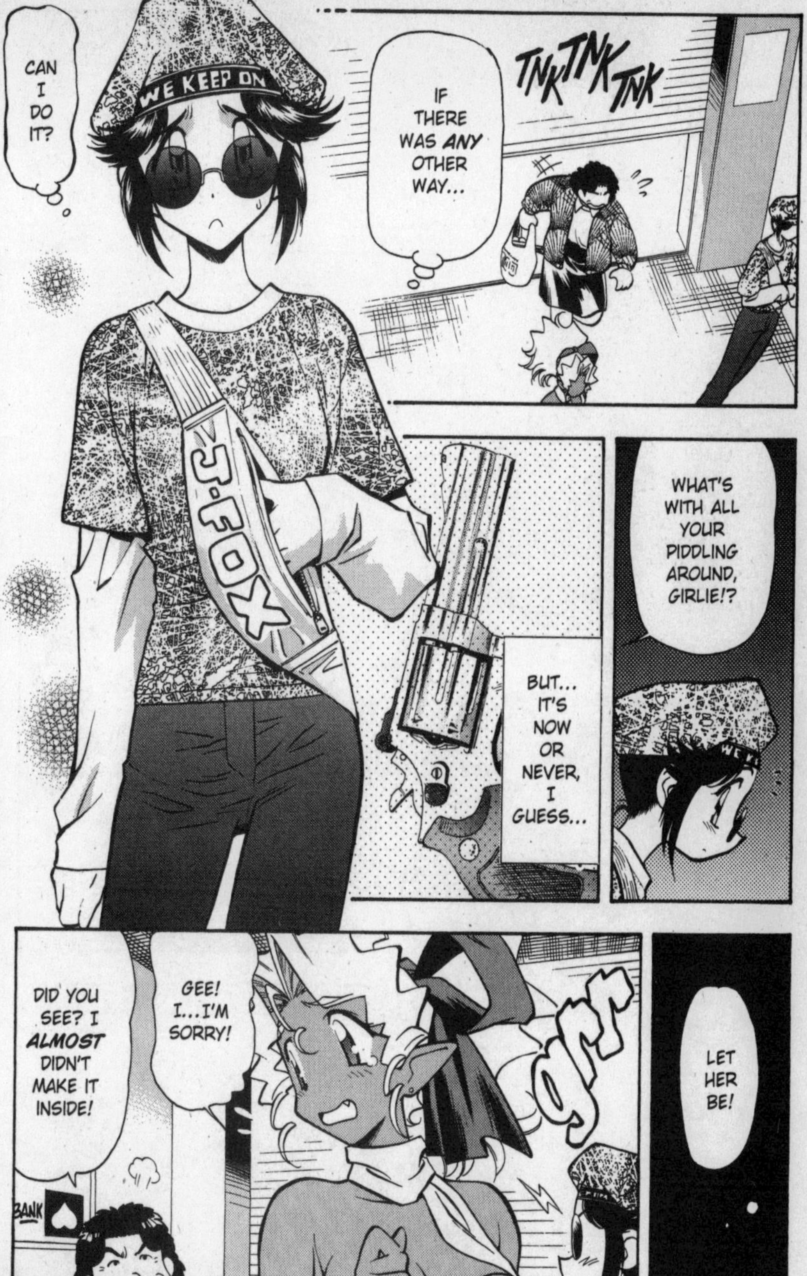
WE KEEP ON
CAN I DO IT?
J-FOX
IF THERE WAS ANY OTHER WAY...
TNK TNK TNK TNK
BUT... IT'S NOW OR NEVER, I GUESS...
WHAT'S WITH ALL YOUR PIDDLING AROUND, GIRLIE!?
DID YOU SEE? I ALMOST DIDN'T MAKE IT INSIDE!
BANK
GEE! I...I'M SORRY!
grr
LET HER BE!

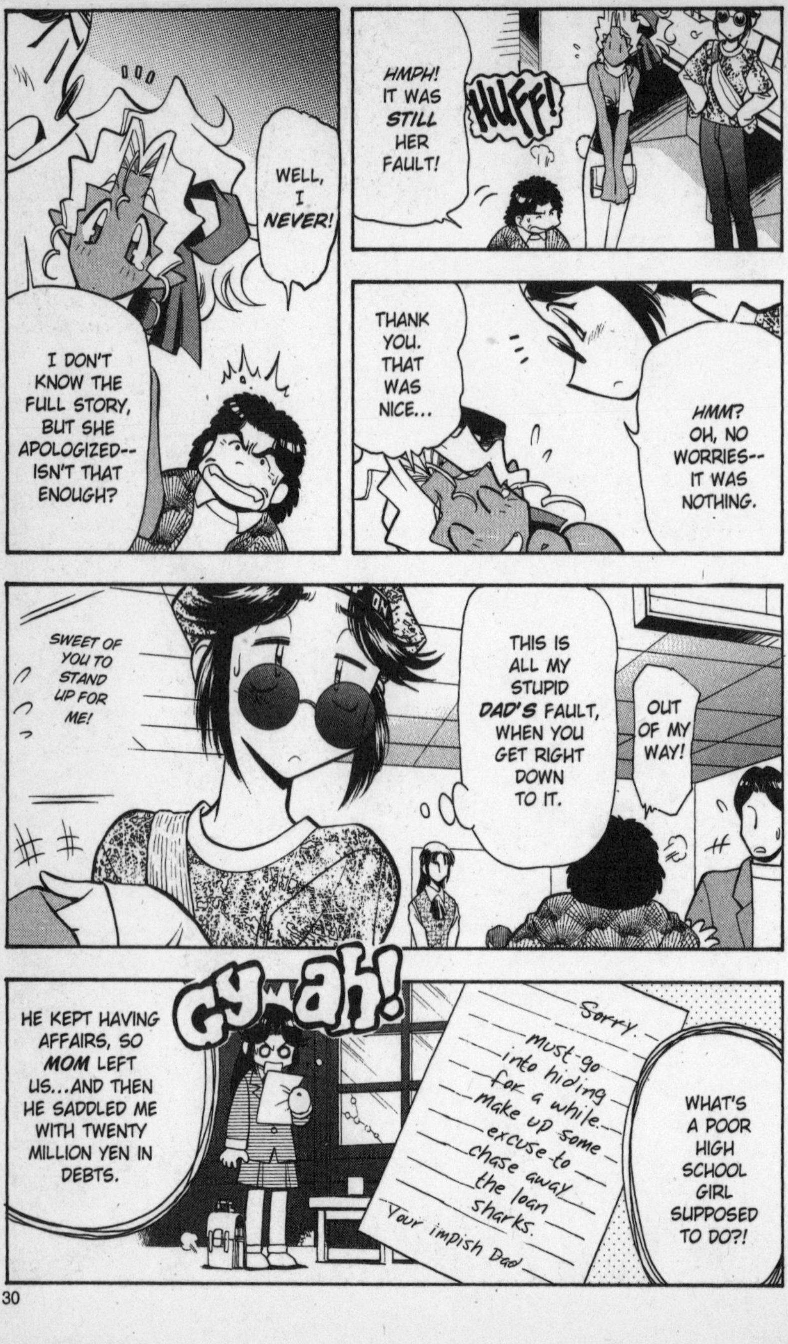

WELL, I NEVER!
I DON'T KNOW THE FULL STORY, BUT SHE APOLOGIZED--ISN'T THAT ENOUGH?
HMPH! IT WAS STILL HER FAULT!
HUFF!
THANK YOU. THAT WAS NICE...
HMM? OH, NO WORRIES--IT WAS NOTHING.
SWEET OF YOU TO STAND UP FOR ME!
THIS IS ALL MY STUPID DAD'S FAULT, WHEN YOU GET RIGHT DOWN TO IT.
OUT OF MY WAY!
HE KEPT HAVING AFFAIRS, SO MOM LEFT US...AND THEN HE SADDLED ME WITH TWENTY MILLION YEN IN DEBTS.
GY-ah!
Sorry. Must go into hiding for a while. Make up some excuse to chase away the loan sharks.
Your impish Dad
WHAT'S A POOR HIGH SCHOOL GIRL SUPPOSED TO DO?!

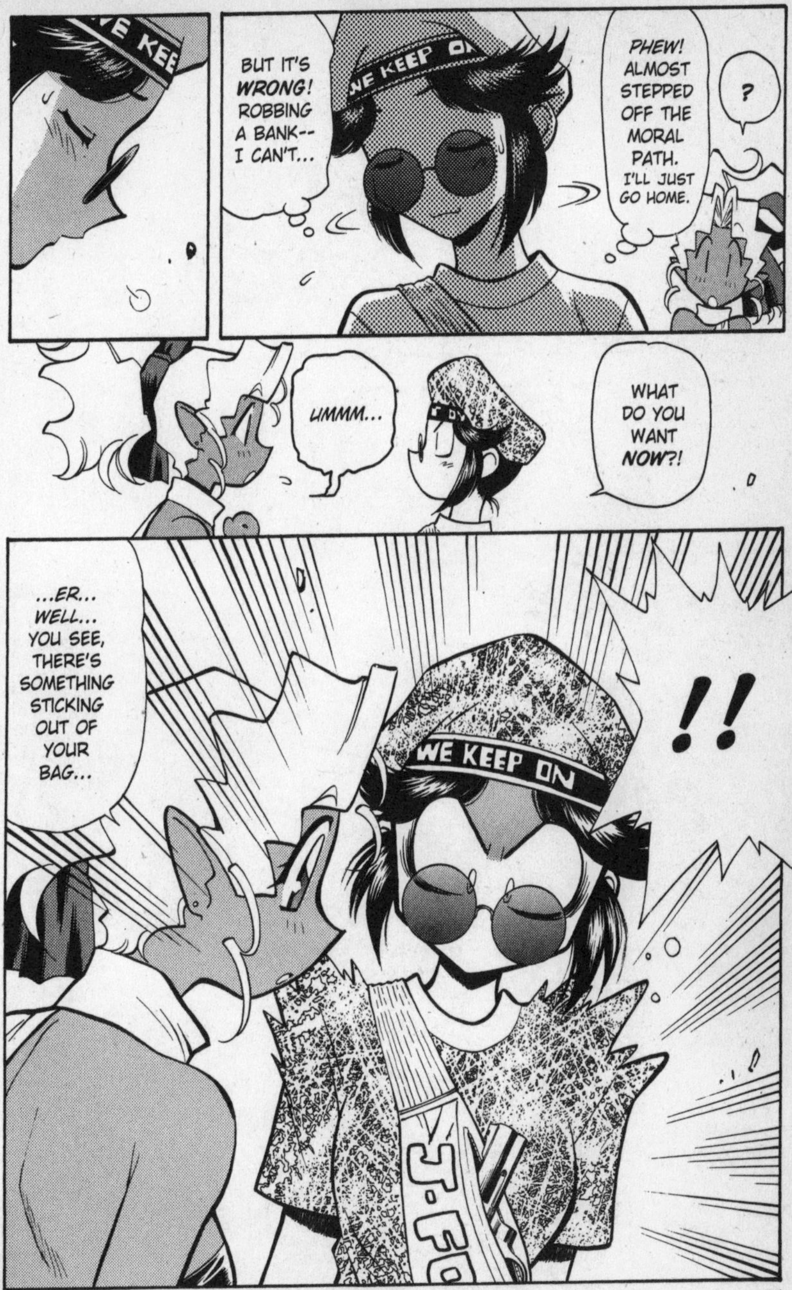
BUT IT'S *WRONG*! ROBBING A BANK-- I CAN'T...
PHEW! ALMOST STEPPED OFF THE MORAL PATH. I'LL JUST GO HOME.
?
UMMM...
WHAT DO YOU WANT *NOW*?!
...ER... WELL... YOU SEE, THERE'S SOMETHING STICKING OUT OF YOUR BAG...
!!
WE KEEP ON

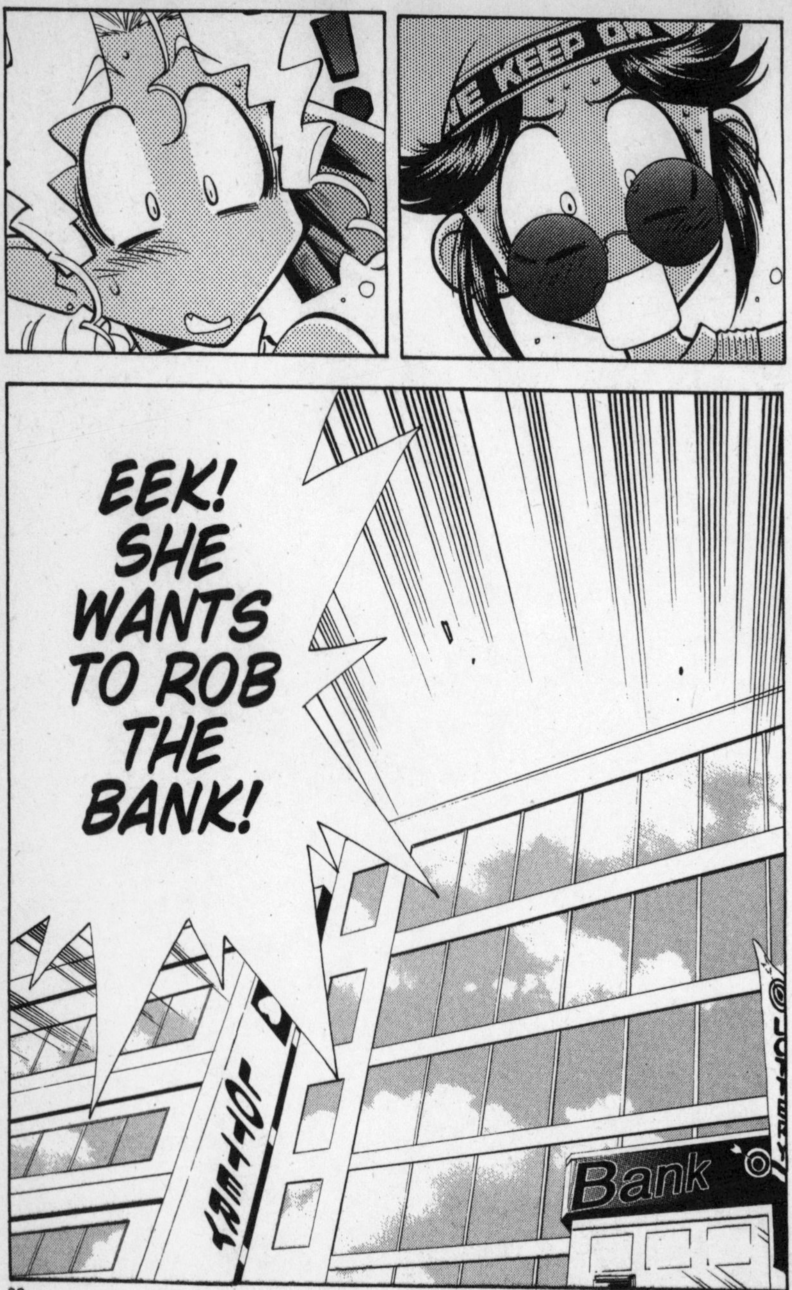
EEK! SHE WANTS TO ROB THE BANK!
Bank

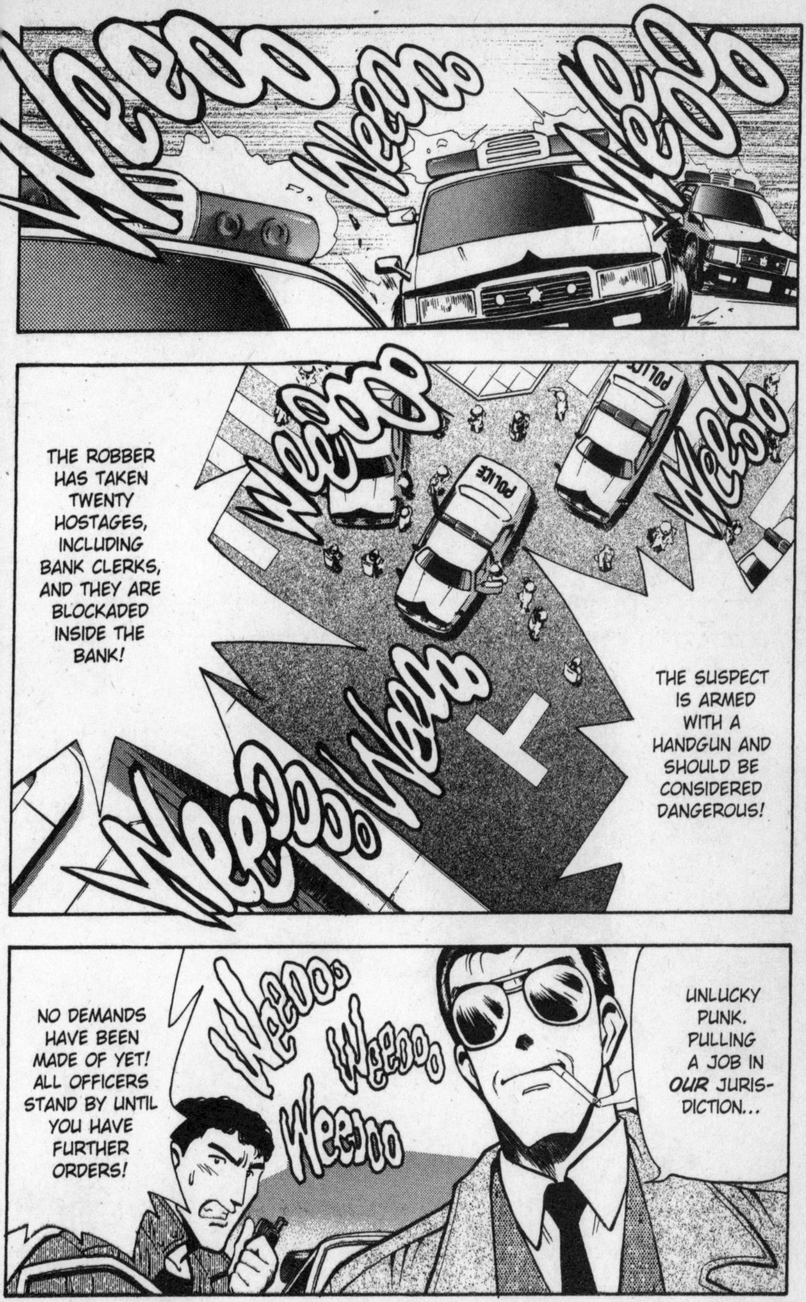

WEEOO
WEEOO
WEEOO
WEEOO
THE ROBBER HAS TAKEN TWENTY HOSTAGES, INCLUDING BANK CLERKS, AND THEY ARE BLOCKADED INSIDE THE BANK!
WEEOO
WEEOOO WEEOO
THE SUSPECT IS ARMED WITH A HANDGUN AND SHOULD BE CONSIDERED DANGEROUS!
NO DEMANDS HAVE BEEN MADE OF YET! ALL OFFICERS STAND BY UNTIL YOU HAVE FURTHER ORDERS!
WEEOO
WEEOO
WEEOO
UNLUCKY PUNK. PULLING A JOB IN *OUR* JURIS-DICTION...

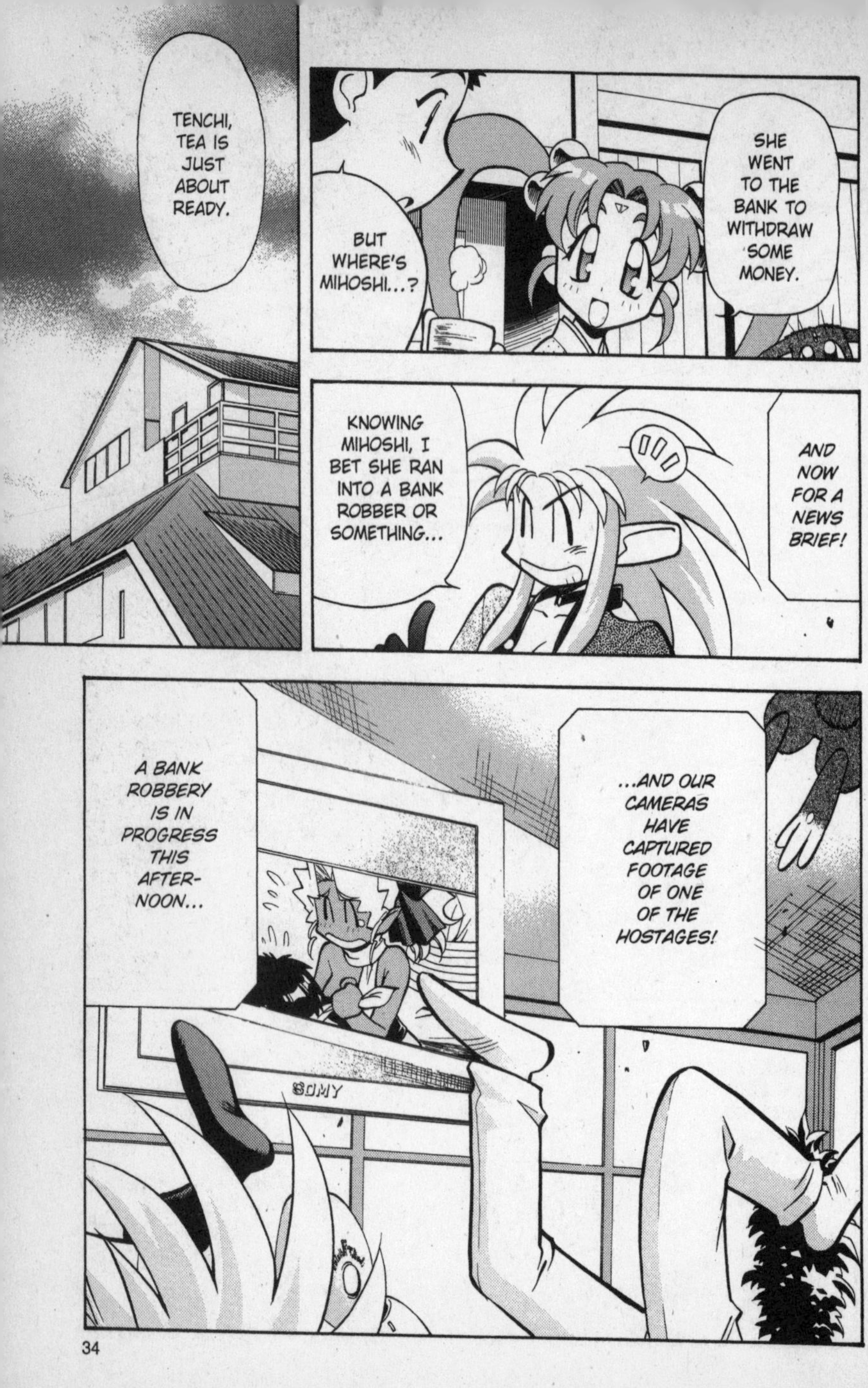
TENCHI, TEA IS JUST ABOUT READY.
BUT WHERE'S MIHOSHI...?
SHE WENT TO THE BANK TO WITHDRAW SOME MONEY.
KNOWING MIHOSHI, I BET SHE RAN INTO A BANK ROBBER OR SOMETHING...
AND NOW FOR A NEWS BRIEF!
A BANK ROBBERY IS IN PROGRESS THIS AFTERNOON...
...AND OUR CAMERAS HAVE CAPTURED FOOTAGE OF ONE OF THE HOSTAGES!
SOMY

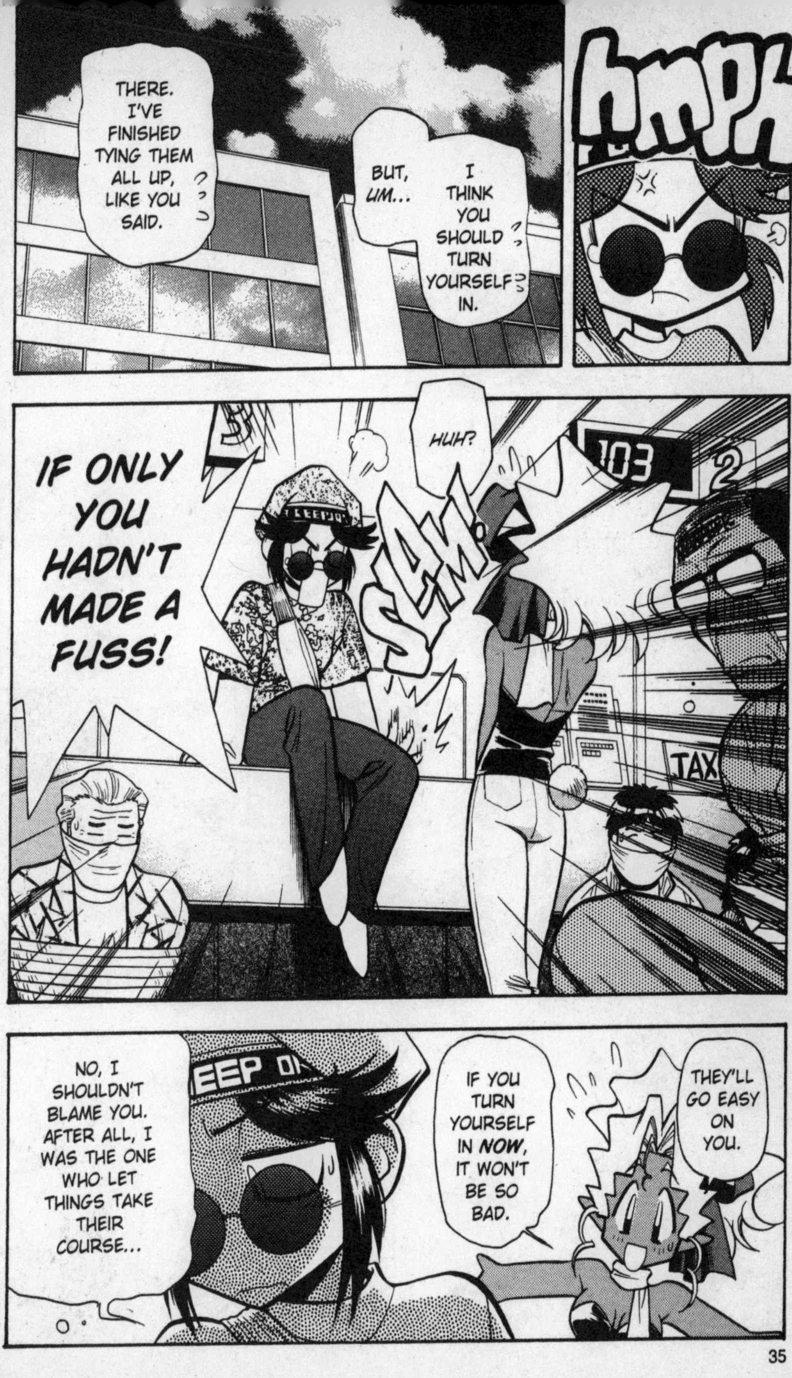
THERE. I'VE FINISHED TYING THEM ALL UP, LIKE YOU SAID.
BUT, UM...
I THINK YOU SHOULD TURN YOURSELF IN.
hmph
IF ONLY YOU HADN'T MADE A FUSS!
HUH?
SLAM
103
2
TAX
NO, I SHOULDN'T BLAME YOU. AFTER ALL, I WAS THE ONE WHO LET THINGS TAKE THEIR COURSE...
EEP O
IF YOU TURN YOURSELF IN NOW, IT WON'T BE SO BAD.
THEY'LL GO EASY ON YOU.

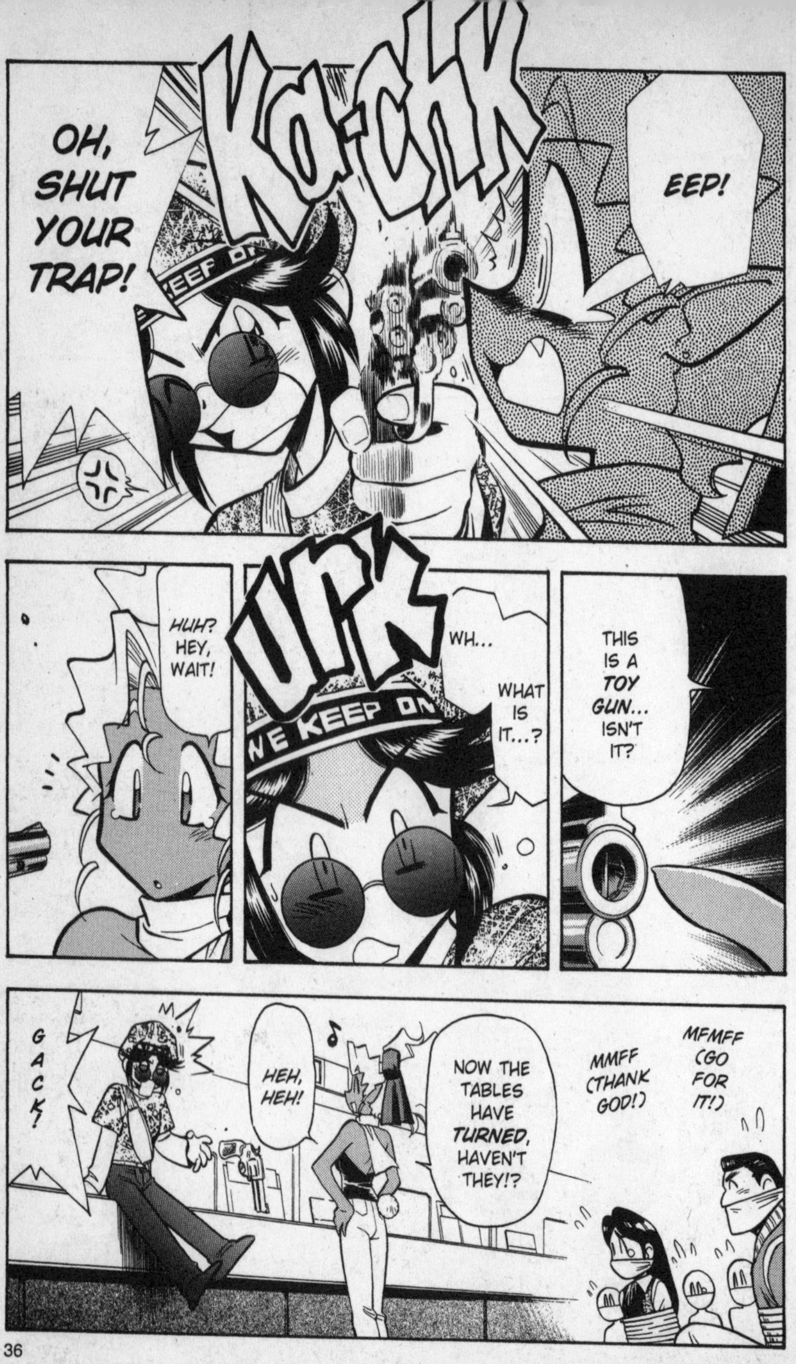

OH, SHUT YOUR TRAP!
KA-CHK
EEP!
HUH? HEY, WAIT!
UP'K
WH...
WHAT IS IT...?
THIS IS A *TOY GUN*... ISN'T IT?
GACK!
HEH, HEH!
NOW THE TABLES HAVE *TURNED*, HAVEN'T THEY!?
MMFF (THANK GOD!)
MFMFF (GO FOR IT!)

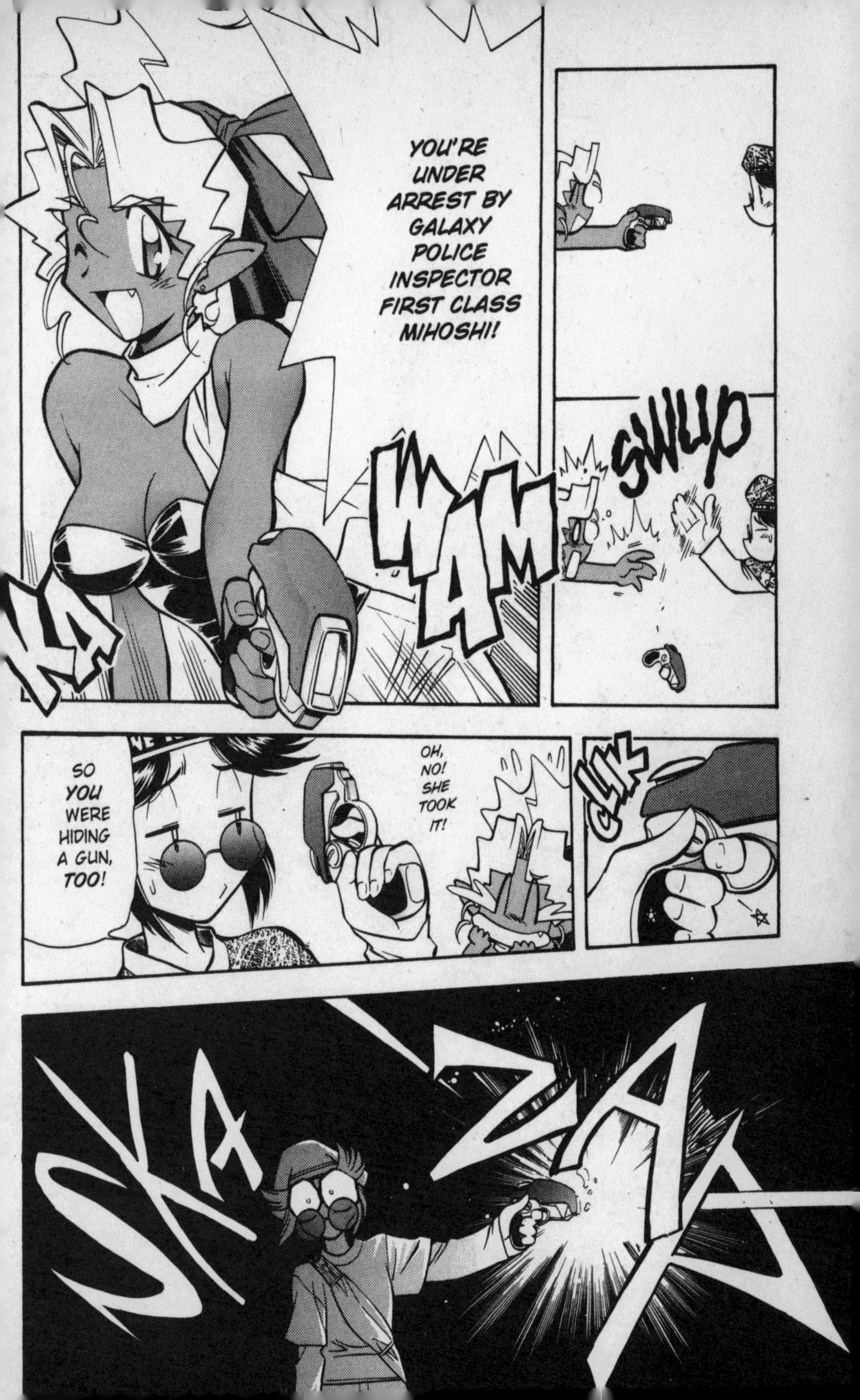
YOU'RE UNDER ARREST BY GALAXY POLICE INSPECTOR FIRST CLASS MIHOSHI!
WAM
SWUP
SO YOU WERE HIDING A GUN, TOO!
OH, NO! SHE TOOK IT!
CLIK

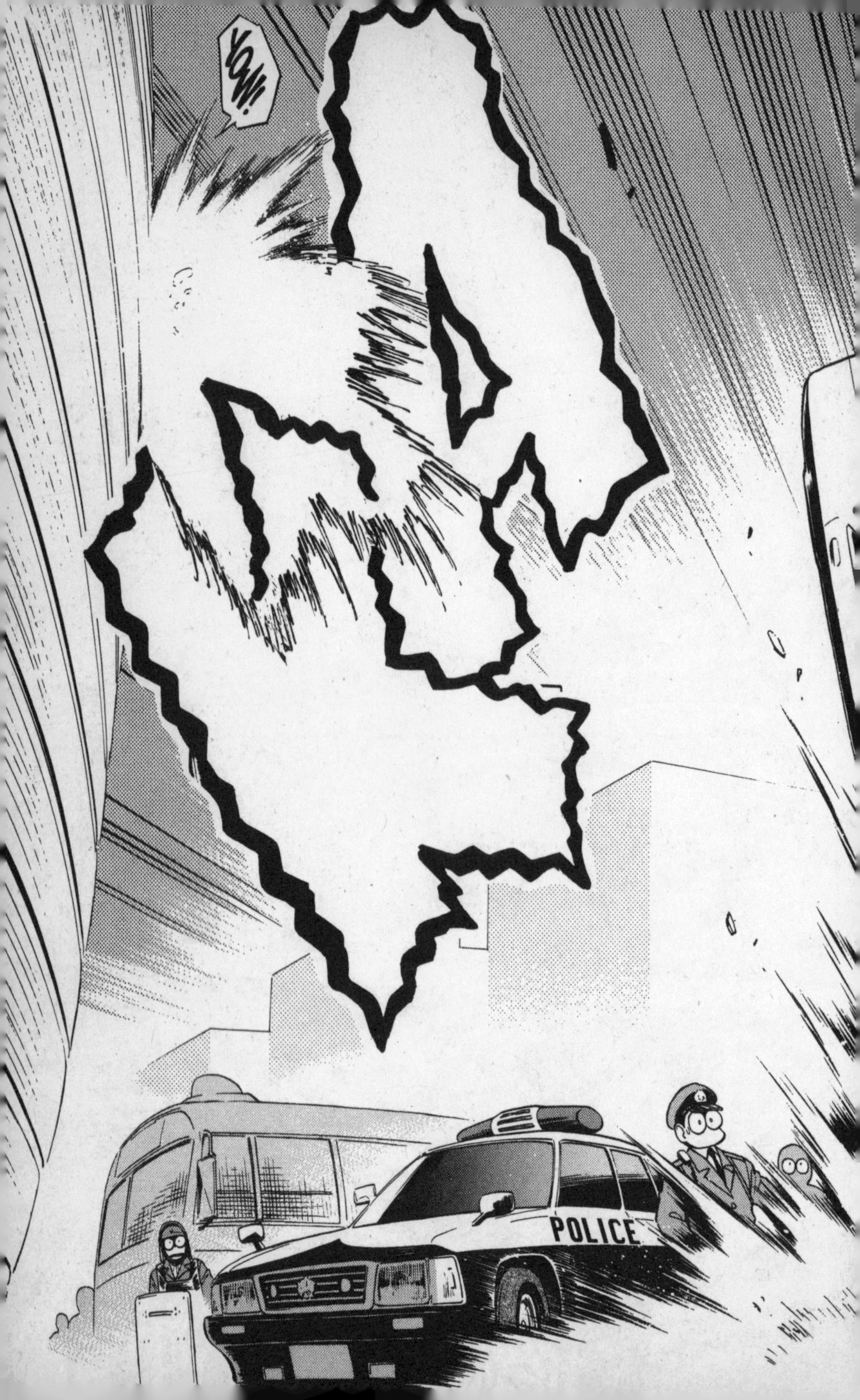
YOW!
POLICE

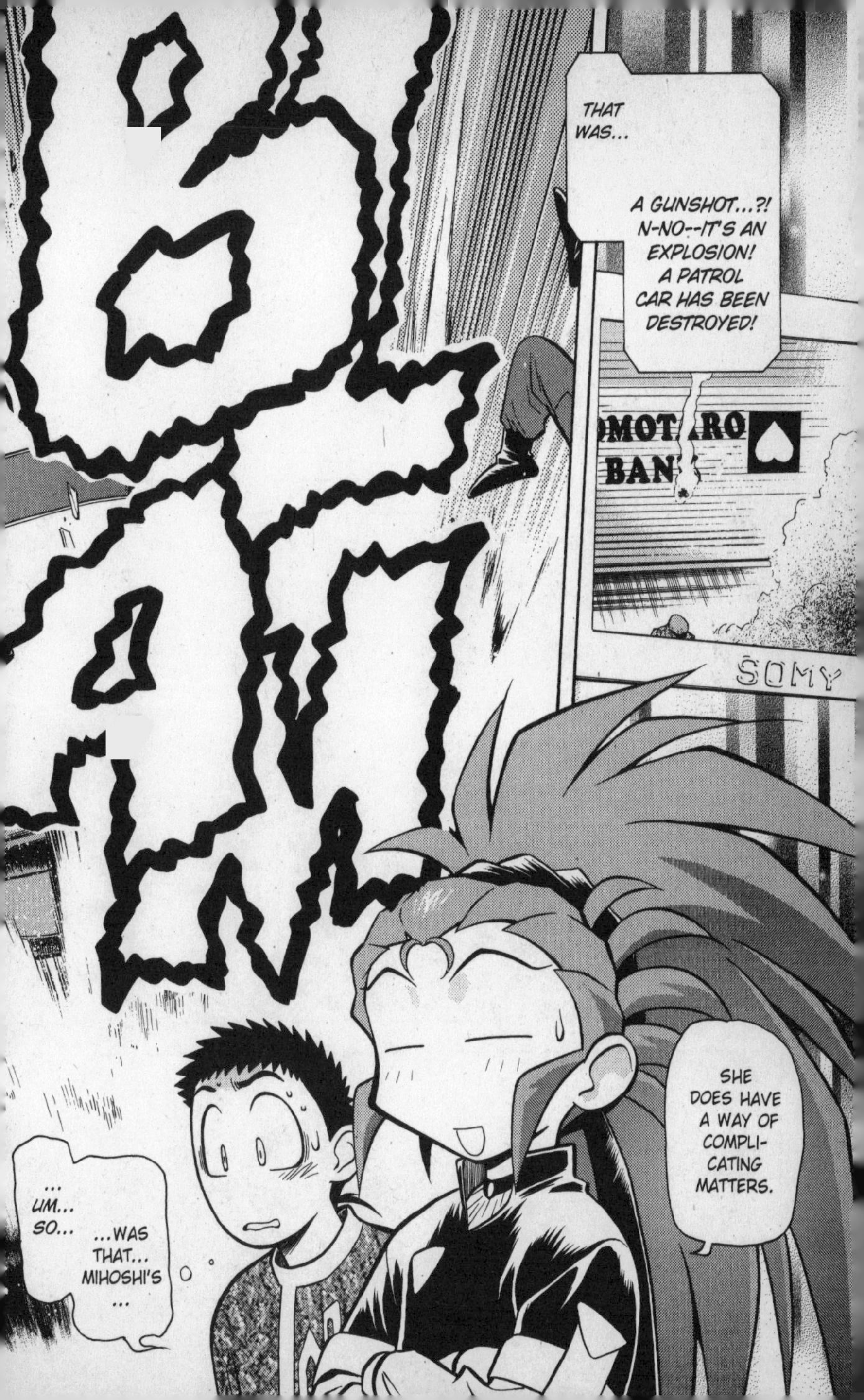
THAT WAS...
A GUNSHOT...?! N-NO--IT'S AN EXPLOSION! A PATROL CAR HAS BEEN DESTROYED!
OMOTARO BAN
SOMY
... UM... SO...
...WAS THAT... MIHOSHI'S ...
SHE DOES HAVE A WAY OF COMPLI-CATING MATTERS.

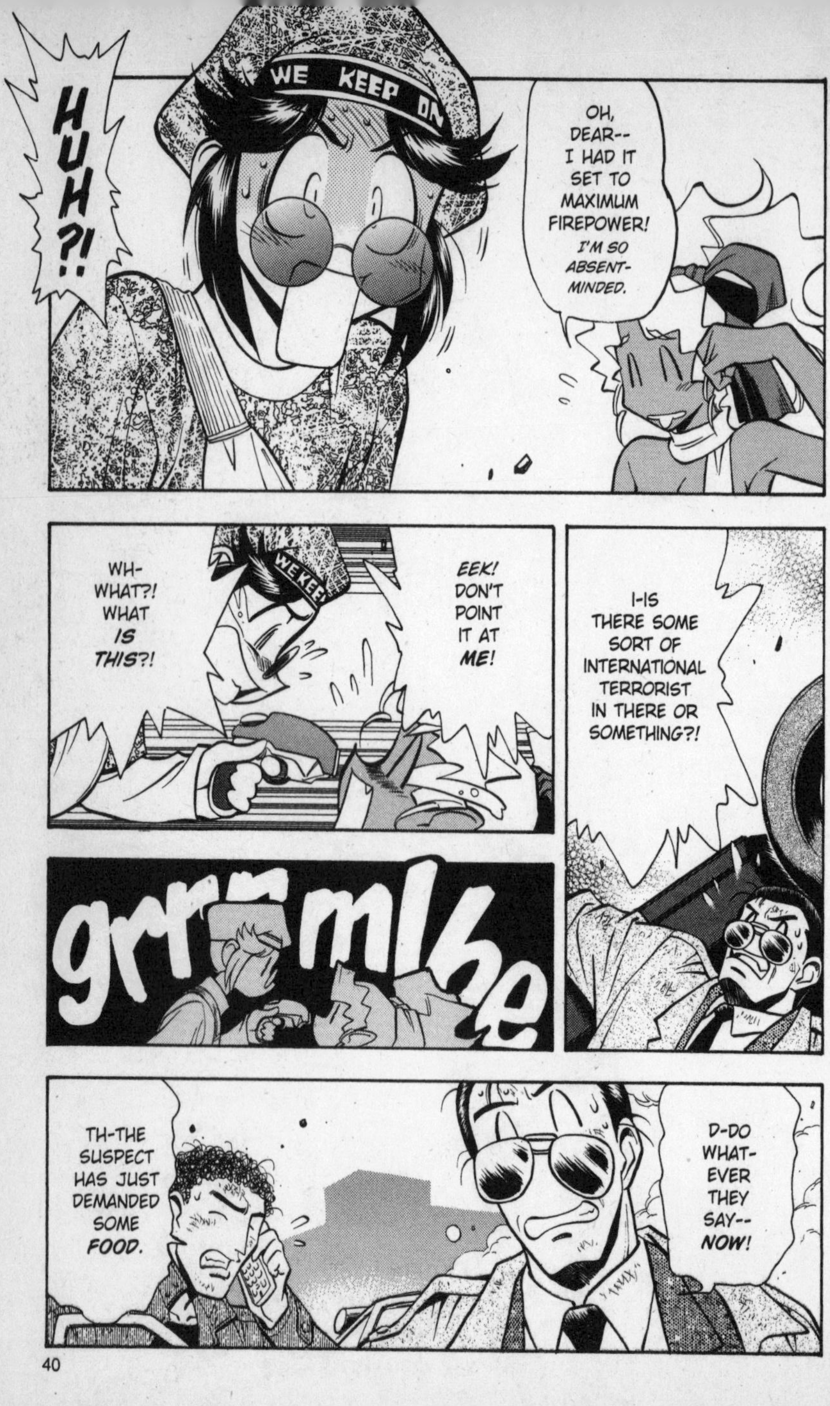
HUH?!
WE KEEP
OH, DEAR-- I HAD IT SET TO MAXIMUM FIREPOWER! I'M SO ABSENT-MINDED.
WH-WHAT?! WHAT IS THIS?!
EEK! DON'T POINT IT AT ME!
I-IS THERE SOME SORT OF INTERNATIONAL TERRORIST IN THERE OR SOMETHING?!
TH-THE SUSPECT HAS JUST DEMANDED SOME FOOD.
D-DO WHAT-EVER THEY SAY-- NOW!

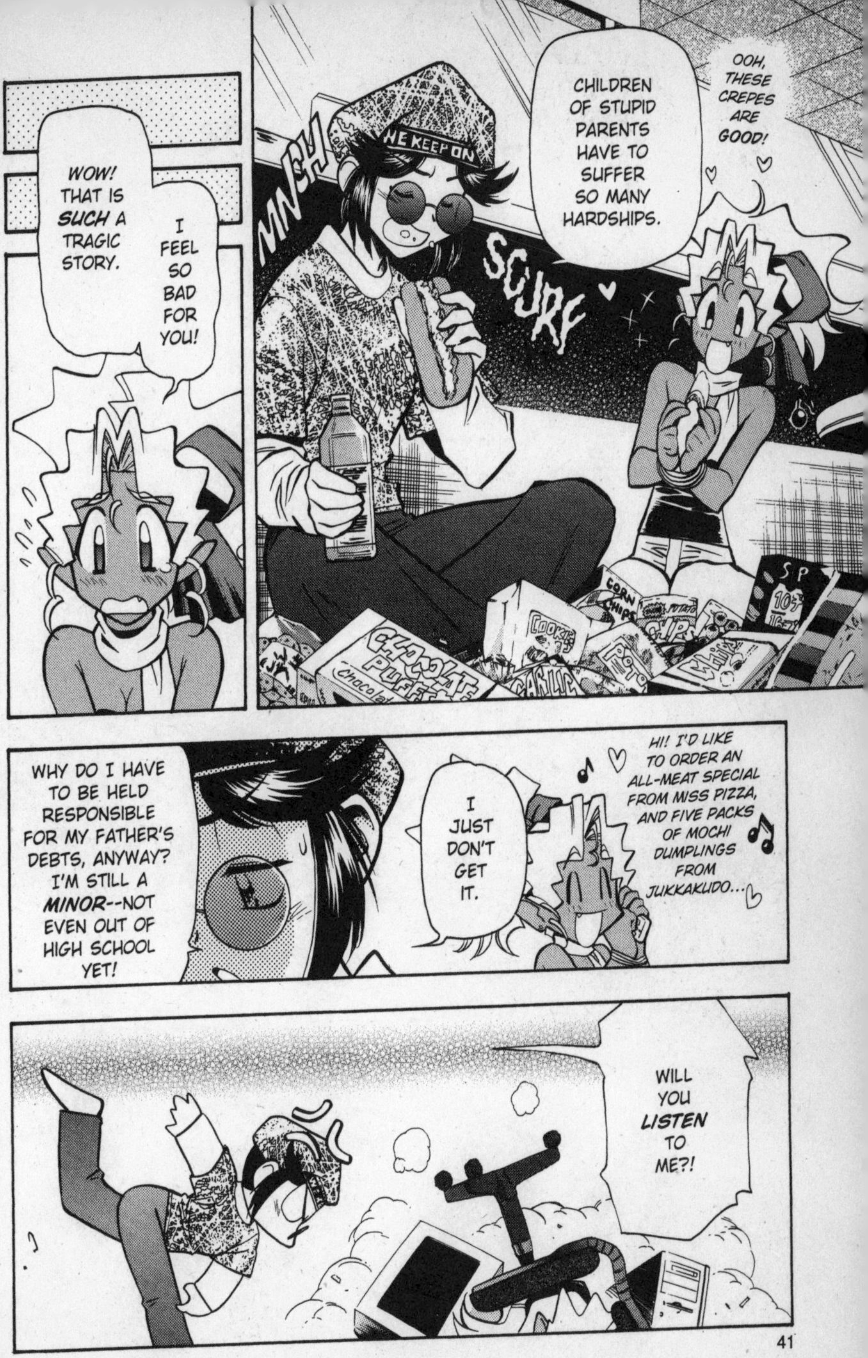
WOW! THAT IS *SUCH* A TRAGIC STORY.
I FEEL SO BAD FOR YOU!
WE KEEP ON
MNCH
CHILDREN OF STUPID PARENTS HAVE TO SUFFER SO MANY HARDSHIPS.
SCURF
OOH, THESE CREPES ARE *GOOD!*
CORN CHIPS
CHOCOLATE PUFFS
WHY DO I HAVE TO BE HELD RESPONSIBLE FOR MY FATHER'S DEBTS, ANYWAY? I'M STILL A *MINOR*--NOT EVEN OUT OF HIGH SCHOOL YET!
I JUST DON'T GET IT.
HI! I'D LIKE TO ORDER AN ALL-MEAT SPECIAL FROM MISS PIZZA, AND FIVE PACKS OF MOCHI DUMPLINGS FROM JUKKAKUDO...
WILL YOU *LISTEN* TO ME?!

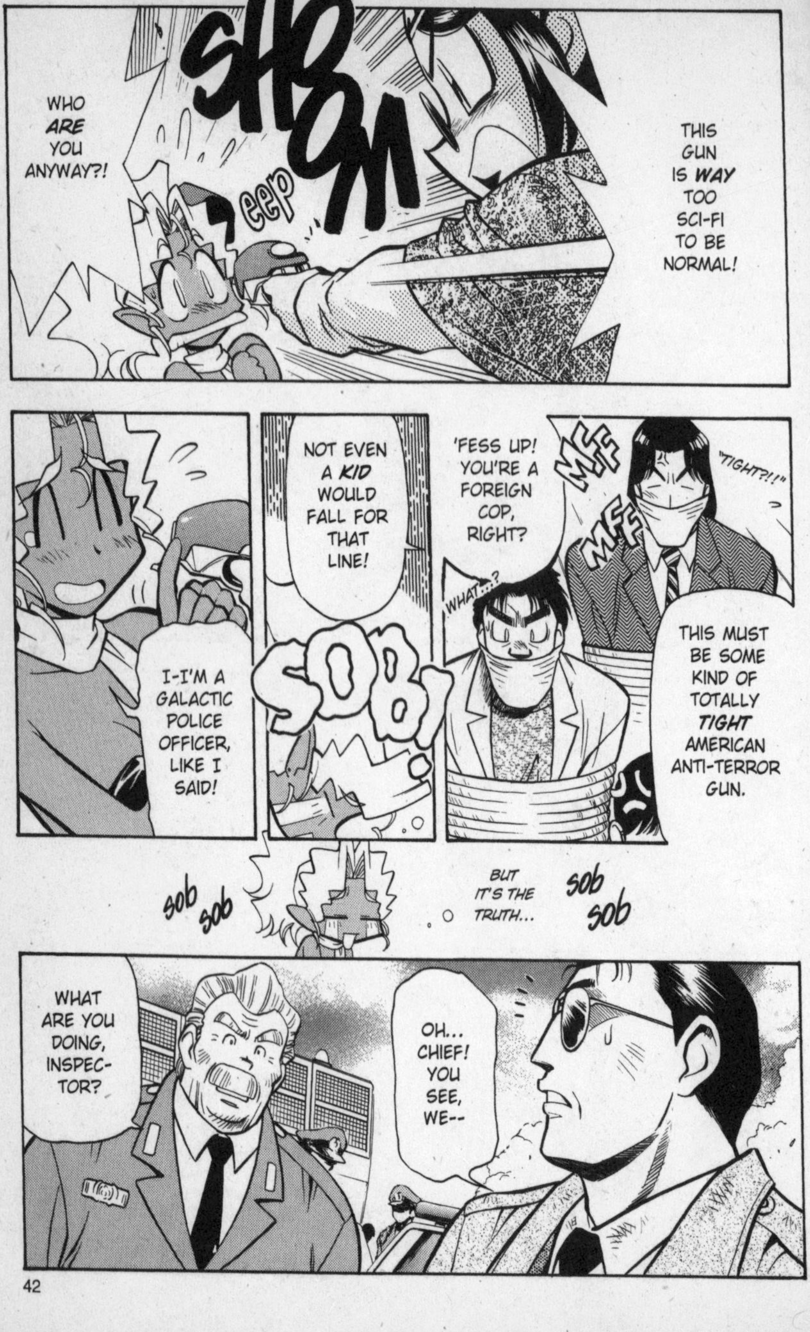
WHO *ARE* YOU ANYWAY?!
eep
THIS GUN IS *WAY* TOO SCI-FI TO BE NORMAL!
I-I'M A GALACTIC POLICE OFFICER, LIKE I SAID!
NOT EVEN A *KID* WOULD FALL FOR THAT LINE!
SOB!
'FESS UP! YOU'RE A FOREIGN COP, RIGHT?
MFF
MFF
WHAT...?
"TIGHT?!"
THIS MUST BE SOME KIND OF TOTALLY *TIGHT* AMERICAN ANTI-TERROR GUN.
sob sob
BUT IT'S THE TRUTH...
sob sob
WHAT ARE YOU DOING, INSPECTOR?
OH... CHIEF! YOU SEE, WE--

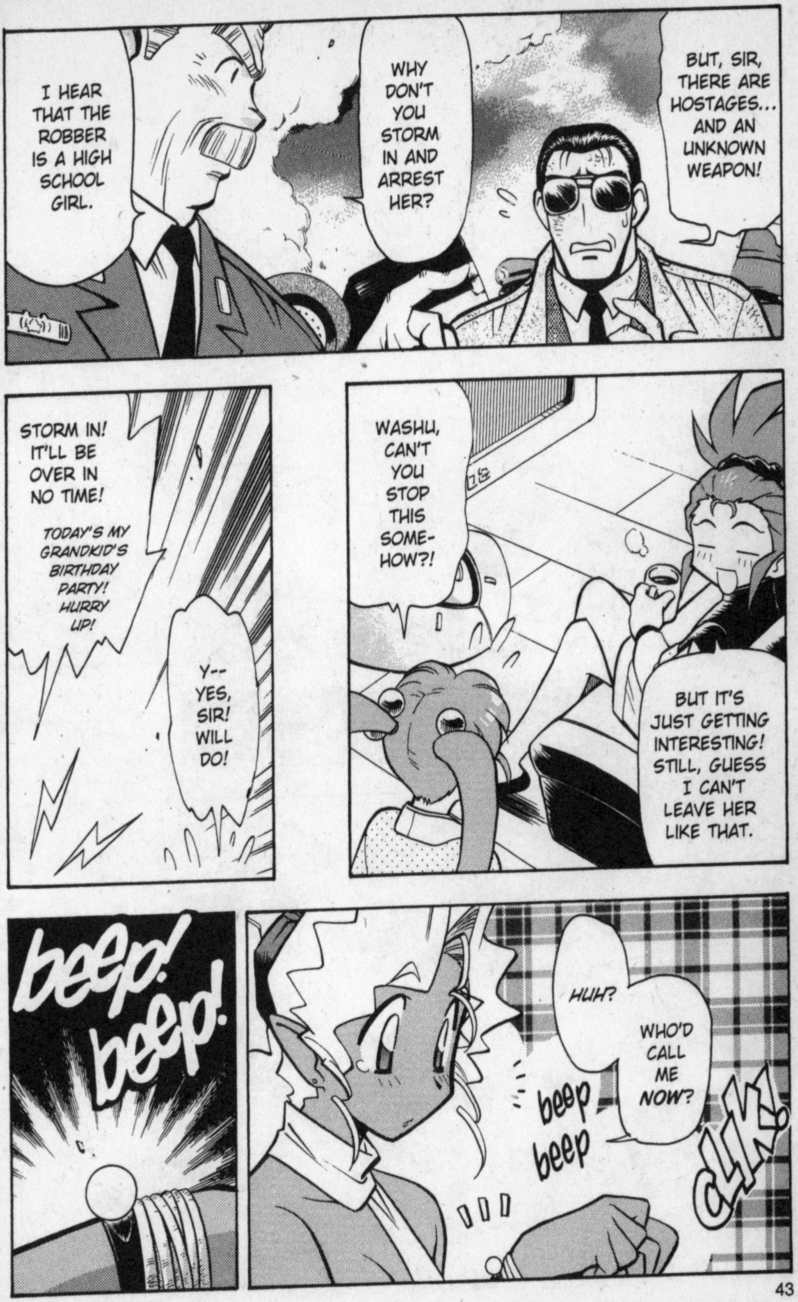
I HEAR THAT THE ROBBER IS A HIGH SCHOOL GIRL.
WHY DON'T YOU STORM IN AND ARREST HER?
BUT, SIR, THERE ARE HOSTAGES... AND AN UNKNOWN WEAPON!
STORM IN! IT'LL BE OVER IN NO TIME!
TODAY'S MY GRANDKID'S BIRTHDAY PARTY! HURRY UP!
Y-- YES, SIR! WILL DO!
WASHU, CAN'T YOU STOP THIS SOME-HOW?!
BUT IT'S JUST GETTING INTERESTING! STILL, GUESS I CAN'T LEAVE HER LIKE THAT.
beep! beep!
HUH?
WHO'D CALL ME NOW?
beep beep
CLIK!

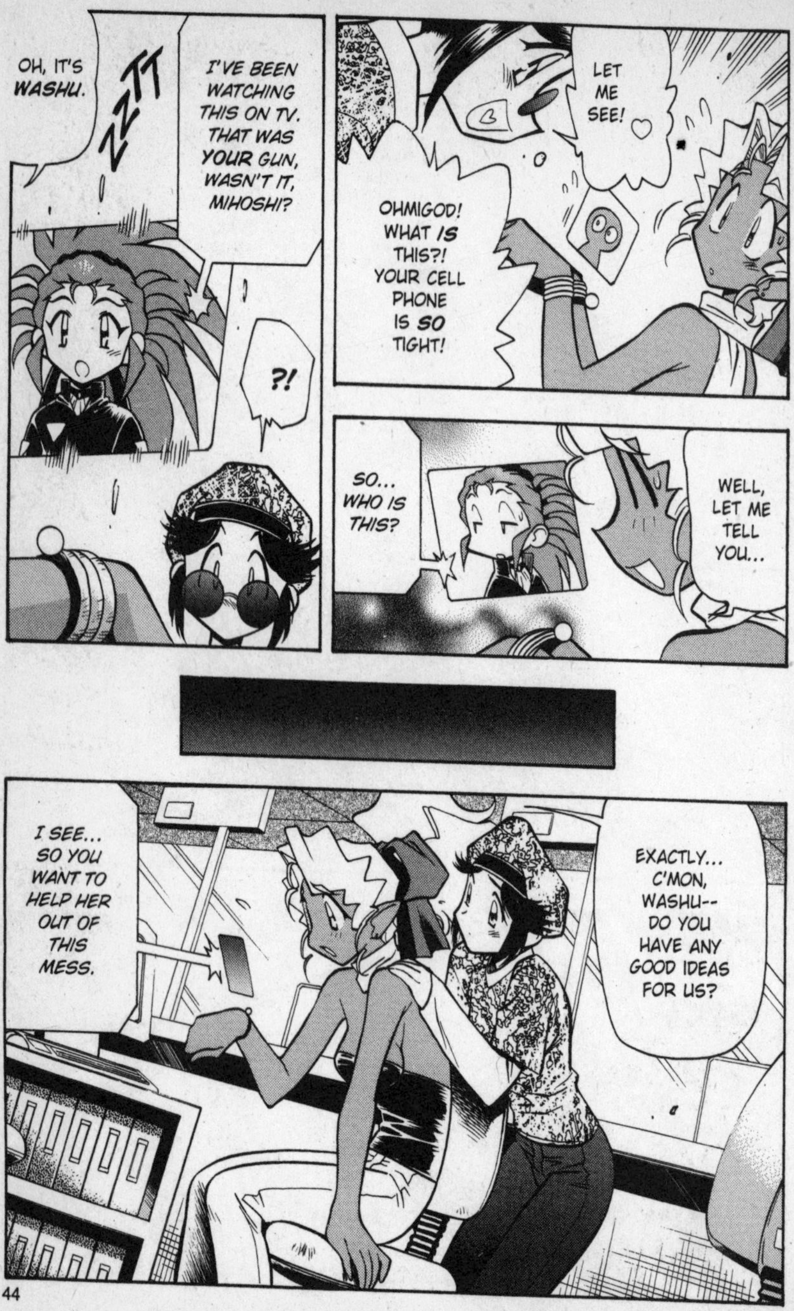
OH, IT'S WASHU.
ZZTT
I'VE BEEN WATCHING THIS ON TV. THAT WAS YOUR GUN, WASN'T IT, MIHOSHI?
LET ME SEE!
OHMIGOD! WHAT IS THIS?! YOUR CELL PHONE IS SO TIGHT!
?!
SO... WHO IS THIS?
WELL, LET ME TELL YOU...
I SEE... SO YOU WANT TO HELP HER OUT OF THIS MESS.
EXACTLY... C'MON, WASHU-- DO YOU HAVE ANY GOOD IDEAS FOR US?

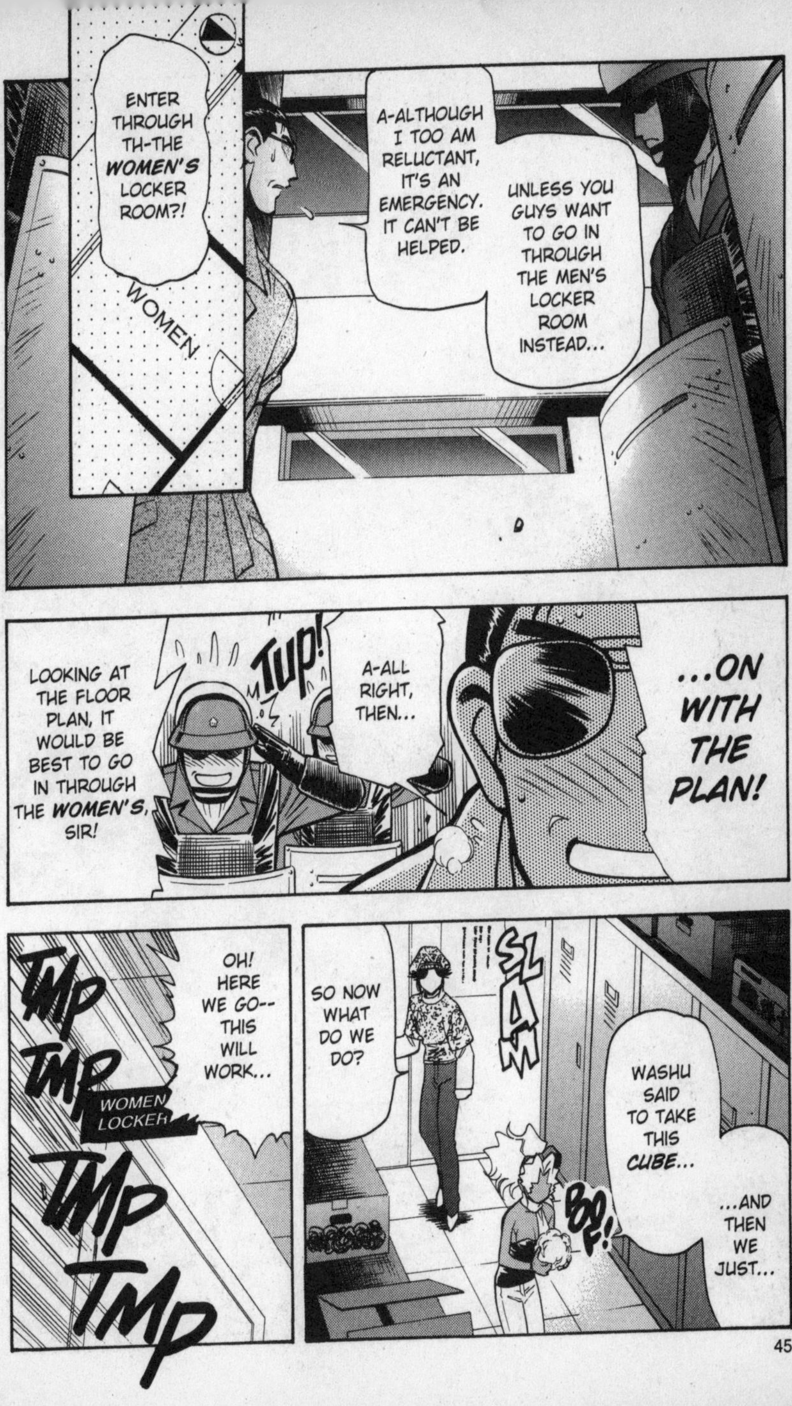
ENTER THROUGH TH-THE WOMEN'S LOCKER ROOM?!
WOMEN
A-ALTHOUGH I TOO AM RELUCTANT, IT'S AN EMERGENCY. IT CAN'T BE HELPED.
UNLESS YOU GUYS WANT TO GO IN THROUGH THE MEN'S LOCKER ROOM INSTEAD...
LOOKING AT THE FLOOR PLAN, IT WOULD BE BEST TO GO IN THROUGH THE WOMEN'S, SIR!
TUP!
A-ALL RIGHT, THEN...
...ON WITH THE PLAN!
TMP TMP TMP TMP
WOMEN LOCKER
OH! HERE WE GO-- THIS WILL WORK...
SO NOW WHAT DO WE DO?
SLAM
WASHU SAID TO TAKE THIS CUBE...
POOF!
...AND THEN WE JUST...

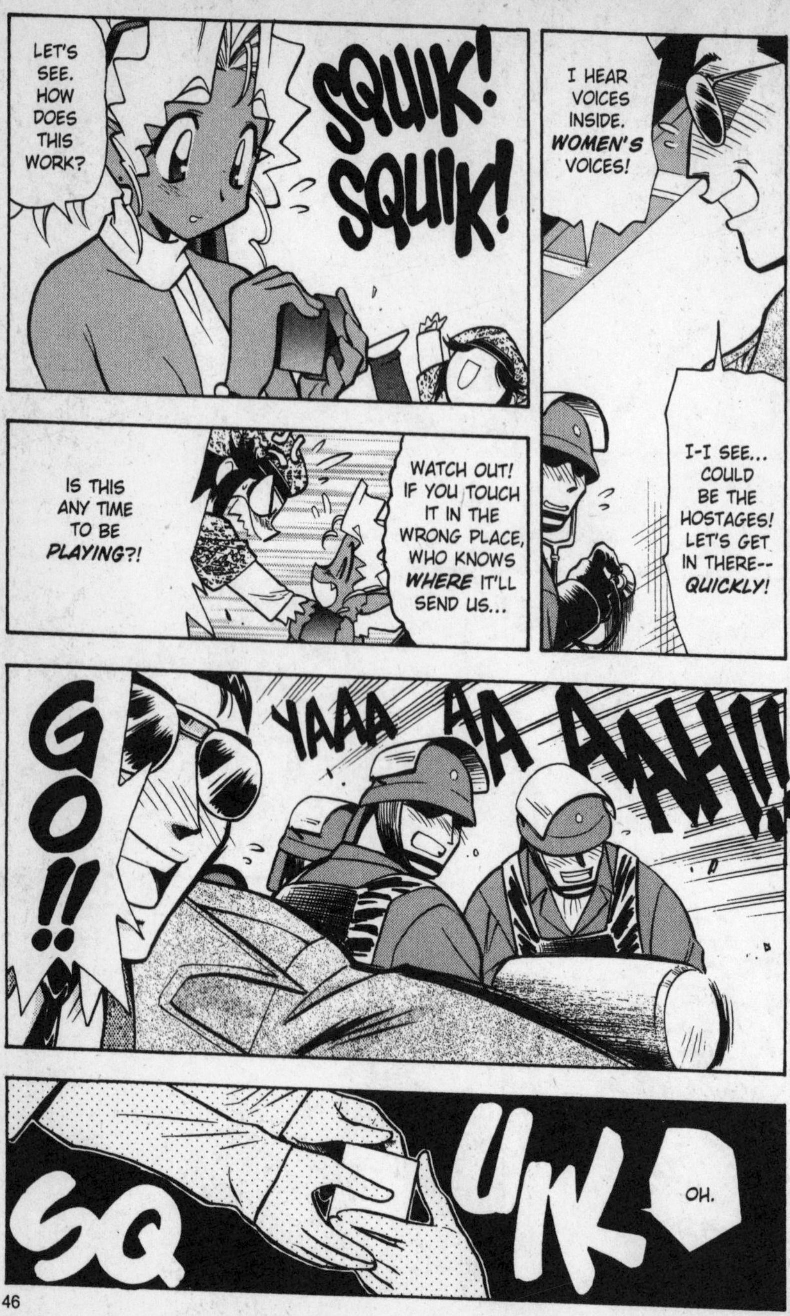
LET'S SEE. HOW DOES THIS WORK?
SQUIK! SQUIK!
I HEAR VOICES INSIDE. WOMEN'S VOICES!
IS THIS ANY TIME TO BE PLAYING?!
WATCH OUT! IF YOU TOUCH IT IN THE WRONG PLACE, WHO KNOWS WHERE IT'LL SEND US...
I-I SEE... COULD BE THE HOSTAGES! LET'S GET IN THERE-- QUICKLY!
GO!!
YAAAAAAAAH!!
SQUIK
OH.

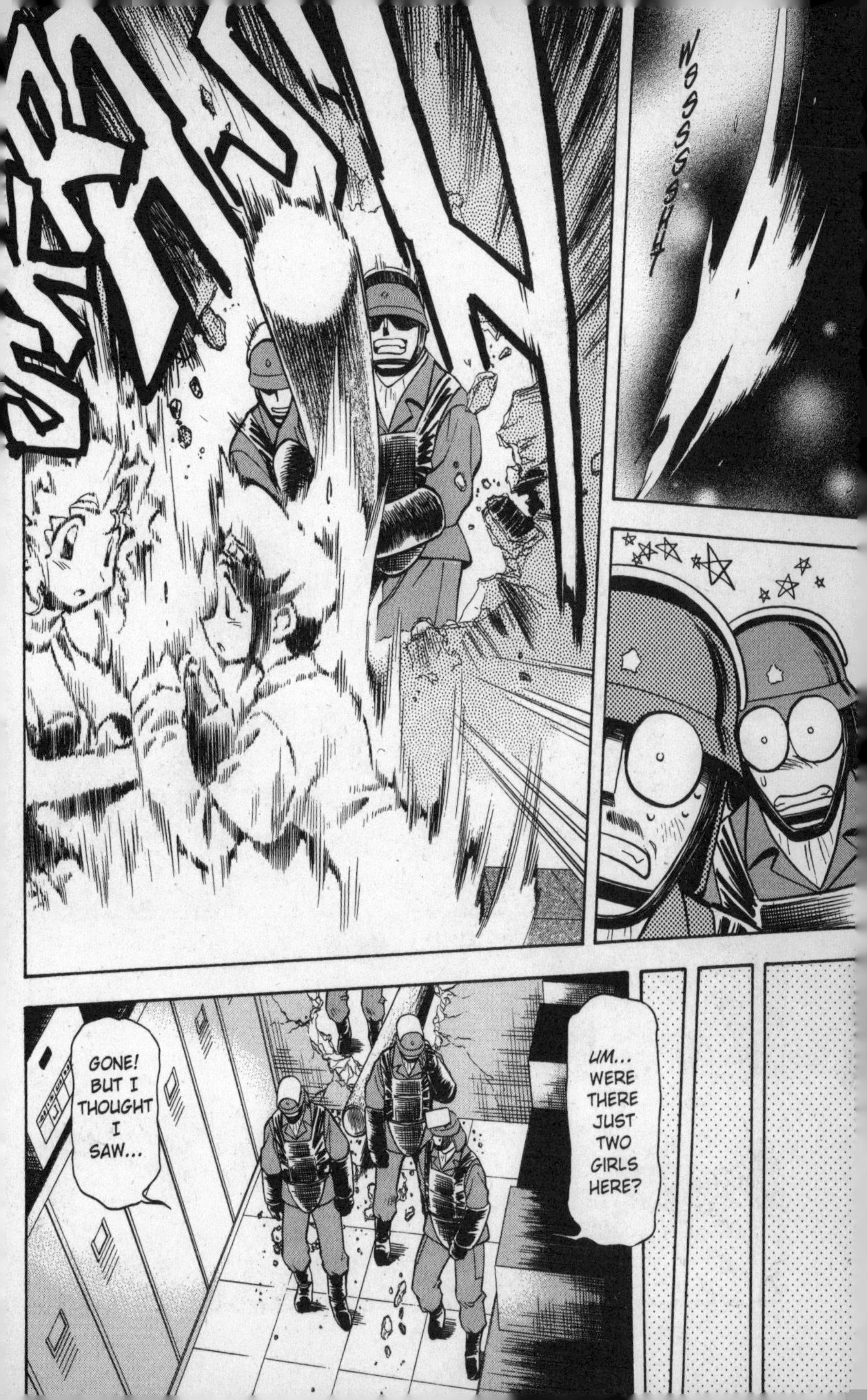
WOSSSSSHH
GONE! BUT I THOUGHT I SAW...
UM... WERE THERE JUST TWO GIRLS HERE?

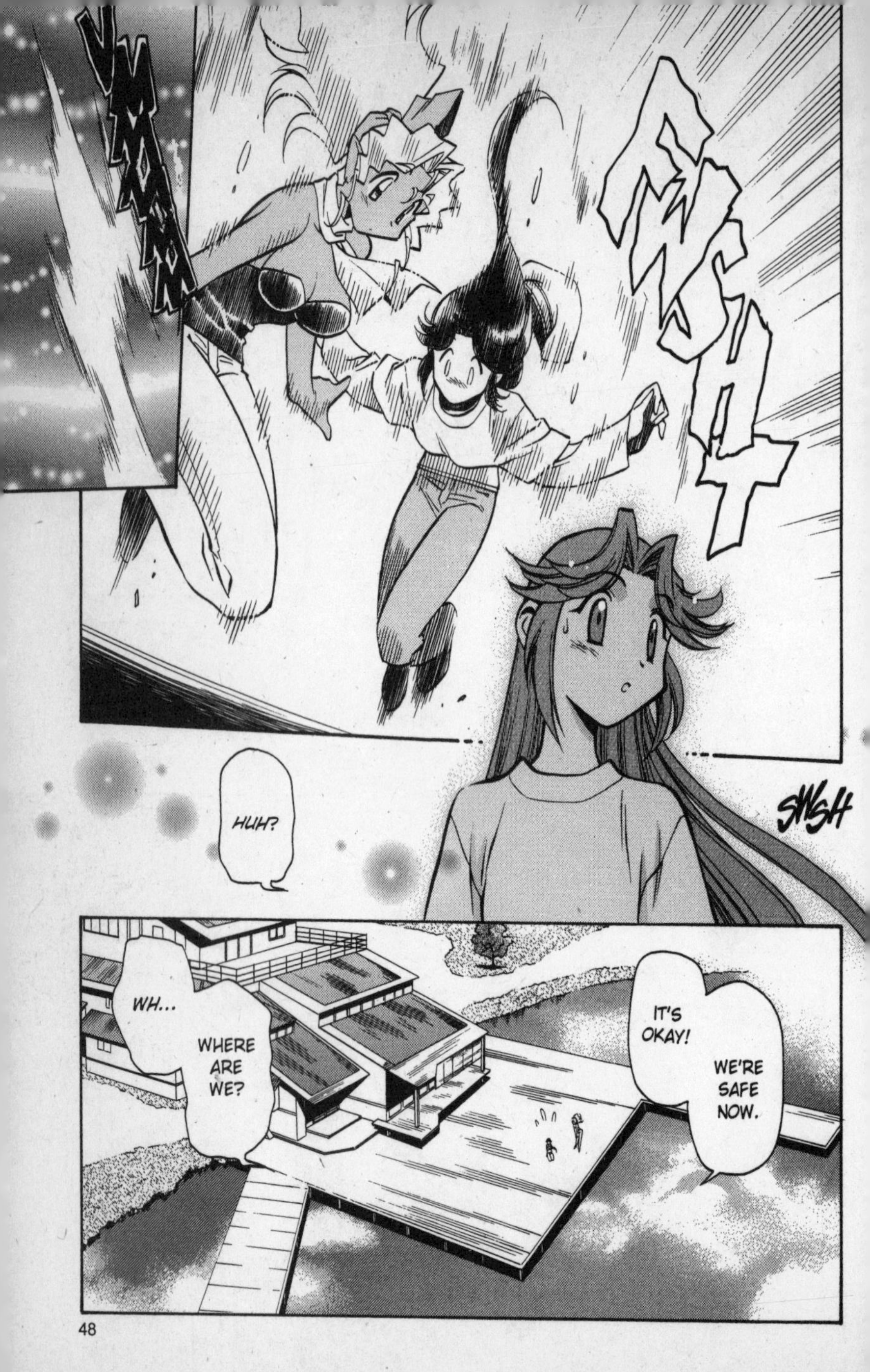
VWOOOM
FWSH
HUH?
SWSH
WH...
WHERE ARE WE?
IT'S OKAY!
WE'RE SAFE NOW.

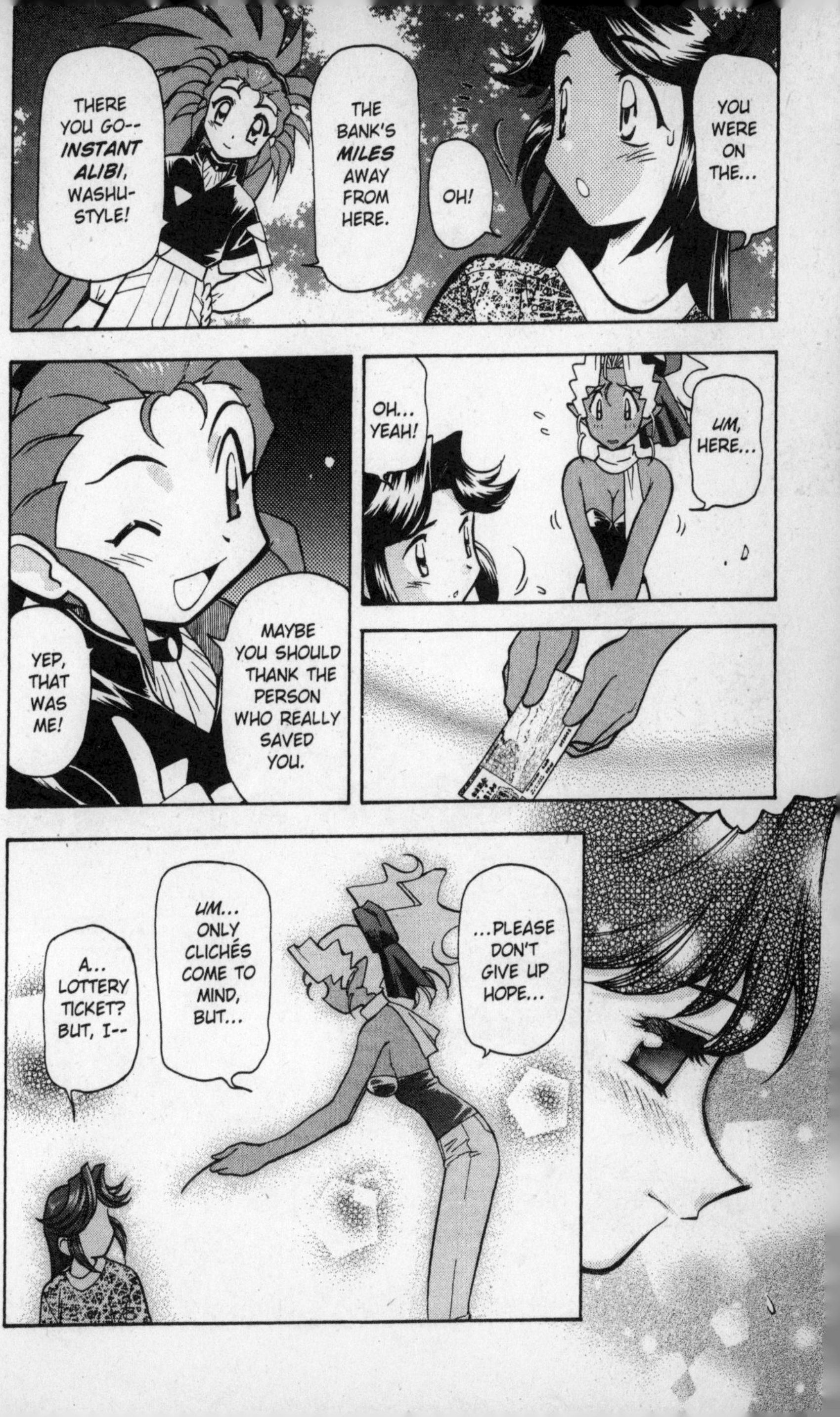
THERE YOU GO-- INSTANT ALIBI, WASHU-STYLE!
THE BANK'S MILES AWAY FROM HERE.
OH!
YOU WERE ON THE...
YEP, THAT WAS ME!
MAYBE YOU SHOULD THANK THE PERSON WHO REALLY SAVED YOU.
OH... YEAH!
UM, HERE...
A... LOTTERY TICKET? BUT, I--
UM... ONLY CLICHÉS COME TO MIND, BUT...
...PLEASE DON'T GIVE UP HOPE...

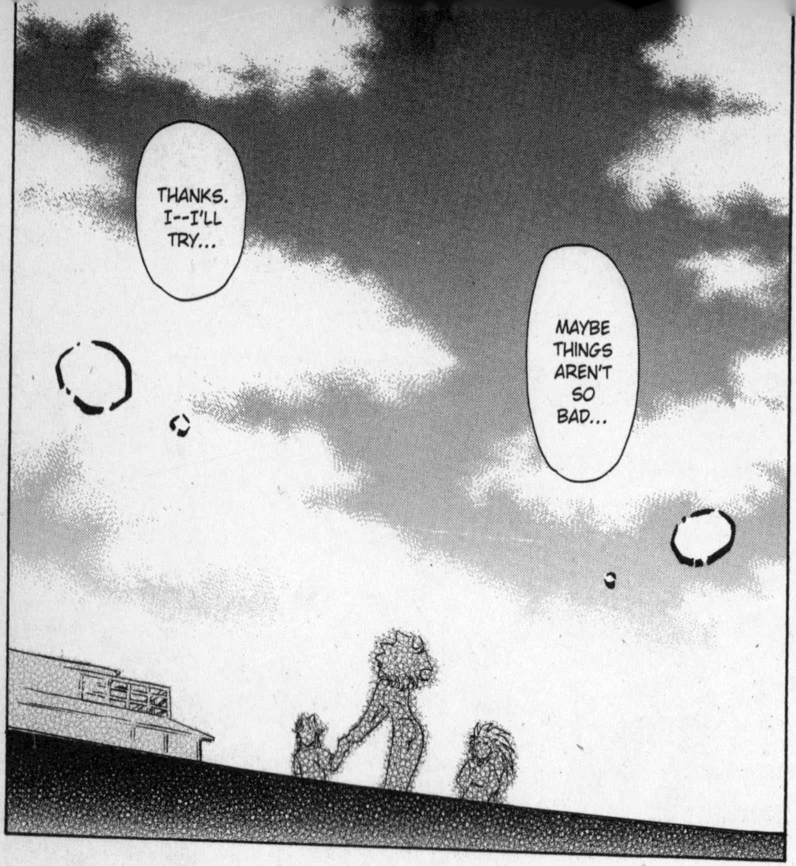
THANKS. I--I'LL TRY...
MAYBE THINGS AREN'T SO BAD...

...AND LATER...

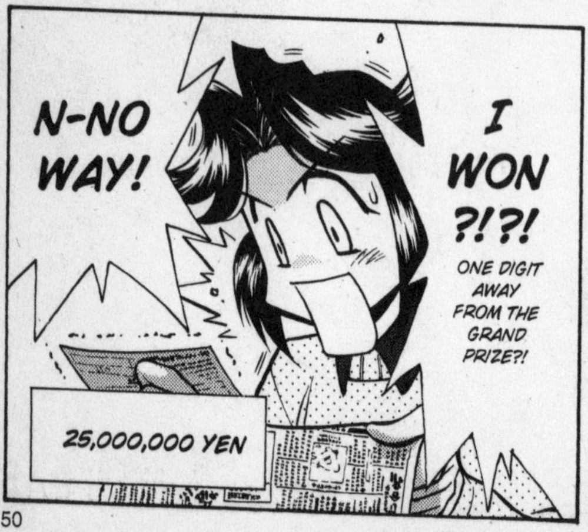
N-NO WAY!
I WON ?!?!
ONE DIGIT AWAY FROM THE GRAND PRIZE?!
25,000,000 YEN

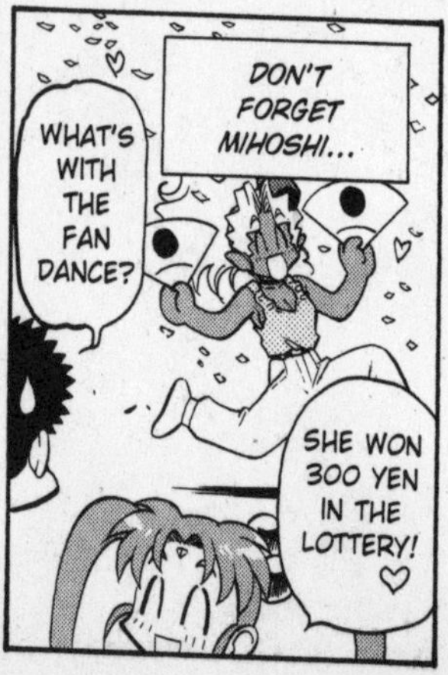
WHAT'S WITH THE FAN DANCE?
DON'T FORGET MIHOSHI...
SHE WON 300 YEN IN THE LOTTERY! ♡

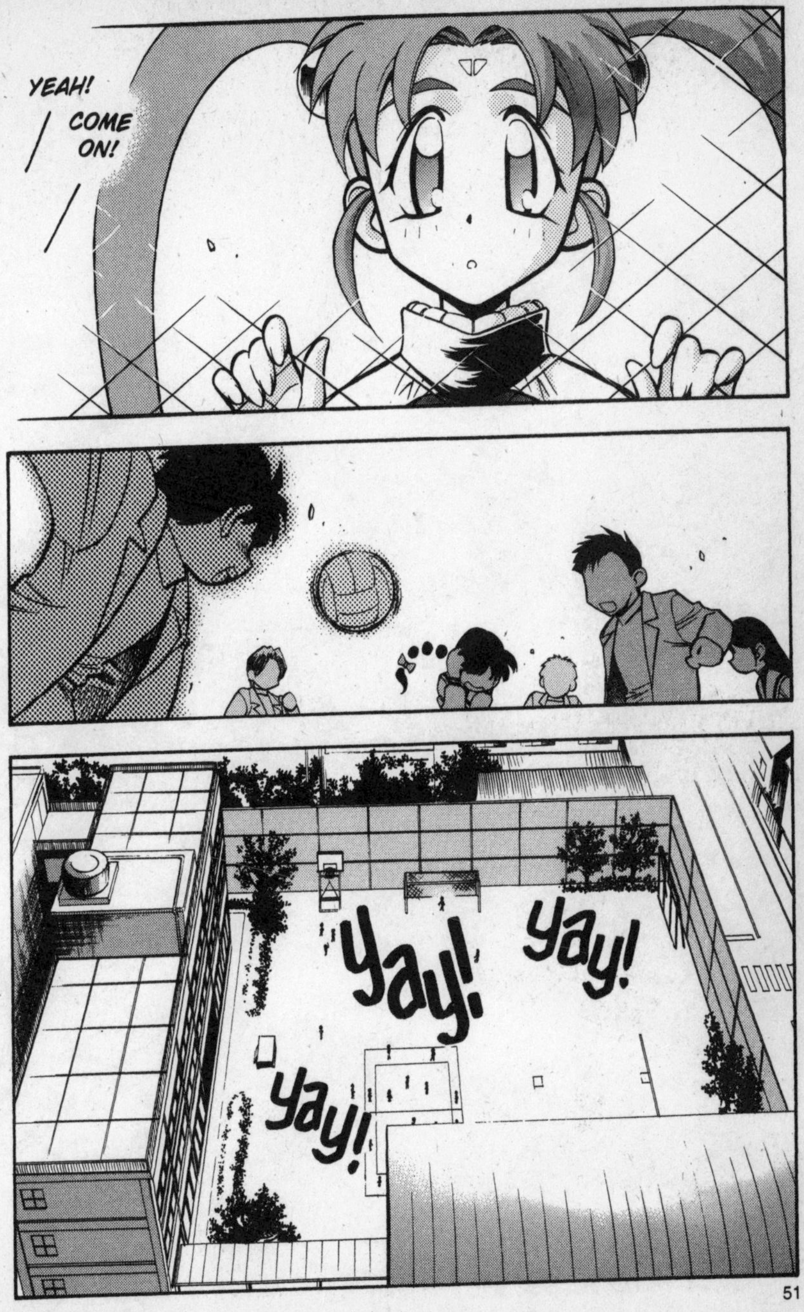
YEAH!
COME ON!
Yay!
yay!
yay!

Chapter 3: MASS CONFUSION

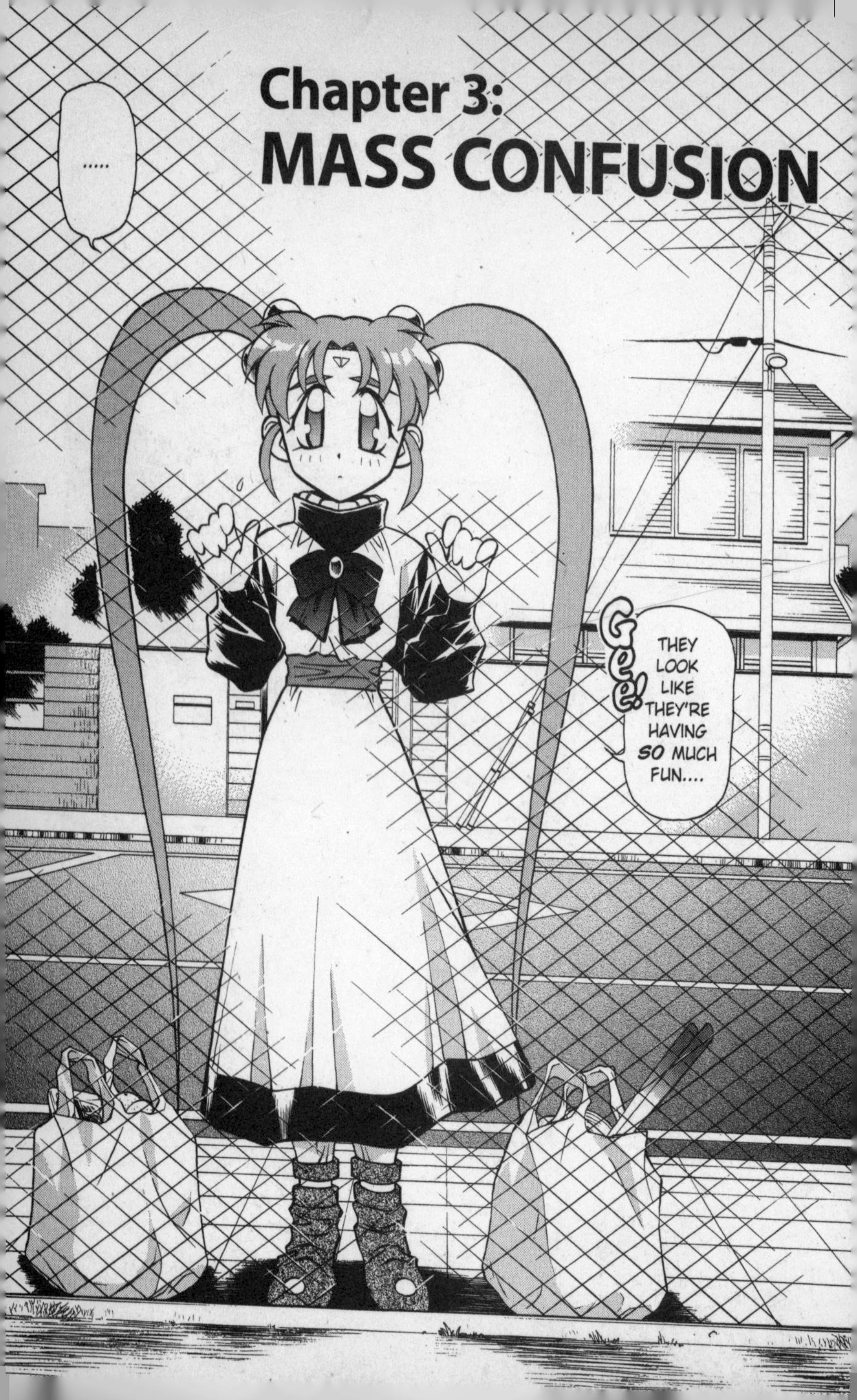
.....
Gee!
THEY LOOK LIKE THEY'RE HAVING SO MUCH FUN....

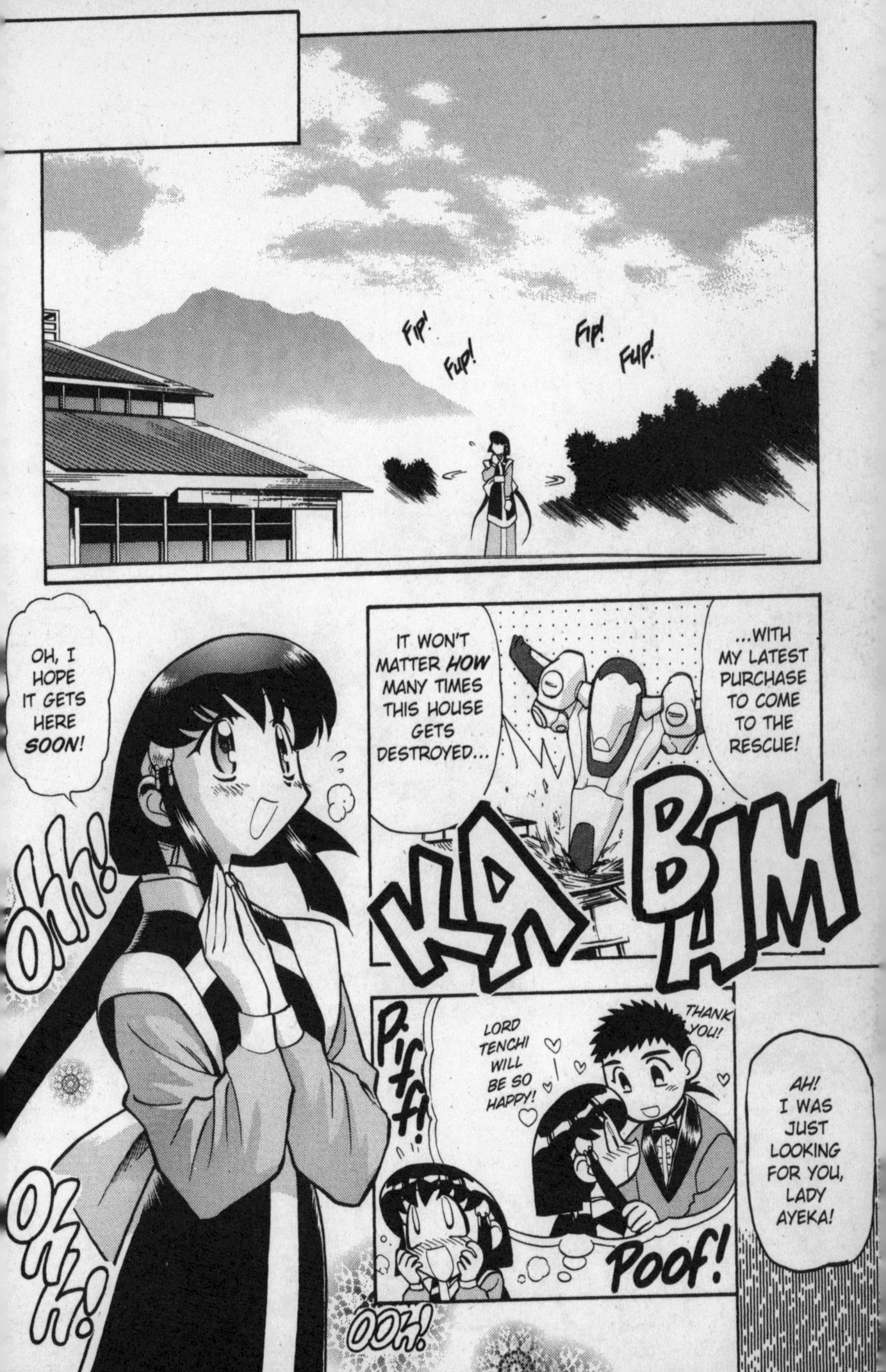

Fip!
Fup!
Fip!
Fup!
OH, I HOPE IT GETS HERE SOON!
Ohh!
Ohh!
OOH!
IT WON'T MATTER HOW MANY TIMES THIS HOUSE GETS DESTROYED...
...WITH MY LATEST PURCHASE TO COME TO THE RESCUE!
KABAM
Piff!
LORD TENCHI WILL BE SO HAPPY!
THANK YOU!
Poof!
AH! I WAS JUST LOOKING FOR YOU, LADY AYEKA!

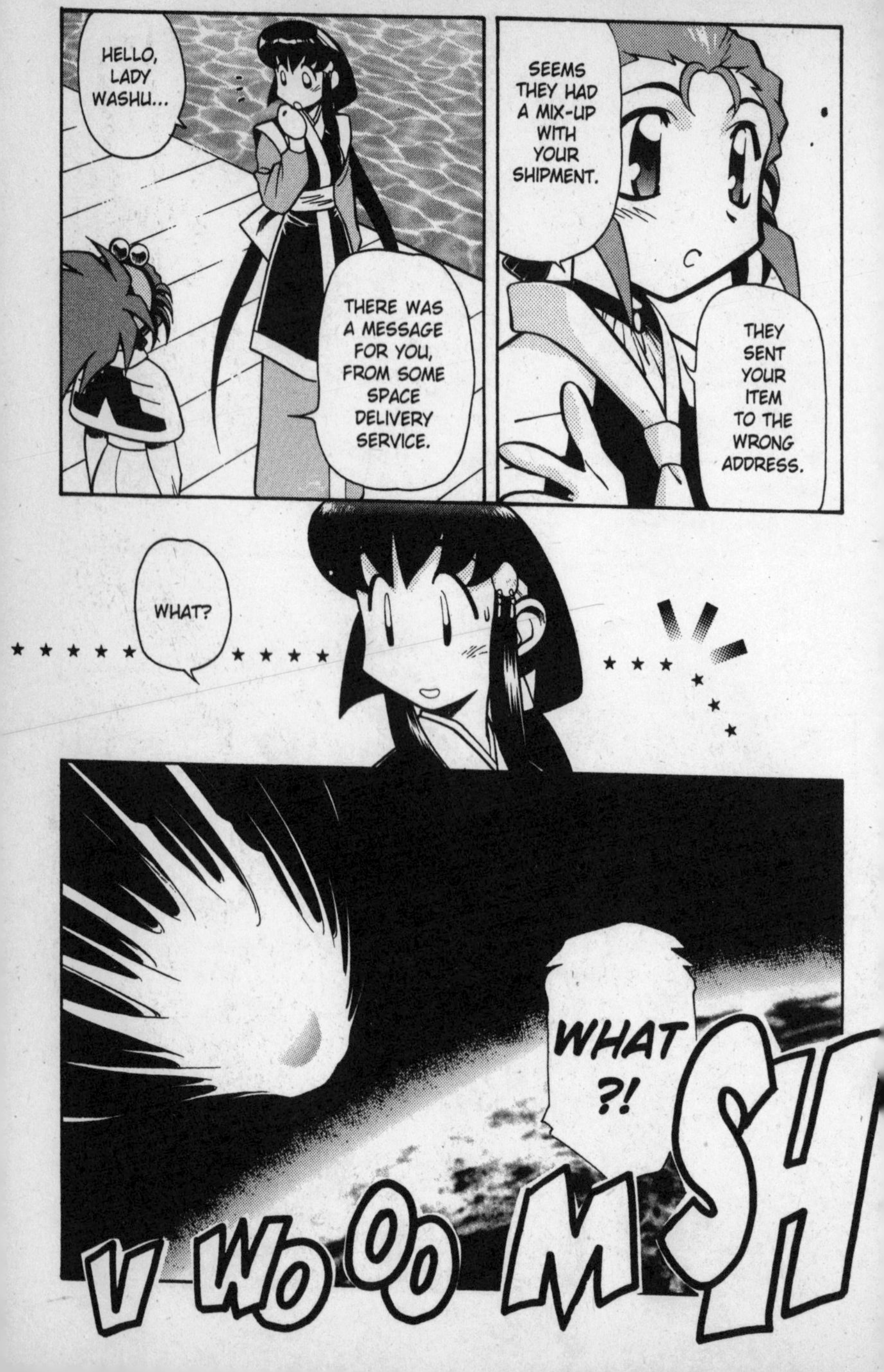
HELLO, LADY WASHU...
THERE WAS A MESSAGE FOR YOU, FROM SOME SPACE DELIVERY SERVICE.
SEEMS THEY HAD A MIX-UP WITH YOUR SHIPMENT.
THEY SENT YOUR ITEM TO THE WRONG ADDRESS.
WHAT?
WHAT?!
VWOOOMSH

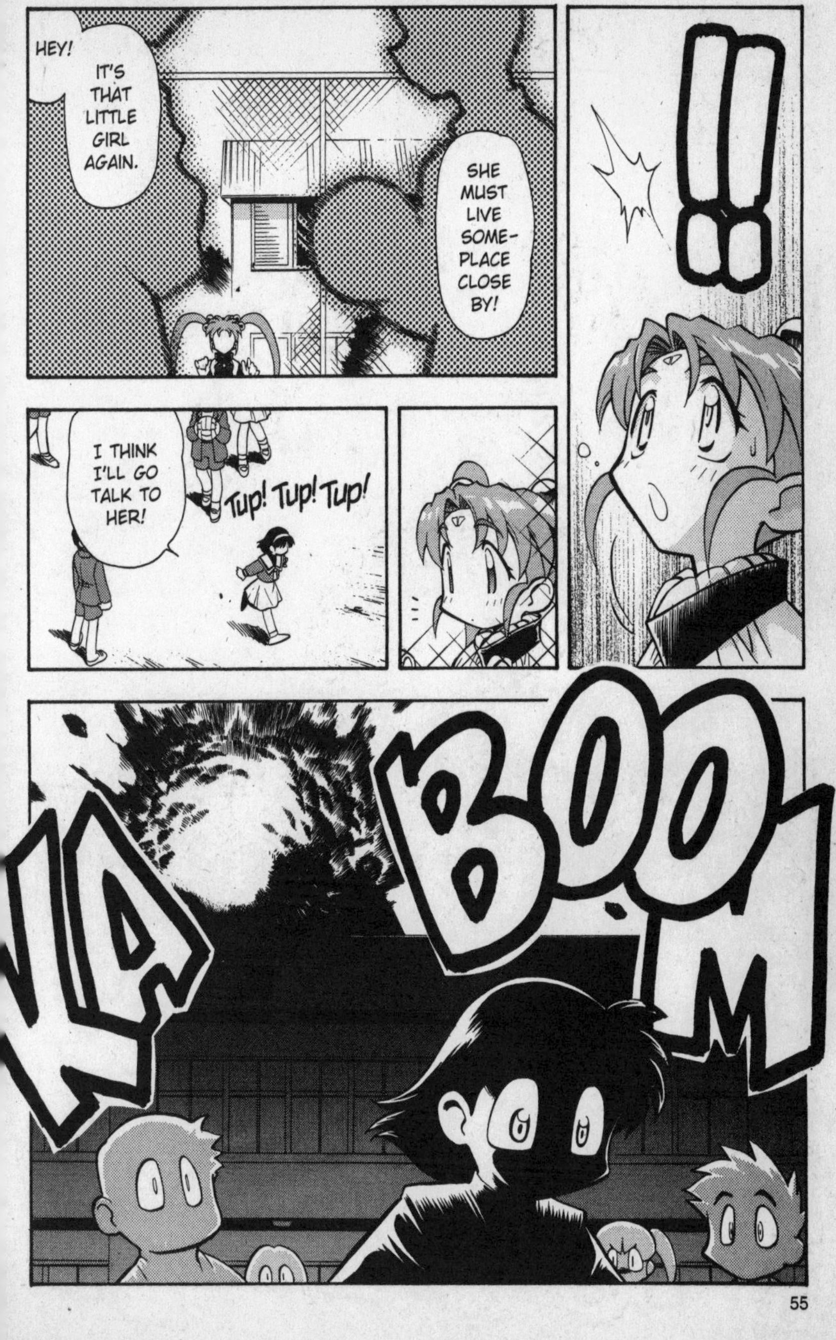
HEY! IT'S THAT LITTLE GIRL AGAIN.
SHE MUST LIVE SOME-PLACE CLOSE BY!
!!
I THINK I'LL GO TALK TO HER!
Tup! Tup! Tup!
KA BOOM

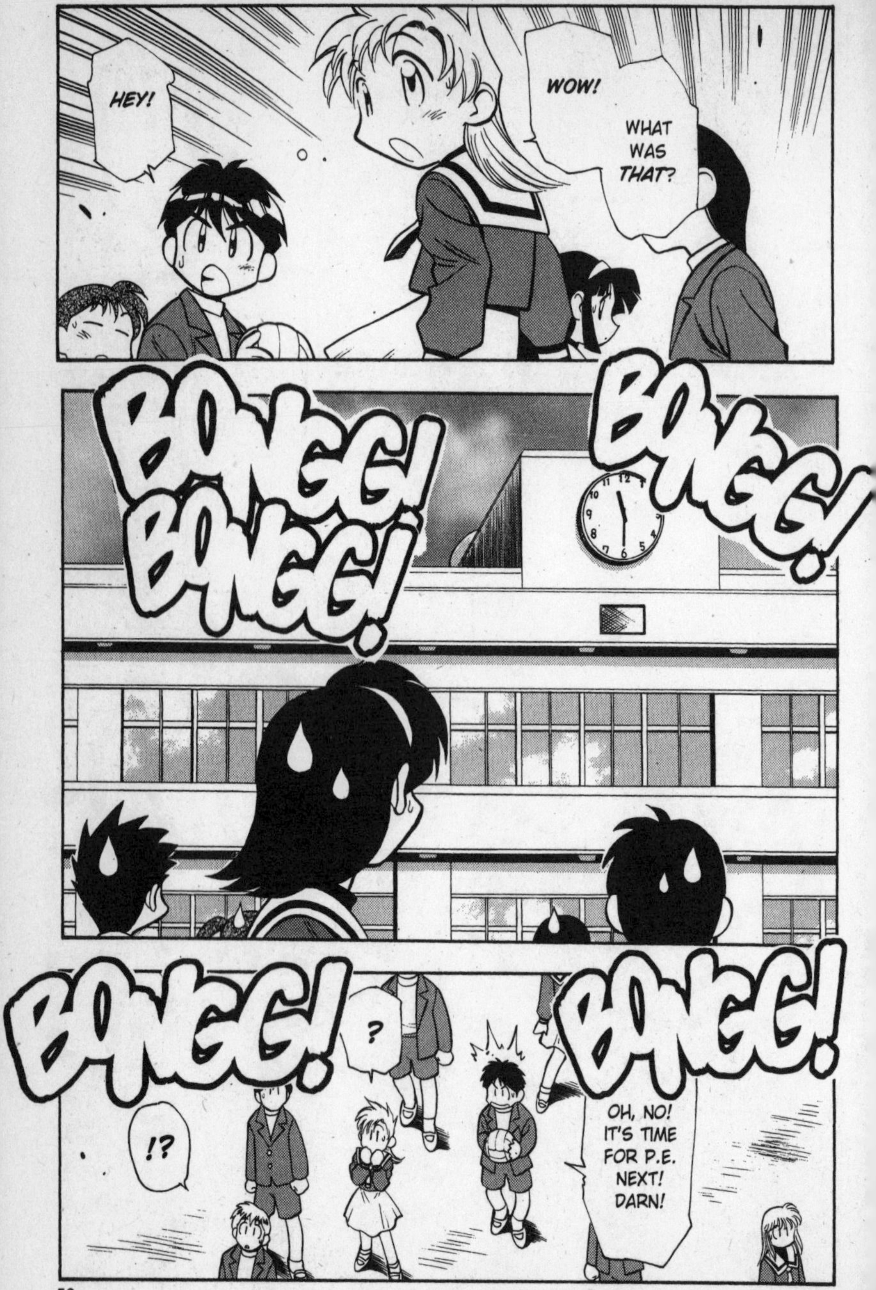
HEY!
WOW!
WHAT WAS THAT?
BONGG! BONGG!
BONGG!
BONGG!
?
BONGG!
!?
OH, NO! IT'S TIME FOR P.E. NEXT! DARN!

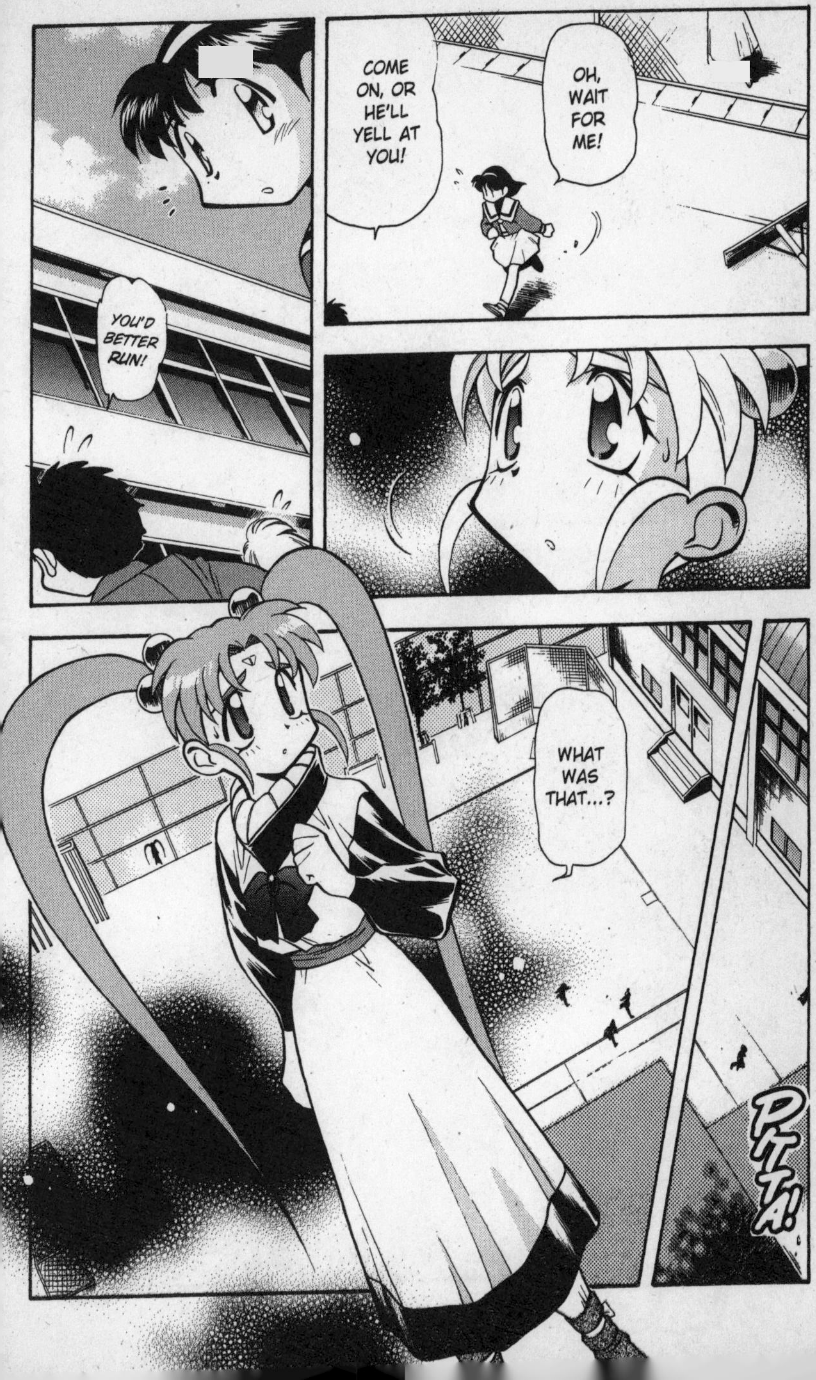
YOU'D BETTER RUN!
COME ON, OR HE'LL YELL AT YOU!
OH, WAIT FOR ME!
WHAT WAS THAT...?
PITTA!

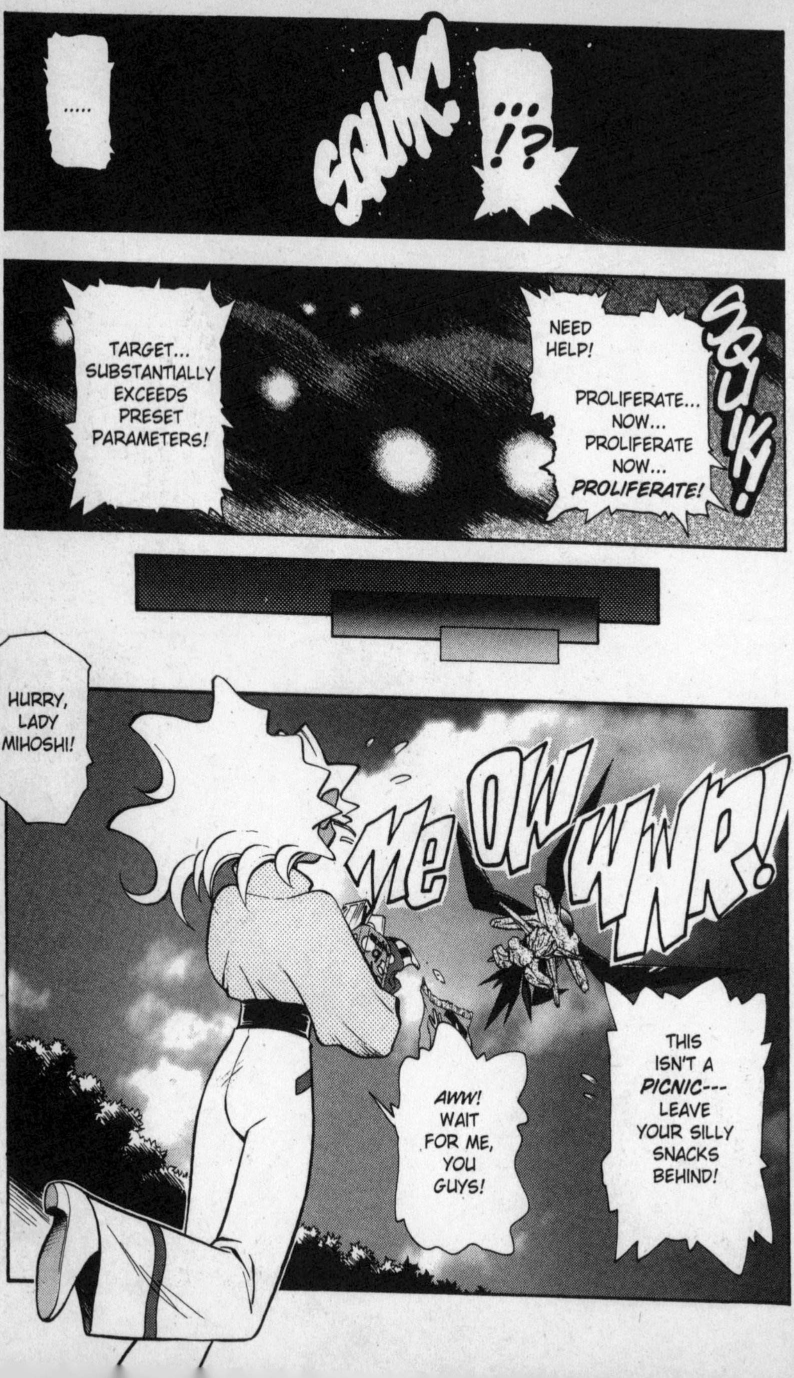

......
SQUIK!
...!?
TARGET... SUBSTANTIALLY EXCEEDS PRESET PARAMETERS!
NEED HELP!
PROLIFERATE... NOW... PROLIFERATE NOW... *PROLIFERATE!*
SQUIK!
HURRY, LADY MIHOSHI!
MEOWWWR!
AWW! WAIT FOR ME, YOU GUYS!
THIS ISN'T A *PICNIC*--- LEAVE YOUR SILLY SNACKS BEHIND!

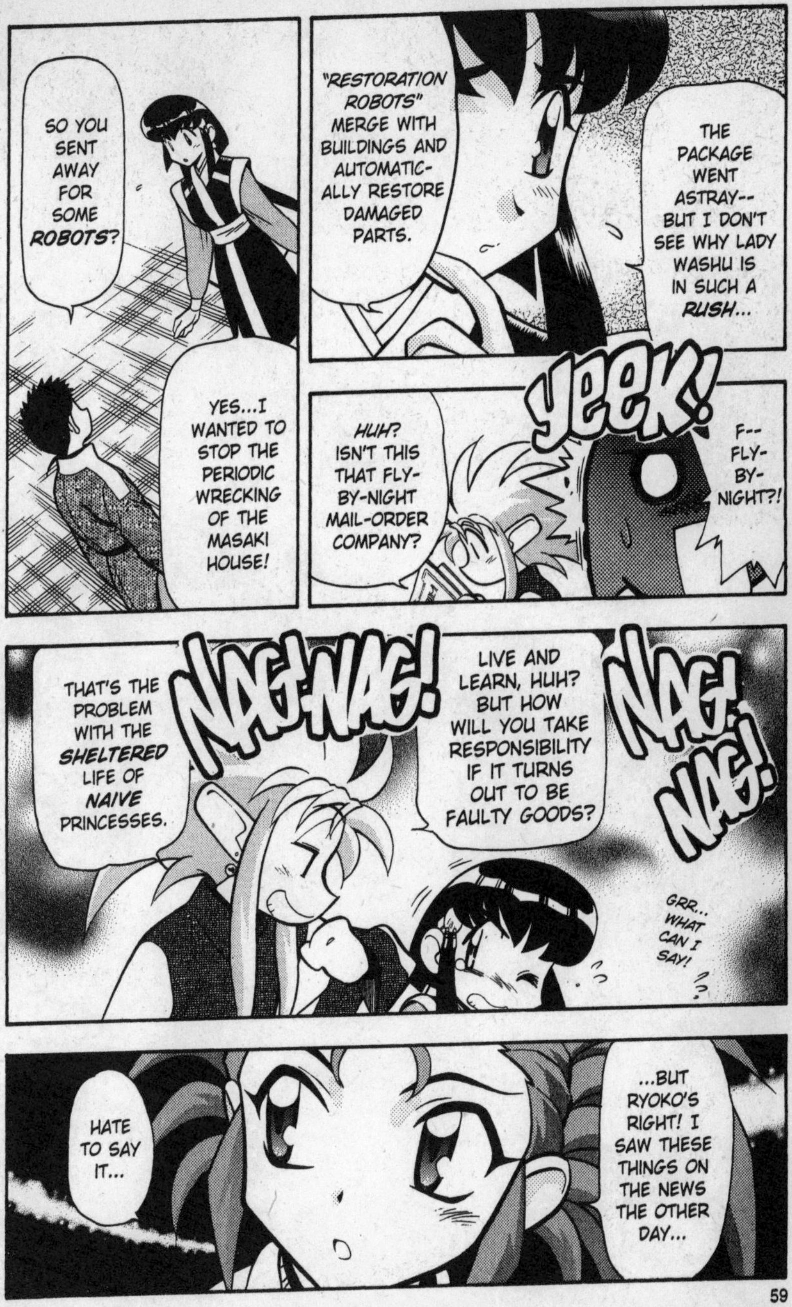
SO YOU SENT AWAY FOR SOME ROBOTS?
YES...I WANTED TO STOP THE PERIODIC WRECKING OF THE MASAKI HOUSE!
"RESTORATION ROBOTS" MERGE WITH BUILDINGS AND AUTOMATIC-ALLY RESTORE DAMAGED PARTS.
THE PACKAGE WENT ASTRAY-- BUT I DON'T SEE WHY LADY WASHU IS IN SUCH A RUSH...
HUH? ISN'T THIS THAT FLY-BY-NIGHT MAIL-ORDER COMPANY?
YEEK!
F-- FLY-BY-NIGHT?!
THAT'S THE PROBLEM WITH THE SHELTERED LIFE OF NAIVE PRINCESSES.
NAG NAG!
LIVE AND LEARN, HUH? BUT HOW WILL YOU TAKE RESPONSIBILITY IF IT TURNS OUT TO BE FAULTY GOODS?
NAG. NAG!
GRR... WHAT CAN I SAY!
HATE TO SAY IT...
...BUT RYOKO'S RIGHT! I SAW THESE THINGS ON THE NEWS THE OTHER DAY...

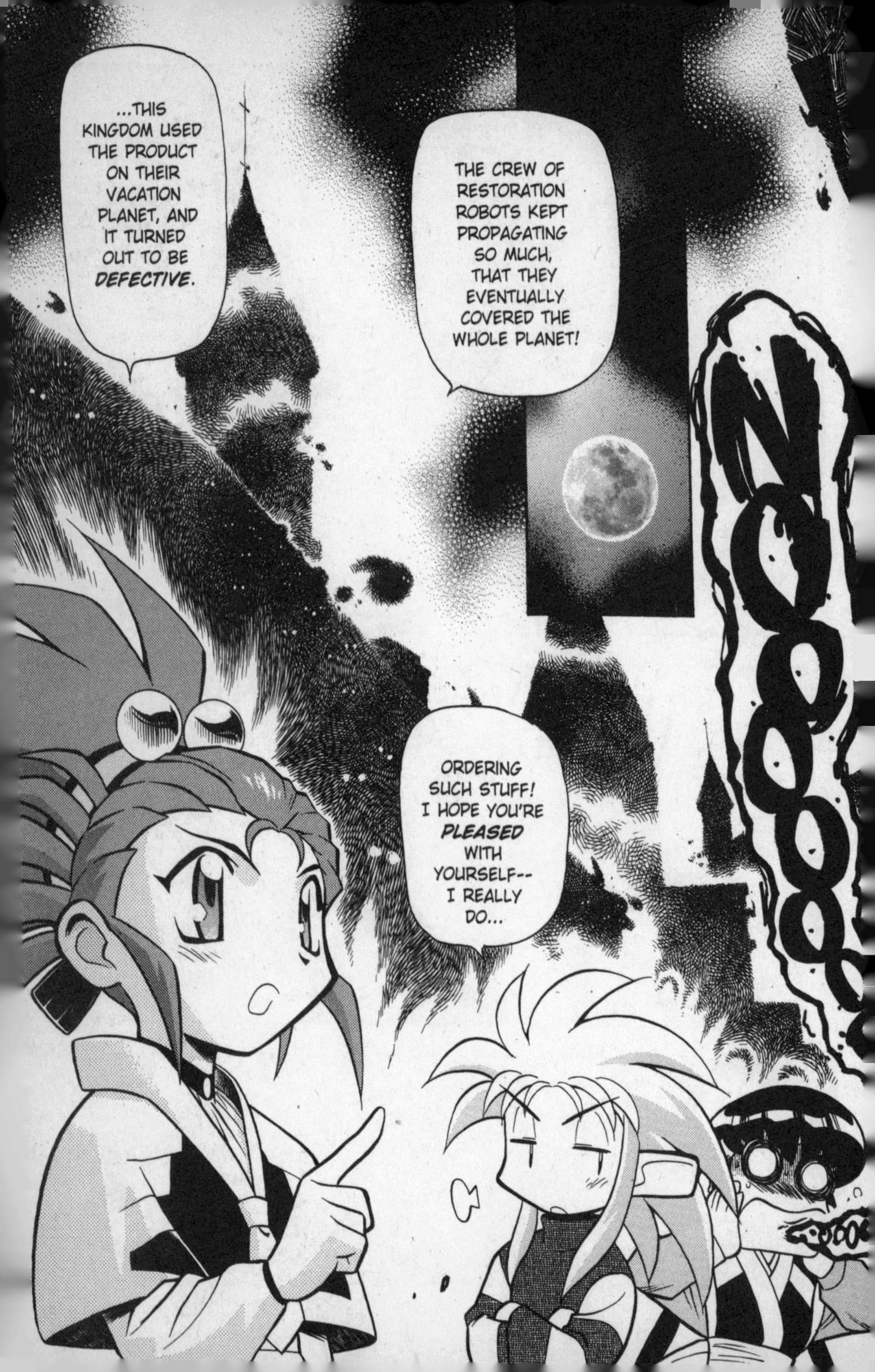
...THIS KINGDOM USED THE PRODUCT ON THEIR VACATION PLANET, AND IT TURNED OUT TO BE ***DEFECTIVE***.
THE CREW OF RESTORATION ROBOTS KEPT PROPAGATING SO MUCH, THAT THEY EVENTUALLY COVERED THE WHOLE PLANET!
NOOOOO
ORDERING SUCH STUFF! I HOPE YOU'RE ***PLEASED*** WITH YOURSELF-- I REALLY DO...

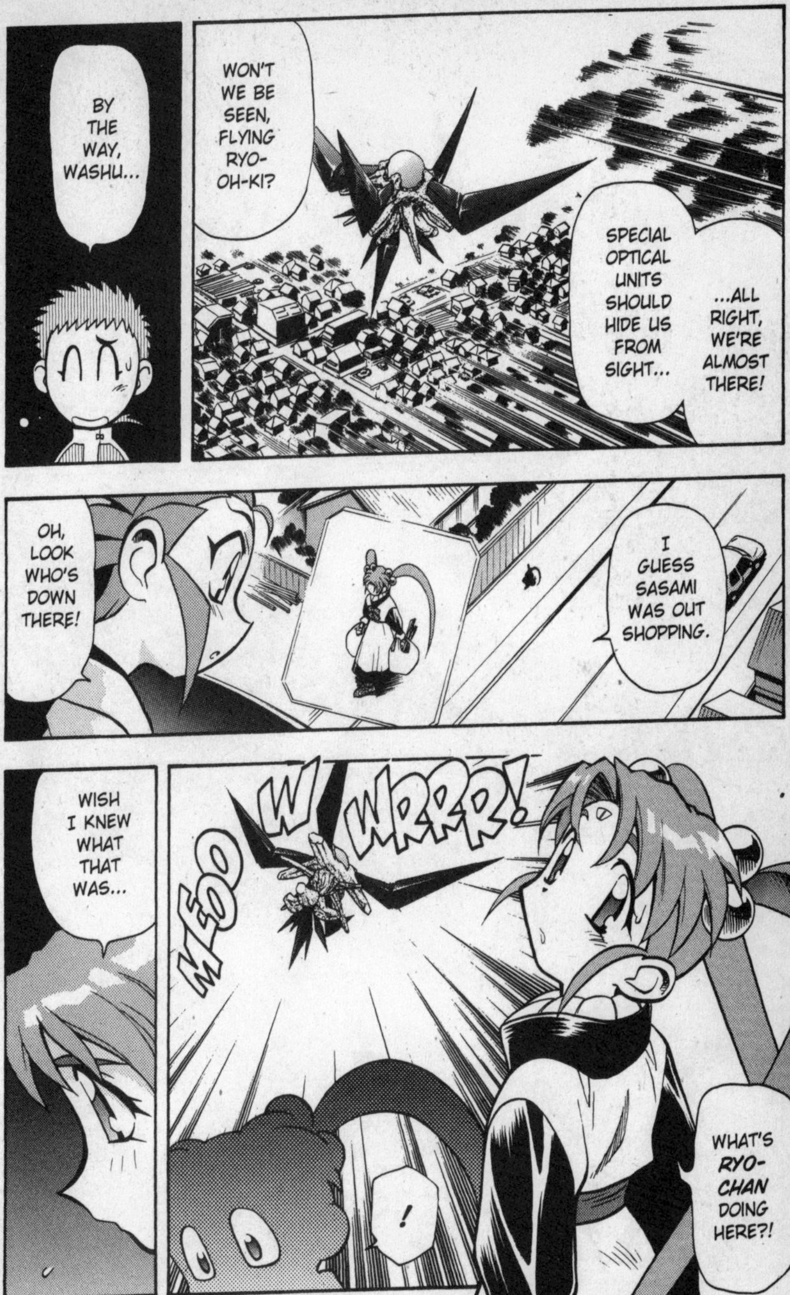
BY THE WAY, WASHU...
WON'T WE BE SEEN, FLYING RYO-OH-KI?
SPECIAL OPTICAL UNITS SHOULD HIDE US FROM SIGHT...
...ALL RIGHT, WE'RE ALMOST THERE!
OH, LOOK WHO'S DOWN THERE!
I GUESS SASAMI WAS OUT SHOPPING.
WISH I KNEW WHAT THAT WAS...
MEOOW
WRRR!
!
WHAT'S *RYO-CHAN* DOING HERE?!

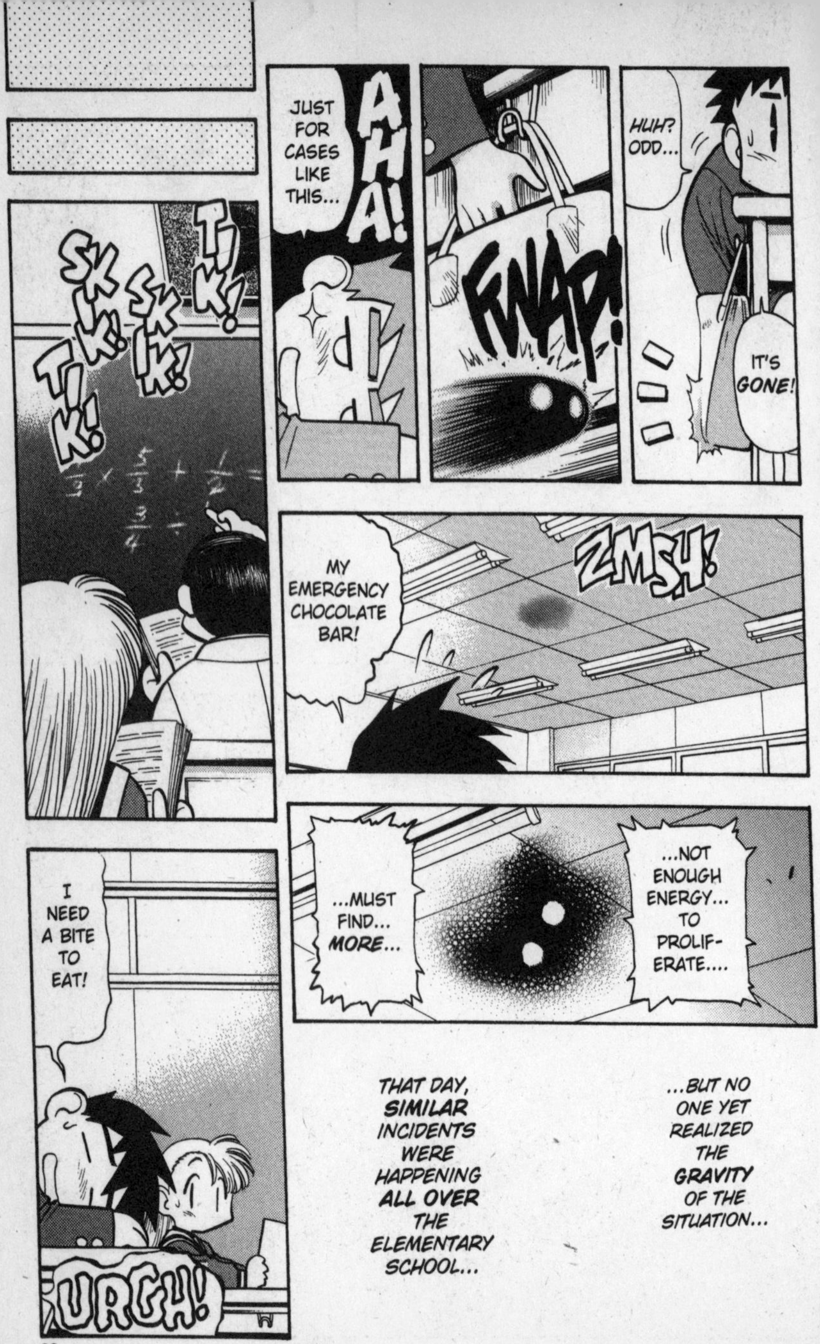
SK SK TIK! SK SK TIK! TIK!
JUST FOR CASES LIKE THIS...
AHA!
FWAP!
HUH? ODD...
IT'S GONE!
MY EMERGENCY CHOCOLATE BAR!
ZMSH!
I NEED A BITE TO EAT!
URGH!
...MUST FIND... MORE...
...NOT ENOUGH ENERGY... TO PROLIF-ERATE....
THAT DAY, SIMILAR INCIDENTS WERE HAPPENING ALL OVER THE ELEMENTARY SCHOOL...
...BUT NO ONE YET REALIZED THE GRAVITY OF THE SITUATION...

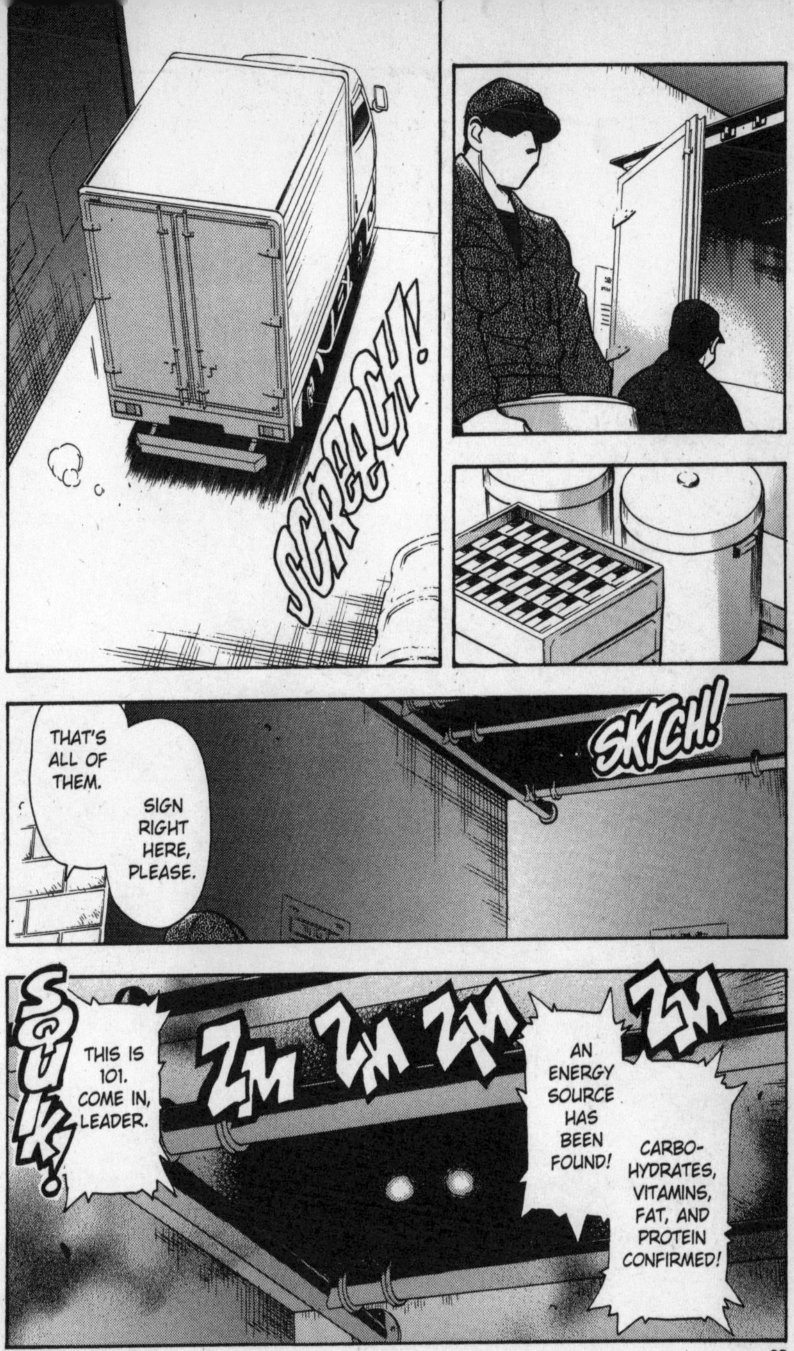
SCREECH!
THAT'S ALL OF THEM.
SIGN RIGHT HERE, PLEASE.
SKTCH!
SQUIK!
THIS IS 101. COME IN, LEADER.
ZM ZM ZM
AN ENERGY SOURCE HAS BEEN FOUND!
ZM
CARBO-HYDRATES, VITAMINS, FAT, AND PROTEIN CONFIRMED!

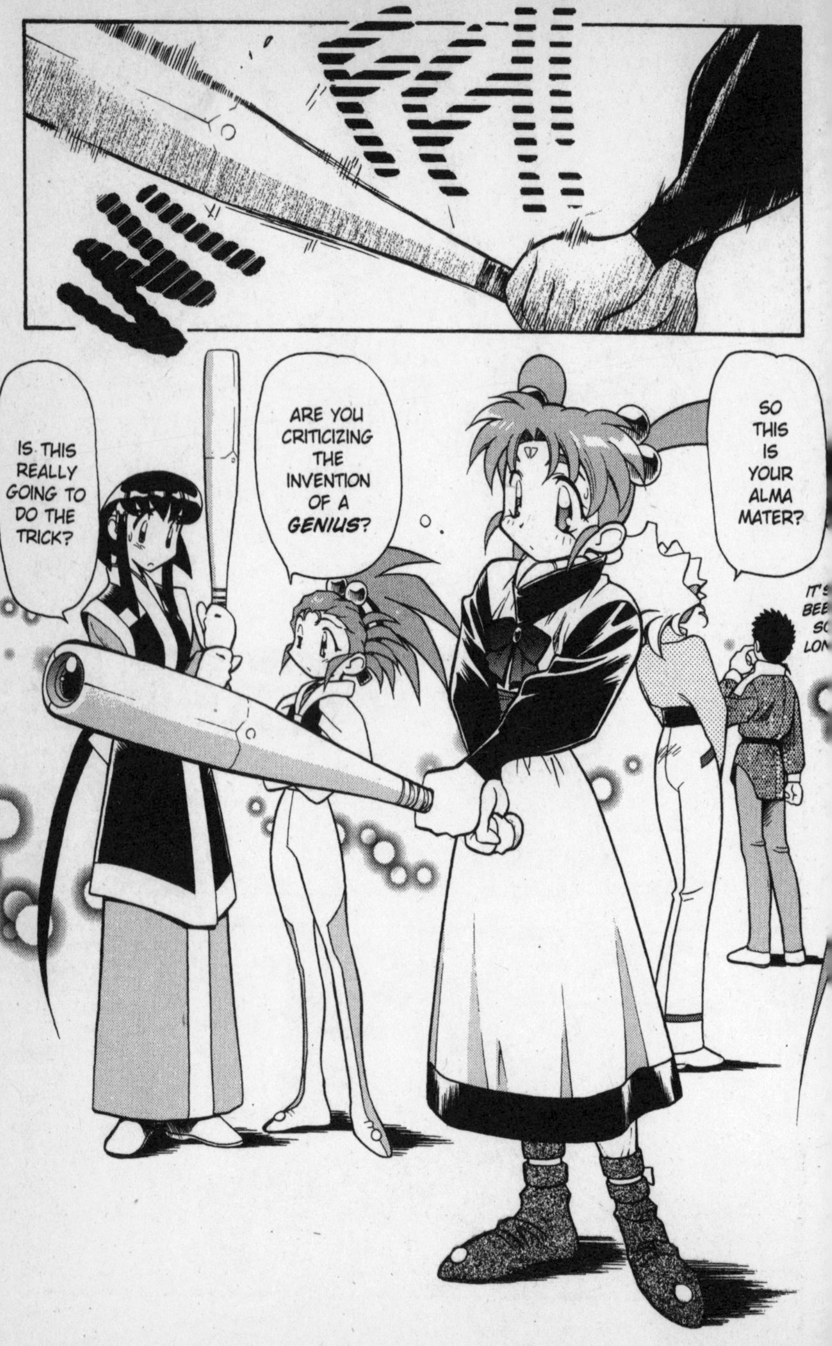
IS THIS REALLY GOING TO DO THE TRICK?
ARE YOU CRITICIZING THE INVENTION OF A *GENIUS*?
SO THIS IS YOUR ALMA MATER?

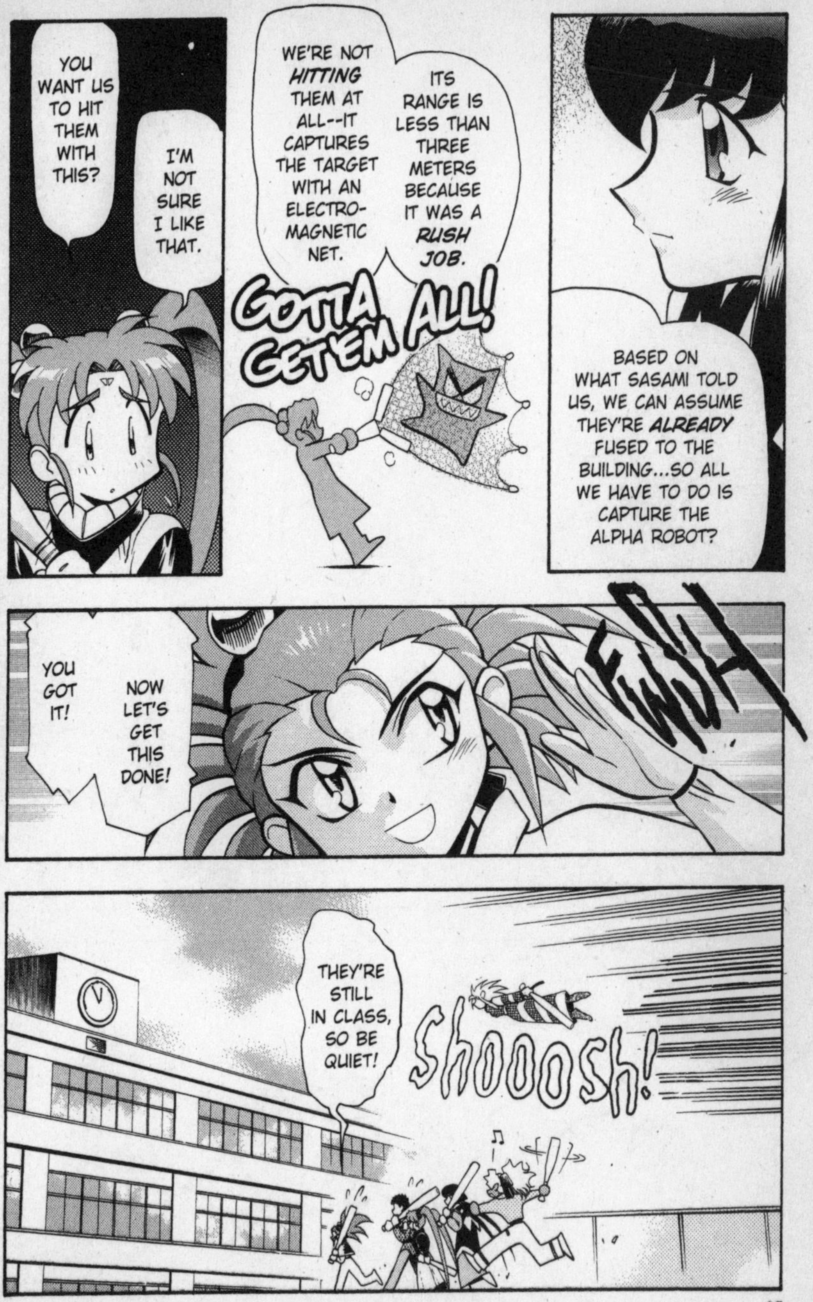
YOU WANT US TO HIT THEM WITH THIS?
I'M NOT SURE I LIKE THAT.
WE'RE NOT HITTING THEM AT ALL--IT CAPTURES THE TARGET WITH AN ELECTRO-MAGNETIC NET.
ITS RANGE IS LESS THAN THREE METERS BECAUSE IT WAS A RUSH JOB.
GOTTA GET'EM ALL!
BASED ON WHAT SASAMI TOLD US, WE CAN ASSUME THEY'RE ALREADY FUSED TO THE BUILDING...SO ALL WE HAVE TO DO IS CAPTURE THE ALPHA ROBOT?
YOU GOT IT!
NOW LET'S GET THIS DONE!
FWISH
THEY'RE STILL IN CLASS, SO BE QUIET!
Shooosh!

OKAY... SO WHERE ARE THE DAMN THINGS?

I'M NOT REALLY SURE.

WHAT'S THAT LOOK?

YOU'RE NOT REALLY *SURE*?!

SHH, QUIET.

THEY'VE FUSED WITH THE BUILDING, SO MY SCANNERS ARE *USELESS.*

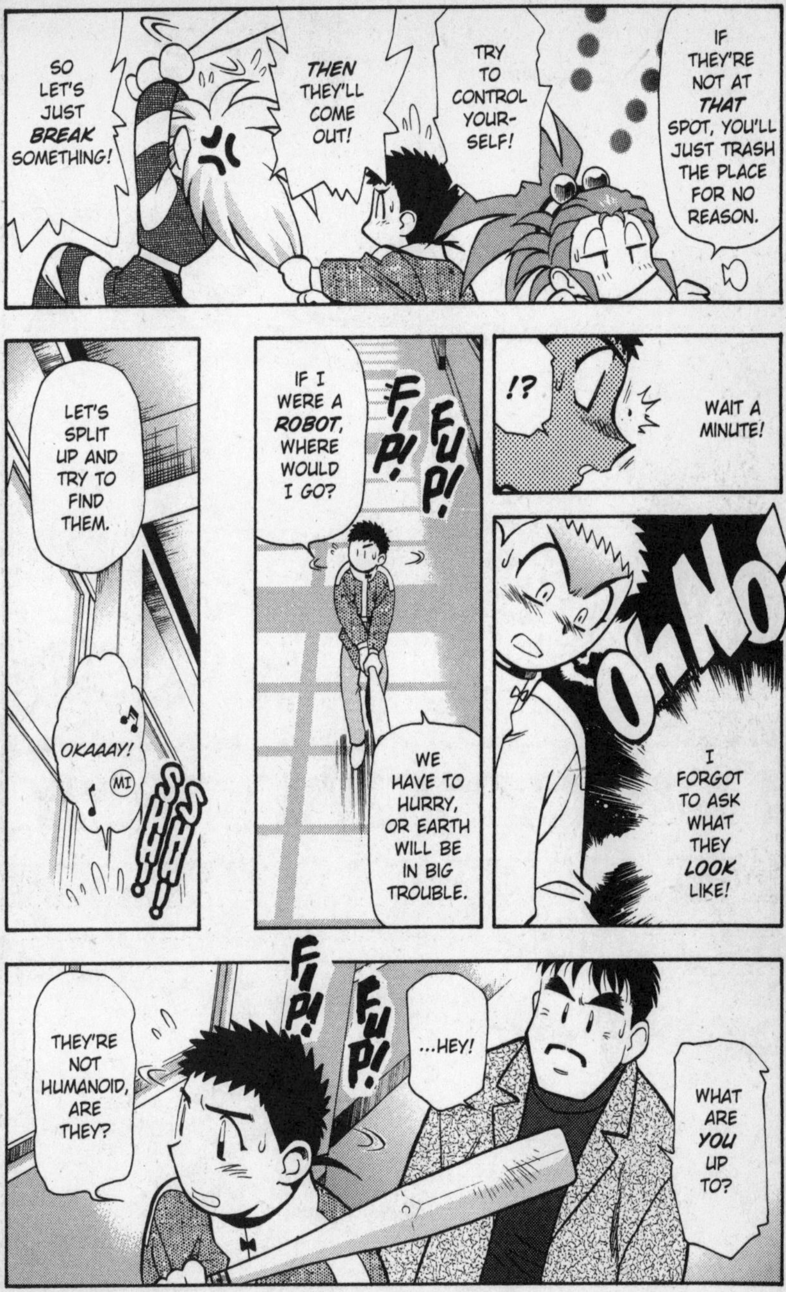
SO LET'S JUST BREAK SOMETHING!
THEN THEY'LL COME OUT!
TRY TO CONTROL YOUR-SELF!
IF THEY'RE NOT AT THAT SPOT, YOU'LL JUST TRASH THE PLACE FOR NO REASON.
LET'S SPLIT UP AND TRY TO FIND THEM.
OKAAAY!
MI
SSHH
SSHH
IF I WERE A ROBOT, WHERE WOULD I GO?
FIP!
FUP!
WE HAVE TO HURRY, OR EARTH WILL BE IN BIG TROUBLE.
!?
WAIT A MINUTE!
OH NO!
I FORGOT TO ASK WHAT THEY LOOK LIKE!
THEY'RE NOT HUMANOID, ARE THEY?
FIP!
FUP!
...HEY!
WHAT ARE YOU UP TO?

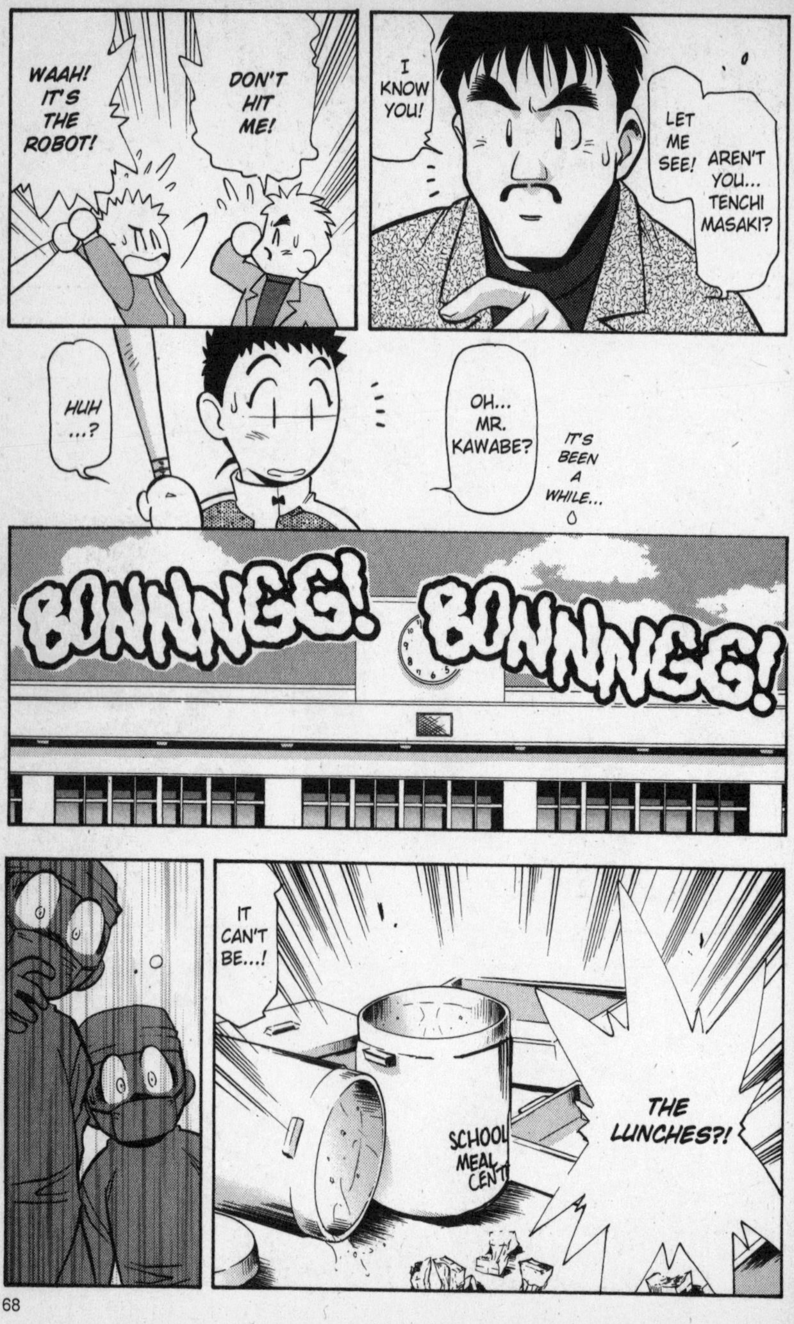
WAAH! IT'S THE ROBOT!
DON'T HIT ME!
I KNOW YOU!
LET ME SEE!
AREN'T YOU... TENCHI MASAKI?
HUH ...?
OH... MR. KAWABE?
IT'S BEEN A WHILE...
BONNNGG!
BONNNGG!
IT CAN'T BE...!
SCHOOL MEAL CENT
THE LUNCHES?!

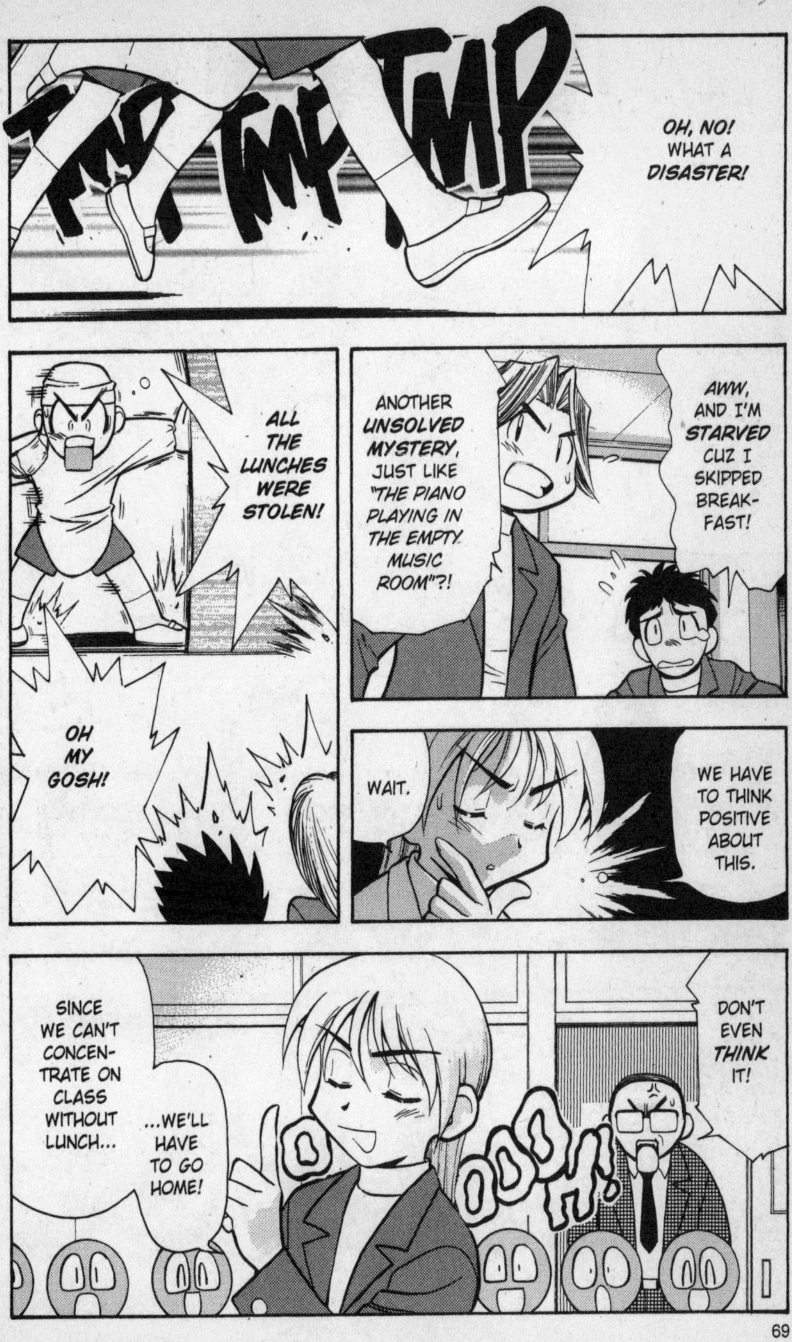
TMP TMP TMP
OH, NO! WHAT A DISASTER!
ALL THE LUNCHES WERE STOLEN!
ANOTHER UNSOLVED MYSTERY, JUST LIKE "THE PIANO PLAYING IN THE EMPTY MUSIC ROOM"?!
AWW, AND I'M STARVED CUZ I SKIPPED BREAK-FAST!
OH MY GOSH!
WAIT.
WE HAVE TO THINK POSITIVE ABOUT THIS.
SINCE WE CAN'T CONCEN-TRATE ON CLASS WITHOUT LUNCH...
...WE'LL HAVE TO GO HOME!
OOOOH!
DON'T EVEN THINK IT!

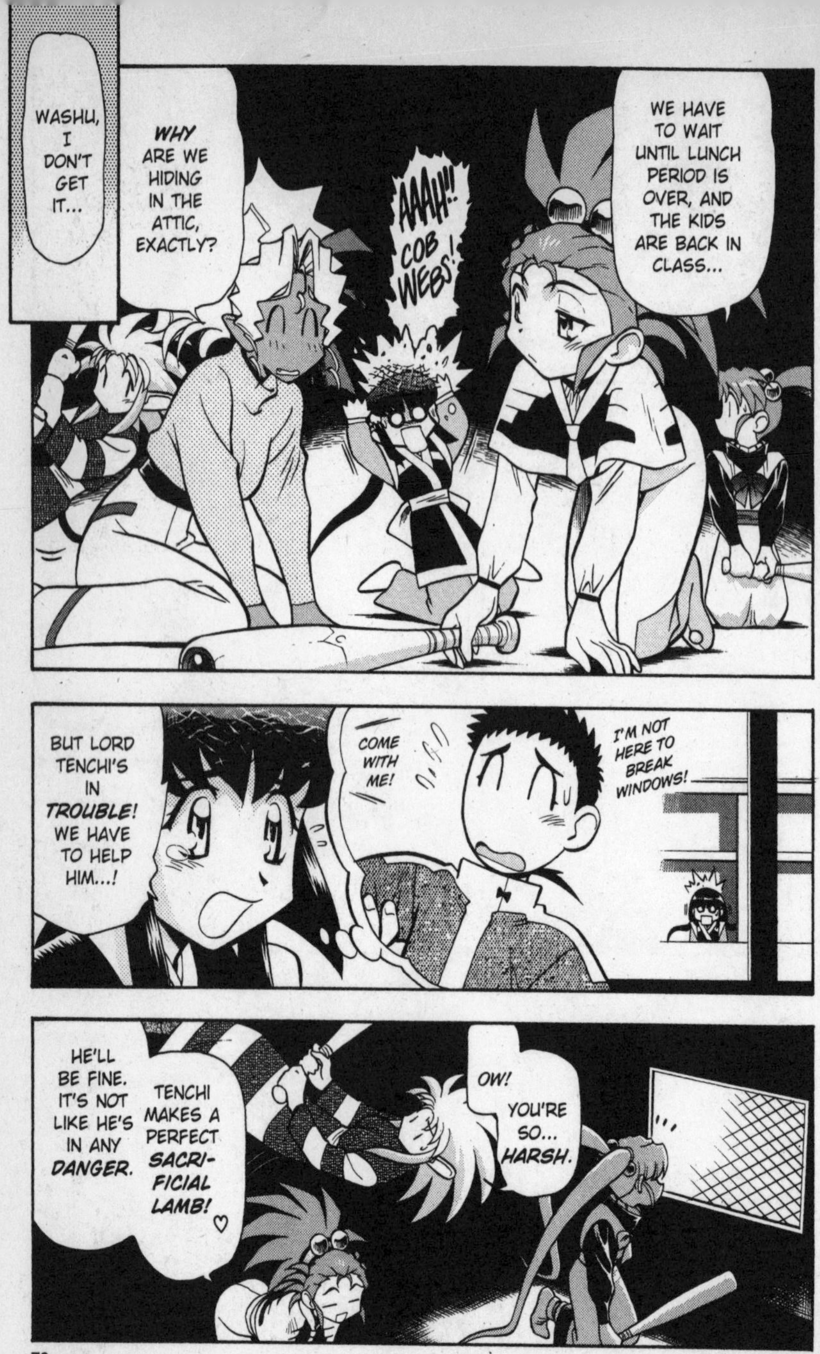
WASHU, I DON'T GET IT...
WHY ARE WE HIDING IN THE ATTIC, EXACTLY?
AAAH!! COB WEBS!
WE HAVE TO WAIT UNTIL LUNCH PERIOD IS OVER, AND THE KIDS ARE BACK IN CLASS...
BUT LORD TENCHI'S IN TROUBLE! WE HAVE TO HELP HIM...!
COME WITH ME!
I'M NOT HERE TO BREAK WINDOWS!
HE'LL BE FINE. IT'S NOT LIKE HE'S IN ANY DANGER.
TENCHI MAKES A PERFECT SACRI-FICIAL LAMB! ♡
OW!
YOU'RE SO... HARSH.
...

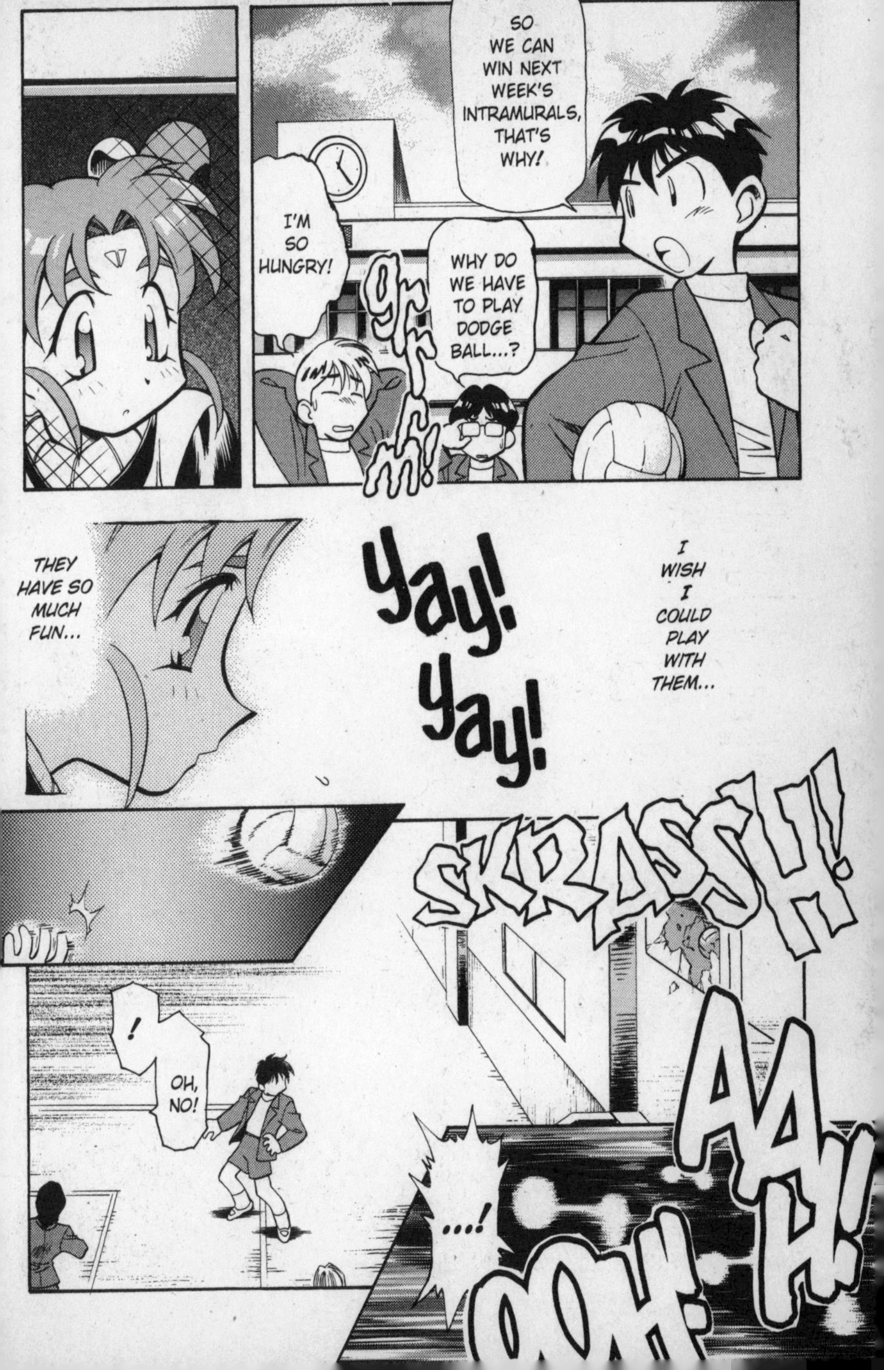
SO WE CAN WIN NEXT WEEK'S INTRAMURALS, THAT'S WHY!
I'M SO HUNGRY!
WHY DO WE HAVE TO PLAY DODGE BALL...?
grrrm!
THEY HAVE SO MUCH FUN...
yay! yay!
I WISH I COULD PLAY WITH THEM...
SKRASSH!
!
OH, NO!
...!
AAH!
OOH!

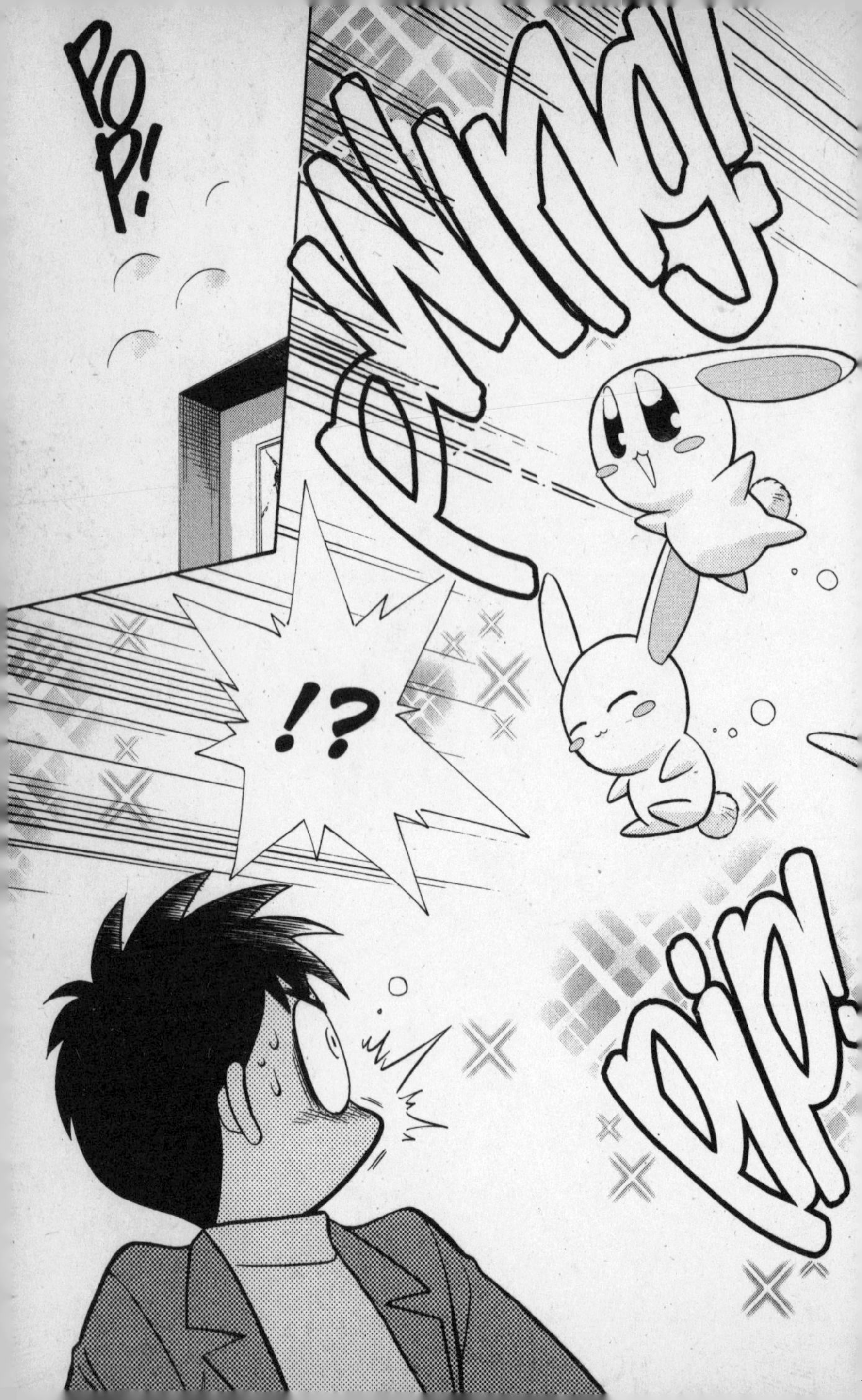
POP!
PWING!
!?
BING!

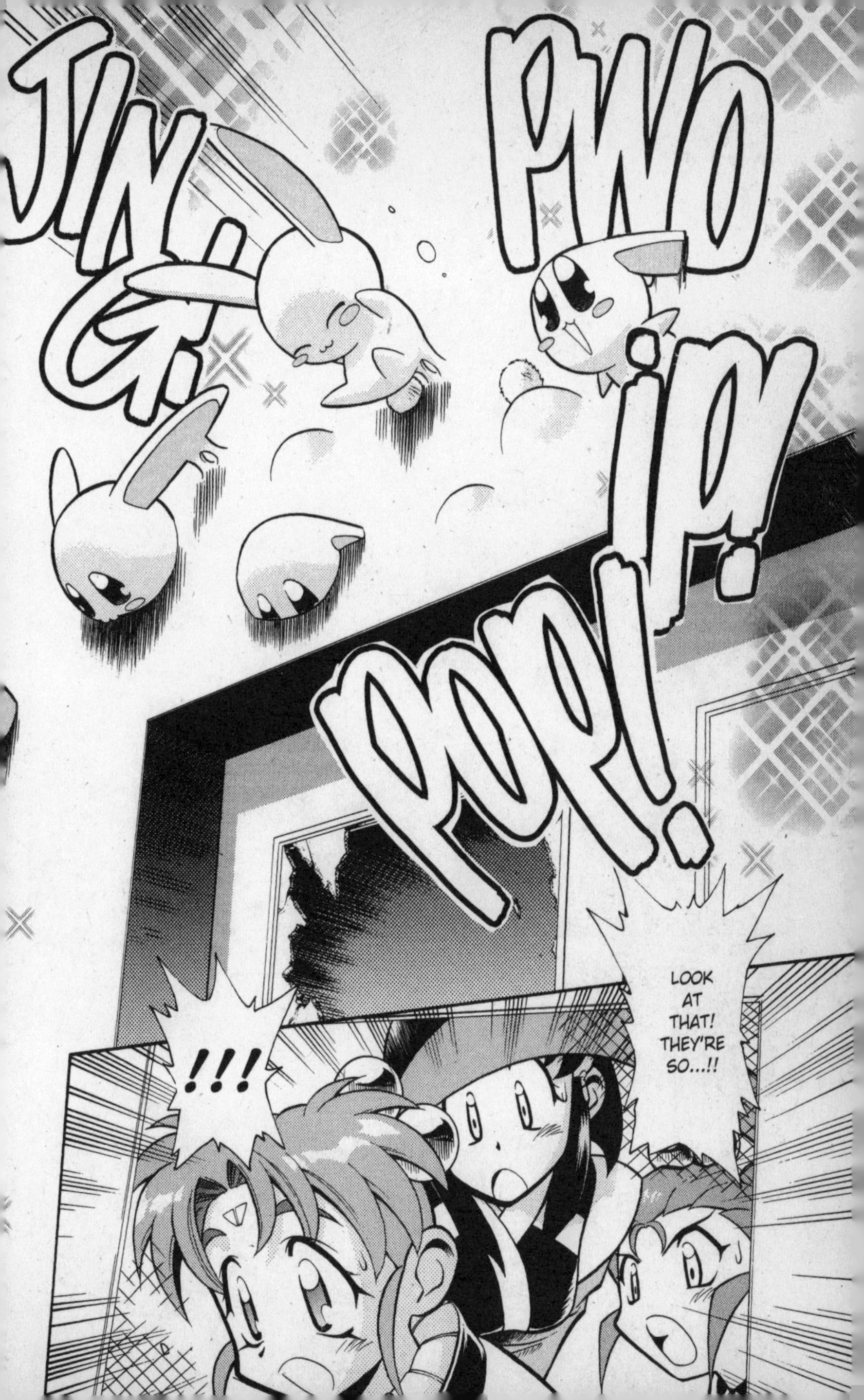
JINGA!
PIWO
POPI POPI!
!!!
LOOK AT THAT! THEY'RE SO...!!

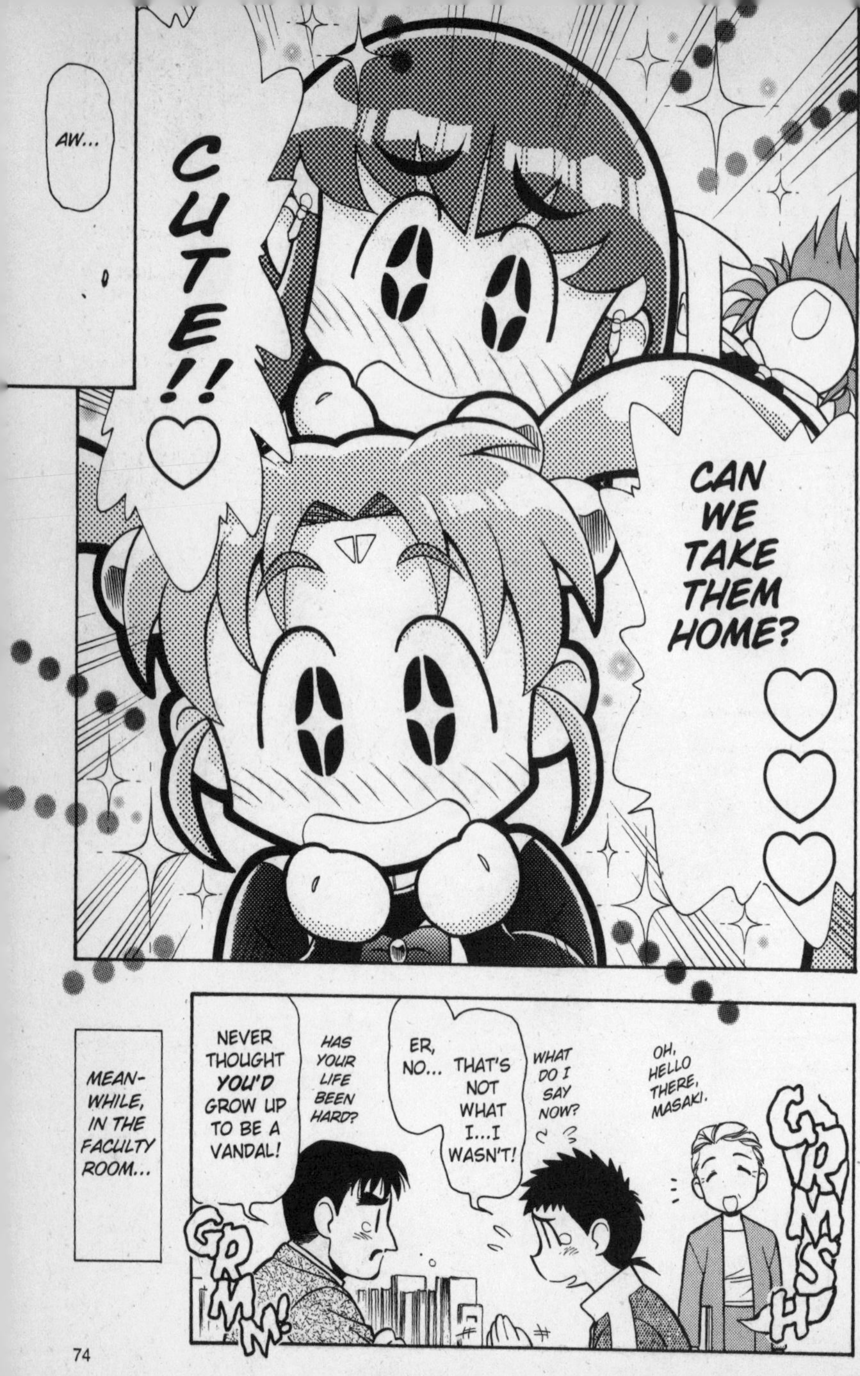
AW...
CUTE!! ♥
CAN WE TAKE THEM HOME? ♥♥♥
MEAN-WHILE, IN THE FACULTY ROOM...
NEVER THOUGHT YOU'D GROW UP TO BE A VANDAL!
GRMM!
HAS YOUR LIFE BEEN HARD?
ER, NO...
THAT'S NOT WHAT I...I WASN'T!
WHAT DO I SAY NOW?
OH, HELLO THERE, MASAKI.
GRMSH

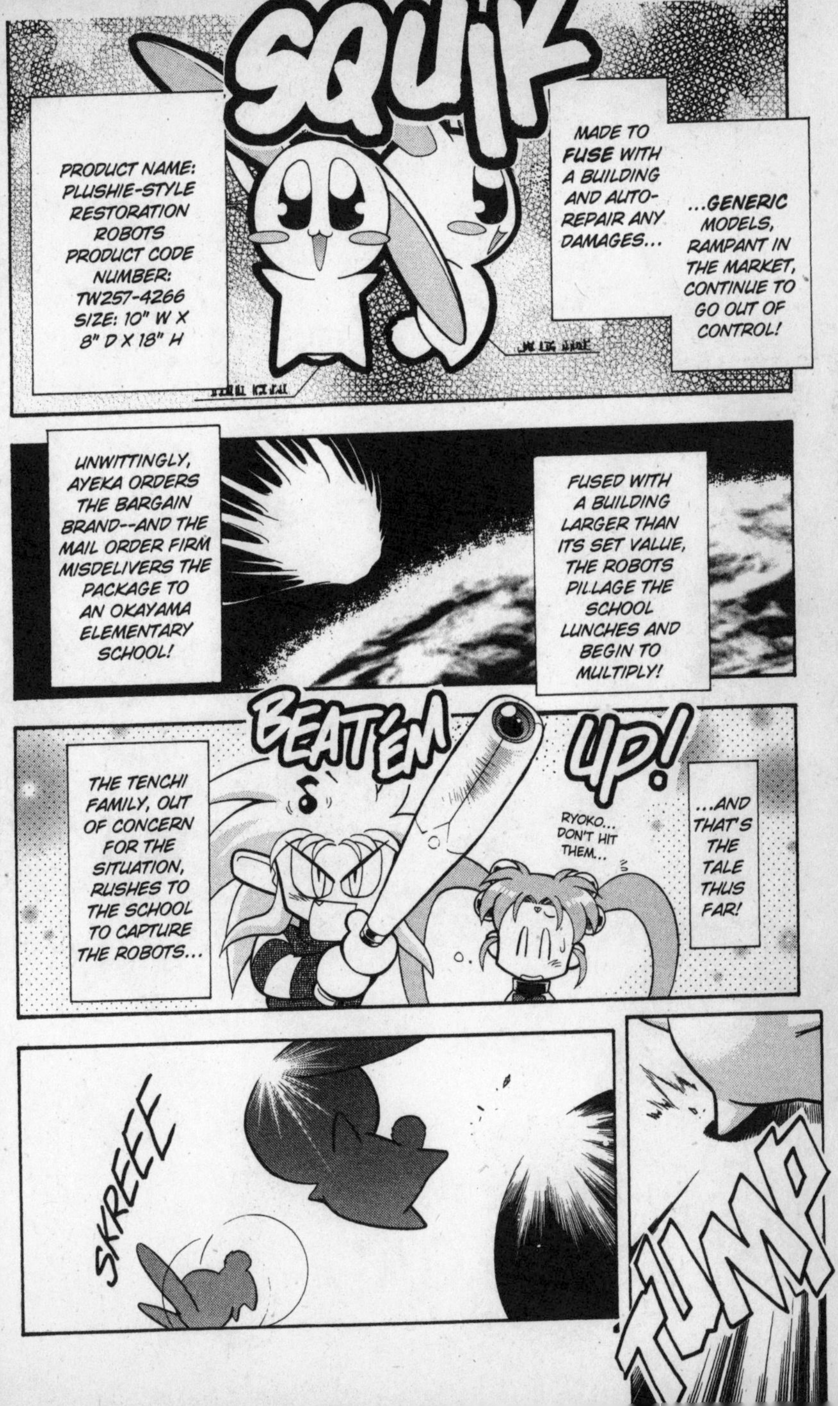
SQUIK
PRODUCT NAME: PLUSHIE-STYLE RESTORATION ROBOTS PRODUCT CODE NUMBER: TW257-4266 SIZE: 10" W X 8" D X 18" H
MADE TO FUSE WITH A BUILDING AND AUTO-REPAIR ANY DAMAGES...
...GENERIC MODELS, RAMPANT IN THE MARKET, CONTINUE TO GO OUT OF CONTROL!
UNWITTINGLY, AYEKA ORDERS THE BARGAIN BRAND--AND THE MAIL ORDER FIRM MISDELIVERS THE PACKAGE TO AN OKAYAMA ELEMENTARY SCHOOL!
FUSED WITH A BUILDING LARGER THAN ITS SET VALUE, THE ROBOTS PILLAGE THE SCHOOL LUNCHES AND BEGIN TO MULTIPLY!
THE TENCHI FAMILY, OUT OF CONCERN FOR THE SITUATION, RUSHES TO THE SCHOOL TO CAPTURE THE ROBOTS...
BEAT'EM UP!
RYOKO... DON'T HIT THEM...
...AND THAT'S THE TALE THUS FAR!
SKREEE
TUMP

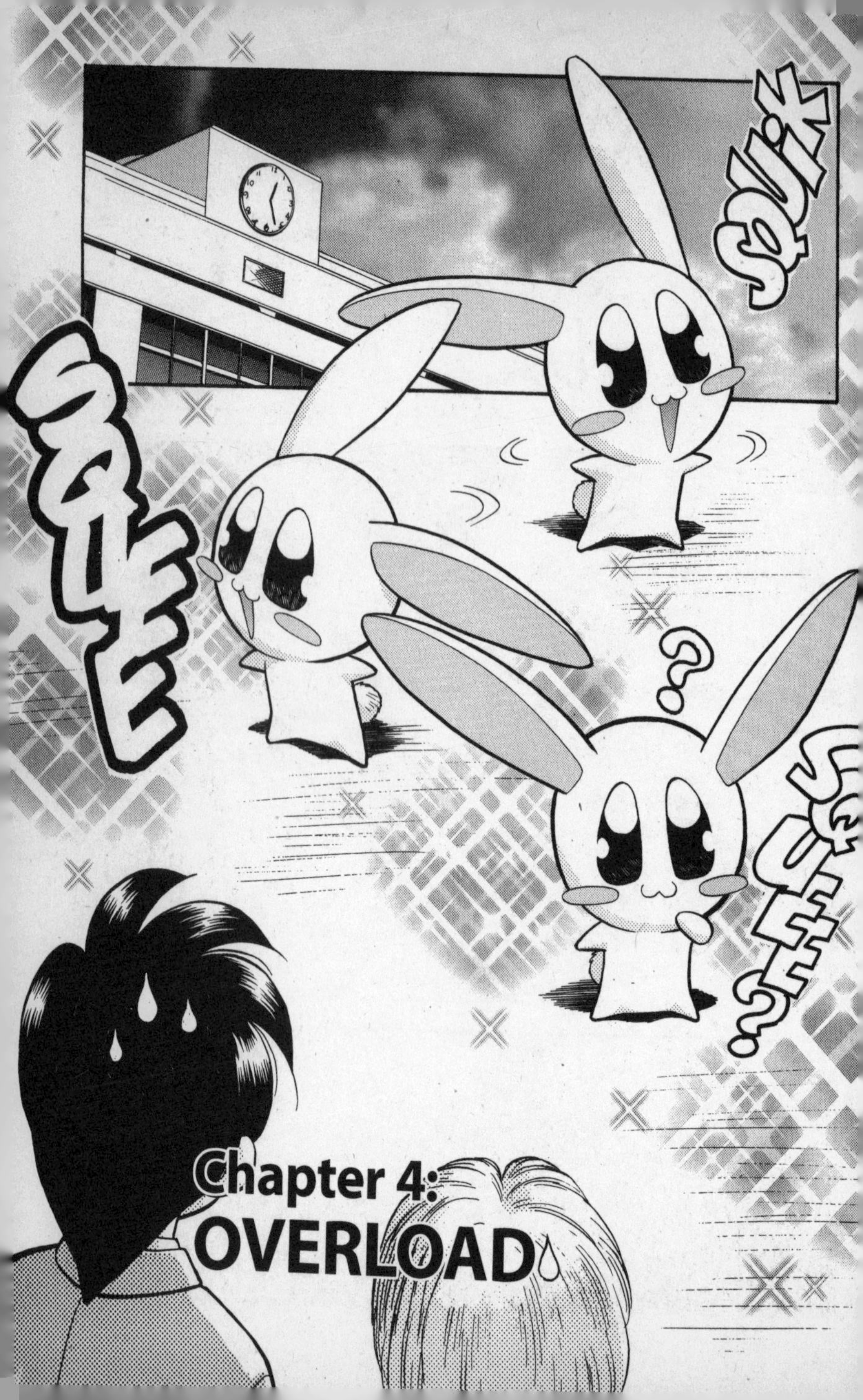
SQUEE
SQUIK
?
SQUEE?

Chapter 4: OVERLOAD

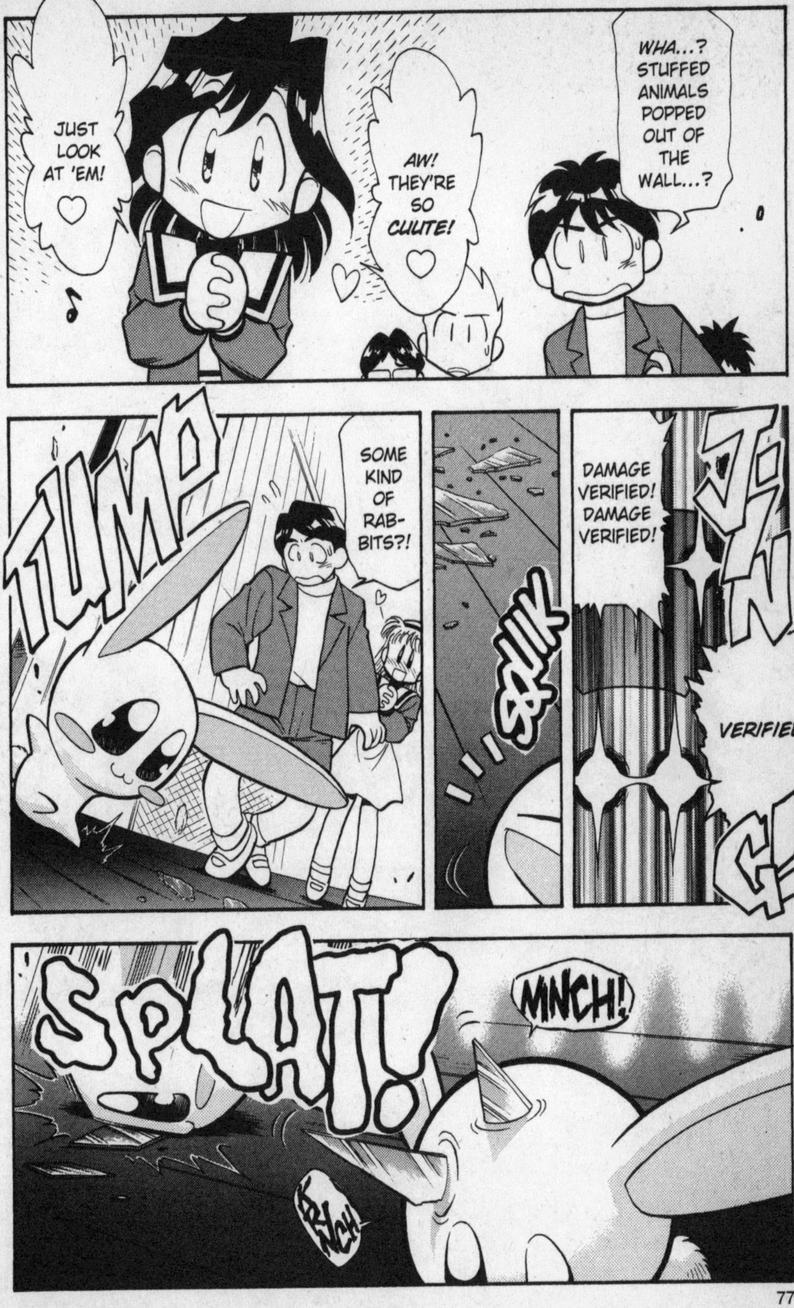
JUST LOOK AT 'EM! ♡
AW! THEY'RE SO CUUTE! ♡
WHA...? STUFFED ANIMALS POPPED OUT OF THE WALL...?
TUMP
SOME KIND OF RAB-BITS?!
SQUIK
DAMAGE VERIFIED! DAMAGE VERIFIED!
VERIFIED!
SPLAT!
MINCH!

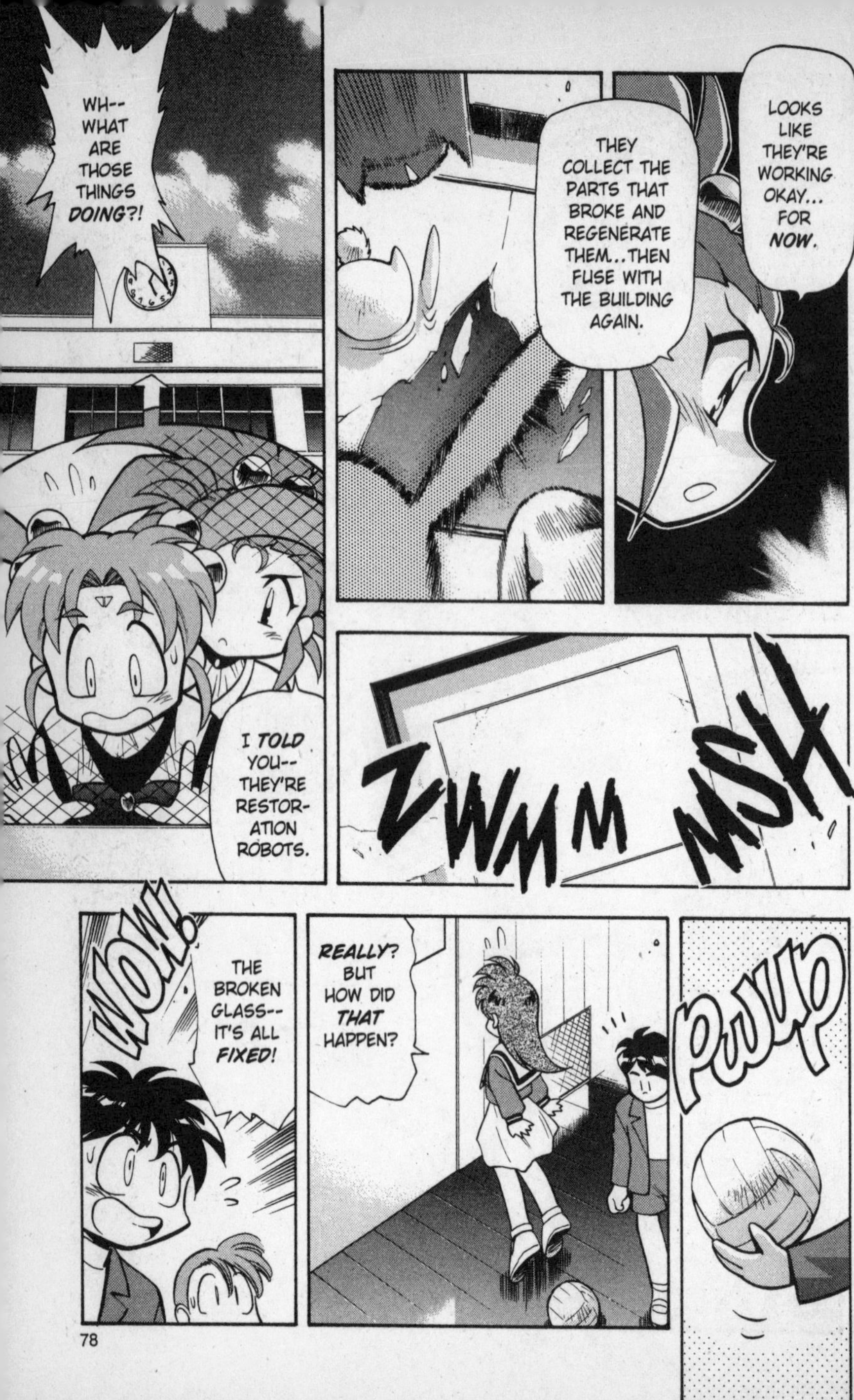
WH-- WHAT ARE THOSE THINGS *DOING*?!
I *TOLD* YOU-- THEY'RE RESTOR-ATION ROBOTS.
THEY COLLECT THE PARTS THAT BROKE AND REGENERATE THEM...THEN FUSE WITH THE BUILDING AGAIN.
LOOKS LIKE THEY'RE WORKING OKAY... FOR ***NOW***.
ZWMM
MSH
WOW!
THE BROKEN GLASS-- IT'S ALL ***FIXED!***
REALLY? BUT HOW DID ***THAT*** HAPPEN?
PWUP

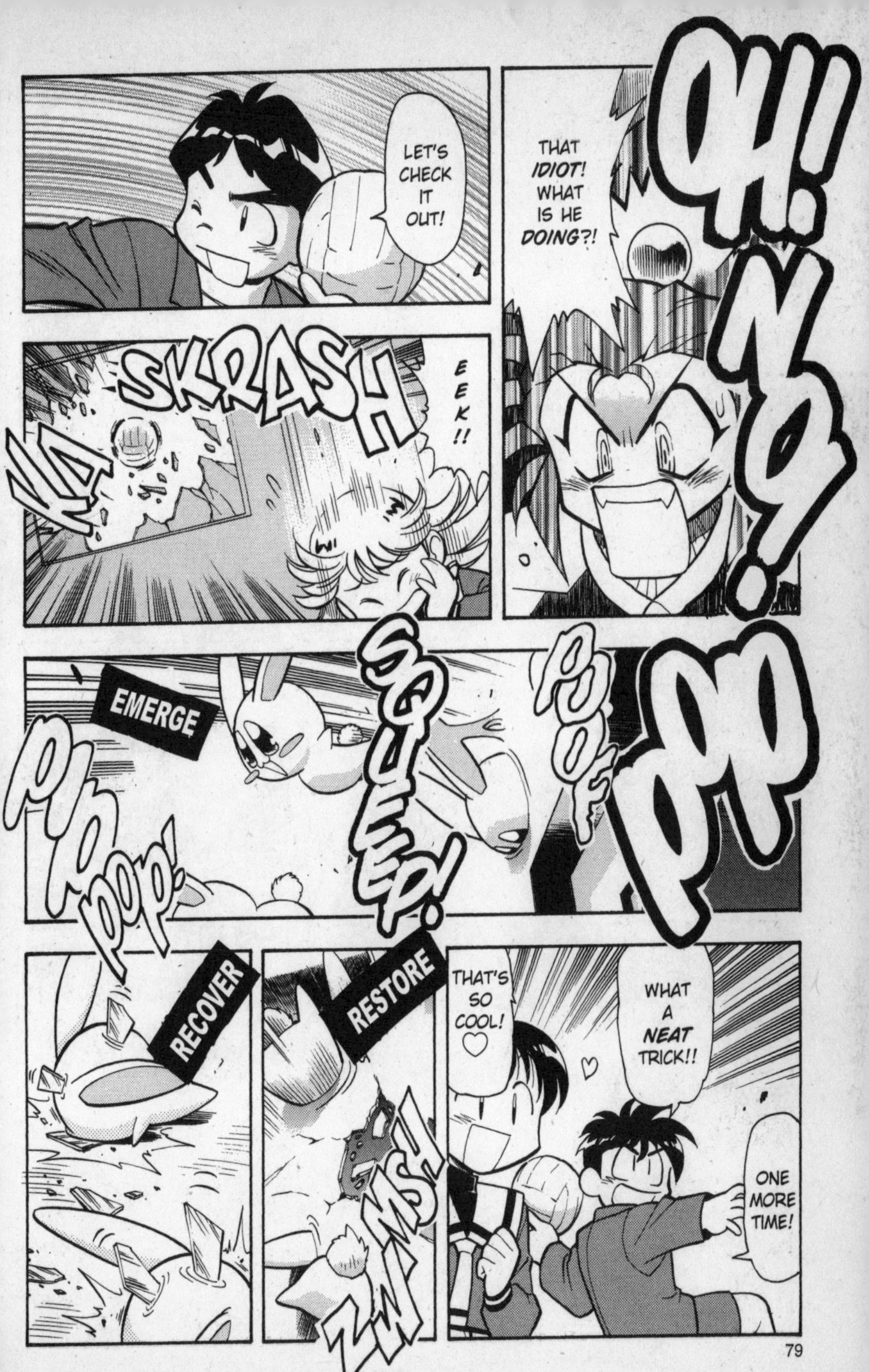
LET'S CHECK IT OUT!
THAT IDIOT! WHAT IS HE DOING?!
OH! NO!
KA-
SKRASH
EEK!!
EMERGE
POP POP!
SQUMP!
POOF
POP
RECOVER
RESTORE
ZWMSH!
THAT'S SO COOL! ♡
WHAT A NEAT TRICK!!
ONE MORE TIME!

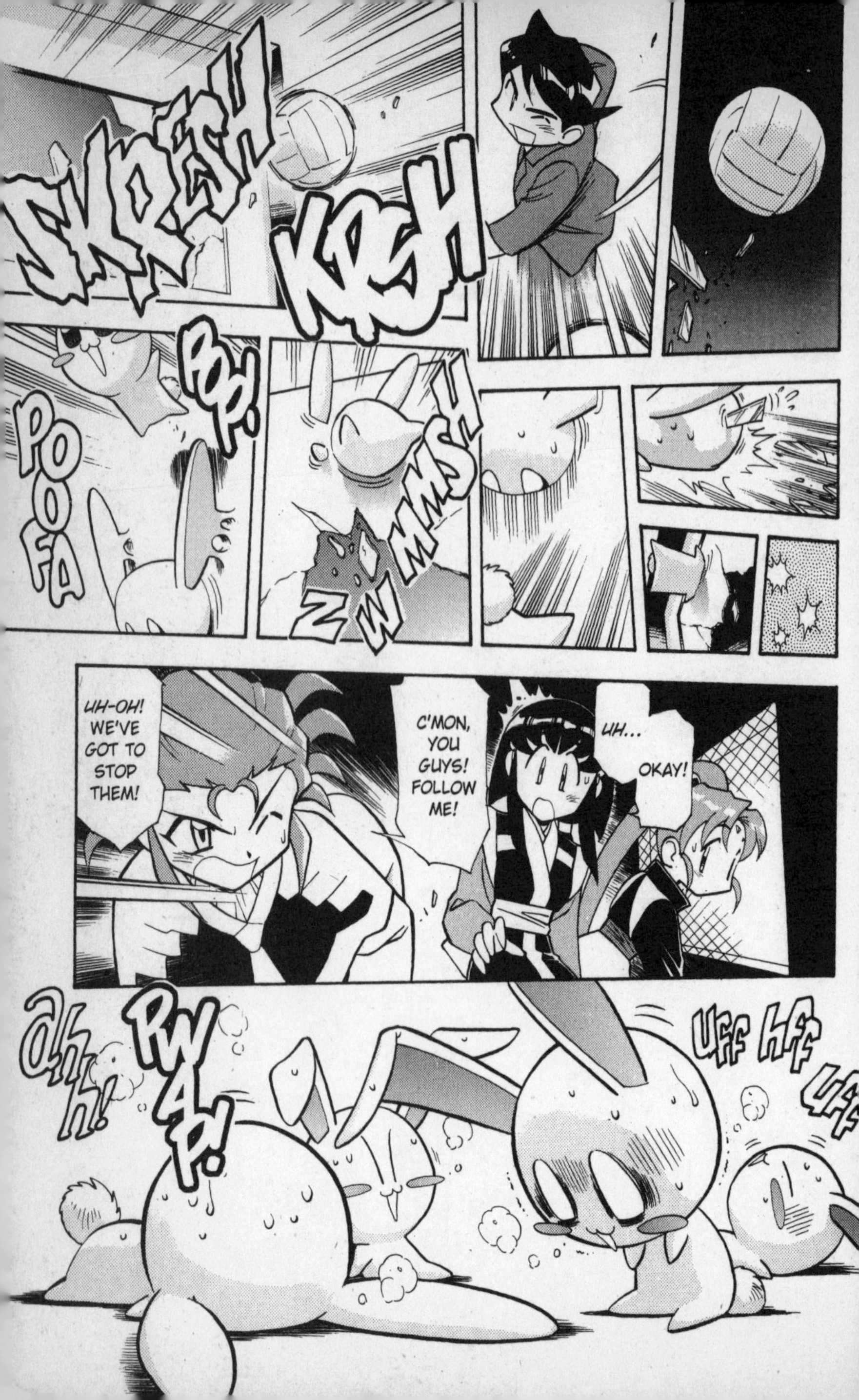
SKRESH
KRSH
POOFA
POP!
ZWMMSH
UH-OH! WE'VE GOT TO STOP THEM!
C'MON, YOU GUYS! FOLLOW ME!
UH...
OKAY!
ahh!
PWAP!
UFF HFF UFF

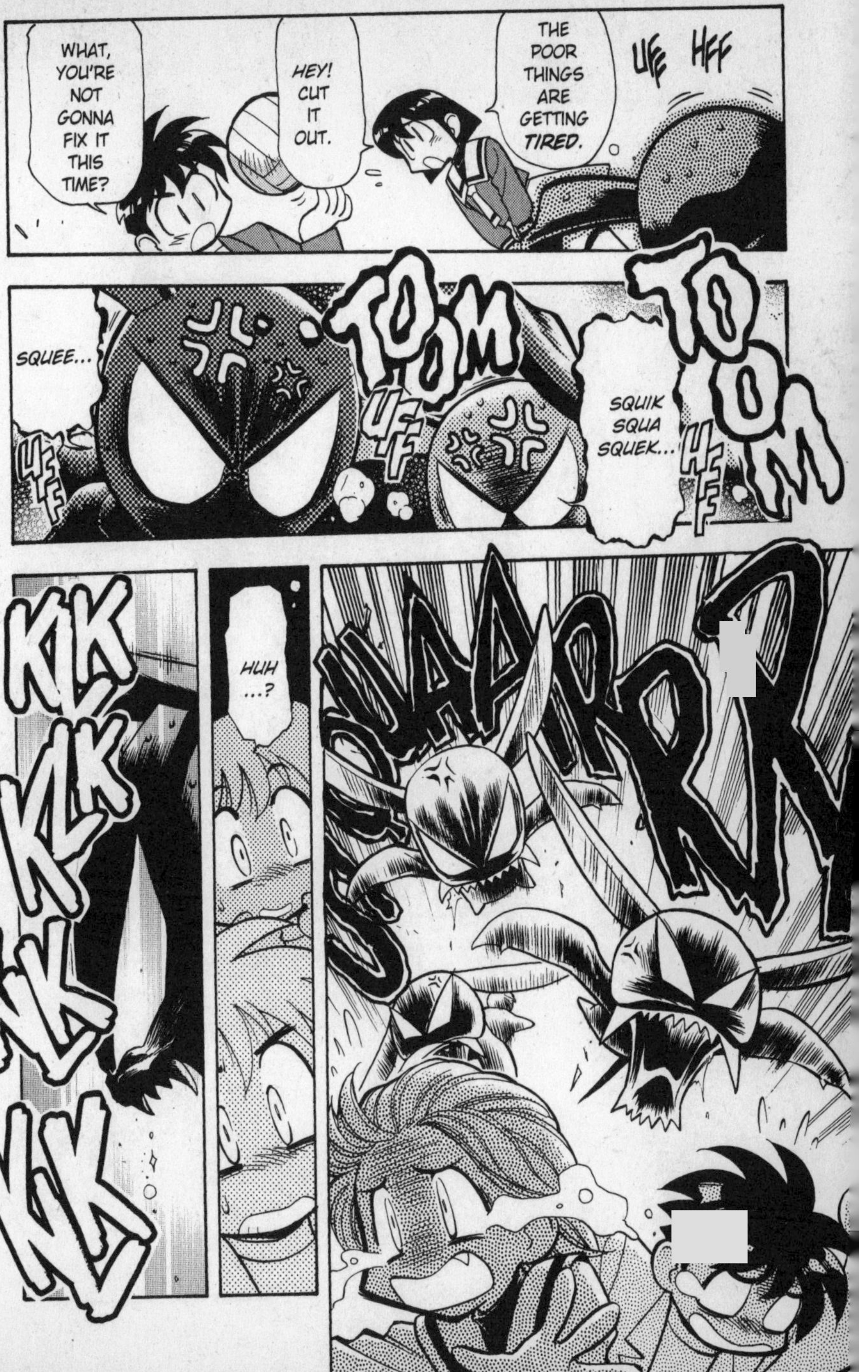
WHAT, YOU'RE NOT GONNA FIX IT THIS TIME?
HEY! CUT IT OUT.
THE POOR THINGS ARE GETTING TIRED.
UFF HFF
SQUEE...
UFF
TOOM
UFF
SQUIK SQUA SQUEK...
TOOM
HFF
KLK KLK KLK KLK
HUH ...?

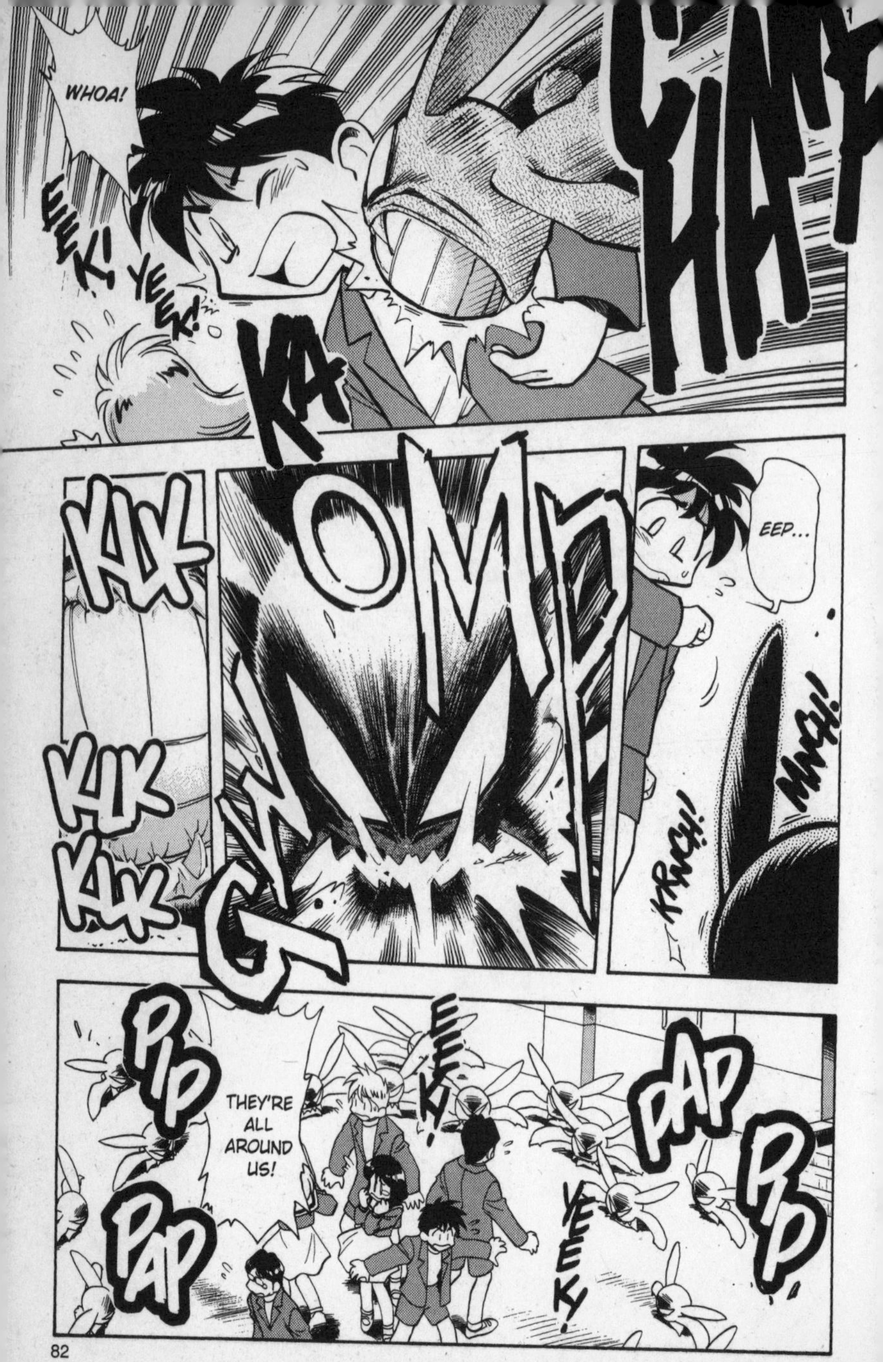
WHOA!
EEK!
YEEK!
KA
CHAP
KLIK
KLIK
KLIK
GOMP
EEP...
KRUNCH!
MUNCH!
PIP
PAP
THEY'RE ALL AROUND US!
EEK!
YEEKY!
PAP
PIP

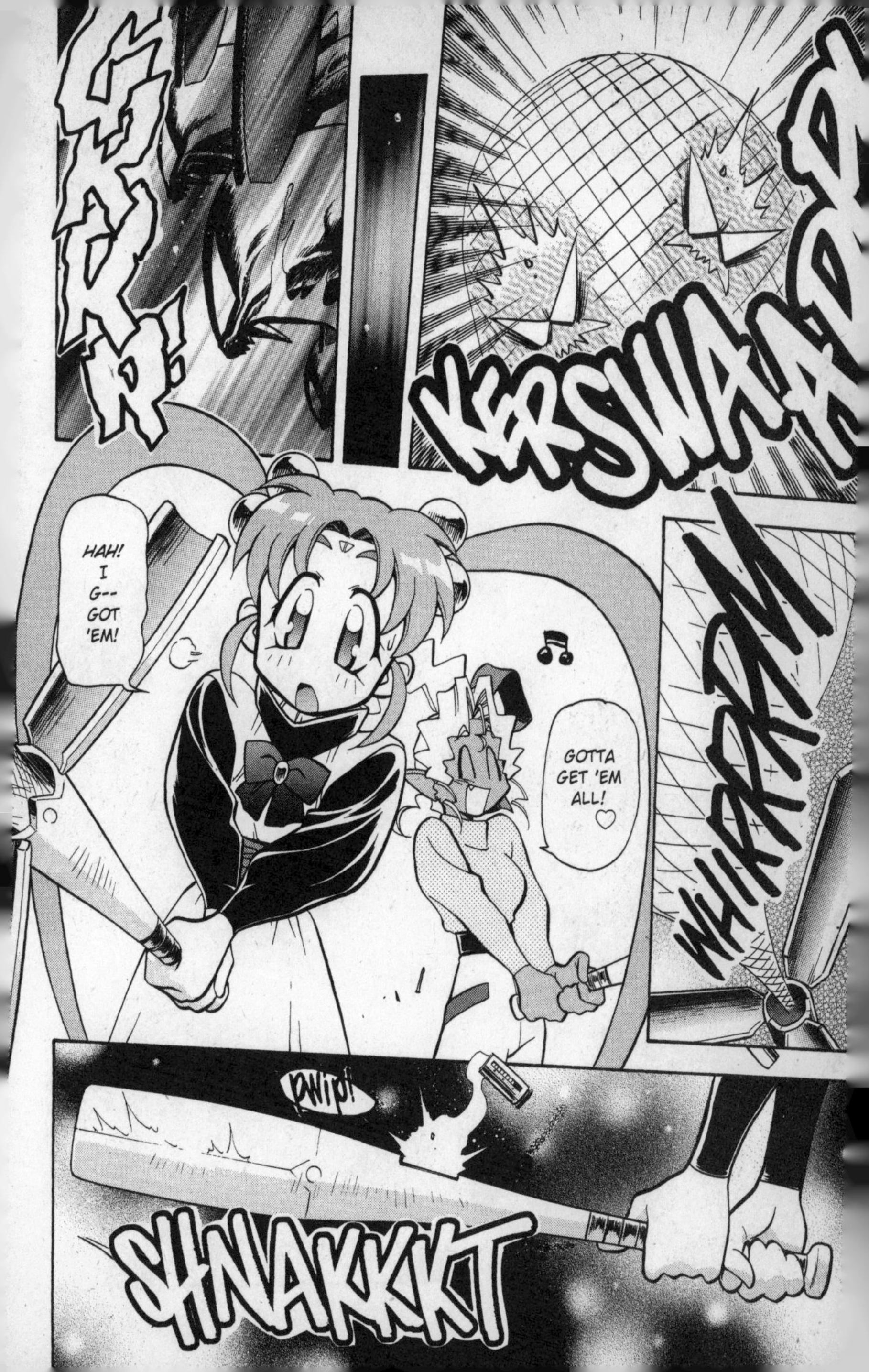

KERSWAP
HAH! I G-- GOT 'EM!
GOTTA GET 'EM ALL!
WHIRRM
PWIP!
SHNAKKKT

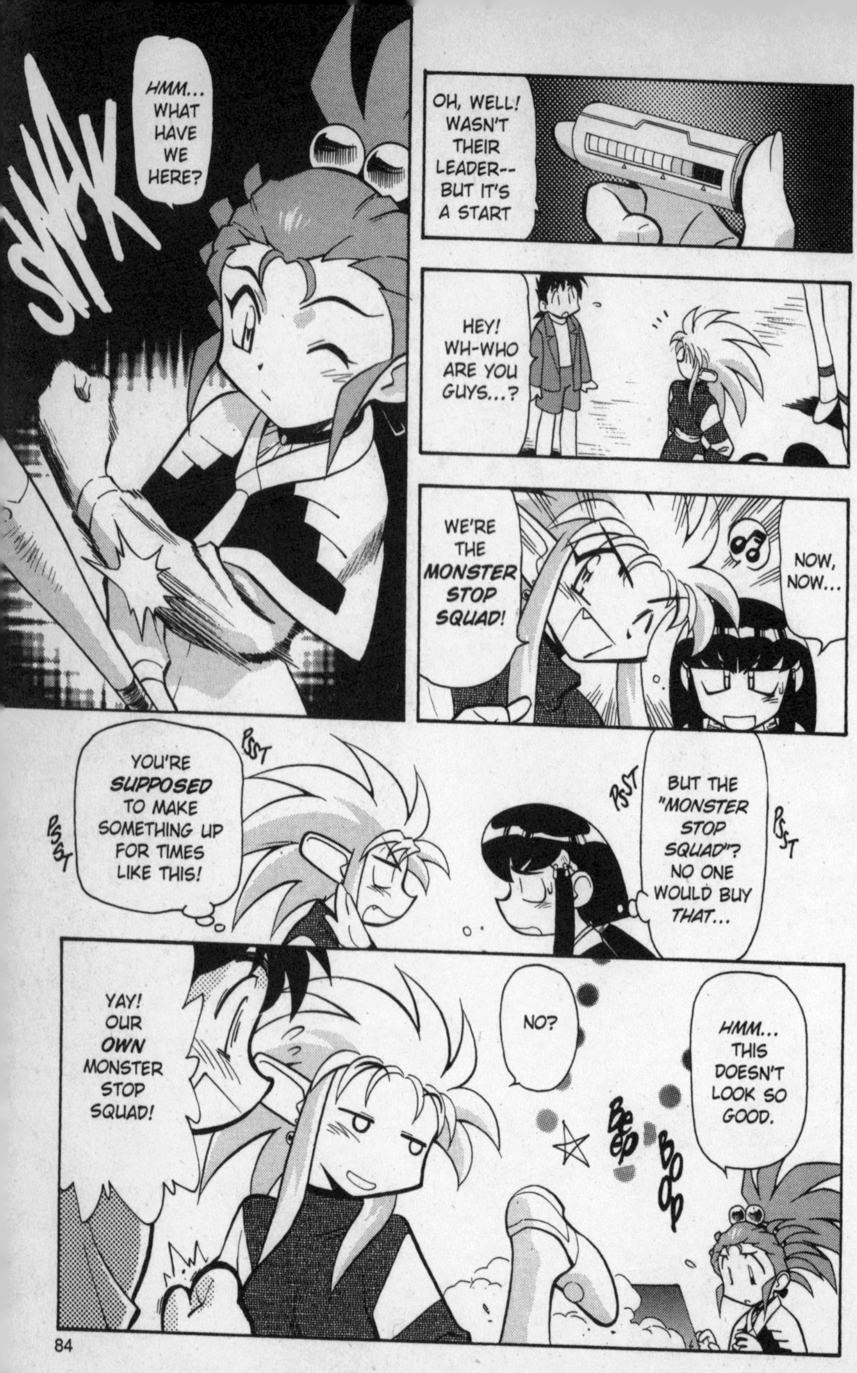
SHAK
HMM... WHAT HAVE WE HERE?
OH, WELL! WASN'T THEIR LEADER-- BUT IT'S A START
HEY! WH-WHO ARE YOU GUYS...?
WE'RE THE **MONSTER STOP SQUAD!**
NOW, NOW...
PSST
YOU'RE **SUPPOSED** TO MAKE SOMETHING UP FOR TIMES LIKE THIS!
PSST
BUT THE "MONSTER STOP SQUAD"? NO ONE WOULD BUY *THAT*...
PSST
YAY! OUR **OWN** MONSTER STOP SQUAD!
NO?
HMM... THIS DOESN'T LOOK SO GOOD.
BEEP
BOOP

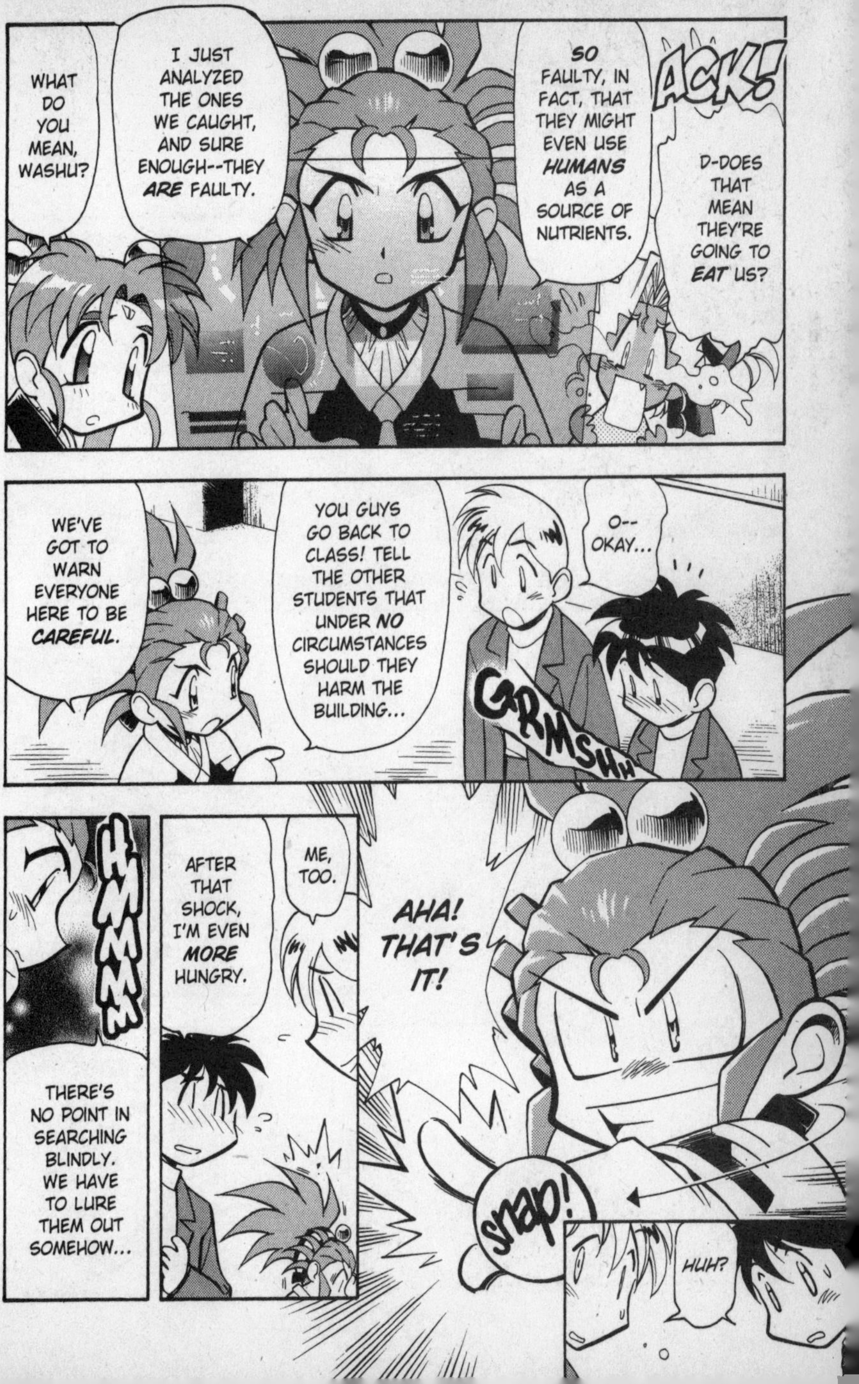
WHAT DO YOU MEAN, WASHU?
I JUST ANALYZED THE ONES WE CAUGHT, AND SURE ENOUGH--THEY *ARE* FAULTY.
SO FAULTY, IN FACT, THAT THEY MIGHT EVEN USE *HUMANS* AS A SOURCE OF NUTRIENTS.
ACK!
D-DOES THAT MEAN THEY'RE GOING TO *EAT* US?
WE'VE GOT TO WARN EVERYONE HERE TO BE *CAREFUL*.
YOU GUYS GO BACK TO CLASS! TELL THE OTHER STUDENTS THAT UNDER *NO* CIRCUMSTANCES SHOULD THEY HARM THE BUILDING...
O-- OKAY...
GRMSHH
HMMMMM
THERE'S NO POINT IN SEARCHING BLINDLY. WE HAVE TO LURE THEM OUT SOMEHOW...
AFTER THAT SHOCK, I'M EVEN *MORE* HUNGRY.
ME, TOO.
AHA! THAT'S IT!
SNAP!
HUH?

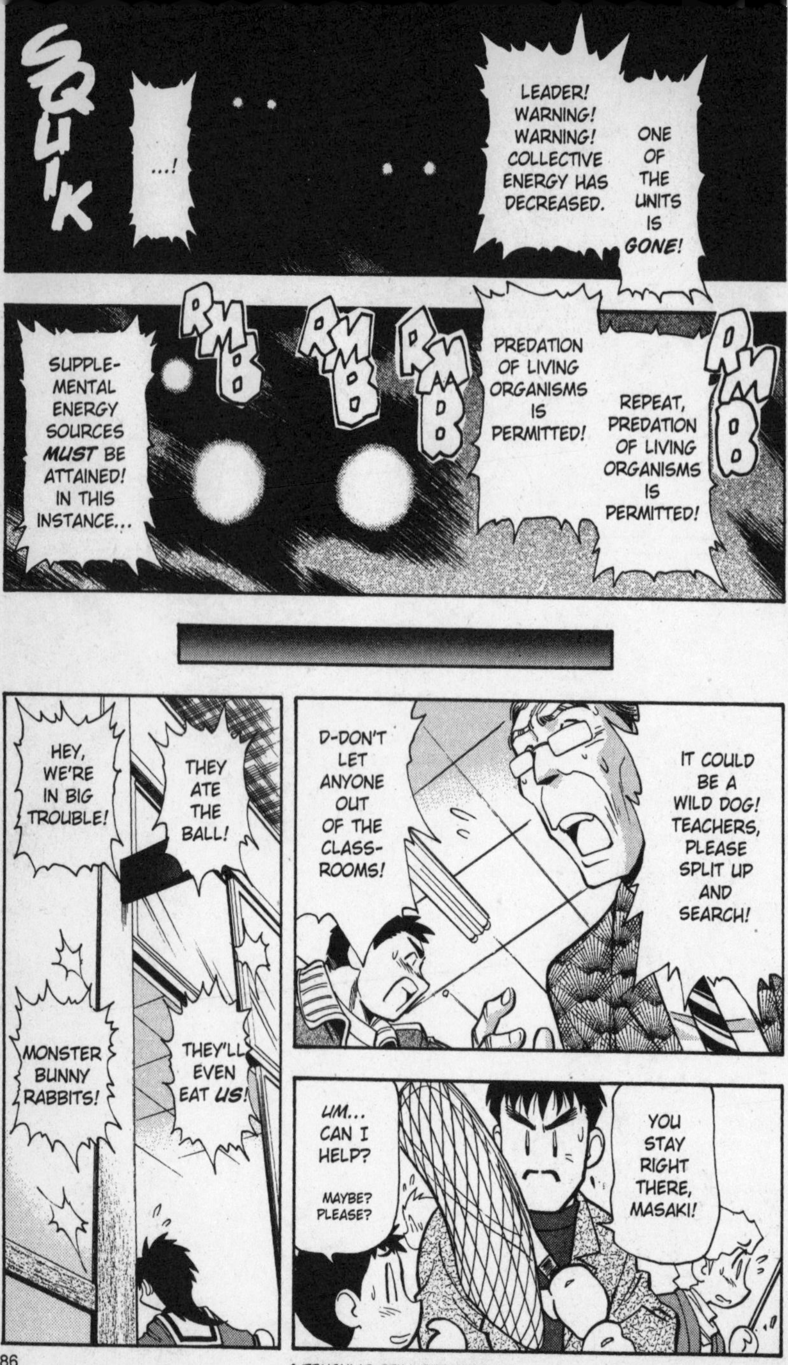
SQUIK
...!
LEADER! WARNING! WARNING! COLLECTIVE ENERGY HAS DECREASED.
ONE OF THE UNITS IS GONE!
SUPPLE-MENTAL ENERGY SOURCES MUST BE ATTAINED! IN THIS INSTANCE...
RMBD RMBD RMBD
PREDATION OF LIVING ORGANISMS IS PERMITTED!
REPEAT, PREDATION OF LIVING ORGANISMS IS PERMITTED!
RMBD
HEY, WE'RE IN BIG TROUBLE!
THEY ATE THE BALL!
MONSTER BUNNY RABBITS!
THEY'LL EVEN EAT US!
D-DON'T LET ANYONE OUT OF THE CLASS-ROOMS!
IT COULD BE A WILD DOG! TEACHERS, PLEASE SPLIT UP AND SEARCH!
UM... CAN I HELP?
MAYBE? PLEASE?
YOU STAY RIGHT THERE, MASAKI!

▲TENCHI IS STILL DETAINED AS A SUSPICIOUS TRESPASSER...◊

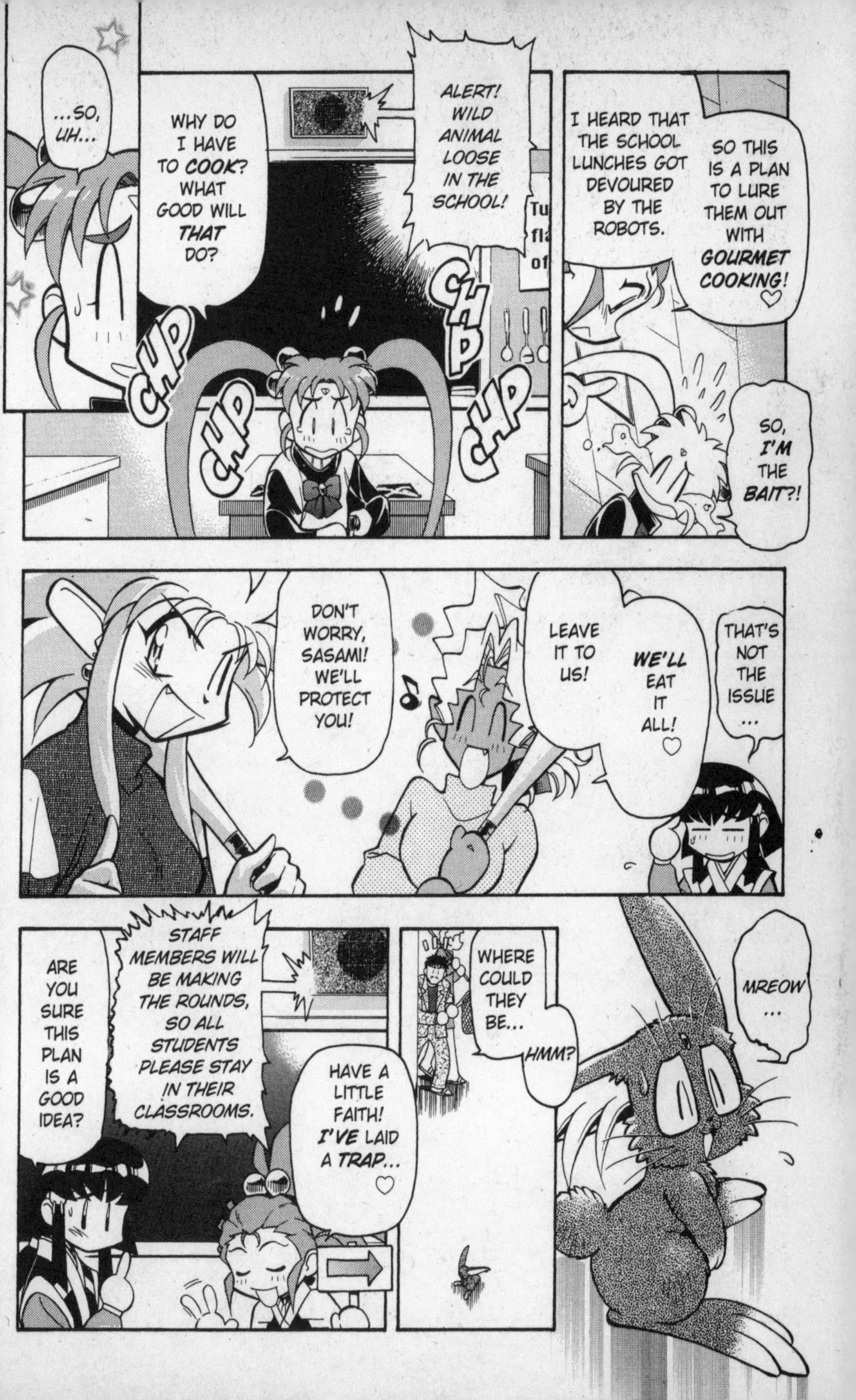
...SO, UH...
WHY DO I HAVE TO COOK? WHAT GOOD WILL THAT DO?
ALERT! WILD ANIMAL LOOSE IN THE SCHOOL!
CHP
CHP
CHP
CHP
I HEARD THAT THE SCHOOL LUNCHES GOT DEVOURED BY THE ROBOTS.
SO THIS IS A PLAN TO LURE THEM OUT WITH GOURMET COOKING! ♡
SO, I'M THE BAIT?!
DON'T WORRY, SASAMI! WE'LL PROTECT YOU!
LEAVE IT TO US!
WE'LL EAT IT ALL! ♡
THAT'S NOT THE ISSUE...
ARE YOU SURE THIS PLAN IS A GOOD IDEA?
STAFF MEMBERS WILL BE MAKING THE ROUNDS, SO ALL STUDENTS PLEASE STAY IN THEIR CLASSROOMS.
HAVE A LITTLE FAITH! I'VE LAID A TRAP... ♡
WHERE COULD THEY BE...
HMM?
MREOW...

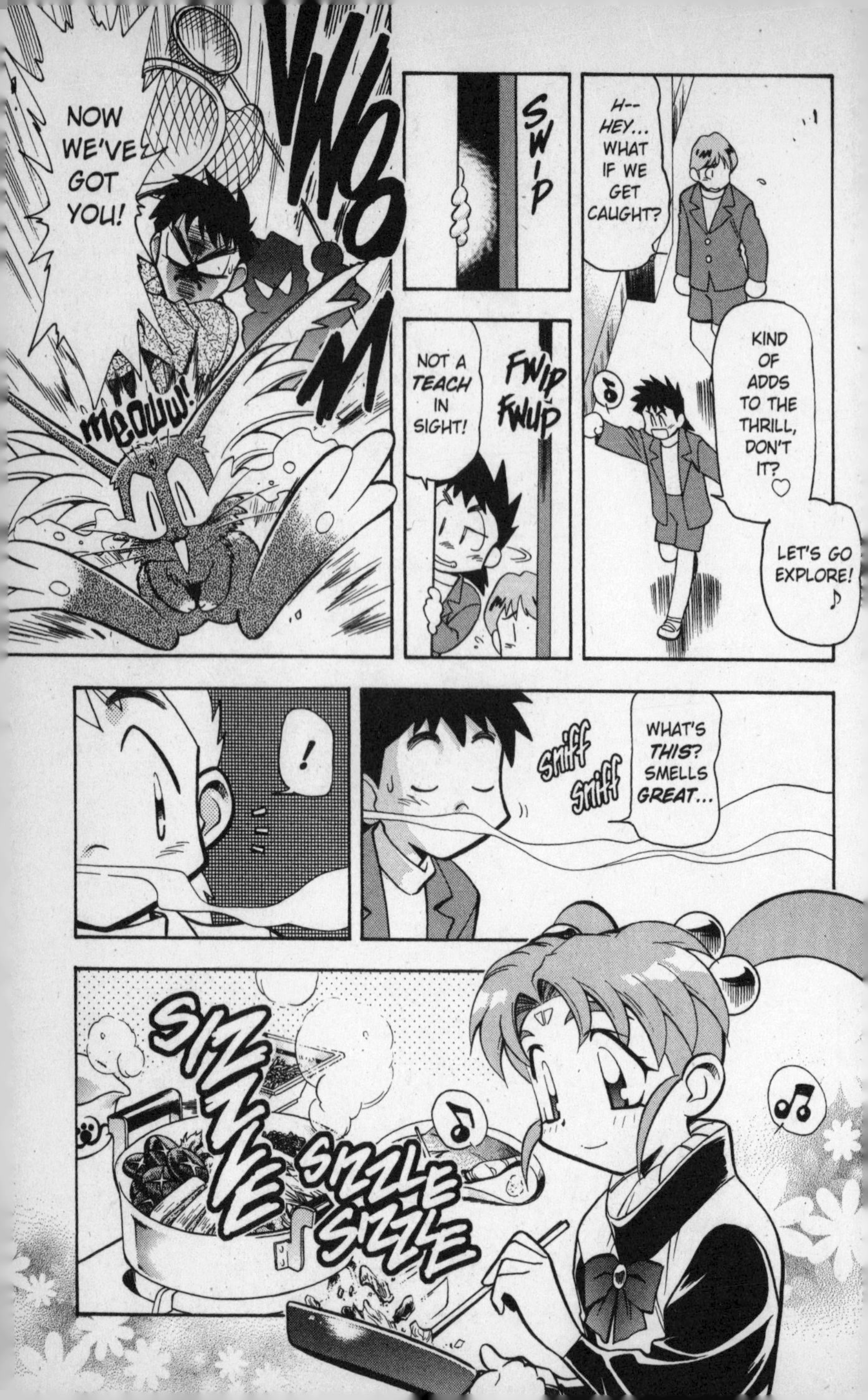
NOW WE'VE GOT YOU!
WHOOM
meoww!
SWIP
NOT A TEACH IN SIGHT!
FWIP FWUP
H-- HEY... WHAT IF WE GET CAUGHT?
KIND OF ADDS TO THE THRILL, DON'T IT? ♡
LET'S GO EXPLORE! ♪
!
sniff sniff
WHAT'S THIS? SMELLS GREAT...
SIZZLE
SIZZLE SIZZLE

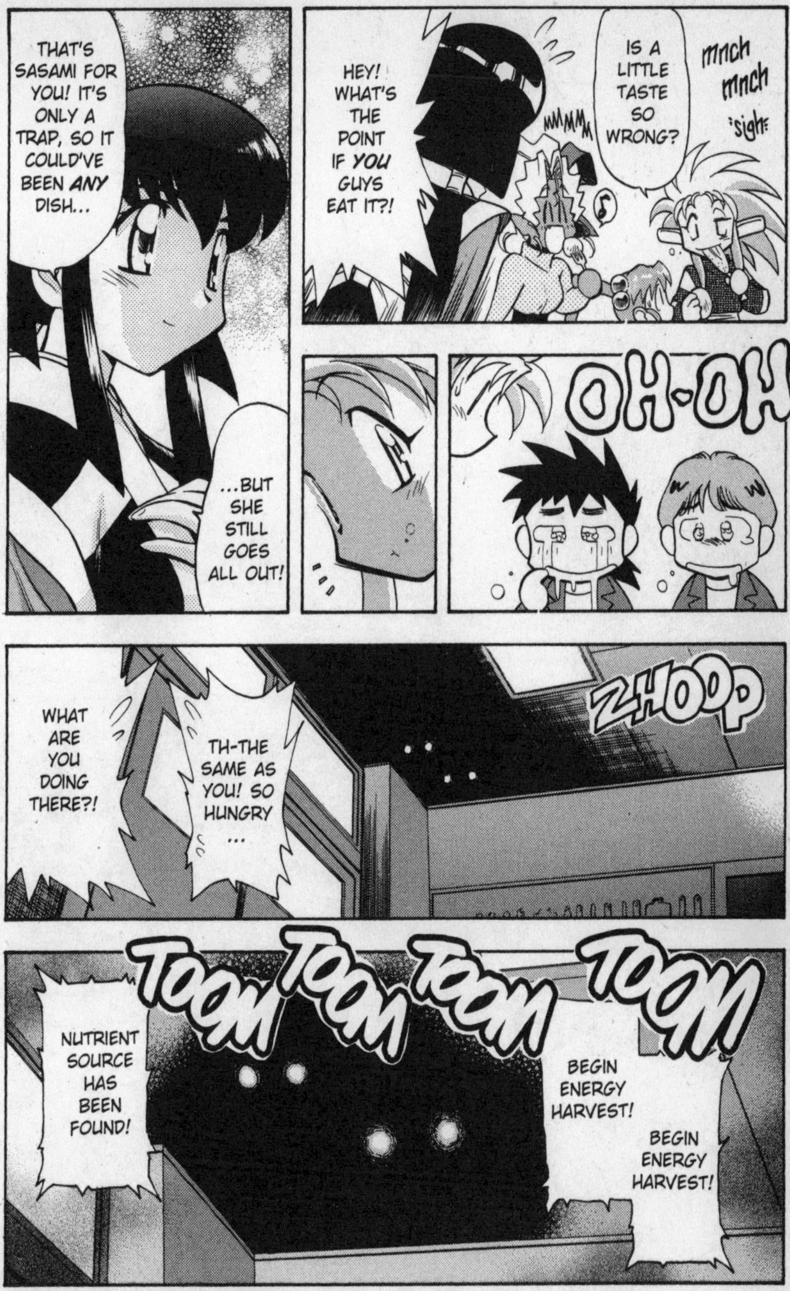
THAT'S SASAMI FOR YOU! IT'S ONLY A TRAP, SO IT COULD'VE BEEN ANY DISH...
...BUT SHE STILL GOES ALL OUT!
HEY! WHAT'S THE POINT IF YOU GUYS EAT IT?!
IS A LITTLE TASTE SO WRONG?
mnch mnch
sigh
OH-OH
WHAT ARE YOU DOING THERE?!
TH-THE SAME AS YOU! SO HUNGRY ...
ZHOOP
TOOM TOOM TOOM TOOM
NUTRIENT SOURCE HAS BEEN FOUND!
BEGIN ENERGY HARVEST!
BEGIN ENERGY HARVEST!

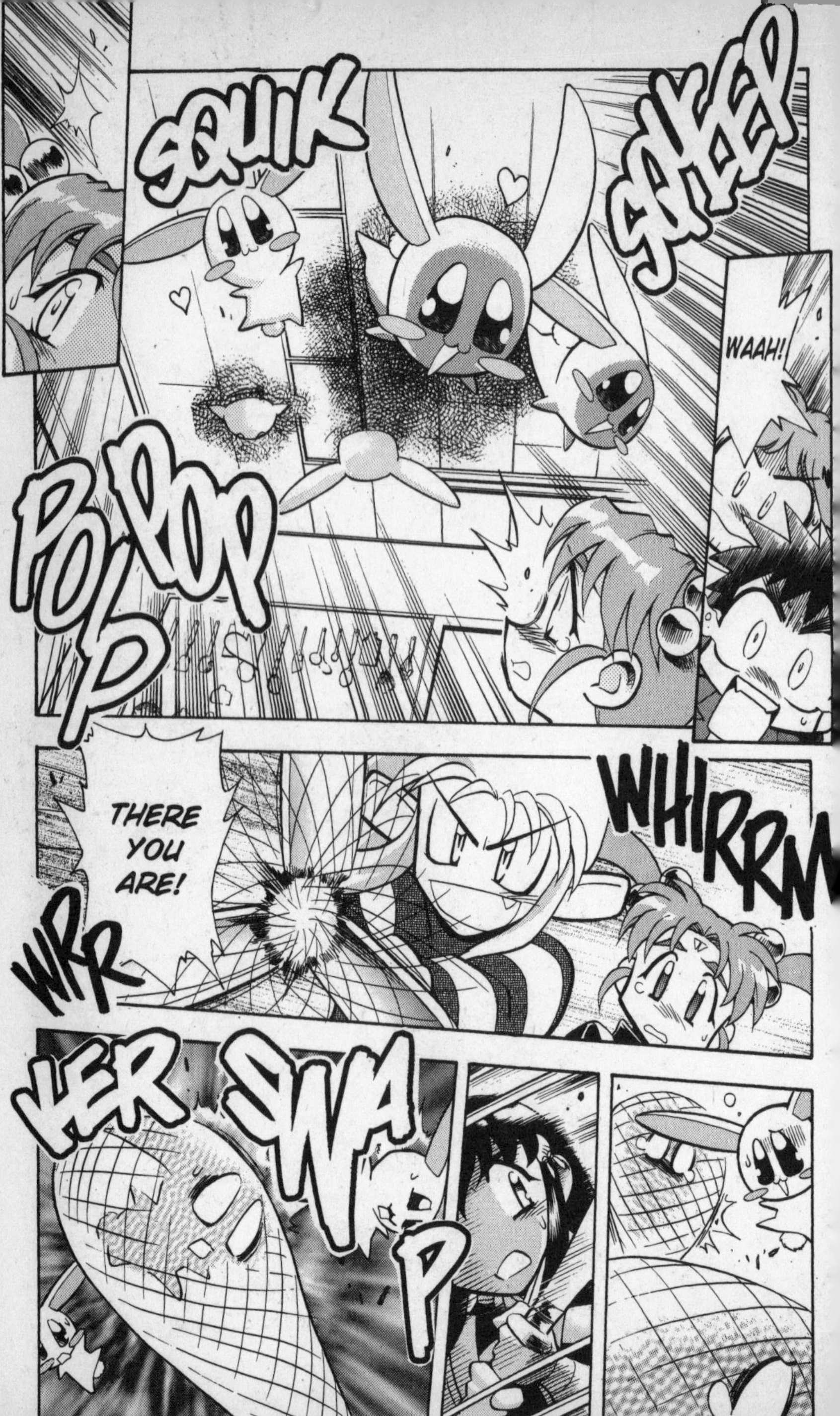
SQUIK
SQUEEP
WAAH!
POP
POP
POP
THERE YOU ARE!
WRR
WHIRRM
KER SWAP

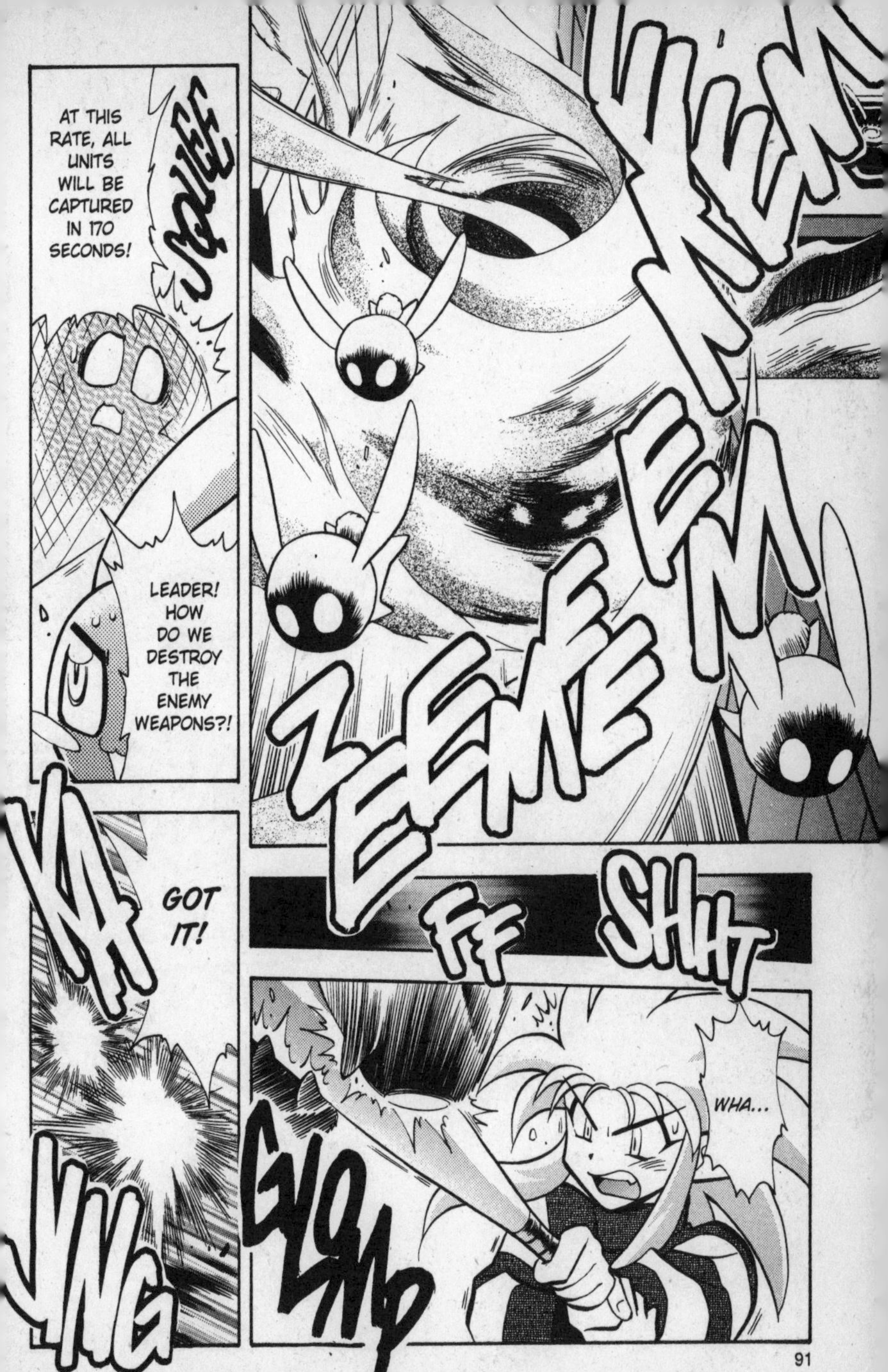
AT THIS RATE, ALL UNITS WILL BE CAPTURED IN 170 SECONDS!
SQUIEE
LEADER! HOW DO WE DESTROY THE ENEMY WEAPONS?!
FF
SHHT
GOT IT!
WHA...

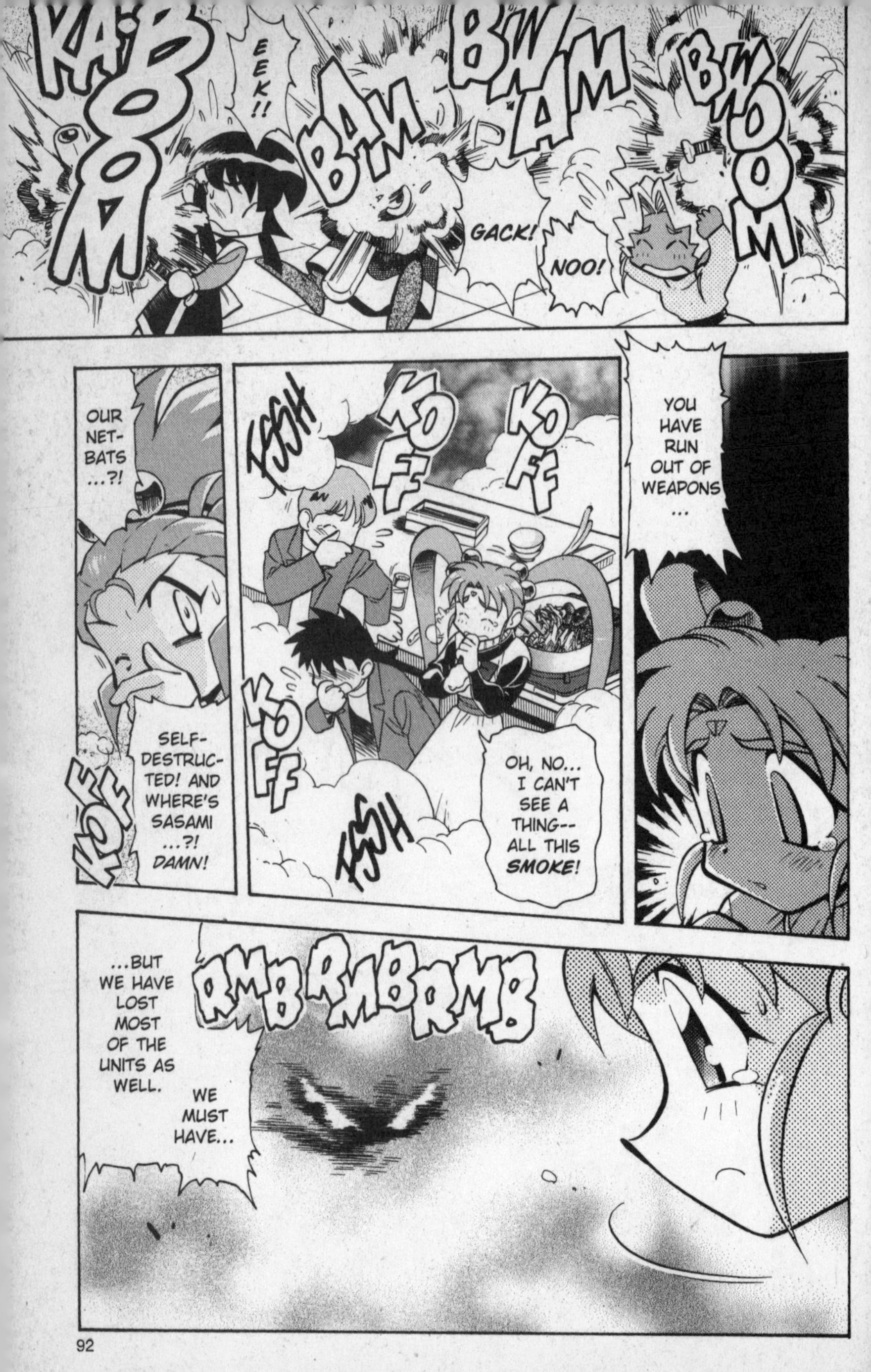
KA-BOOM
EEK!!
BAM
BWAM
BWOOM
GACK!
NOO!
OUR NET-BATS ...?!
SELF-DESTRUCTED! AND WHERE'S SASAMI ...?! DAMN!
KOFF
FSSH
KOFF
KOFF
KOFF
OH, NO... I CAN'T SEE A THING-- ALL THIS SMOKE!
FSSH
YOU HAVE RUN OUT OF WEAPONS ...
...BUT WE HAVE LOST MOST OF THE UNITS AS WELL.
WE MUST HAVE...
RMB RMB RMB

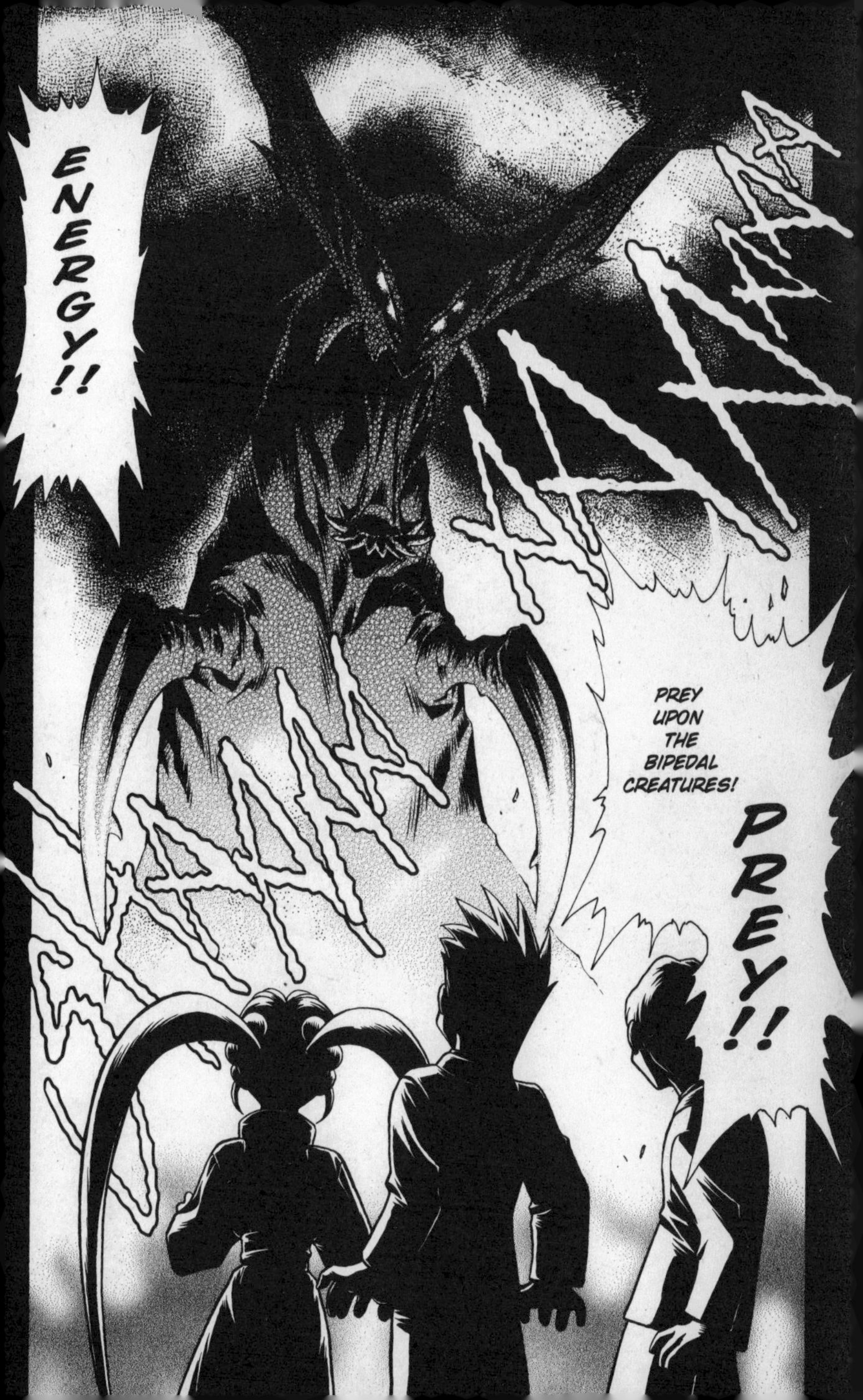
ENERGY!!
PREY UPON THE BIPEDAL CREATURES!
PREY!!

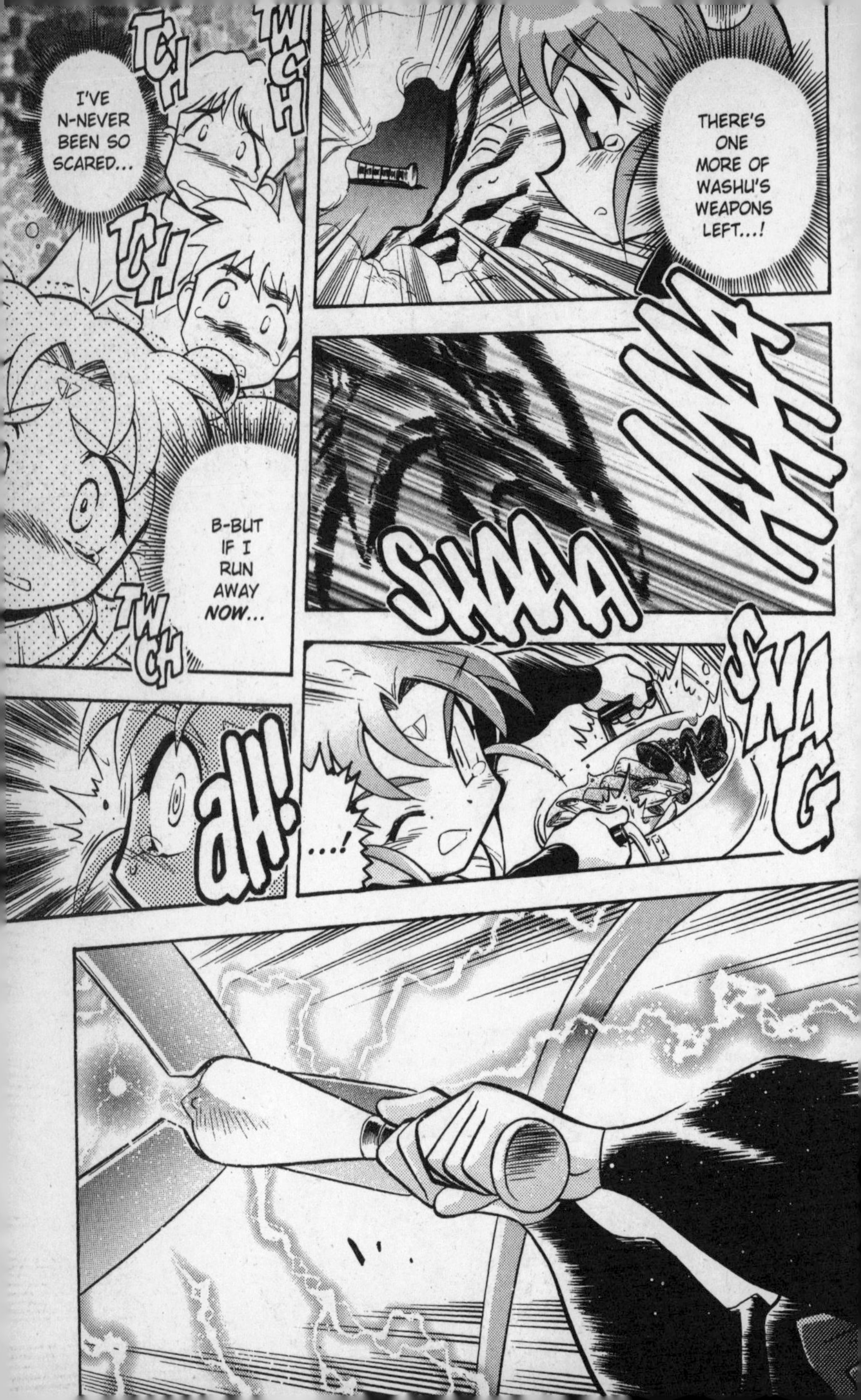
I'VE N-NEVER BEEN SO SCARED...
TCH
TWCH
TCH
THERE'S ONE MORE OF WASHU'S WEAPONS LEFT...!
B-BUT IF I RUN AWAY *NOW*...
TWCH
SHAAA
VWAAA
AH!
...!
SNAG

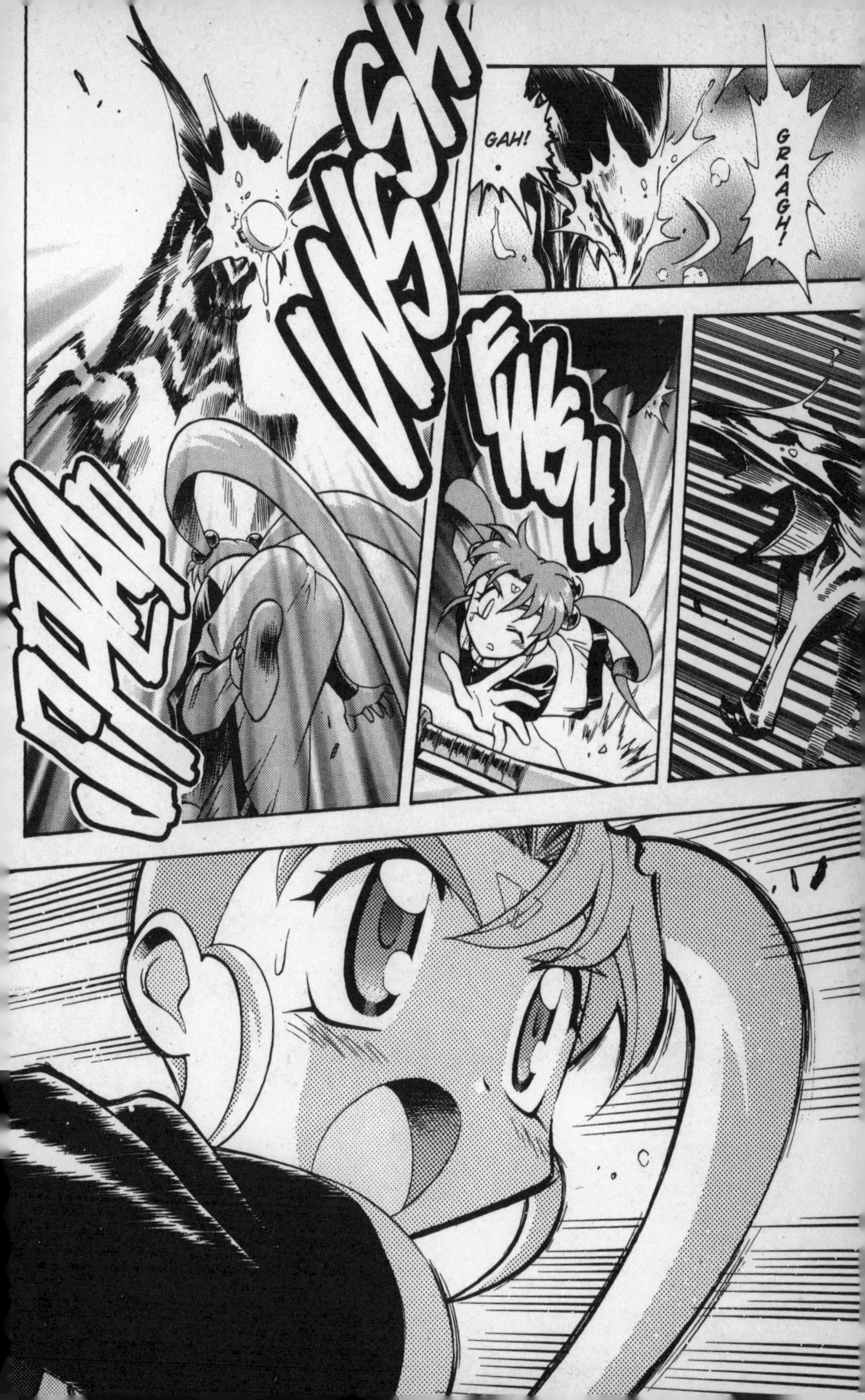
GAH!
GRAAGH!

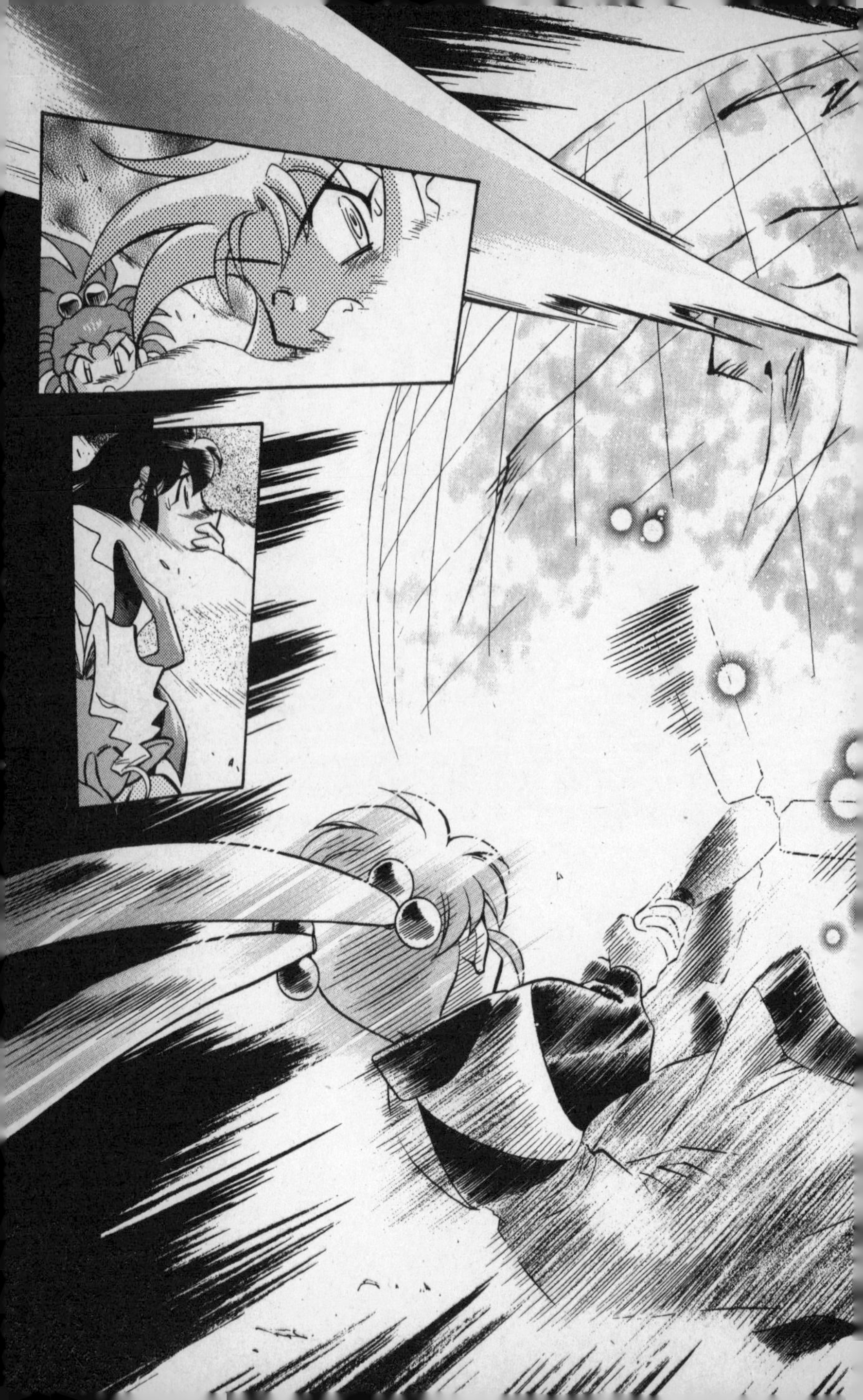

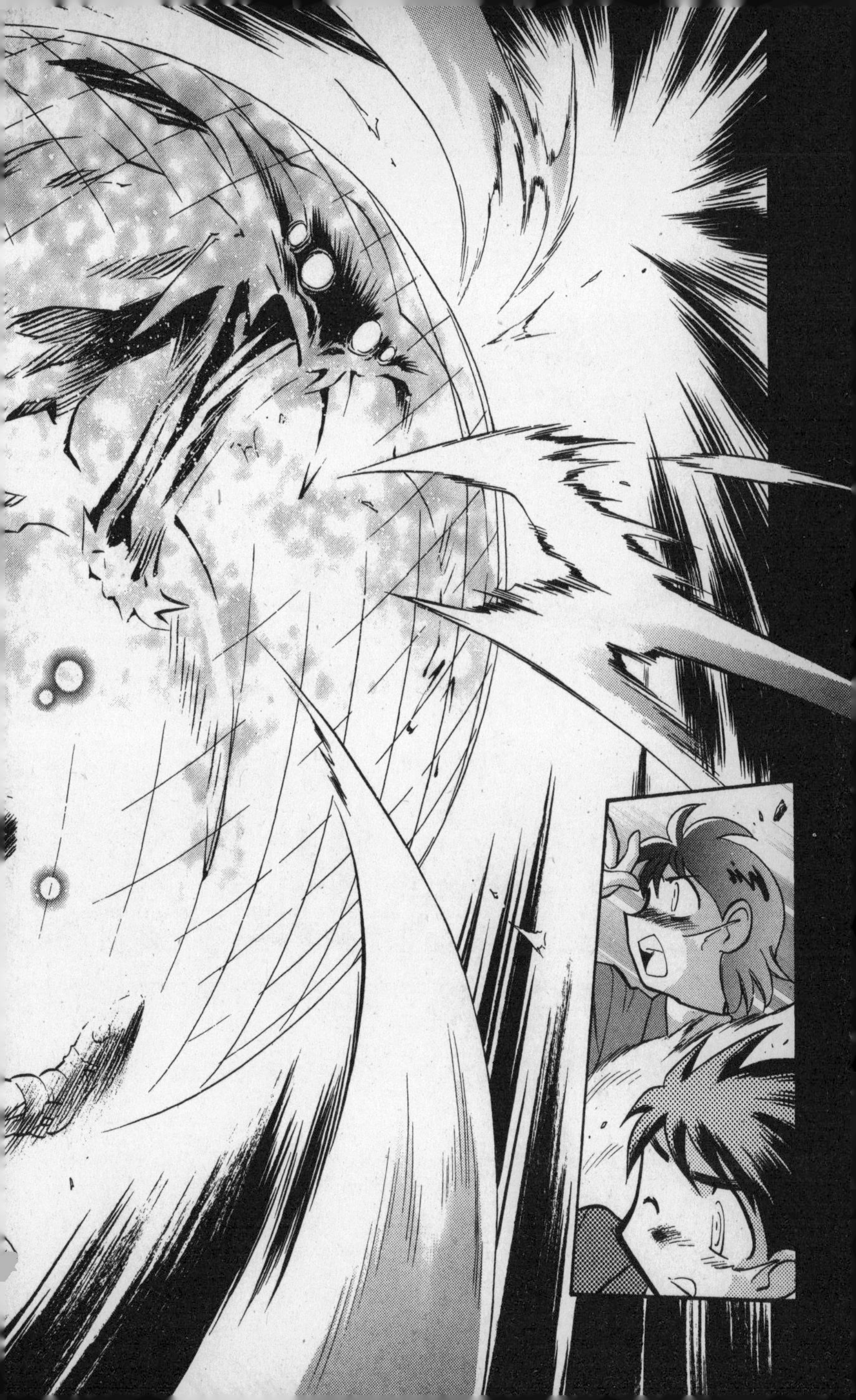

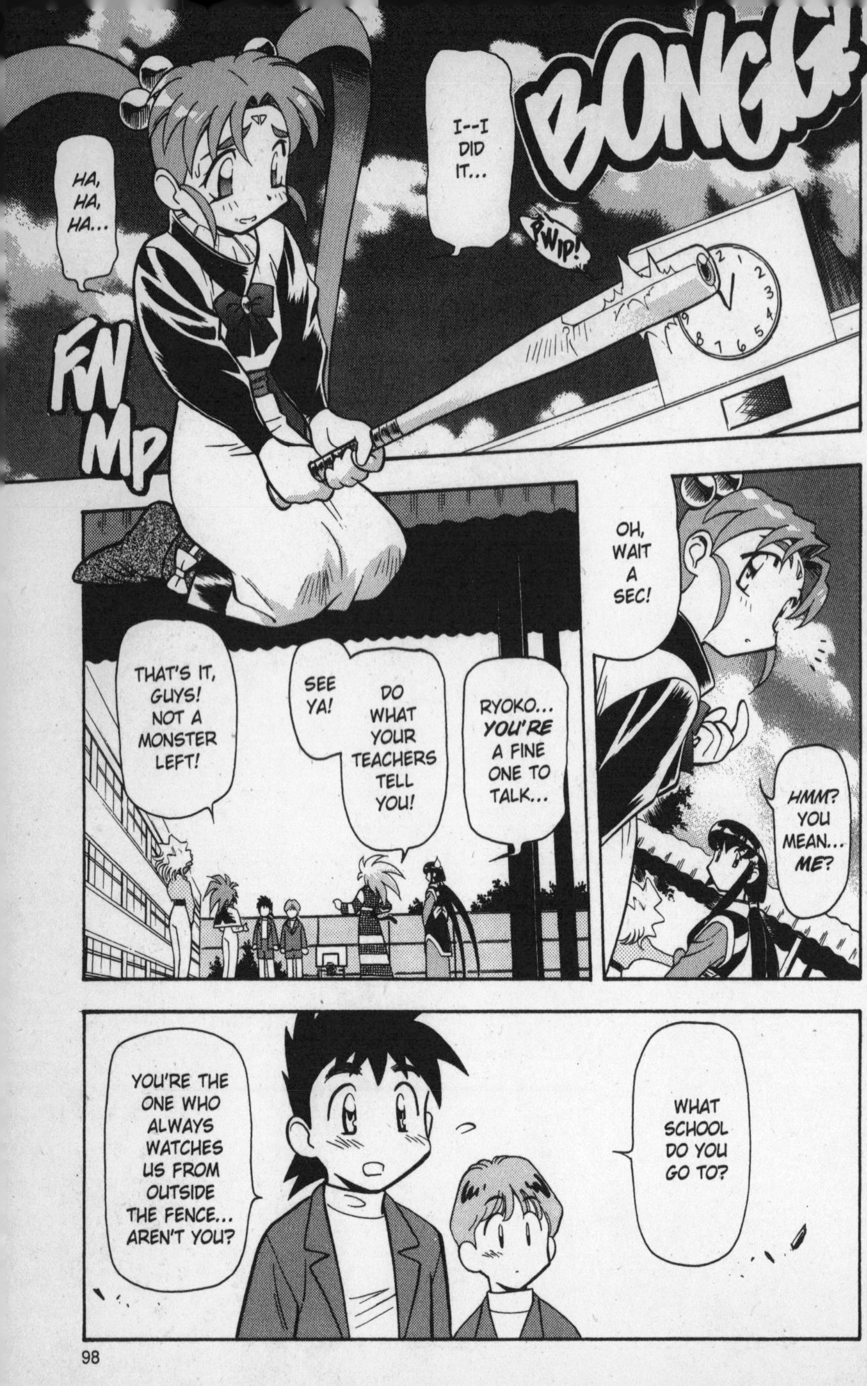

HA, HA, HA...
I--I DID IT...
BONGG!
TWIP!
FWMP
THAT'S IT, GUYS! NOT A MONSTER LEFT!
SEE YA!
DO WHAT YOUR TEACHERS TELL YOU!
RYOKO... *YOU'RE* A FINE ONE TO TALK...
OH, WAIT A SEC!
HMM? YOU MEAN... *ME?*
YOU'RE THE ONE WHO ALWAYS WATCHES US FROM OUTSIDE THE FENCE... AREN'T YOU?
WHAT SCHOOL DO YOU GO TO?

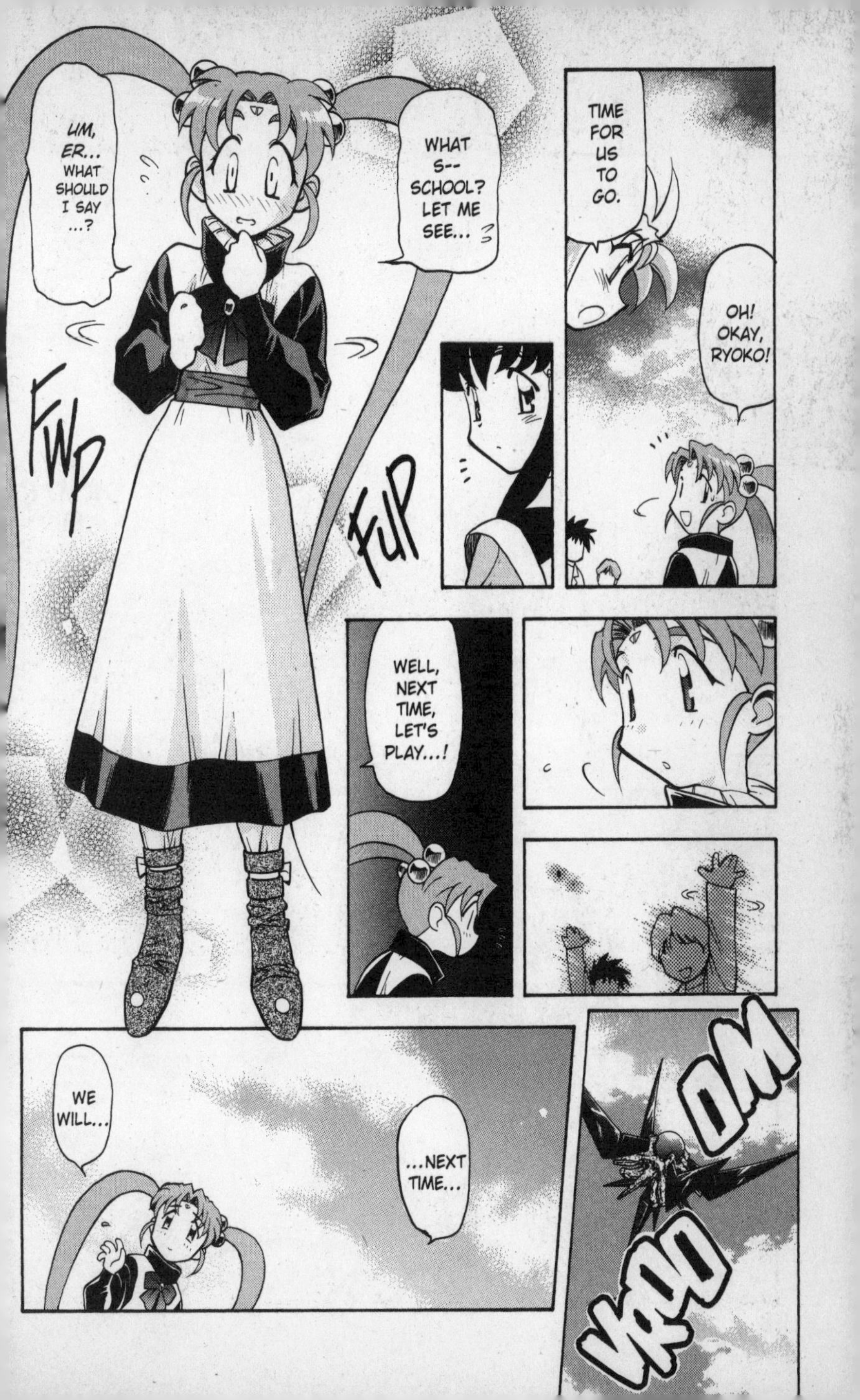
UM, ER... WHAT SHOULD I SAY ...?
WHAT S-- SCHOOL? LET ME SEE...
FWP
FUP
TIME FOR US TO GO.
OH! OKAY, RYOKO!
WELL, NEXT TIME, LET'S PLAY...!
WE WILL...
...NEXT TIME...
VROOOM

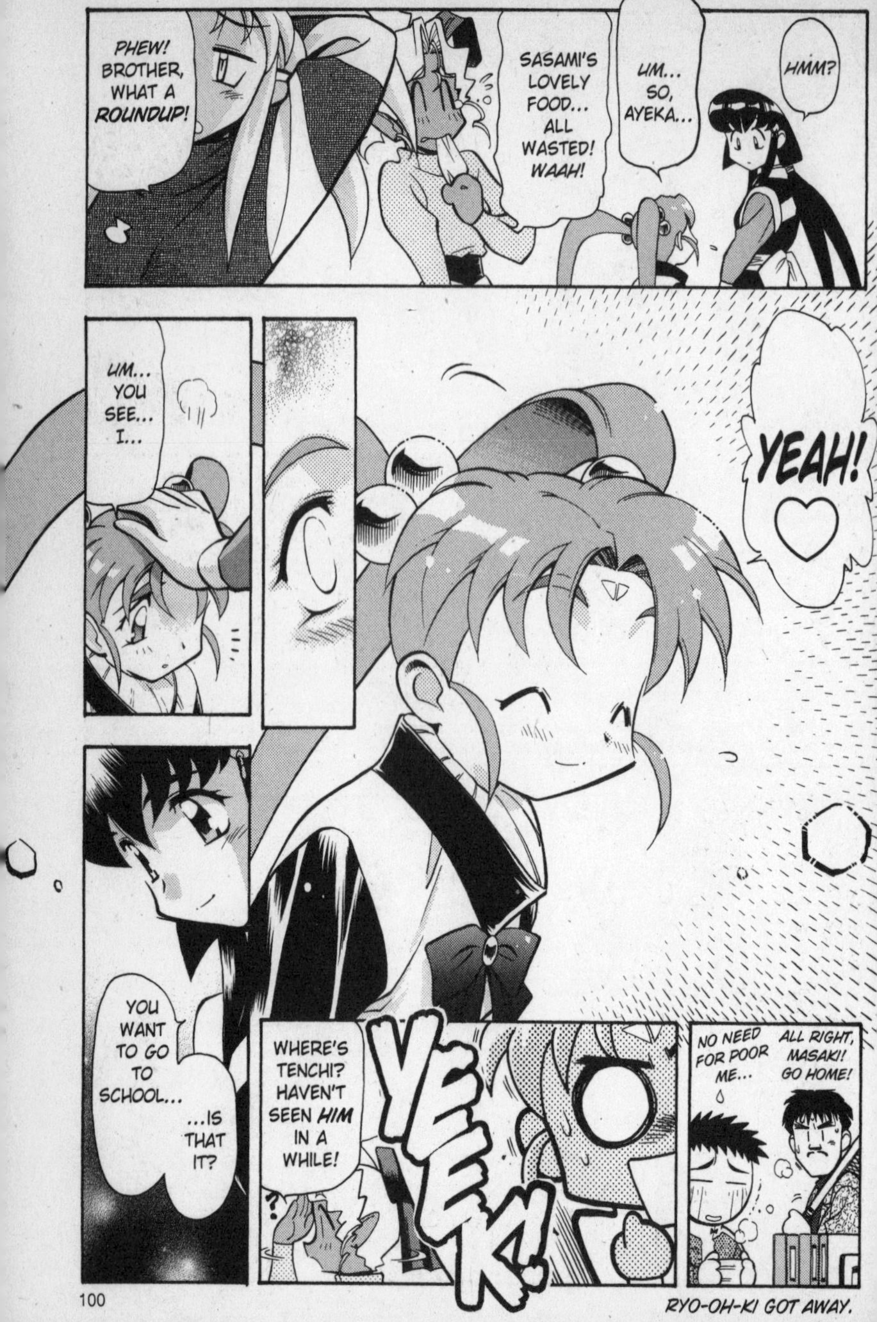
PHEW! BROTHER, WHAT A ROUNDUP!
SASAMI'S LOVELY FOOD... ALL WASTED! WAAH!
UM... SO, AYEKA...
HMM?
UM... YOU SEE... I...
YEAH!
YOU WANT TO GO TO SCHOOL...
...IS THAT IT?
WHERE'S TENCHI? HAVEN'T SEEN HIM IN A WHILE!
YEEK!
NO NEED FOR POOR ME...
ALL RIGHT, MASAKI! GO HOME!

RYO-OH-KI GOT AWAY.

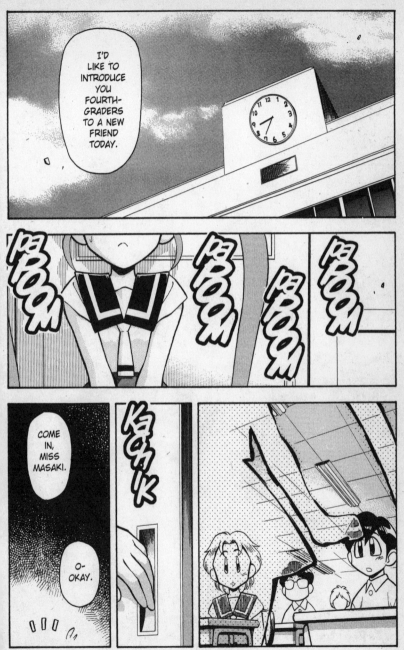

I'D LIKE TO INTRODUCE YOU FOURTH-GRADERS TO A NEW FRIEND TODAY.

pa BOOM pa BOOM pa BOOM pa BOOM

COME IN, MISS MASAKI.

Ka CHAK

O-OKAY.

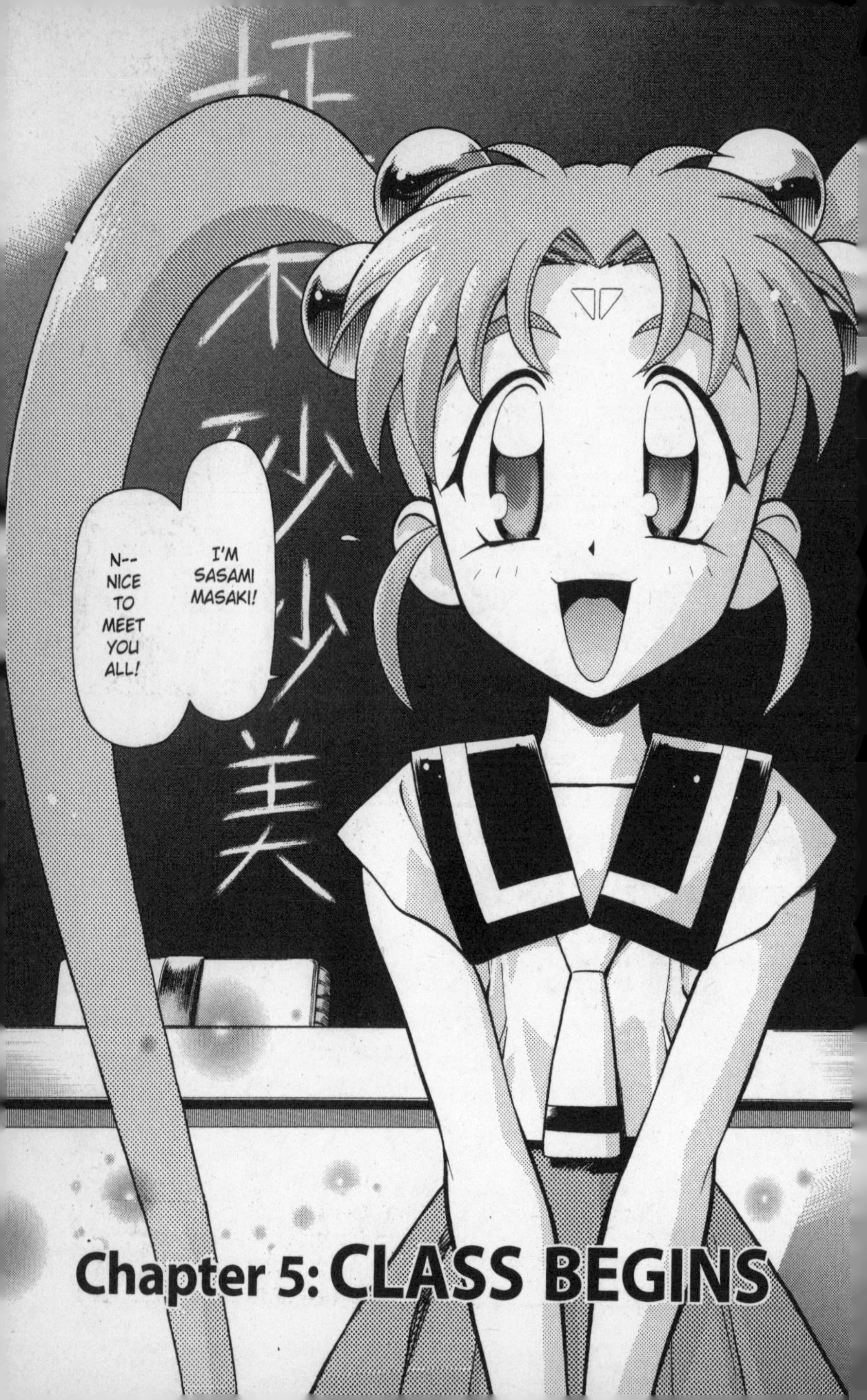
I'M SASAMI MASAKI!
N-- NICE TO MEET YOU ALL!

Chapter 5: CLASS BEGINS

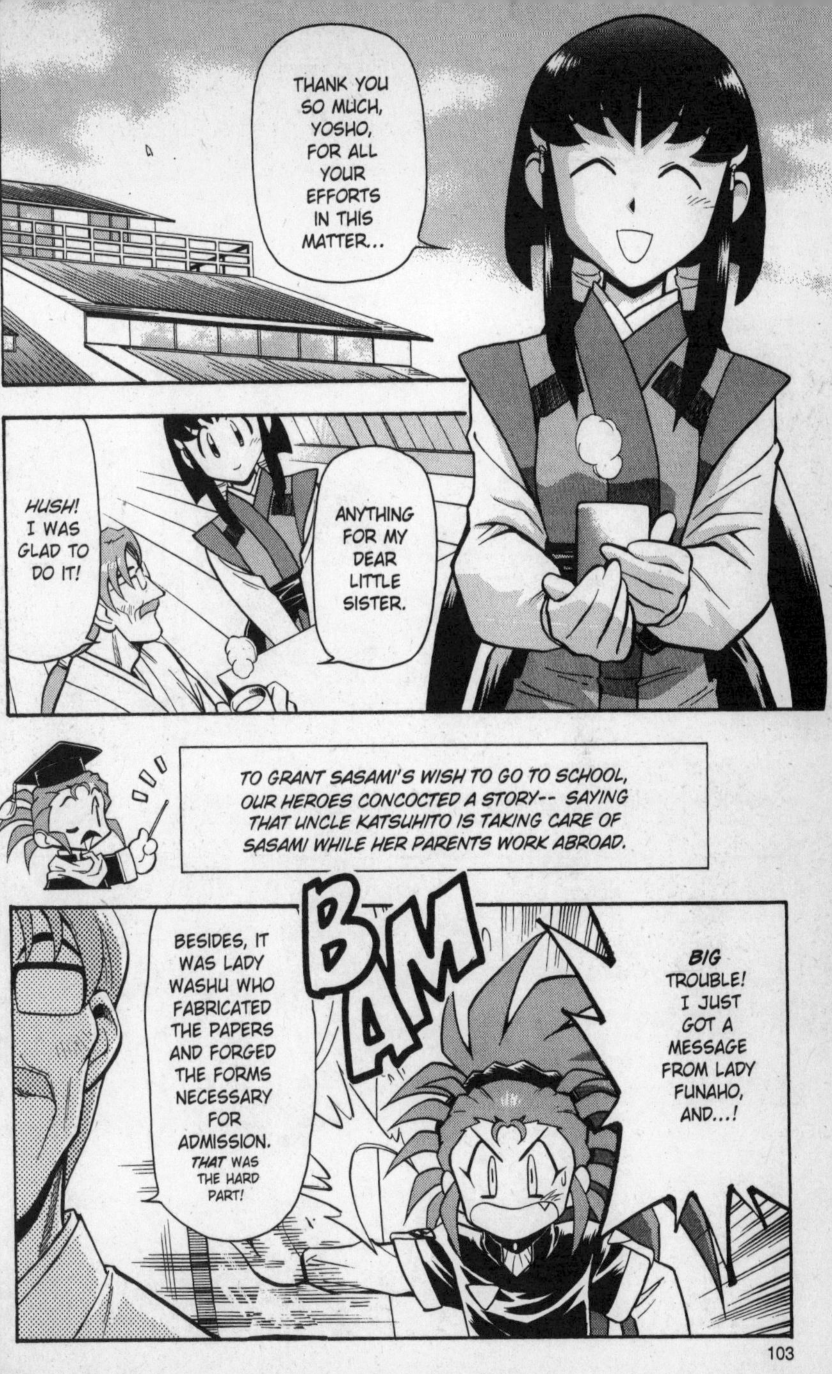
THANK YOU SO MUCH, YOSHO, FOR ALL YOUR EFFORTS IN THIS MATTER...
HUSH! I WAS GLAD TO DO IT!
ANYTHING FOR MY DEAR LITTLE SISTER.
TO GRANT SASAMI'S WISH TO GO TO SCHOOL, OUR HEROES CONCOCTED A STORY-- SAYING THAT UNCLE KATSUHITO IS TAKING CARE OF SASAMI WHILE HER PARENTS WORK ABROAD.
BESIDES, IT WAS LADY WASHU WHO FABRICATED THE PAPERS AND FORGED THE FORMS NECESSARY FOR ADMISSION. *THAT* WAS THE HARD PART!
BAM
BIG TROUBLE! I JUST GOT A MESSAGE FROM LADY FUNAHO, AND...!

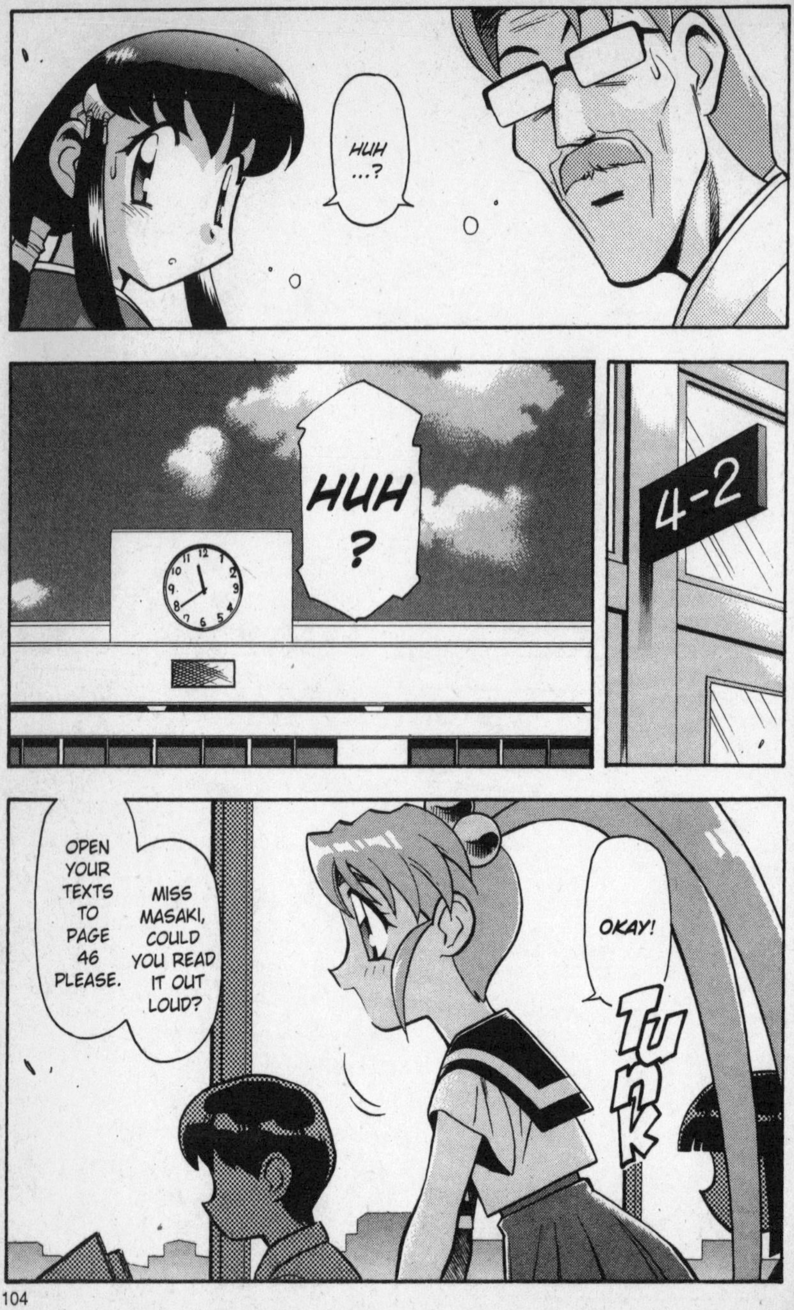
HUH ...?
HUH ?
4-2
OPEN YOUR TEXTS TO PAGE 46 PLEASE.
MISS MASAKI, COULD YOU READ IT OUT LOUD?
OKAY!
TUNK

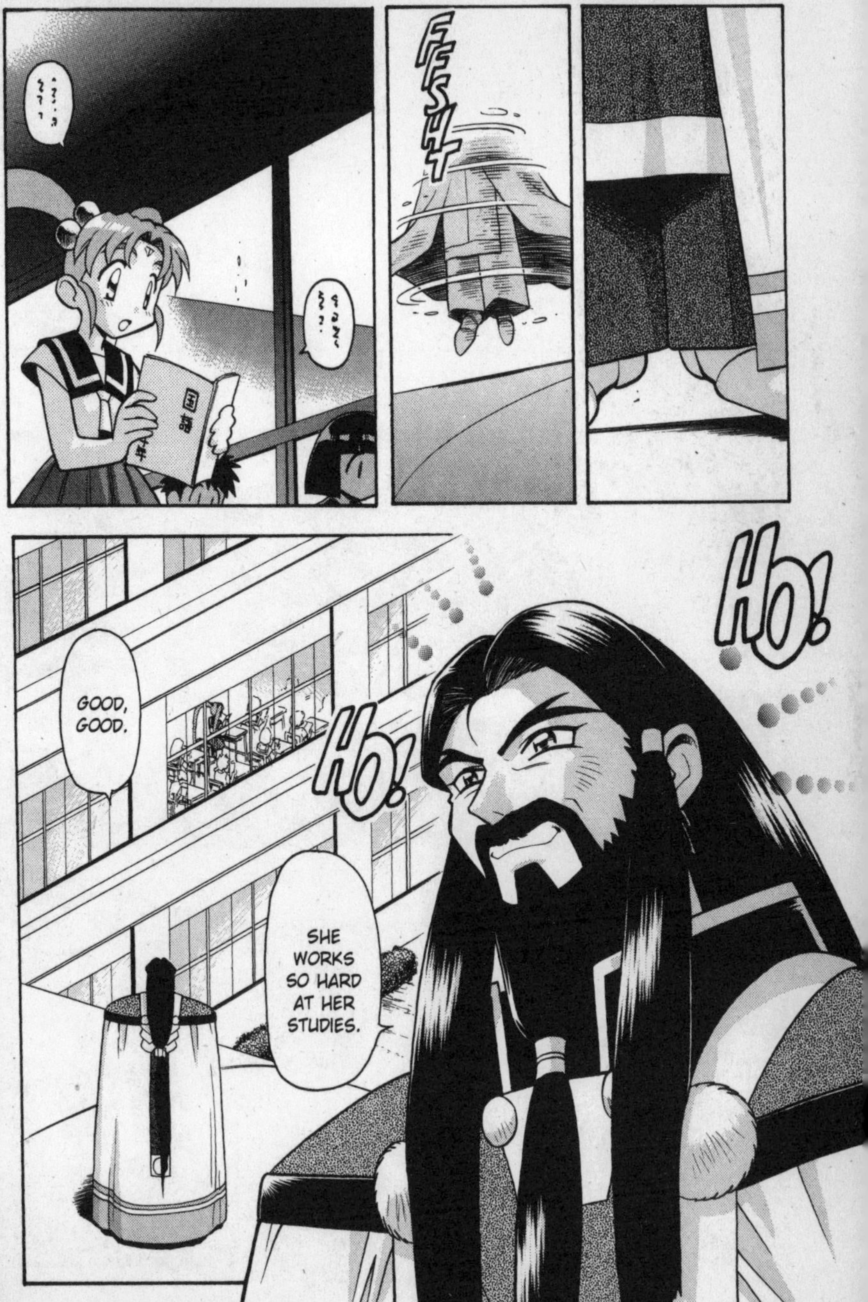
FFSHT
GOOD, GOOD.
HO!
HO!
SHE WORKS SO HARD AT HER STUDIES.

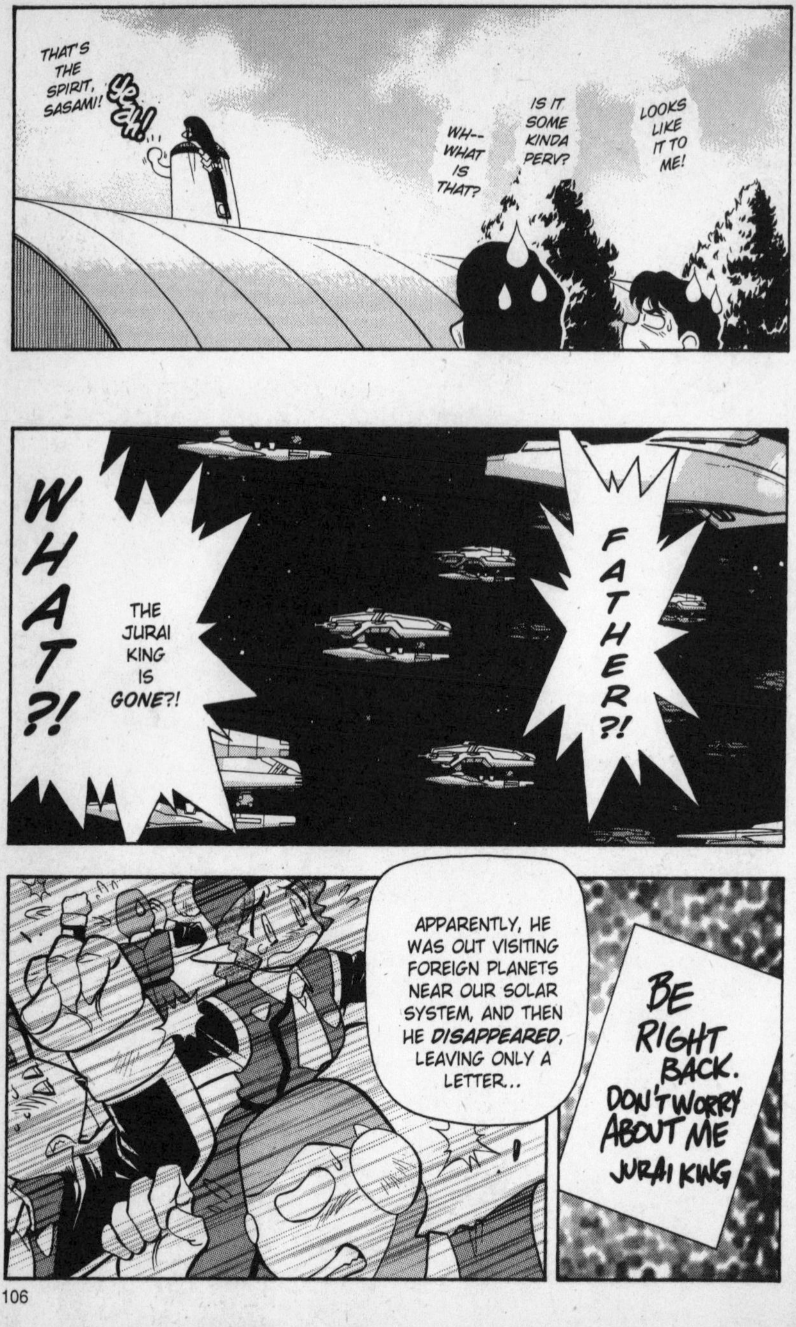
THAT'S THE SPIRIT, SASAMI!
YEAH!
WH-- WHAT IS THAT?
IS IT SOME KINDA PERV?
LOOKS LIKE IT TO ME!
WHAT?!
THE JURAI KING IS GONE?!
FATHER?!
APPARENTLY, HE WAS OUT VISITING FOREIGN PLANETS NEAR OUR SOLAR SYSTEM, AND THEN HE DISAPPEARED, LEAVING ONLY A LETTER...
BE RIGHT BACK. DON'T WORRY ABOUT ME
JURAI KING

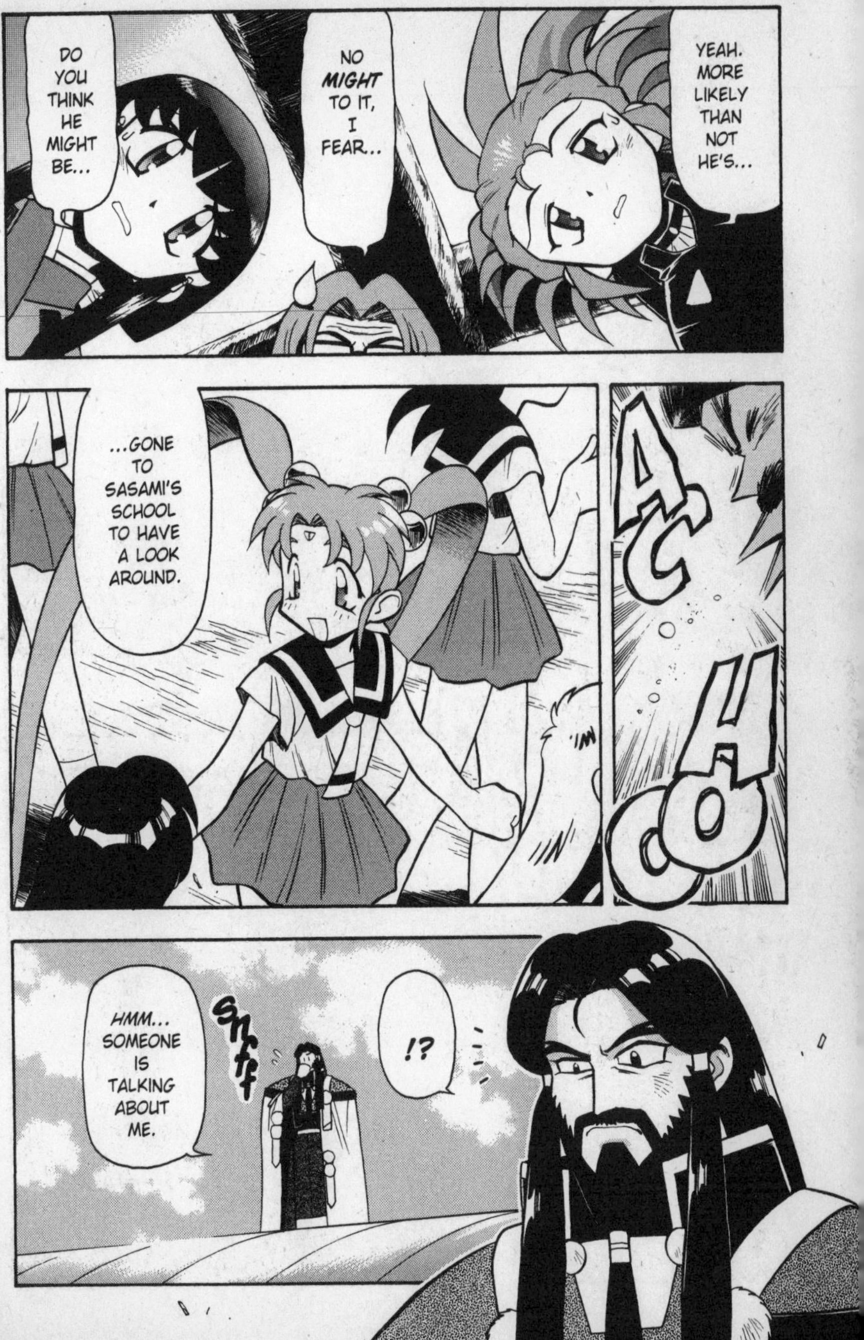
DO YOU THINK HE MIGHT BE...
NO *MIGHT* TO IT, I FEAR...
YEAH. MORE LIKELY THAN NOT HE'S...
...GONE TO SASAMI'S SCHOOL TO HAVE A LOOK AROUND.
ACHOO
HMM... SOMEONE IS TALKING ABOUT ME.
Sniff
!?

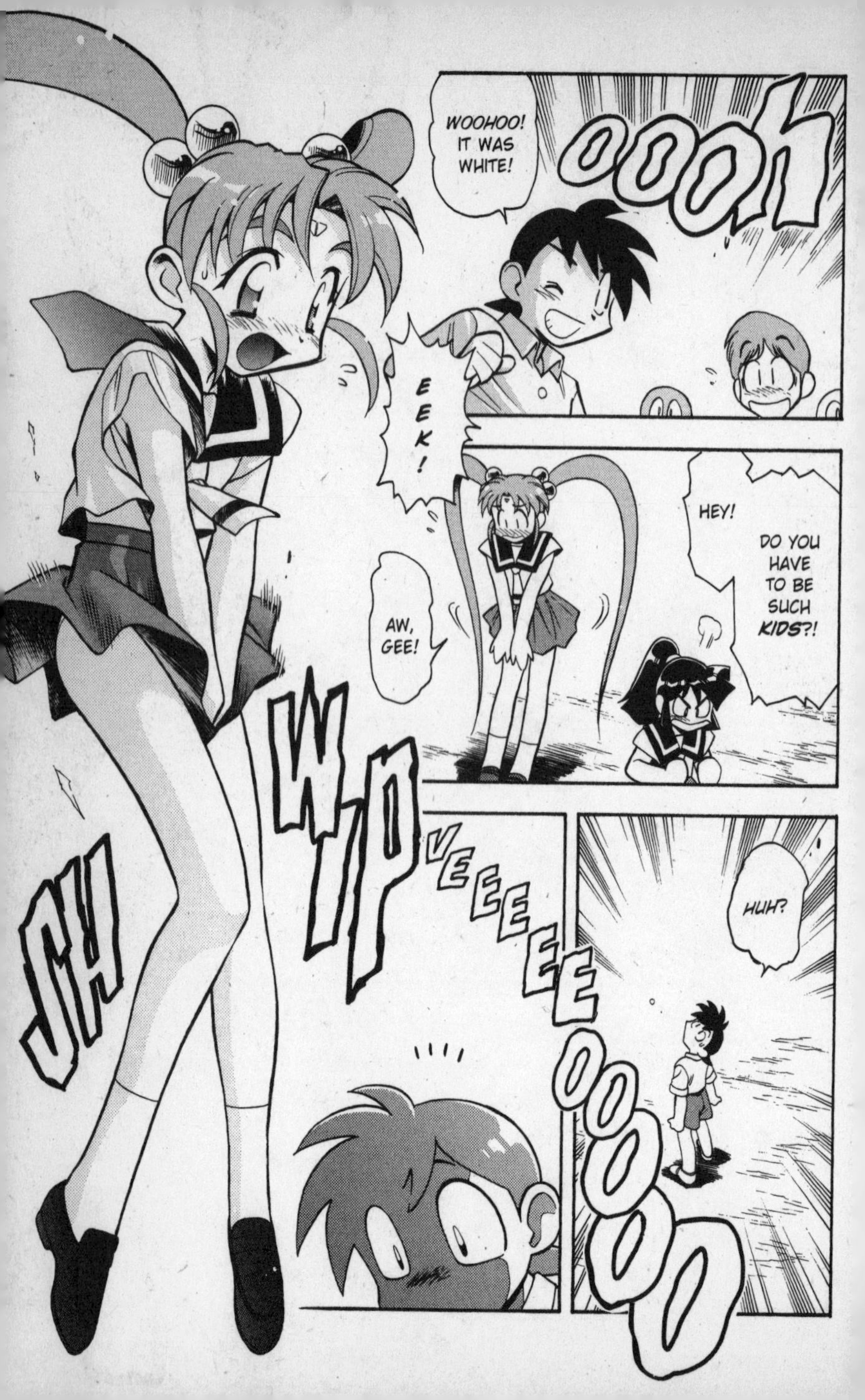
EEK!
WOOHOO! IT WAS WHITE!
oooh
AW, GEE!
HEY!
DO YOU HAVE TO BE SUCH KIDS?!
HUH?

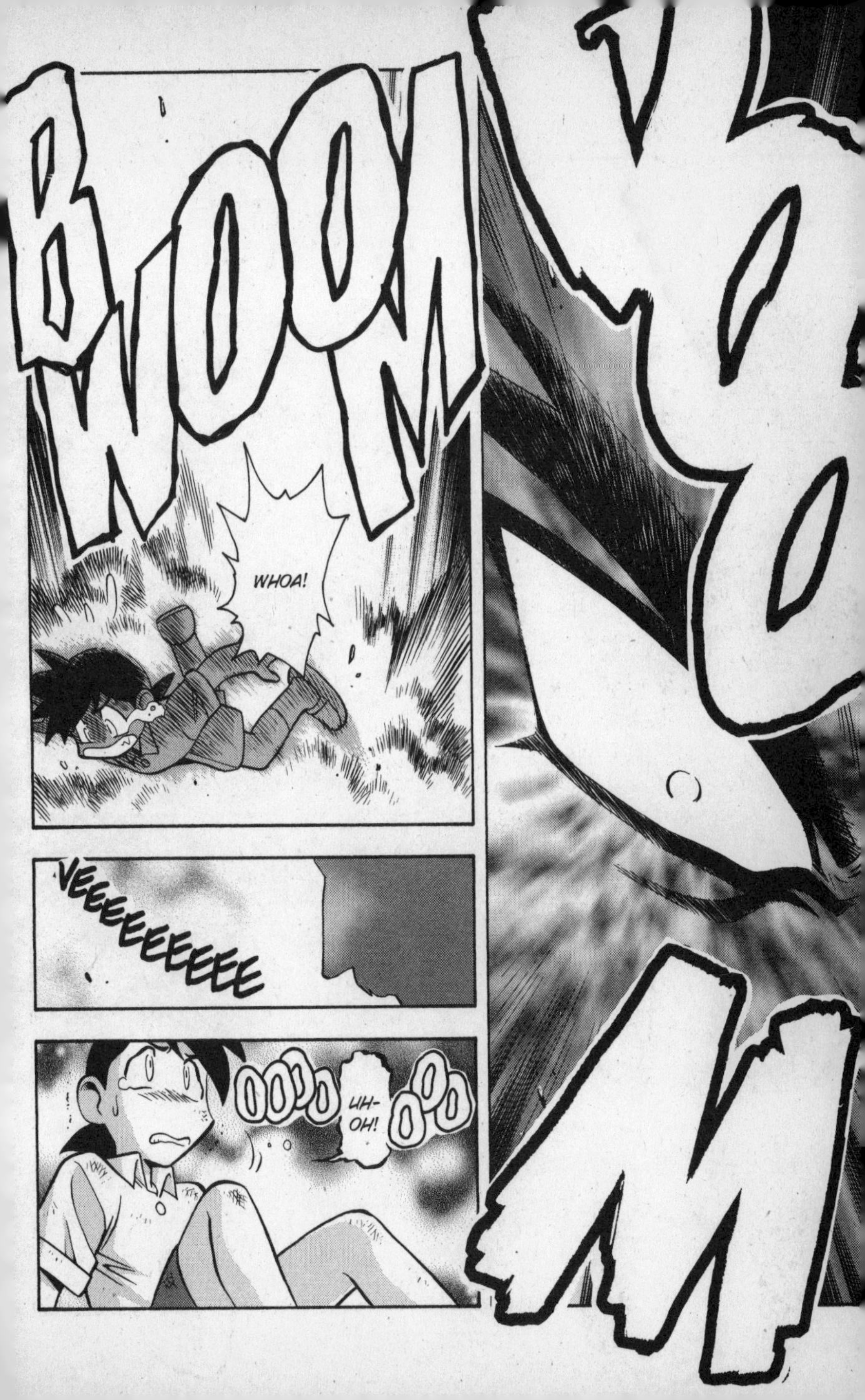
BOOOM
WHOA!
VEEEEEEEEE
UH-OH!

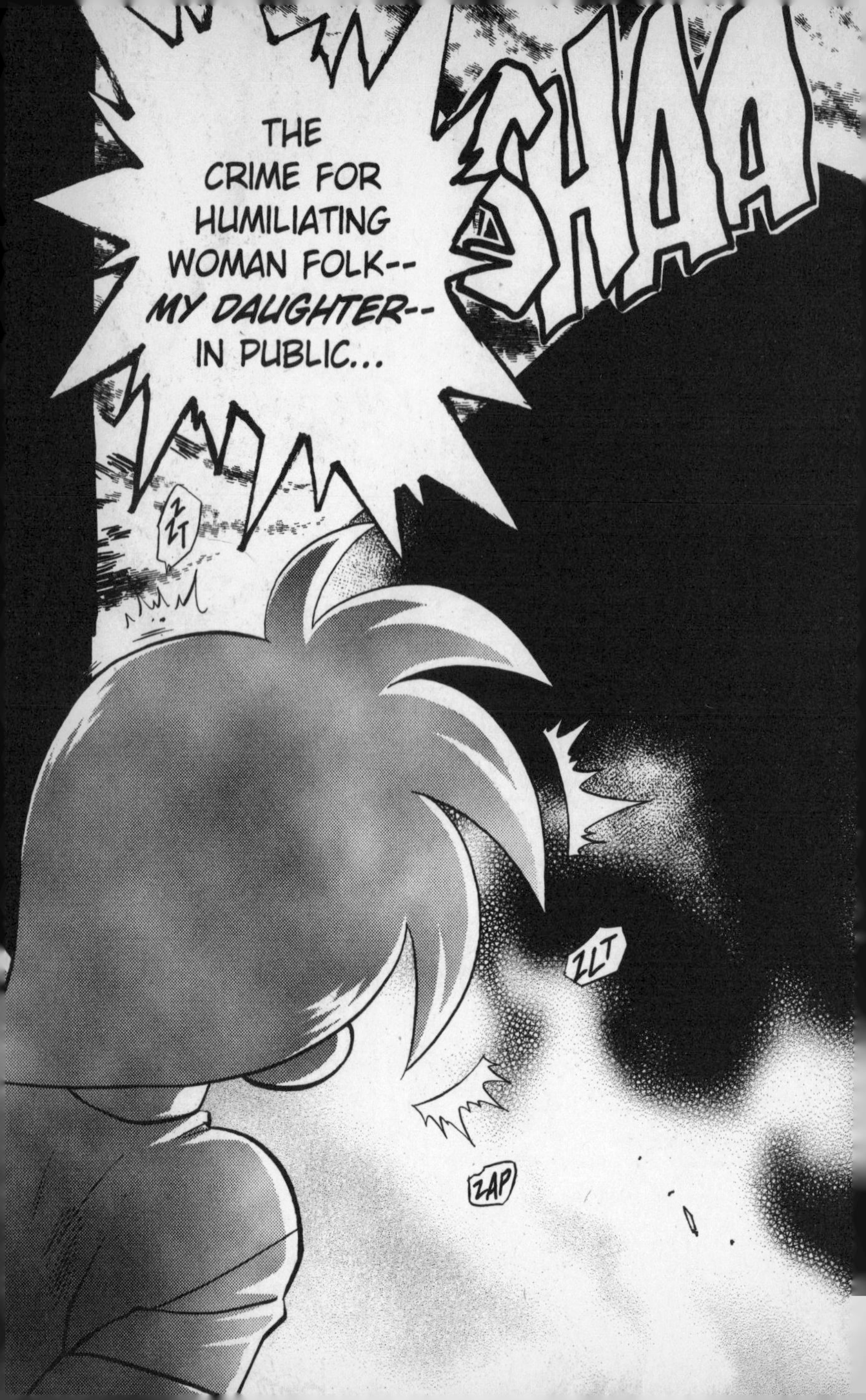
THE CRIME FOR HUMILIATING WOMAN FOLK-- *MY DAUGHTER*-- IN PUBLIC...
SHAA
ZZT
ZZT
ZAP

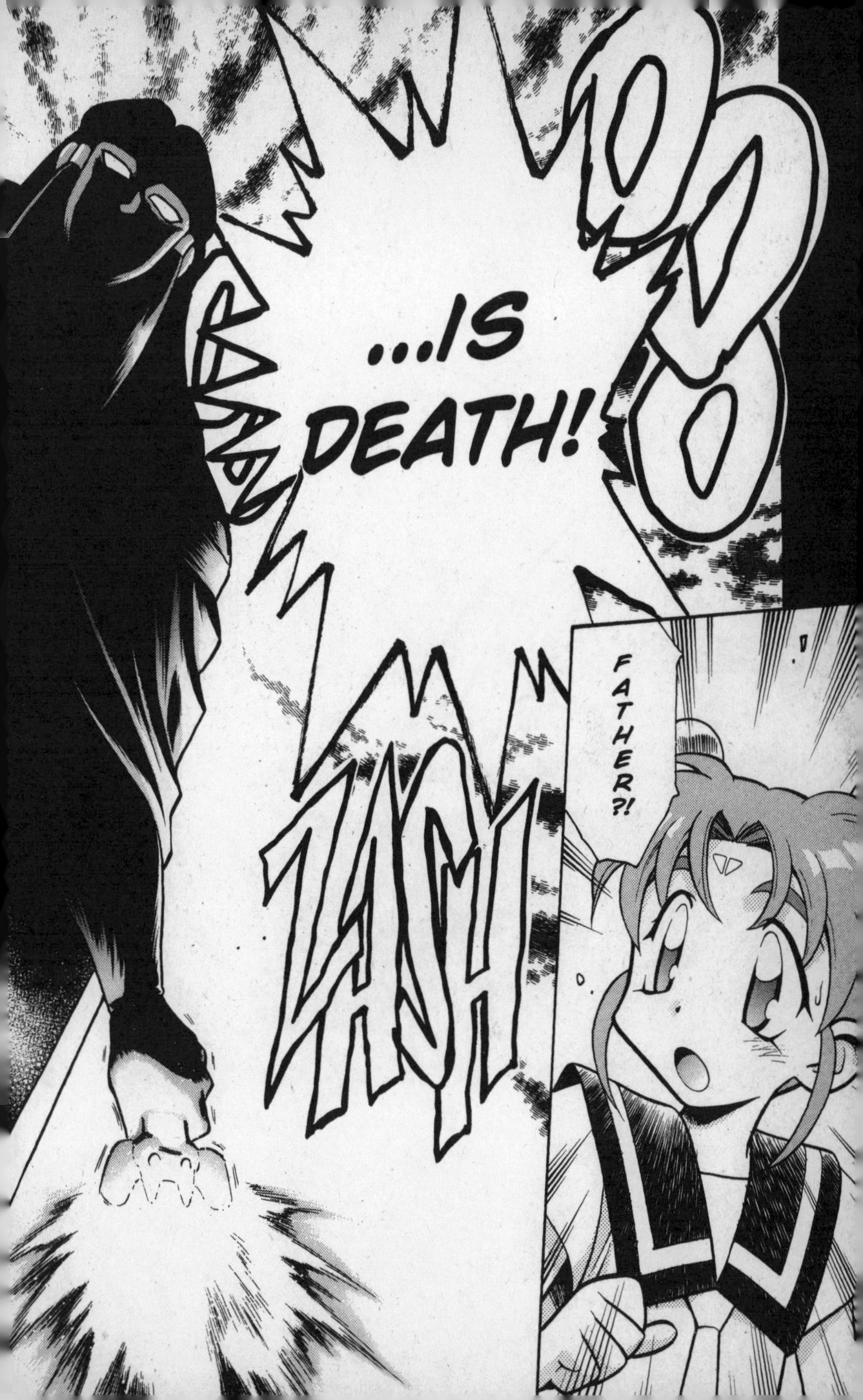
...IS DEATH!
ZASH
FATHER?!

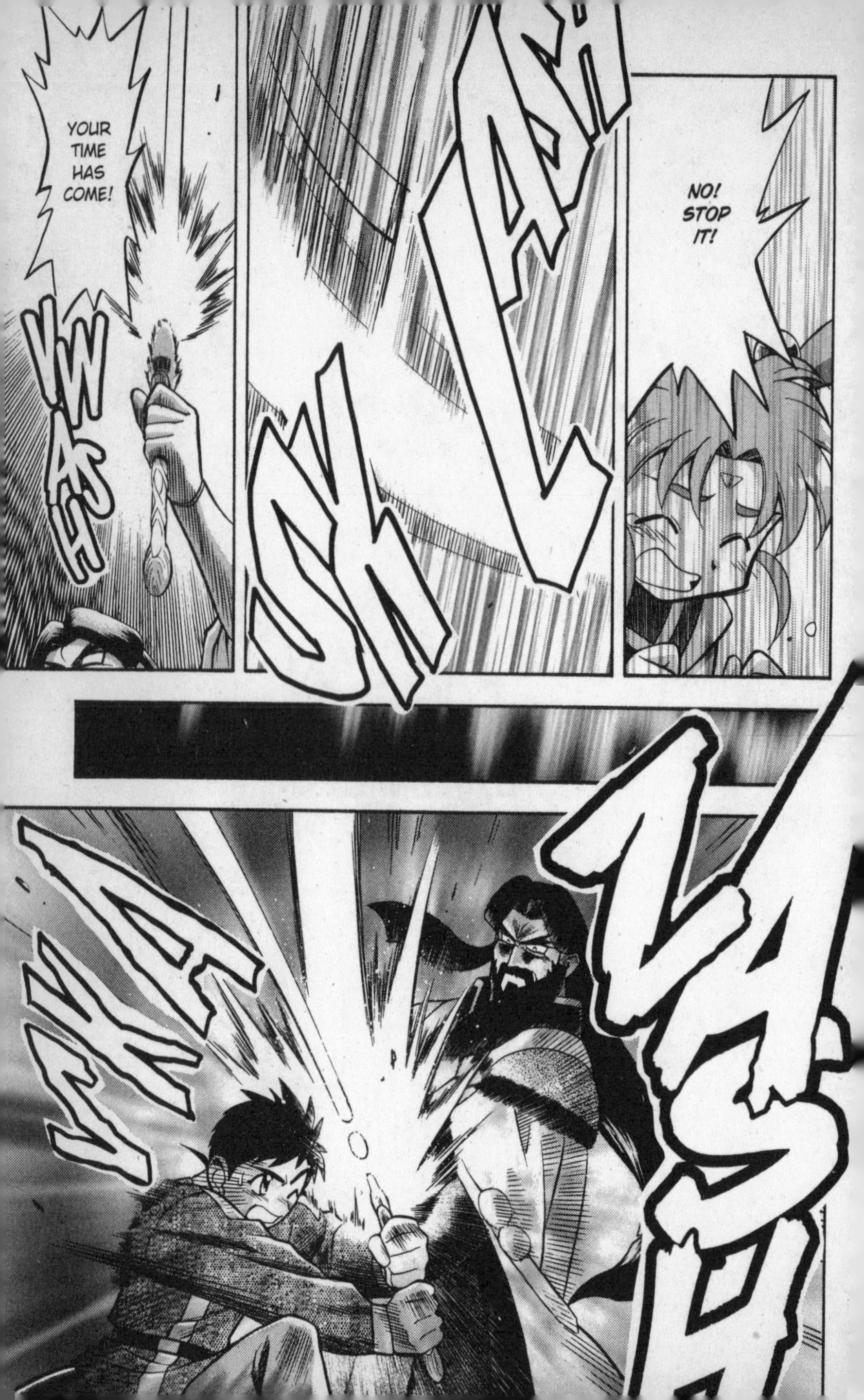
YOUR TIME HAS COME!
VWASH
NO! STOP IT!

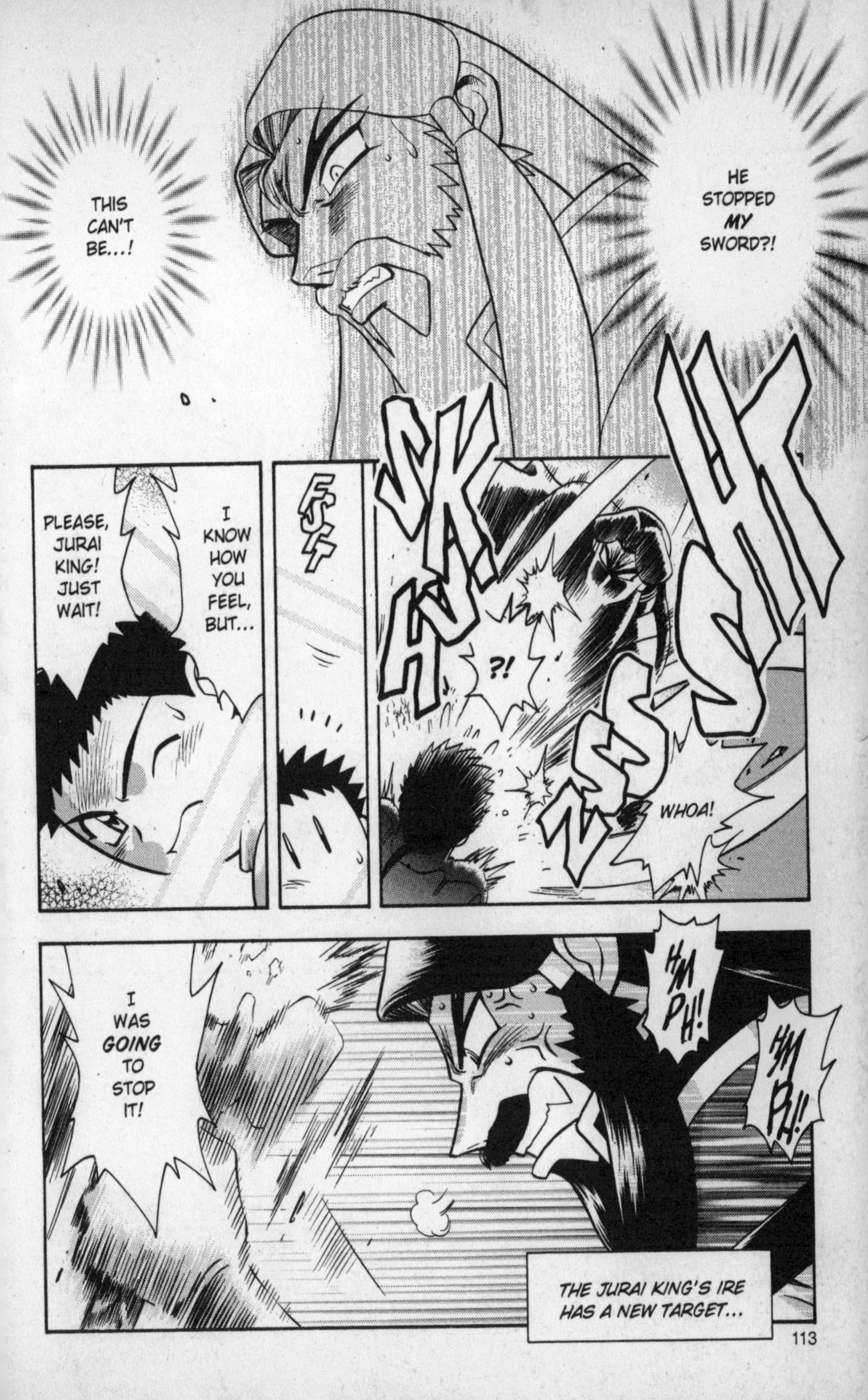
THIS CAN'T BE...!
HE STOPPED MY SWORD?!
PLEASE, JURAI KING! JUST WAIT!
I KNOW HOW YOU FEEL, BUT...
FSST
SKAH
?!
ZSSH
WHOA!
I WAS GOING TO STOP IT!
HMPH!
HMPH!!
THE JURAI KING'S IRE HAS A NEW TARGET...

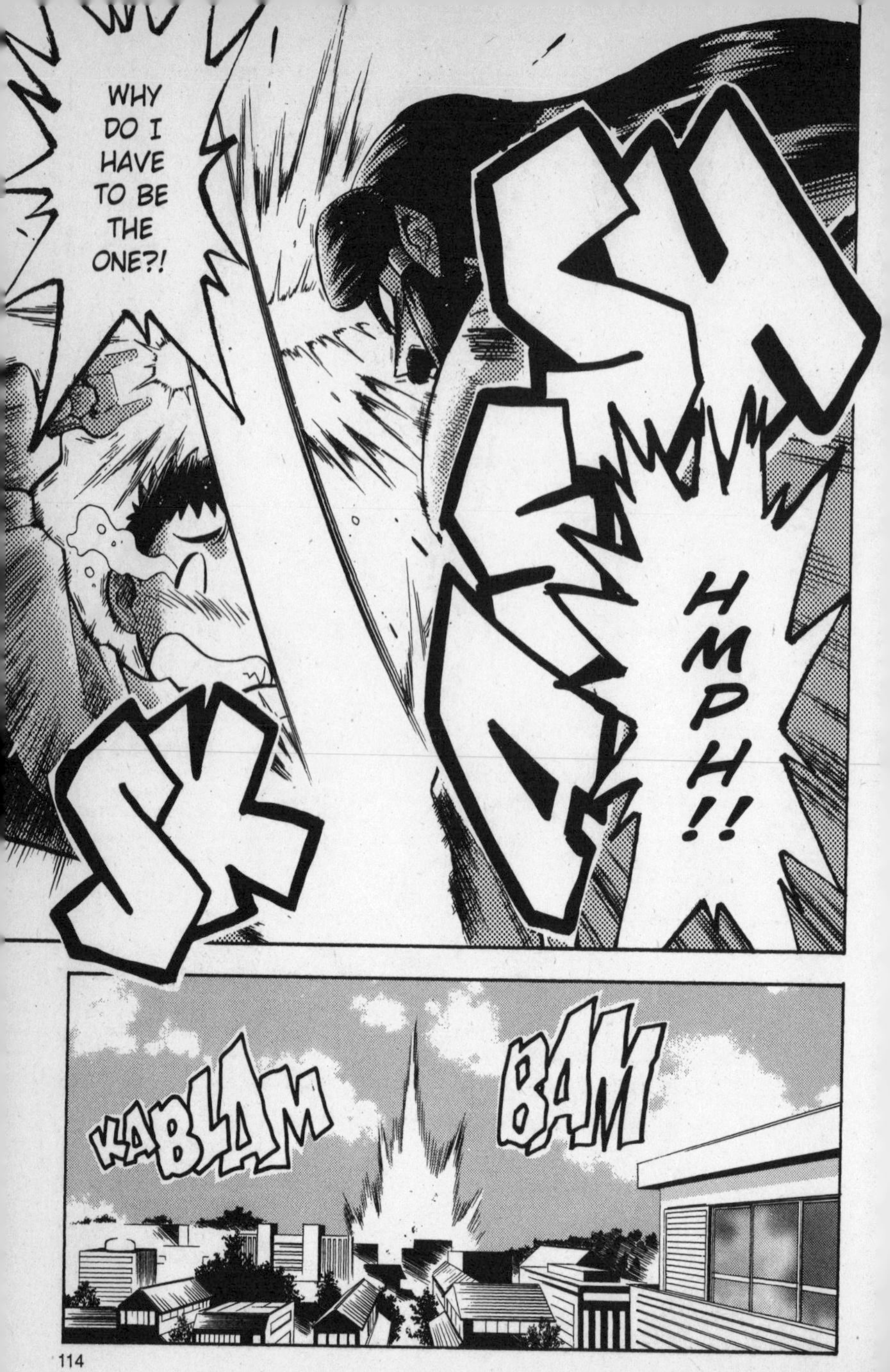
WHY DO I HAVE TO BE THE ONE?!
HMPH!!
KABLAM
BAM

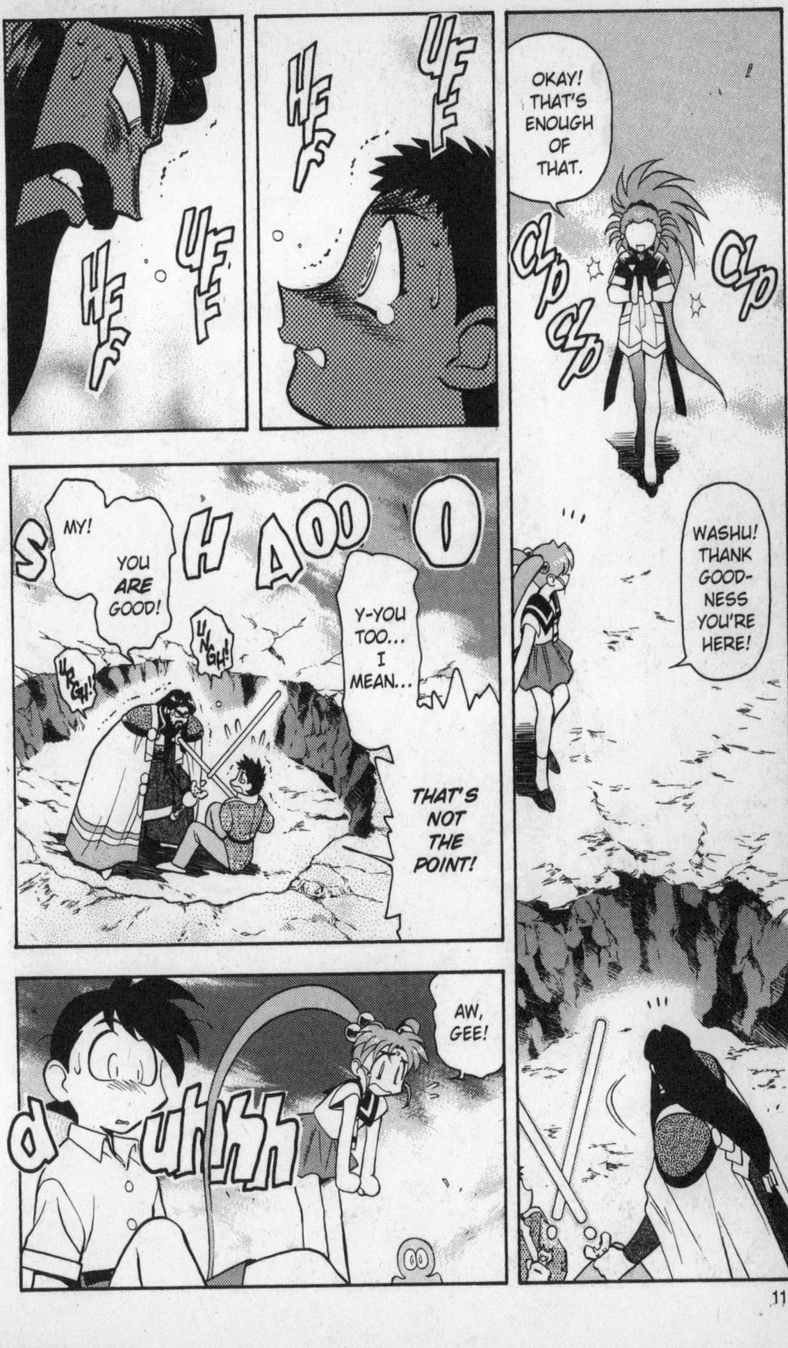
HFF
UFF
HFF
UFF
SHAOOO
MY! YOU ARE GOOD!
URGH!
UNGH!
Y-YOU TOO... I MEAN...
THAT'S NOT THE POINT!
OKAY! THAT'S ENOUGH OF THAT.
CLP
CLP
CLP
WASHU! THANK GOOD-NESS YOU'RE HERE!
DUHHH
AW, GEE!

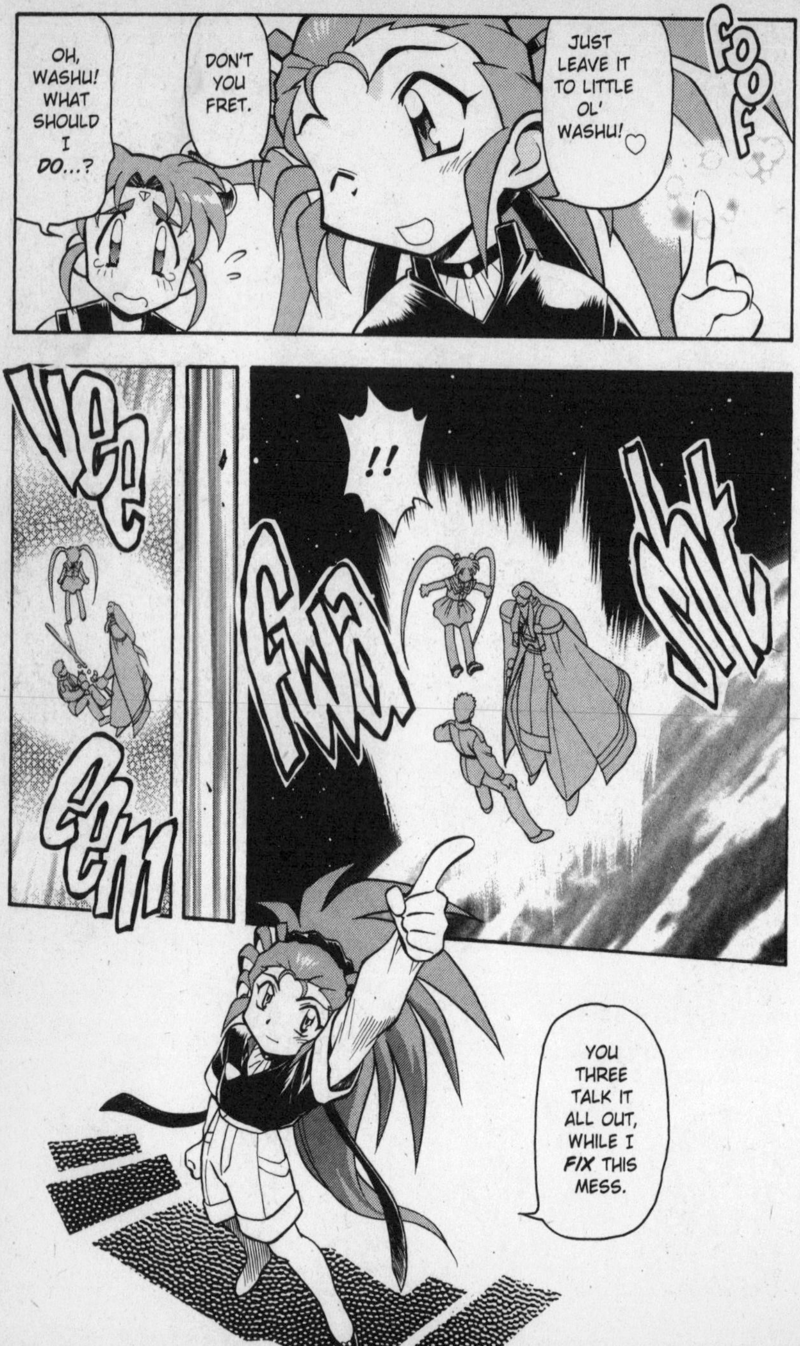
OH, WASHU! WHAT SHOULD I DO...?
DON'T YOU FRET.
JUST LEAVE IT TO LITTLE OL' WASHU! ♡
FOOF
Vee
eem
!!
Fwa
YOU THREE TALK IT ALL OUT, WHILE I *FIX* THIS MESS.

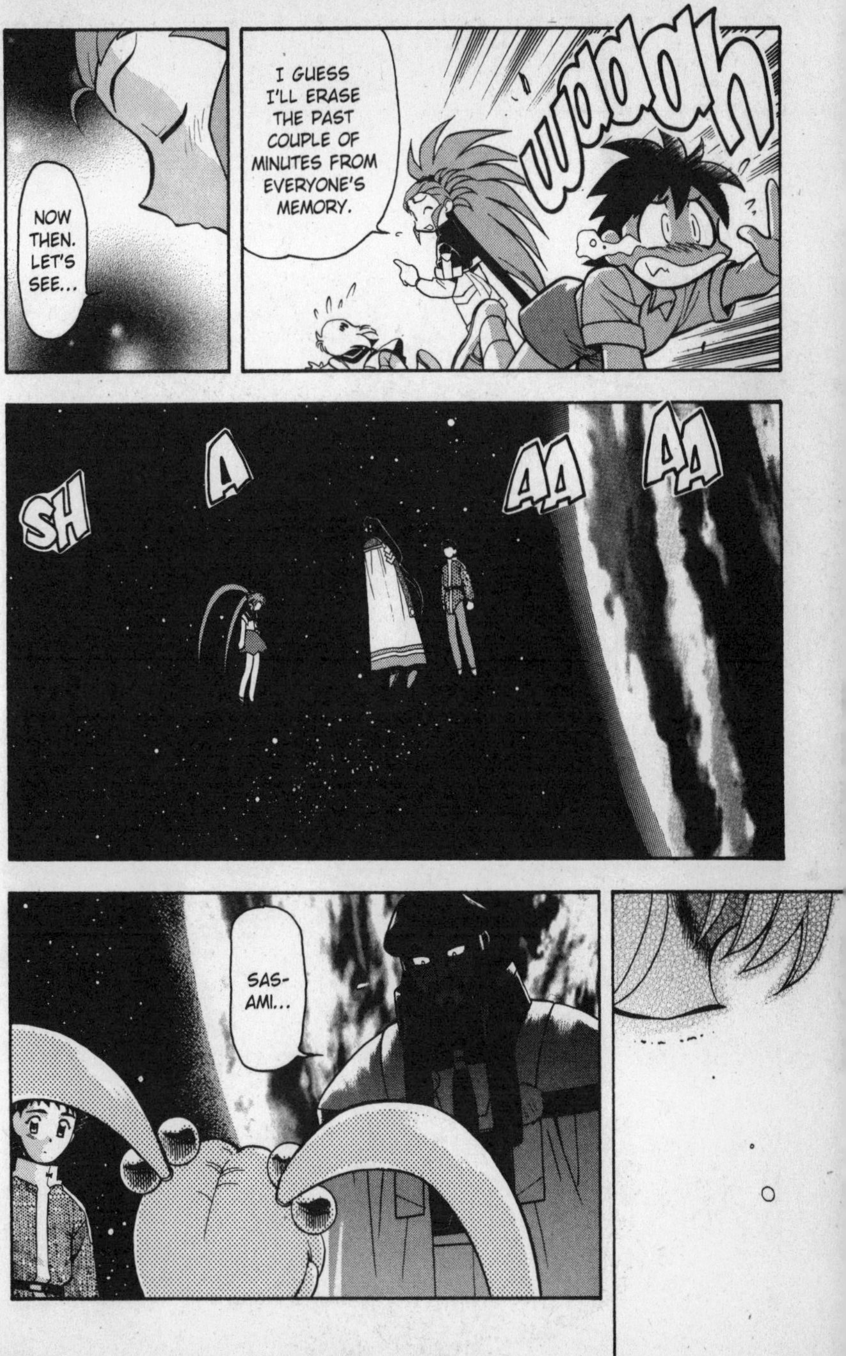
NOW THEN. LET'S SEE...
I GUESS I'LL ERASE THE PAST COUPLE OF MINUTES FROM EVERYONE'S MEMORY.
WAAAH
SH
A
AA
AA
SAS-AMI...

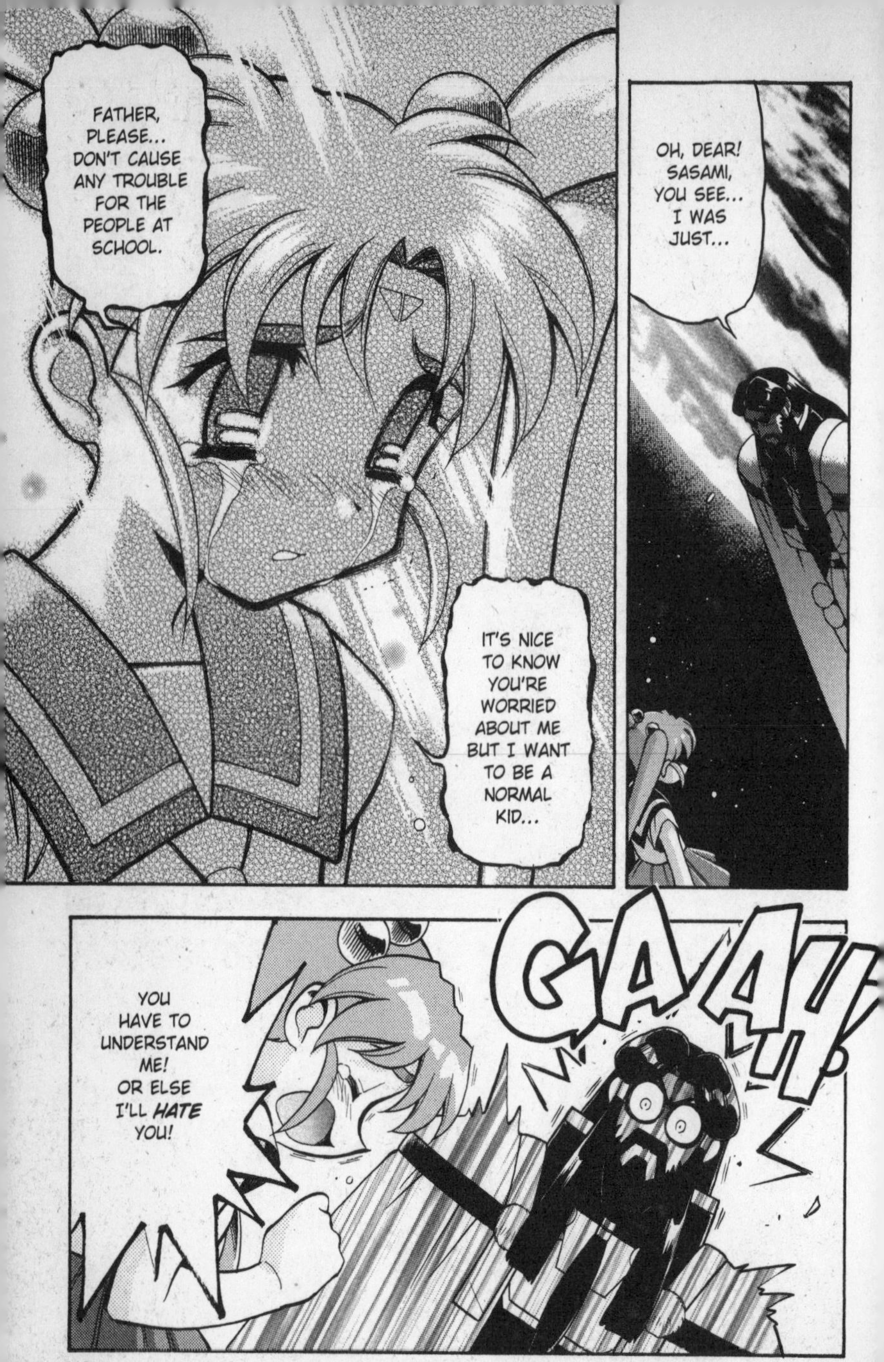
FATHER, PLEASE... DON'T CAUSE ANY TROUBLE FOR THE PEOPLE AT SCHOOL.
IT'S NICE TO KNOW YOU'RE WORRIED ABOUT ME BUT I WANT TO BE A NORMAL KID...
OH, DEAR! SASAMI, YOU SEE... I WAS JUST...
YOU HAVE TO UNDERSTAND ME! OR ELSE I'LL *HATE* YOU!
GAAH!

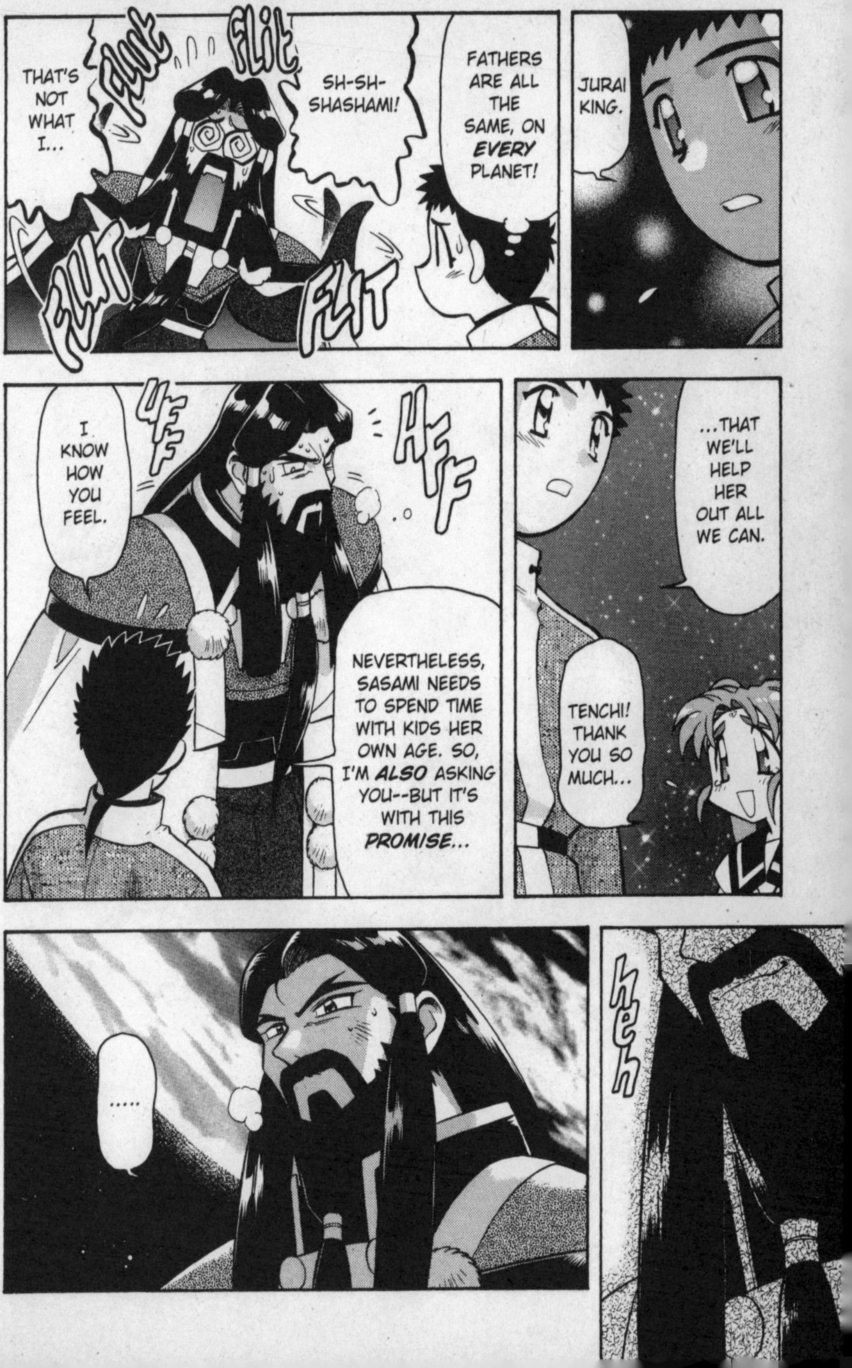
THAT'S NOT WHAT I...
FLUT
FLIT
SH-SH-SHASHAMI!
FLUT
FLIT
FATHERS ARE ALL THE SAME, ON *EVERY* PLANET!
JURAI KING.
I KNOW HOW YOU FEEL.
UFF
HEF
NEVERTHELESS, SASAMI NEEDS TO SPEND TIME WITH KIDS HER OWN AGE. SO, I'M *ALSO* ASKING YOU--BUT IT'S WITH THIS *PROMISE*...
...THAT WE'LL HELP HER OUT ALL WE CAN.
TENCHI! THANK YOU SO MUCH...
.....
heh

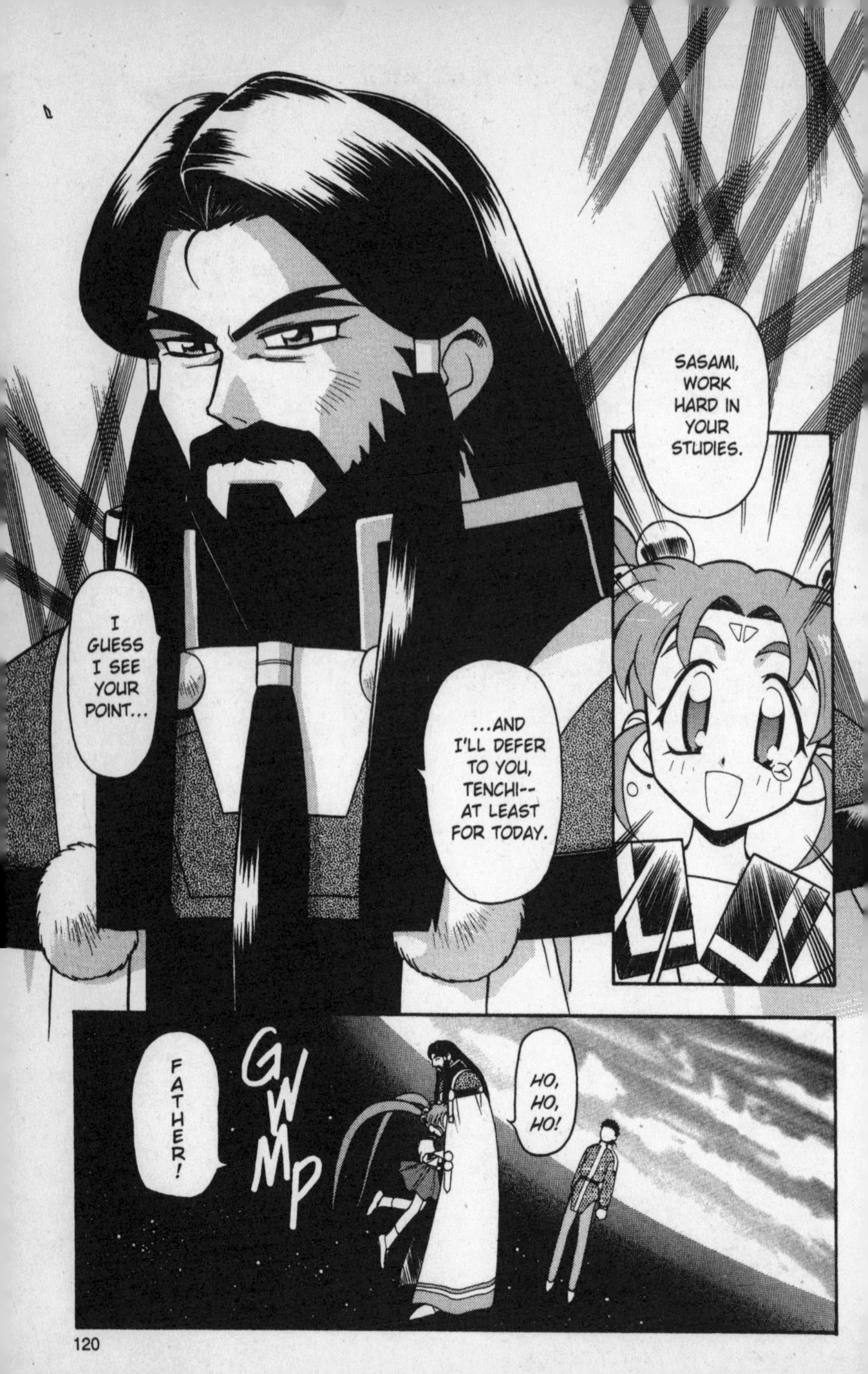

I GUESS I SEE YOUR POINT...
...AND I'LL DEFER TO YOU, TENCHI-- AT LEAST FOR TODAY.
SASAMI, WORK HARD IN YOUR STUDIES.
FATHER!
GWMP
HO, HO, HO!

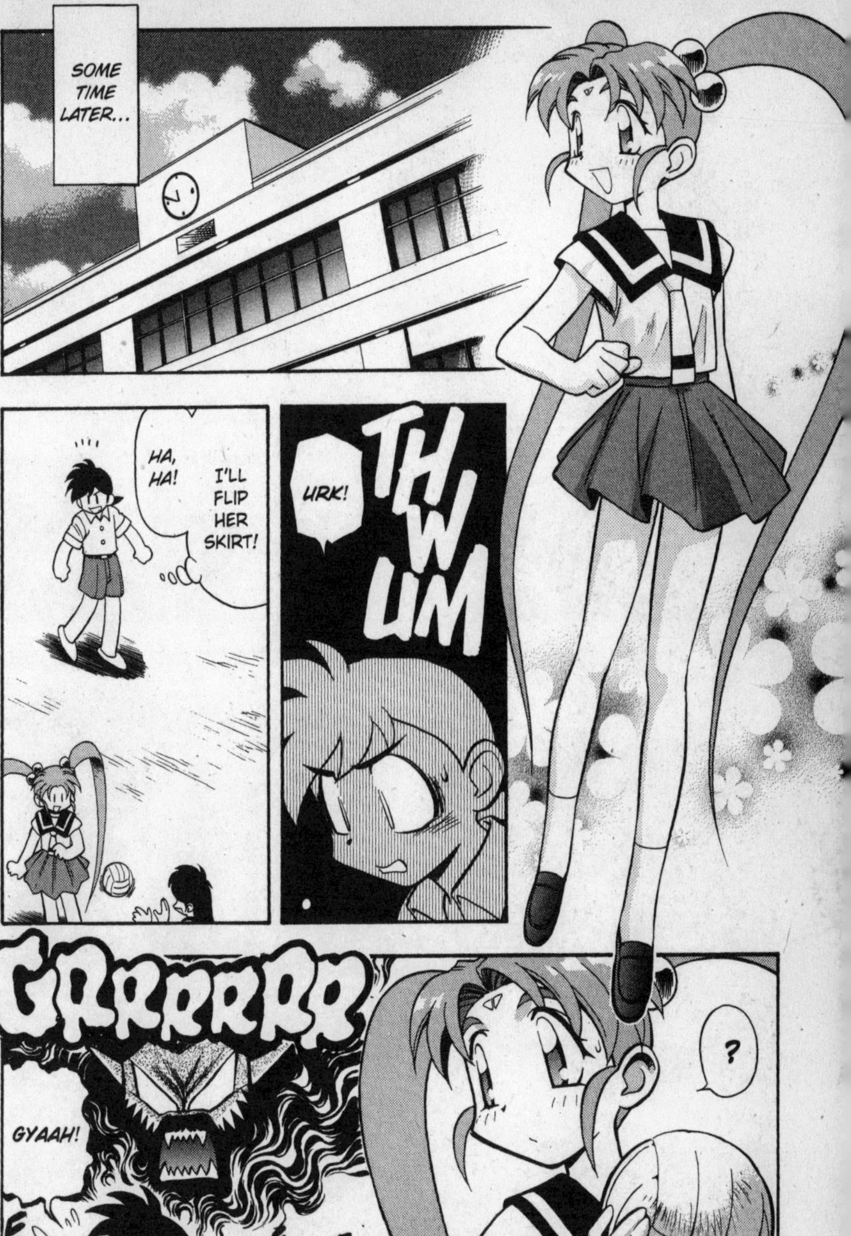
SOME TIME LATER...
HA, HA!
I'LL FLIP HER SKIRT!
URK!
THWUM
GRRRRRR
GYAAH!
?
FAP
Flip
Flip
WASHU HAD PLANTED THE JURAI KING'S ANGER INTO HIS SUBCONSCIOUS.

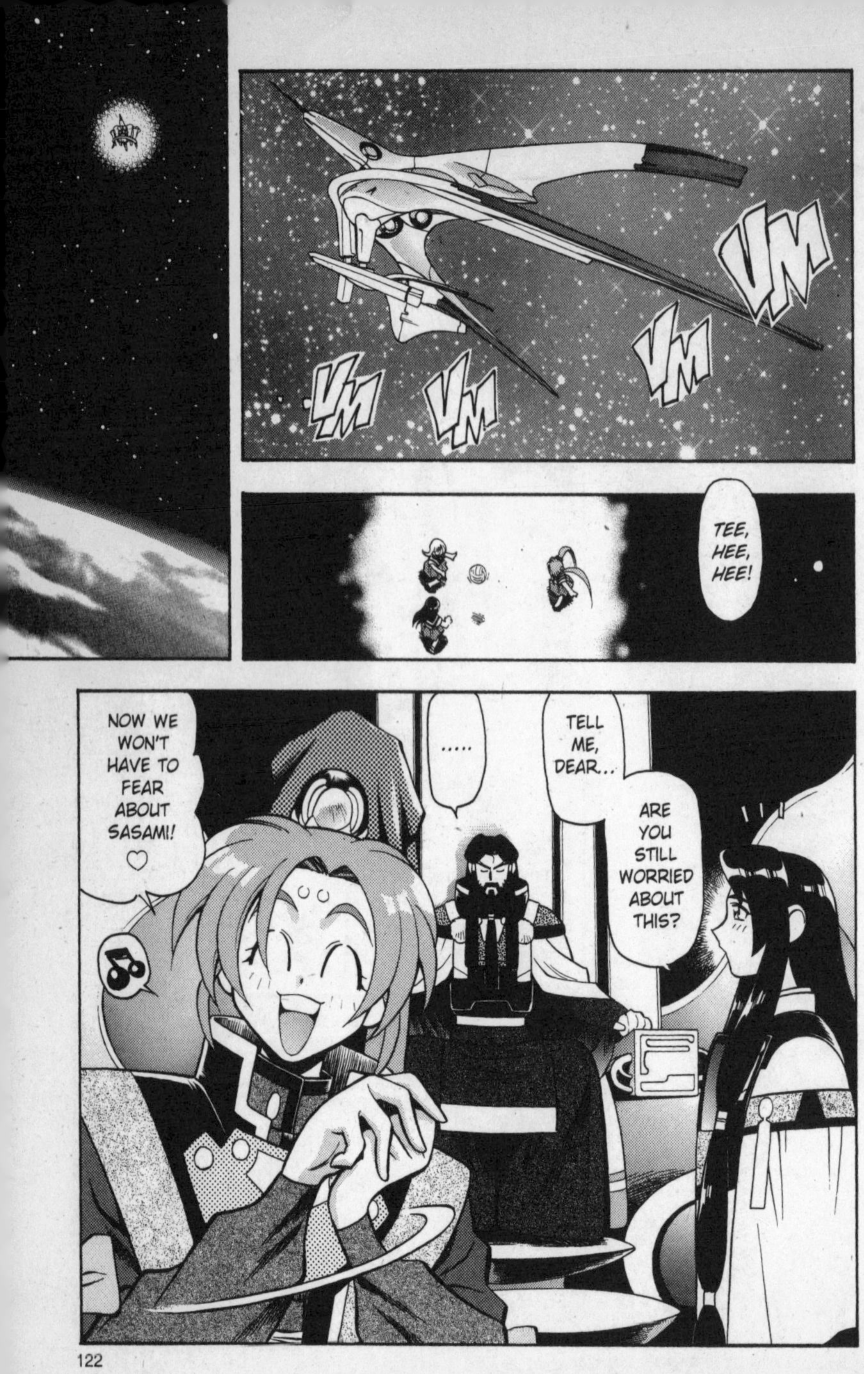

VM
VM
VM
VM
TEE, HEE, HEE!
NOW WE WON'T HAVE TO FEAR ABOUT SASAMI! ♡
.....
TELL ME, DEAR...
ARE YOU STILL WORRIED ABOUT THIS?

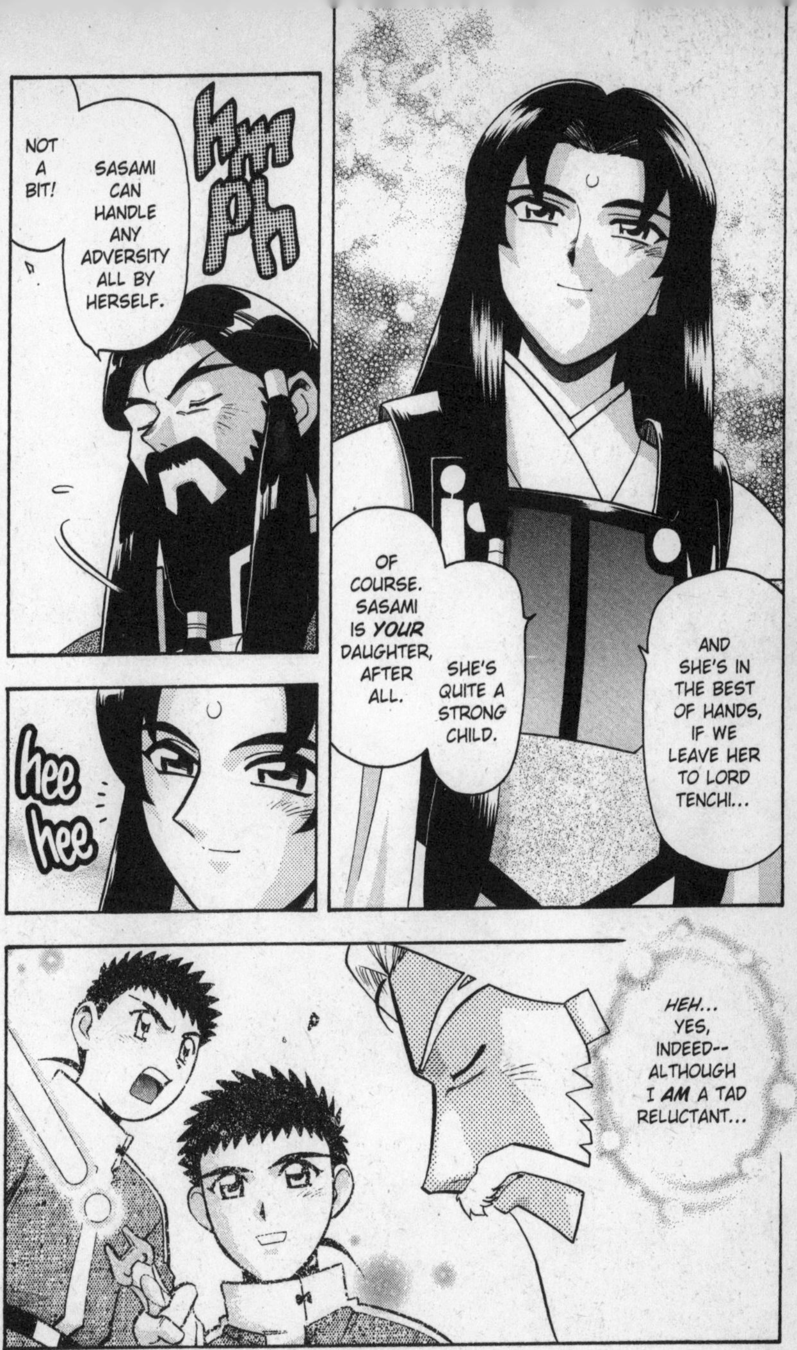

NOT A BIT!
SASAMI CAN HANDLE ANY ADVERSITY ALL BY HERSELF.
hmph
hee hee
OF COURSE. SASAMI IS *YOUR* DAUGHTER, AFTER ALL.
SHE'S QUITE A STRONG CHILD.
AND SHE'S IN THE BEST OF HANDS, IF WE LEAVE HER TO LORD TENCHI...
HEH... YES, INDEED-- ALTHOUGH I *AM* A TAD RELUCTANT...

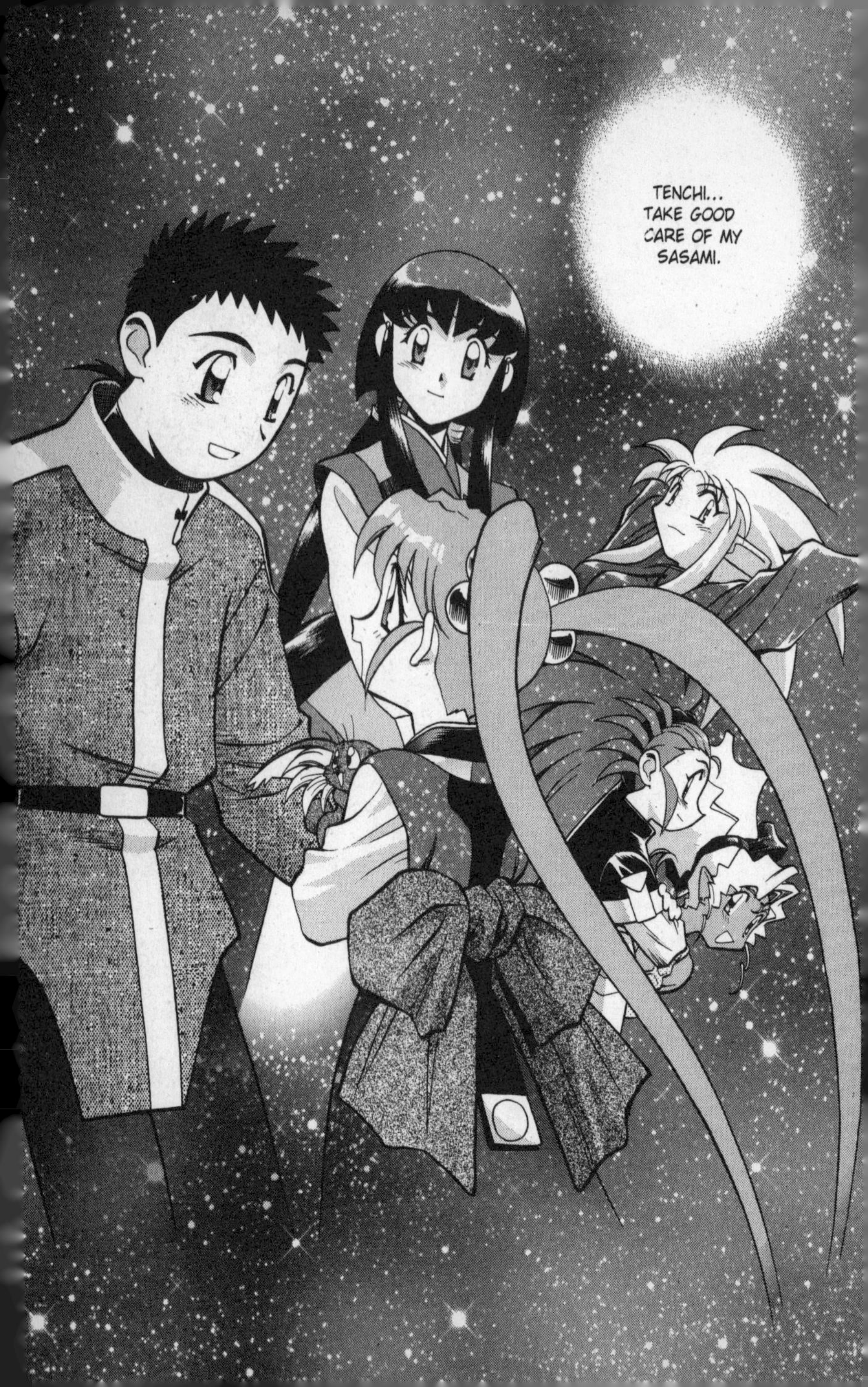
TENCHI...
TAKE GOOD
CARE OF MY
SASAMI.

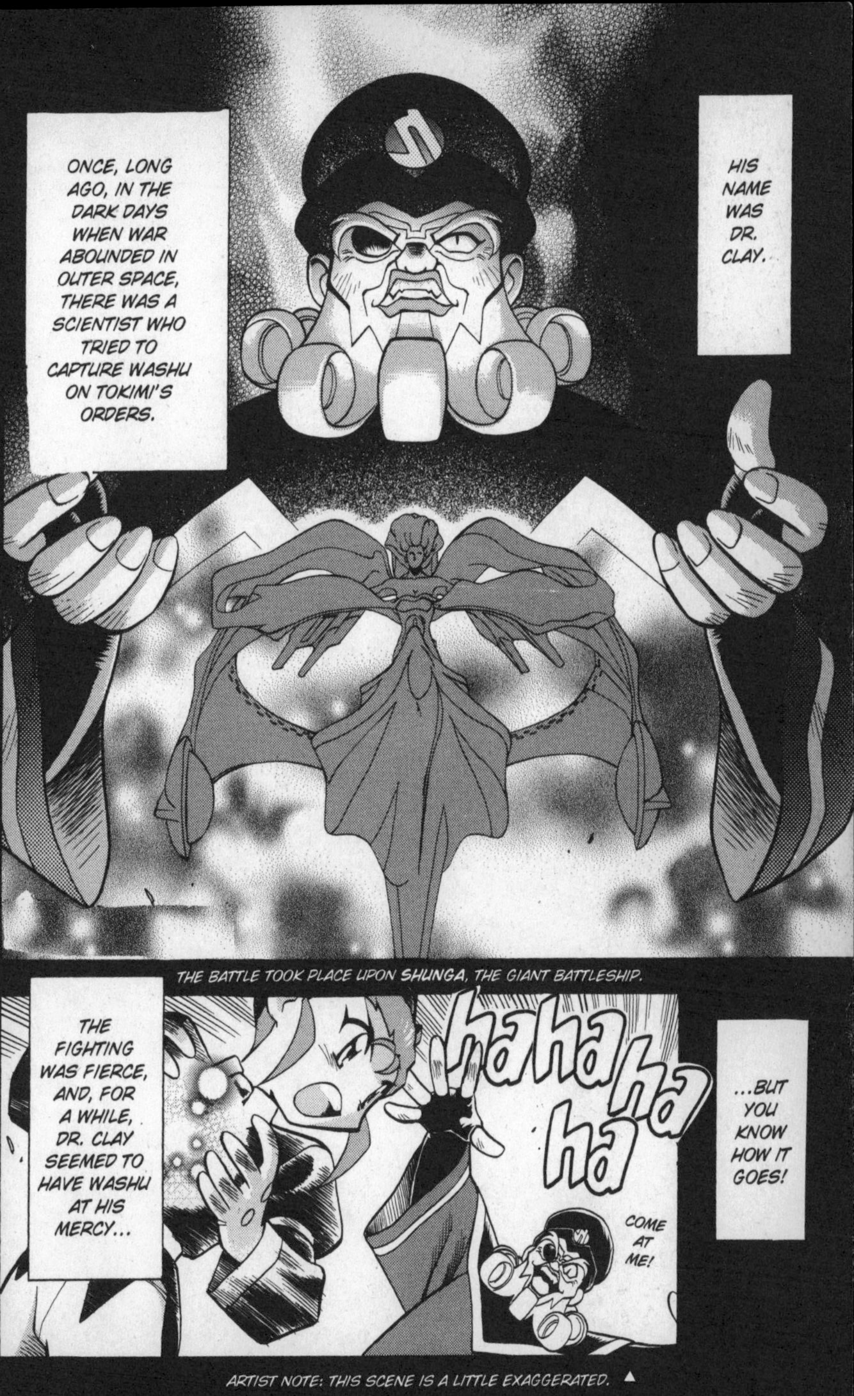
ONCE, LONG AGO, IN THE DARK DAYS WHEN WAR ABOUNDED IN OUTER SPACE, THERE WAS A SCIENTIST WHO TRIED TO CAPTURE WASHU ON TOKIMI'S ORDERS.
HIS NAME WAS DR. CLAY.
THE BATTLE TOOK PLACE UPON SHUNGA, THE GIANT BATTLESHIP.
THE FIGHTING WAS FIERCE, AND, FOR A WHILE, DR. CLAY SEEMED TO HAVE WASHU AT HIS MERCY...
hahahahaha
COME AT ME!
...BUT YOU KNOW HOW IT GOES!
ARTIST NOTE: THIS SCENE IS A LITTLE EXAGGERATED.

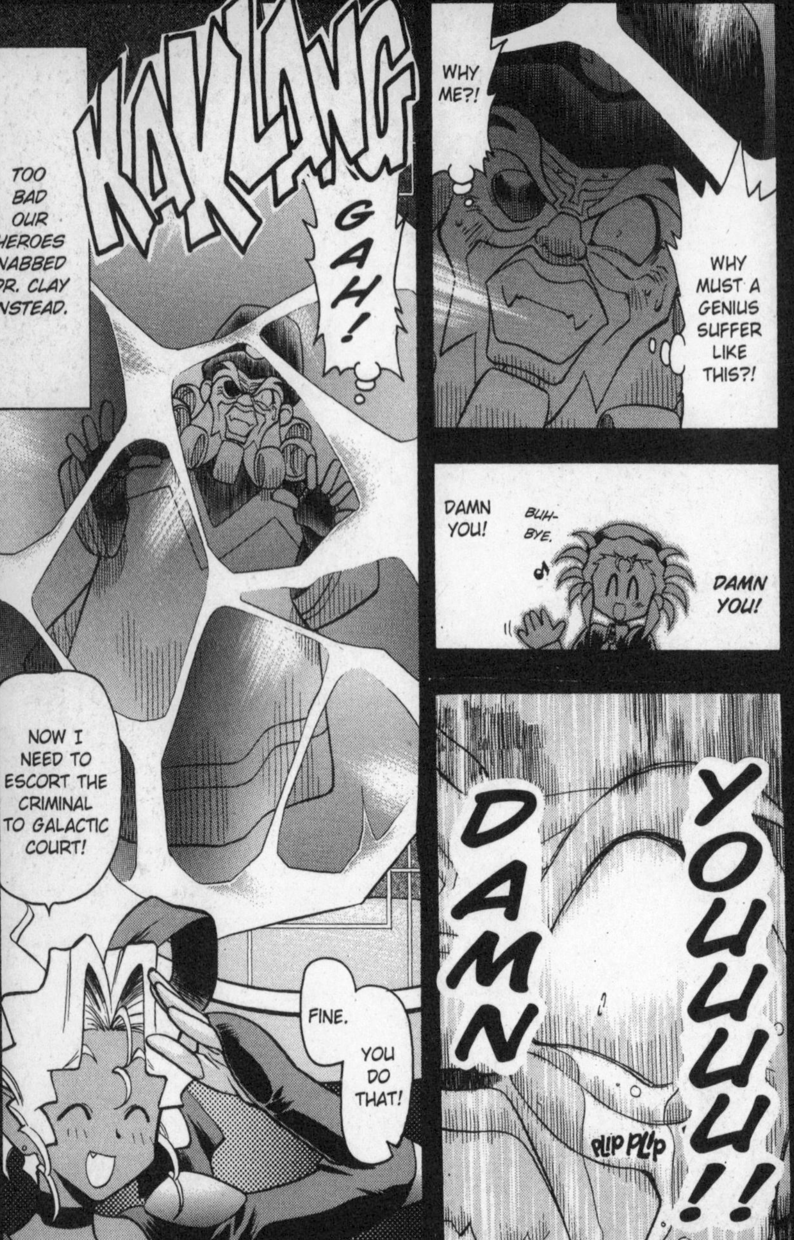
TOO BAD OUR HEROES NABBED DR. CLAY INSTEAD.
KAKLANG
GAH!
NOW I NEED TO ESCORT THE CRIMINAL TO GALACTIC COURT!
FINE.
YOU DO THAT!
WHY ME?!
WHY MUST A GENIUS SUFFER LIKE THIS?!
DAMN YOU!
BUH-BYE.
DAMN YOU!
DAMN YOUUUU!!
PLIP PLIP

Chapter 6: SOWING THE SEEDS

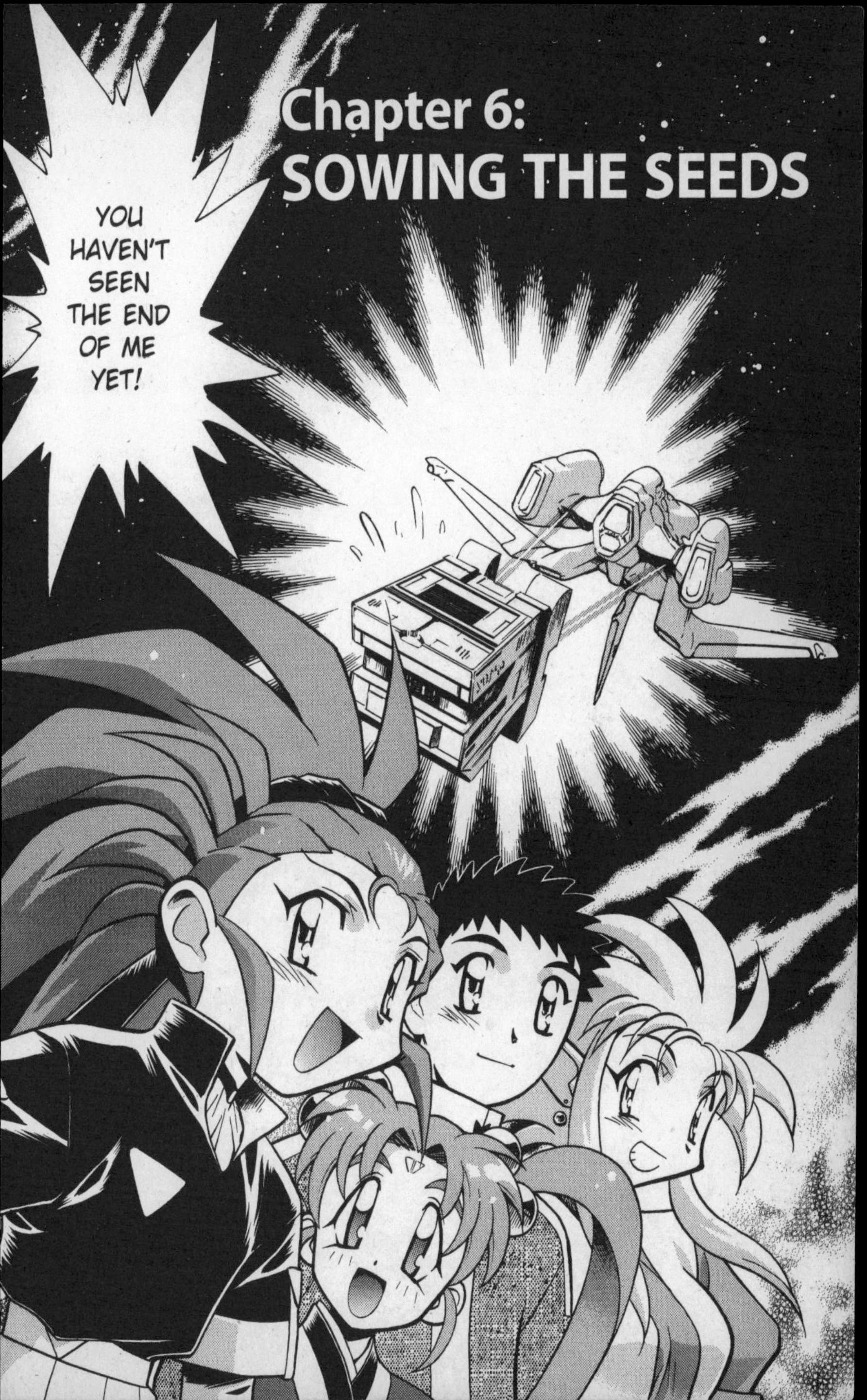
YOU HAVEN'T SEEN THE END OF ME YET!

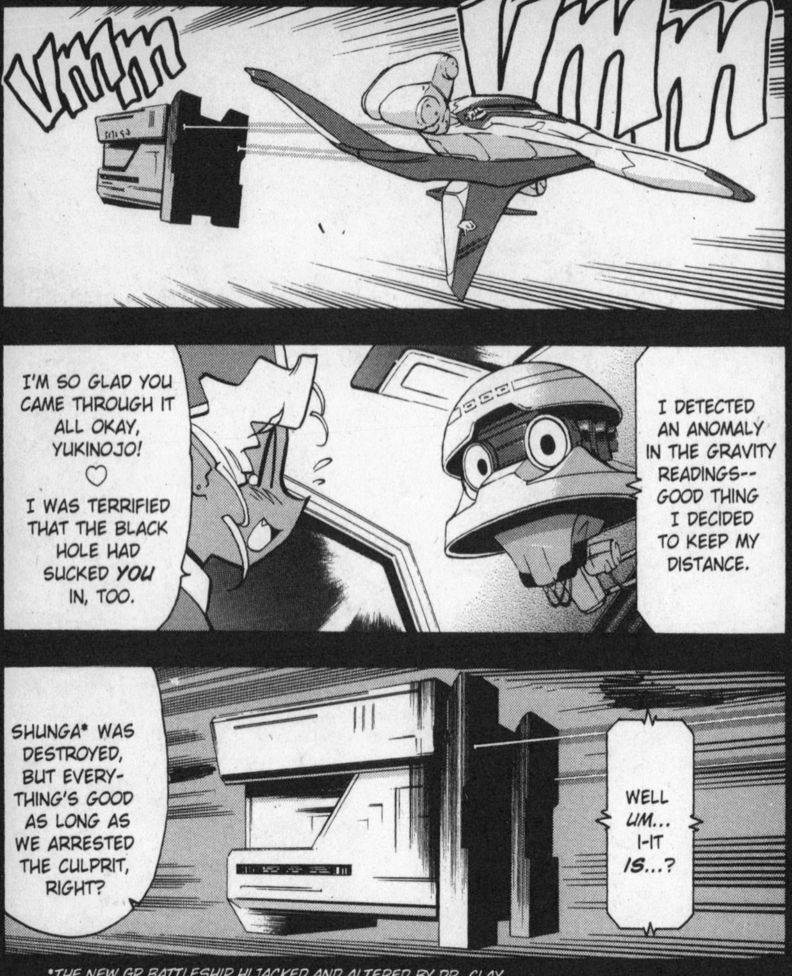
VMMM
VMM
I'M SO GLAD YOU CAME THROUGH IT ALL OKAY, YUKINOJO! ♡
I WAS TERRIFIED THAT THE BLACK HOLE HAD SUCKED *YOU* IN, TOO.
I DETECTED AN ANOMALY IN THE GRAVITY READINGS-- GOOD THING I DECIDED TO KEEP MY DISTANCE.
SHUNGA* WAS DESTROYED, BUT EVERYTHING'S GOOD AS LONG AS WE ARRESTED THE CULPRIT, RIGHT?
WELL *UM*... I-IT *IS*...?

*THE NEW GP BATTLESHIP HIJACKED AND ALTERED BY DR. CLAY.

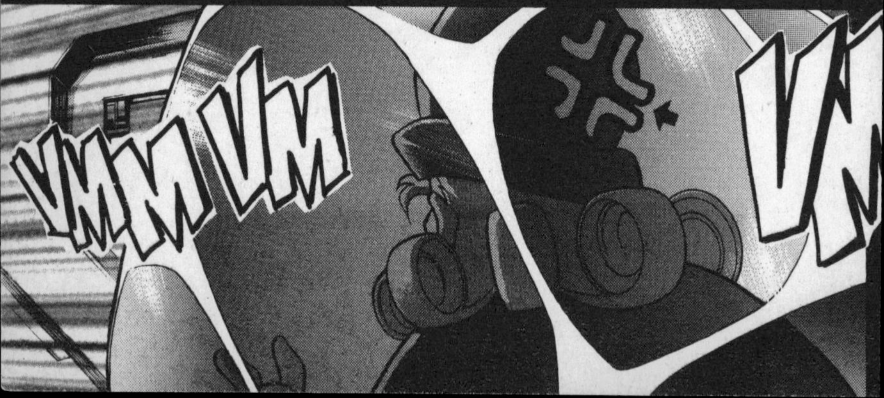
VMM VM

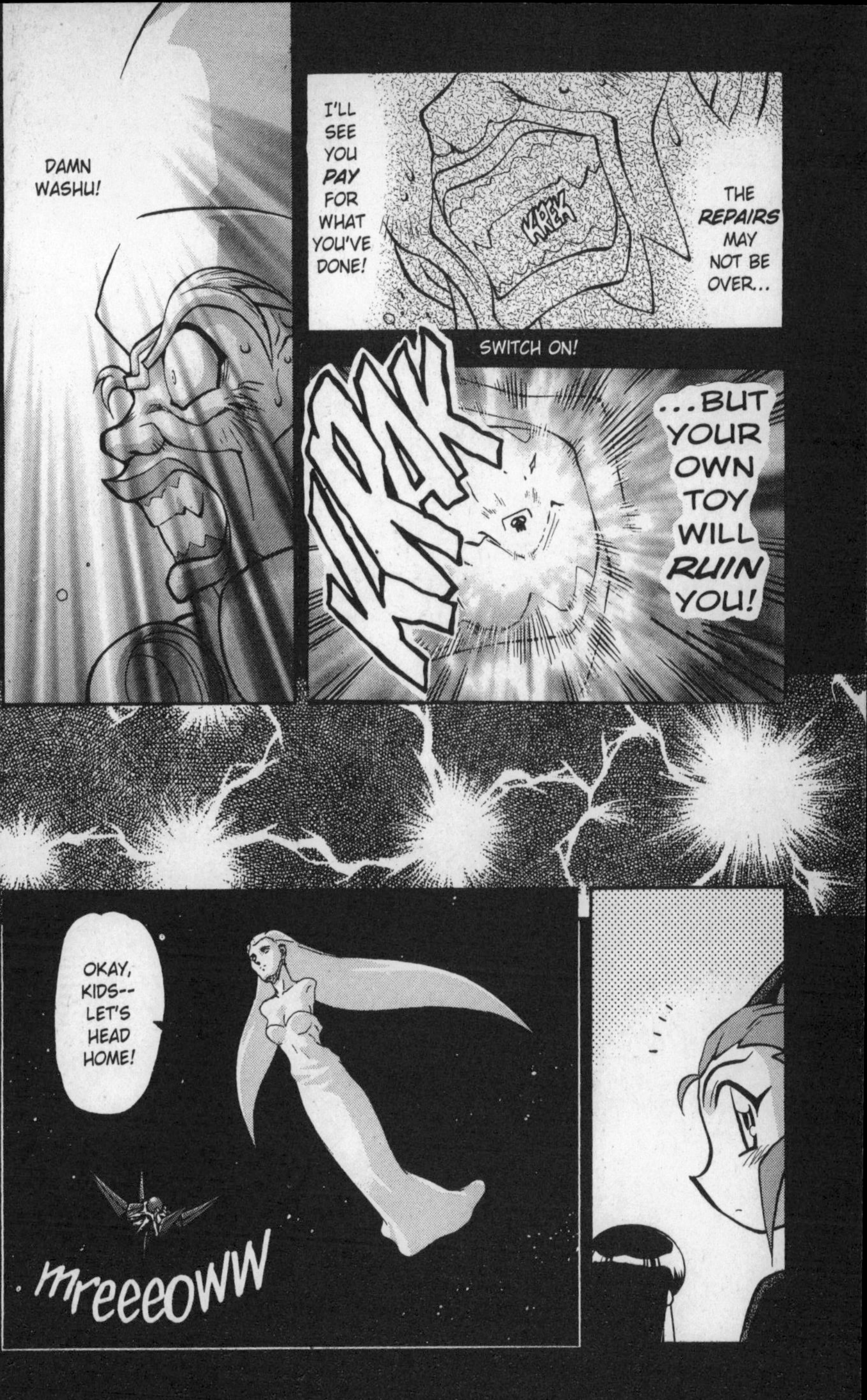
THE REPAIRS MAY NOT BE OVER...
I'LL SEE YOU PAY FOR WHAT YOU'VE DONE!
SWITCH ON!
...BUT YOUR OWN TOY WILL RUIN YOU!
DAMN WASHU!
OKAY, KIDS-- LET'S HEAD HOME!
mreeeoww

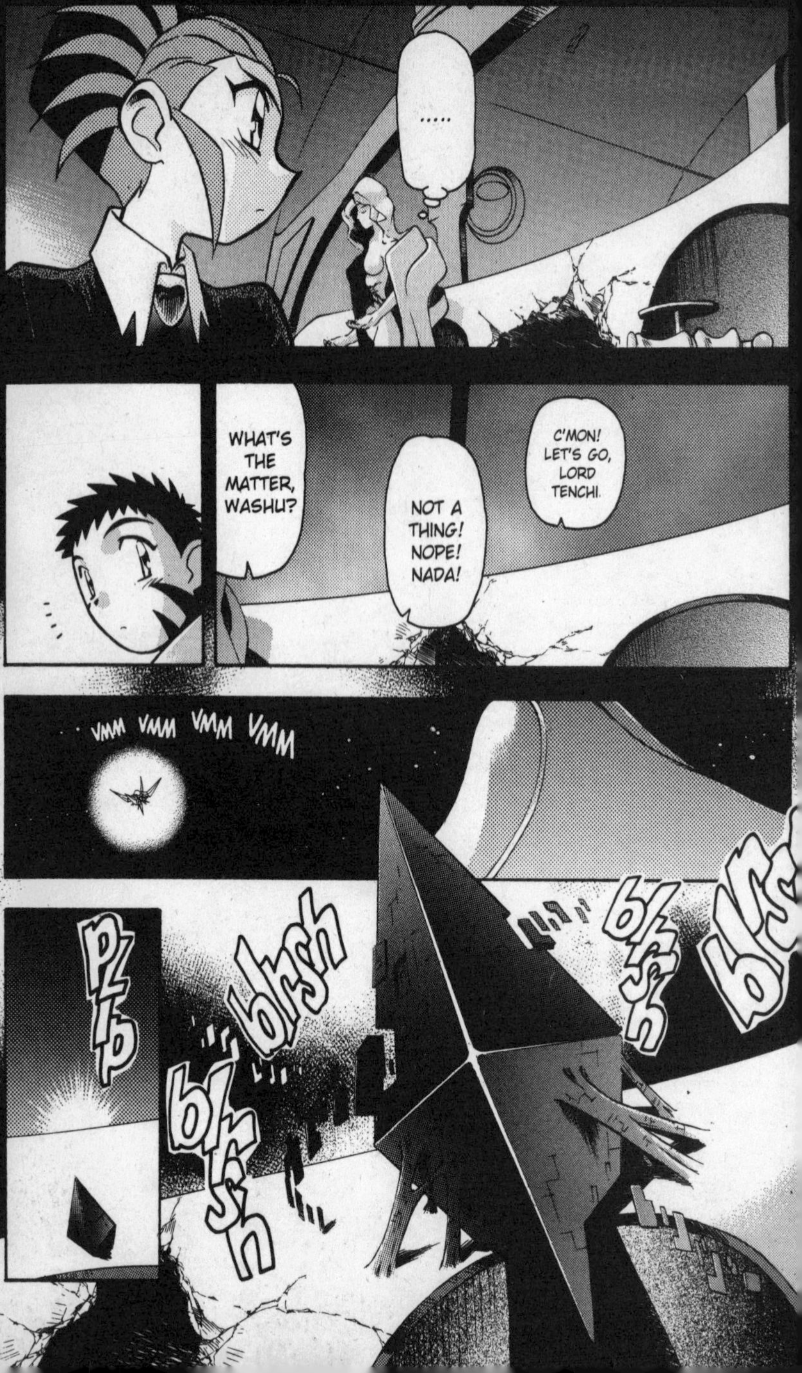
.....
WHAT'S THE MATTER, WASHU?
NOT A THING! NOPE! NADA!
C'MON! LET'S GO, LORD TENCHI.
VMM VMM VMM VMM
plip
blrsh
blrsh
blrsh
blrsh

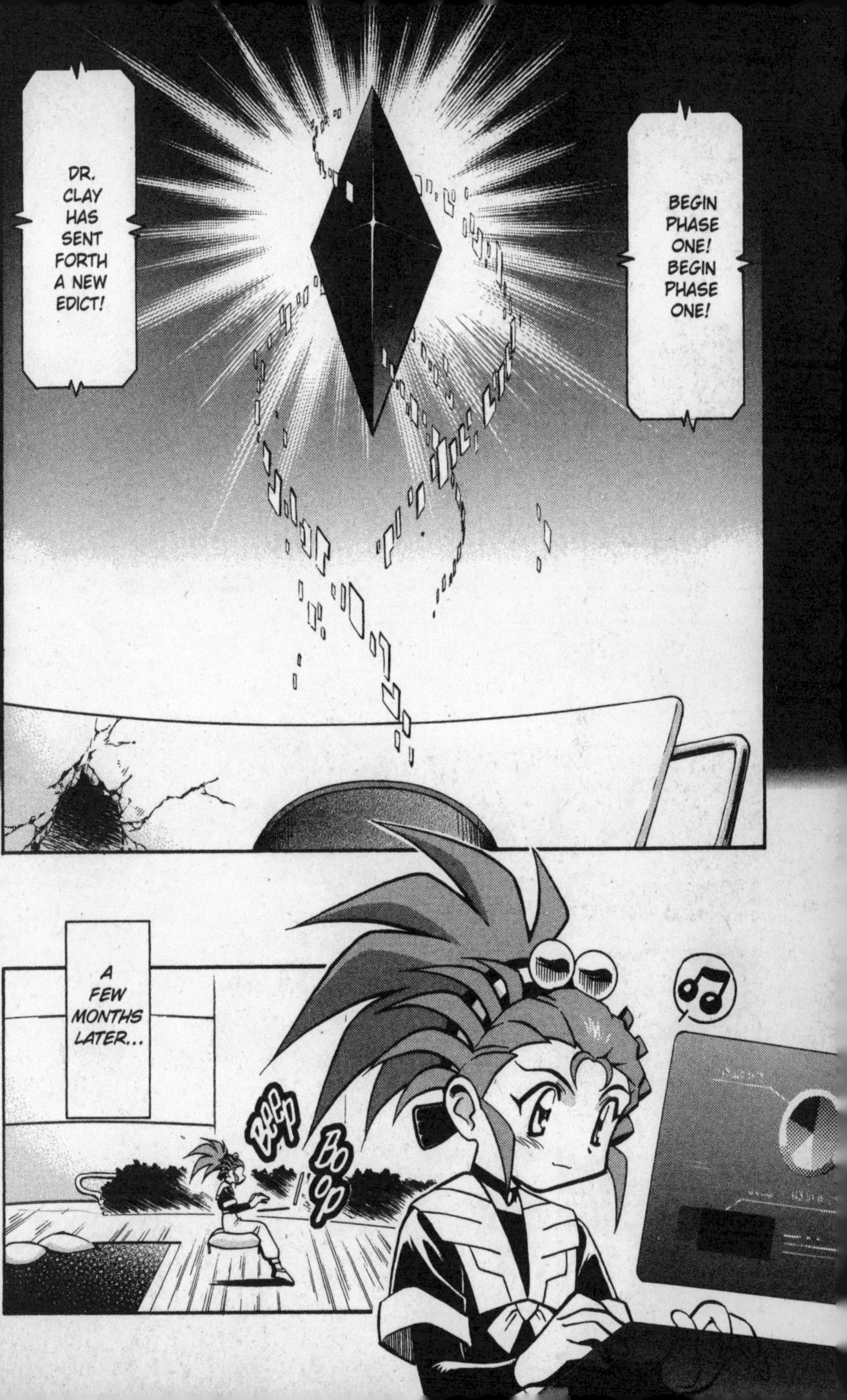
DR. CLAY HAS SENT FORTH A NEW EDICT!
BEGIN PHASE ONE! BEGIN PHASE ONE!
A FEW MONTHS LATER...
BEEP
BOOP
♫

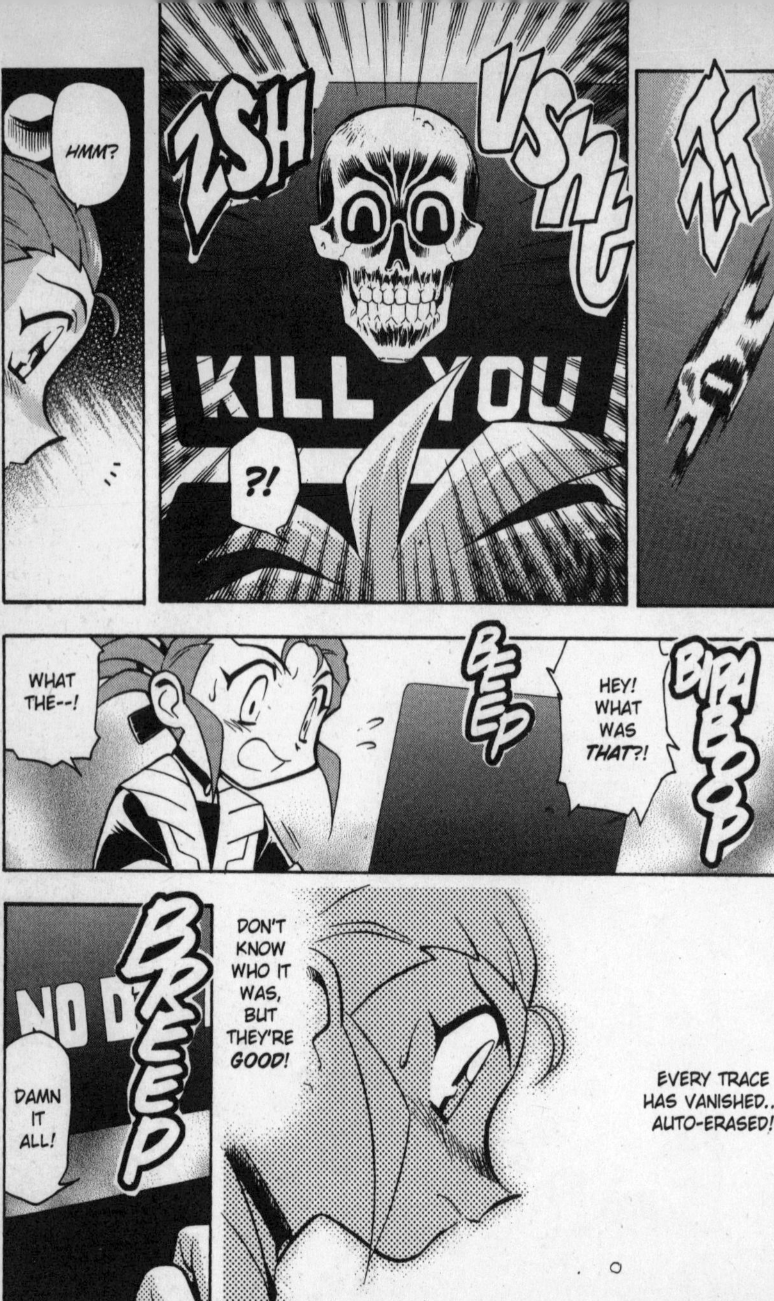

HMM?
ZSH
USHT
KILL YOU
?!
ZT
WHAT THE--!
BEEP
HEY! WHAT WAS THAT?!
BIPA BOOP
NO D
BREEEP
DAMN IT ALL!
DON'T KNOW WHO IT WAS, BUT THEY'RE GOOD!
EVERY TRACE HAS VANISHED... AUTO-ERASED!

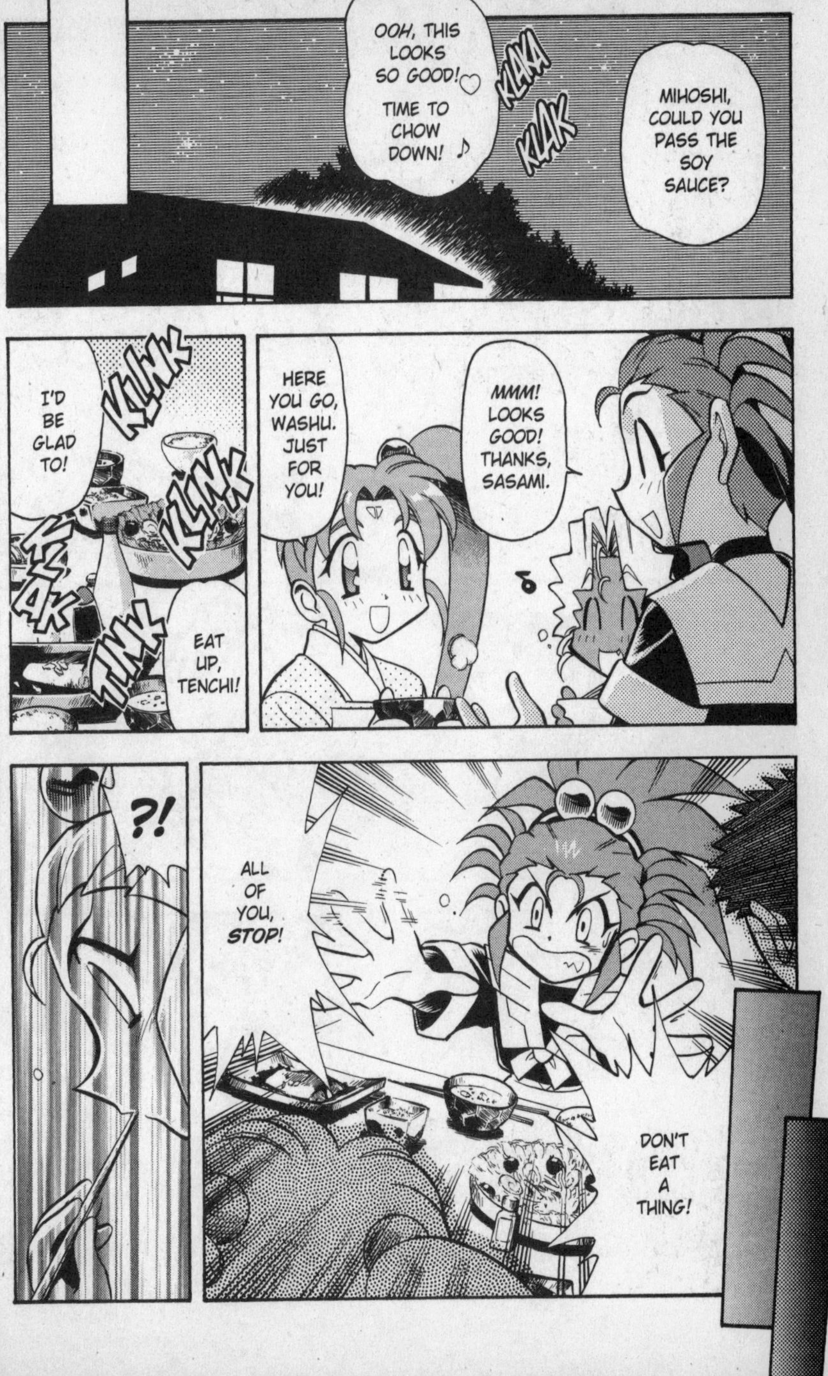
OOH, THIS LOOKS SO GOOD! ♡
TIME TO CHOW DOWN! ♪
KLAKA
KLAK
MIHOSHI, COULD YOU PASS THE SOY SAUCE?
I'D BE GLAD TO!
KLINK
KLINK
KLAK
TINK
EAT UP, TENCHI!
HERE YOU GO, WASHU. JUST FOR YOU!
MMM! LOOKS GOOD! THANKS, SASAMI.
?!
ALL OF YOU, STOP!
DON'T EAT A THING!

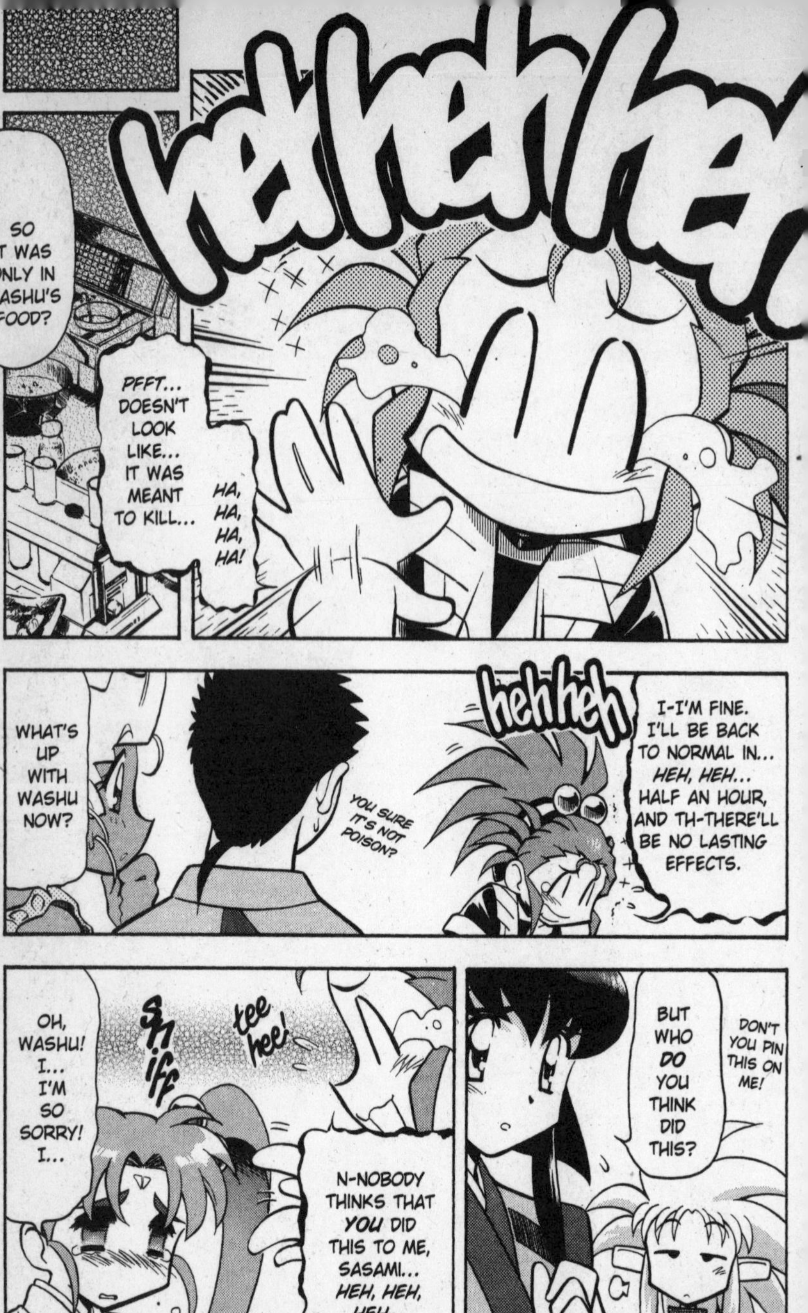
SO IT WAS ONLY IN WASHU'S FOOD?
PFFT... DOESN'T LOOK LIKE... IT WAS MEANT TO KILL...
HA, HA, HA, HA!
WHAT'S UP WITH WASHU NOW?
YOU SURE IT'S NOT POISON?
heh heh
I-I'M FINE. I'LL BE BACK TO NORMAL IN... *HEH, HEH...* HALF AN HOUR, AND TH-THERE'LL BE NO LASTING EFFECTS.
OH, WASHU! I... I'M SO SORRY! I...
sniff
tee hee!
N-NOBODY THINKS THAT *YOU* DID THIS TO ME, SASAMI... *HEH, HEH, HEH...*
BUT WHO *DO* YOU THINK DID THIS?
DON'T YOU PIN THIS ON ME!

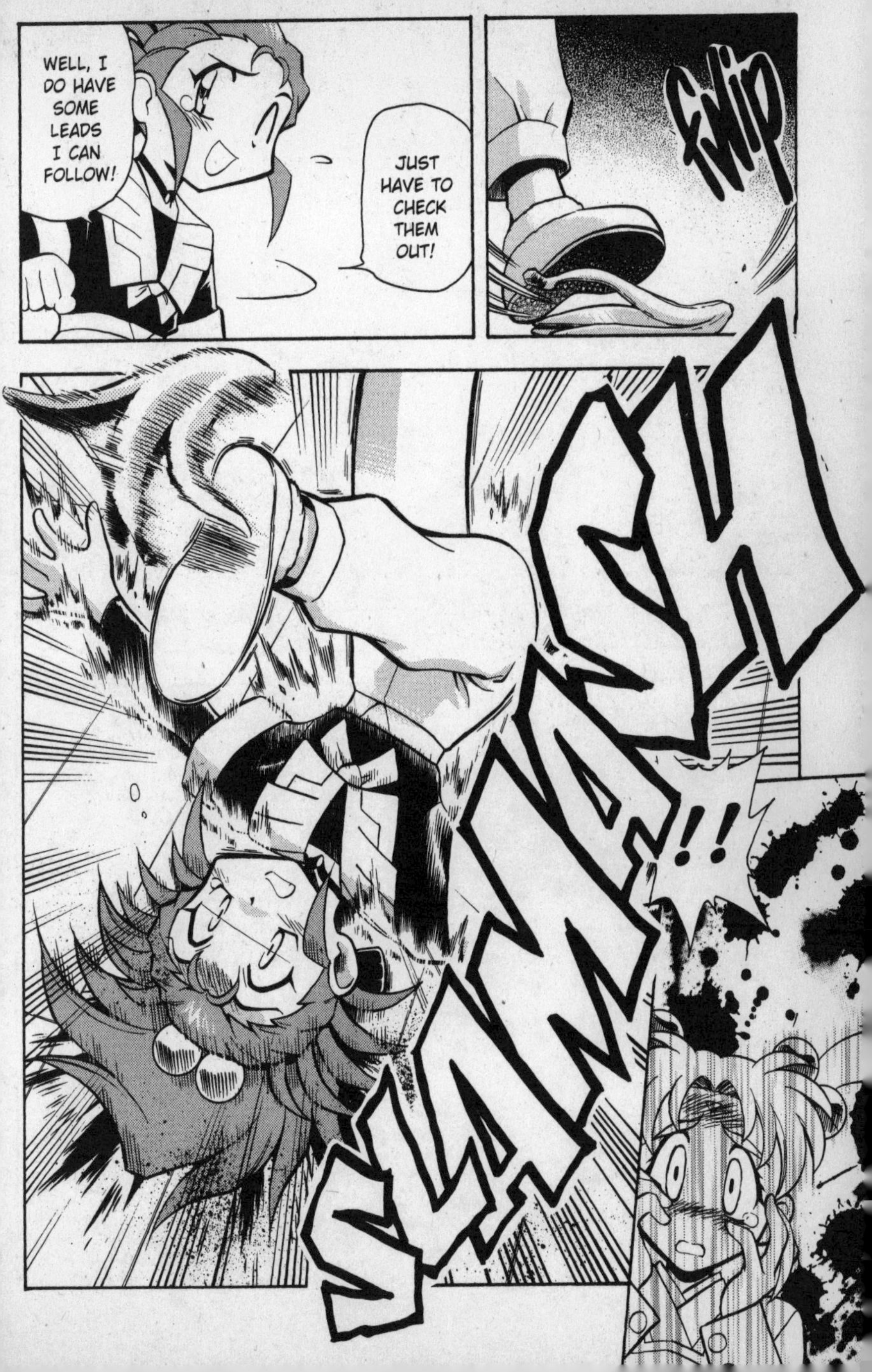
WELL, I DO HAVE SOME LEADS I CAN FOLLOW!
JUST HAVE TO CHECK THEM OUT!
FWIP
SLAMMM!!!

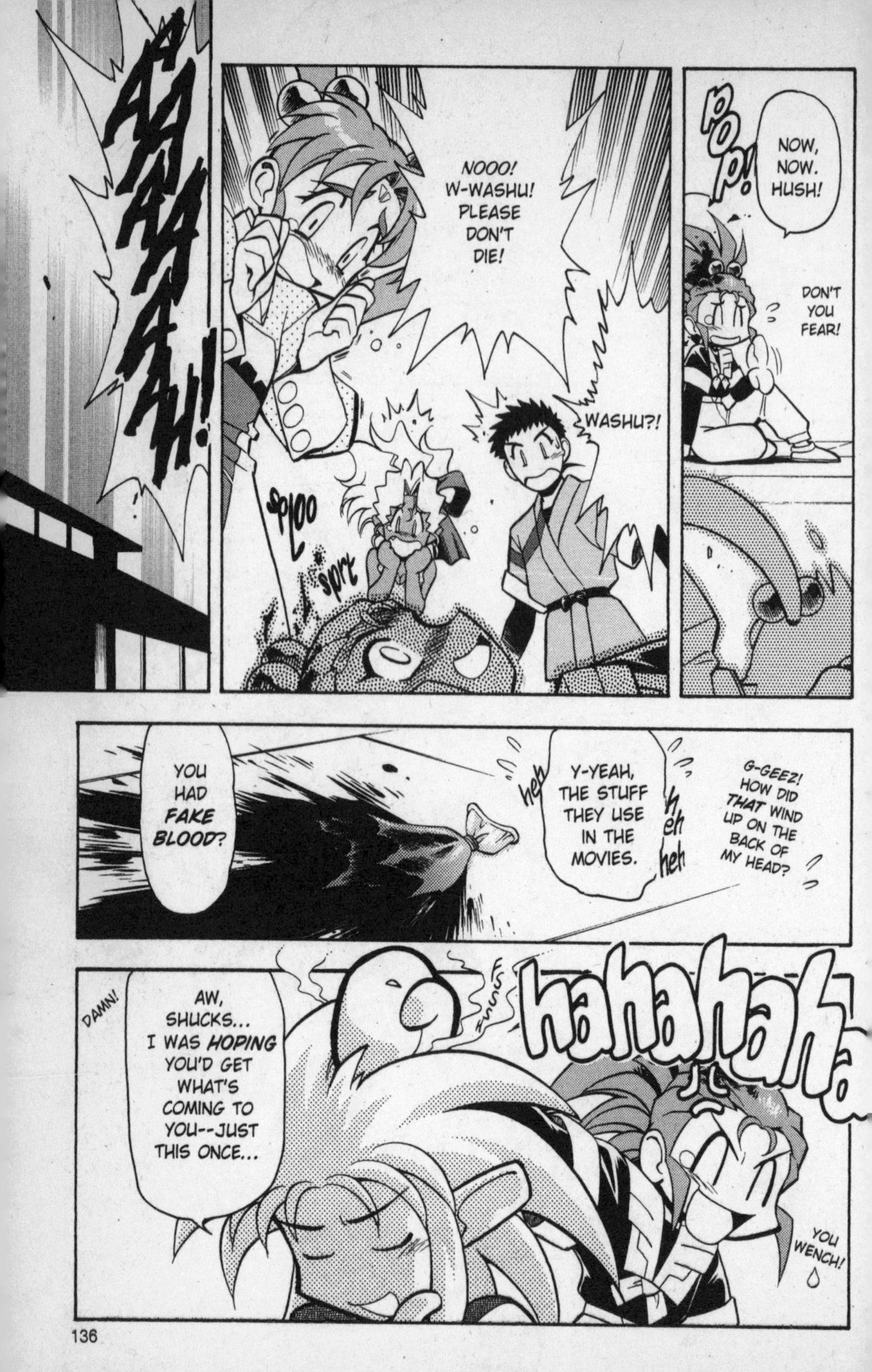
AAAAAAAH!
NOOO! W-WASHU! PLEASE DON'T DIE!
WASHU?!
sploo
sprt
pop!
NOW, NOW. HUSH!
DON'T YOU FEAR!
YOU HAD FAKE BLOOD?
heh heh heh
Y-YEAH, THE STUFF THEY USE IN THE MOVIES.
G-GEEZ! HOW DID THAT WIND UP ON THE BACK OF MY HEAD?
DAMN!
AW, SHUCKS... I WAS HOPING YOU'D GET WHAT'S COMING TO YOU--JUST THIS ONCE...
hahahaha
YOU WENCH!

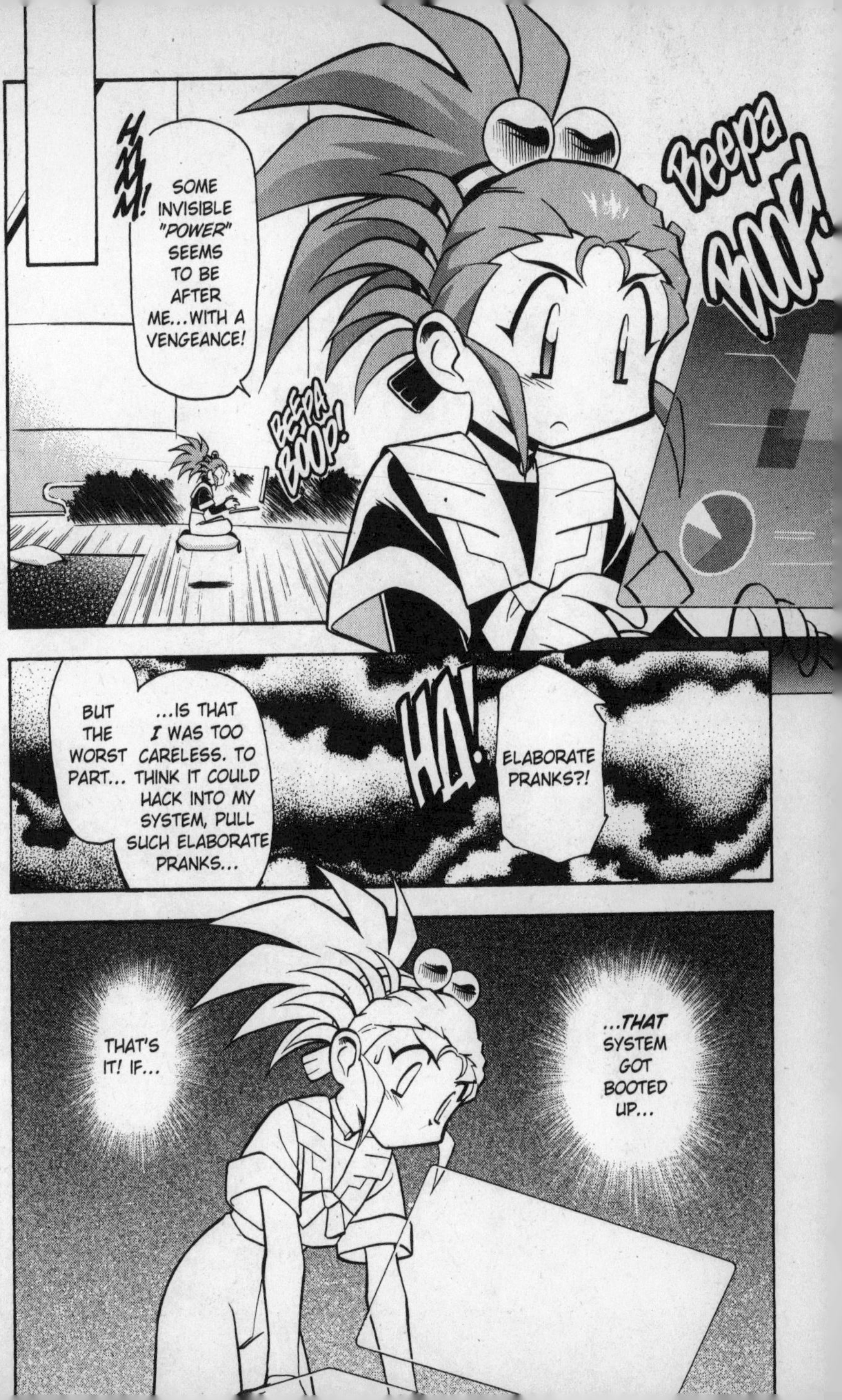
HMMM!
SOME INVISIBLE "POWER" SEEMS TO BE AFTER ME...WITH A VENGEANCE!
BEEPA BOOP!
Beepa BOOP!
BUT THE WORST PART...
...IS THAT I WAS TOO CARELESS. TO THINK IT COULD HACK INTO MY SYSTEM, PULL SUCH ELABORATE PRANKS...
HA!
ELABORATE PRANKS?!
THAT'S IT! IF...
...THAT SYSTEM GOT BOOTED UP...

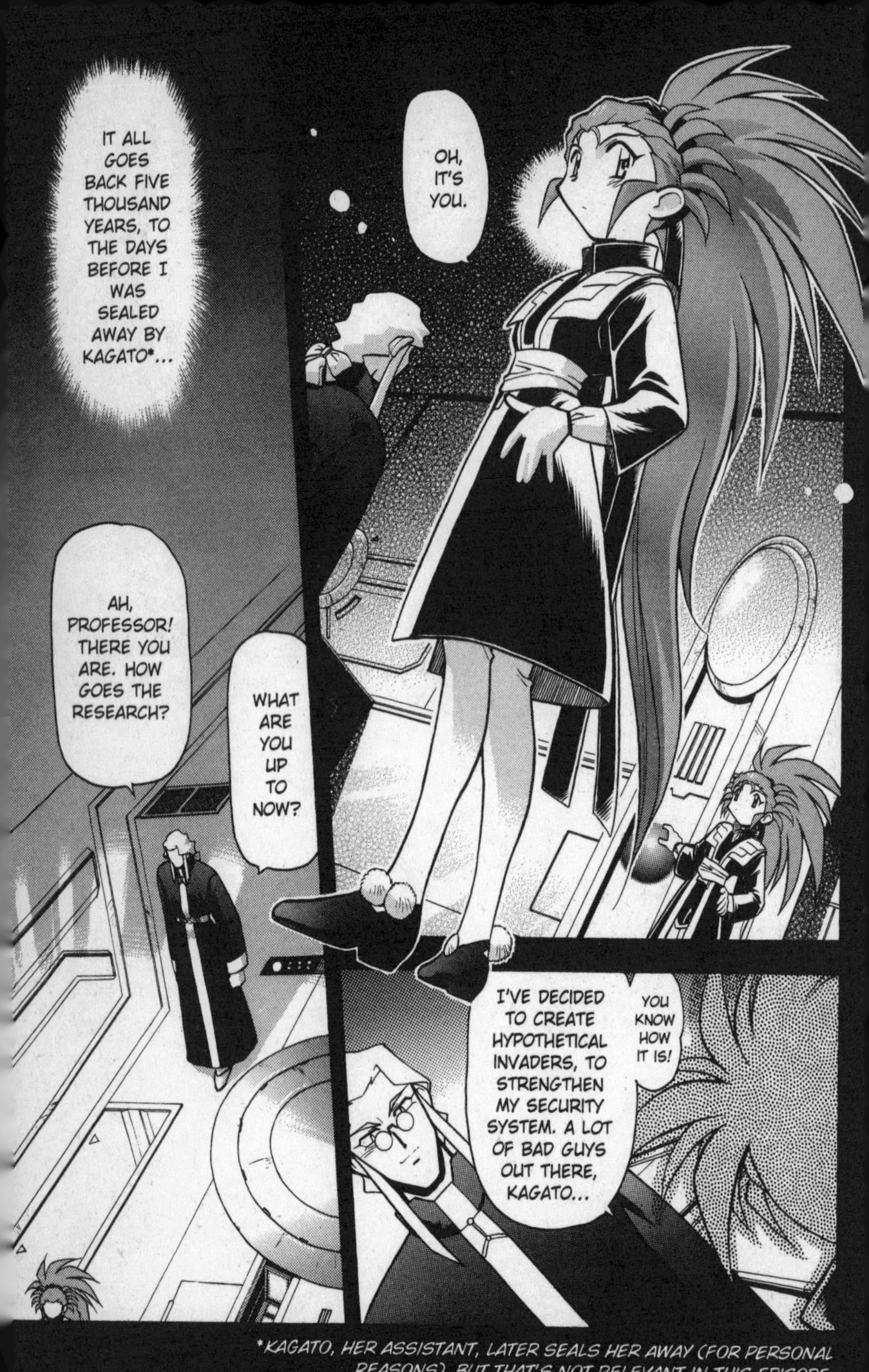
IT ALL GOES BACK FIVE THOUSAND YEARS, TO THE DAYS BEFORE I WAS SEALED AWAY BY KAGATO*...
AH, PROFESSOR! THERE YOU ARE. HOW GOES THE RESEARCH?
WHAT ARE YOU UP TO NOW?
OH, IT'S YOU.
I'VE DECIDED TO CREATE HYPOTHETICAL INVADERS, TO STRENGTHEN MY SECURITY SYSTEM. A LOT OF BAD GUYS OUT THERE, KAGATO...
YOU KNOW HOW IT IS!

*KAGATO, HER ASSISTANT, LATER SEALS HER AWAY (FOR PERSONAL REASONS), BUT THAT'S NOT RELEVANT IN THIS EPISODE.

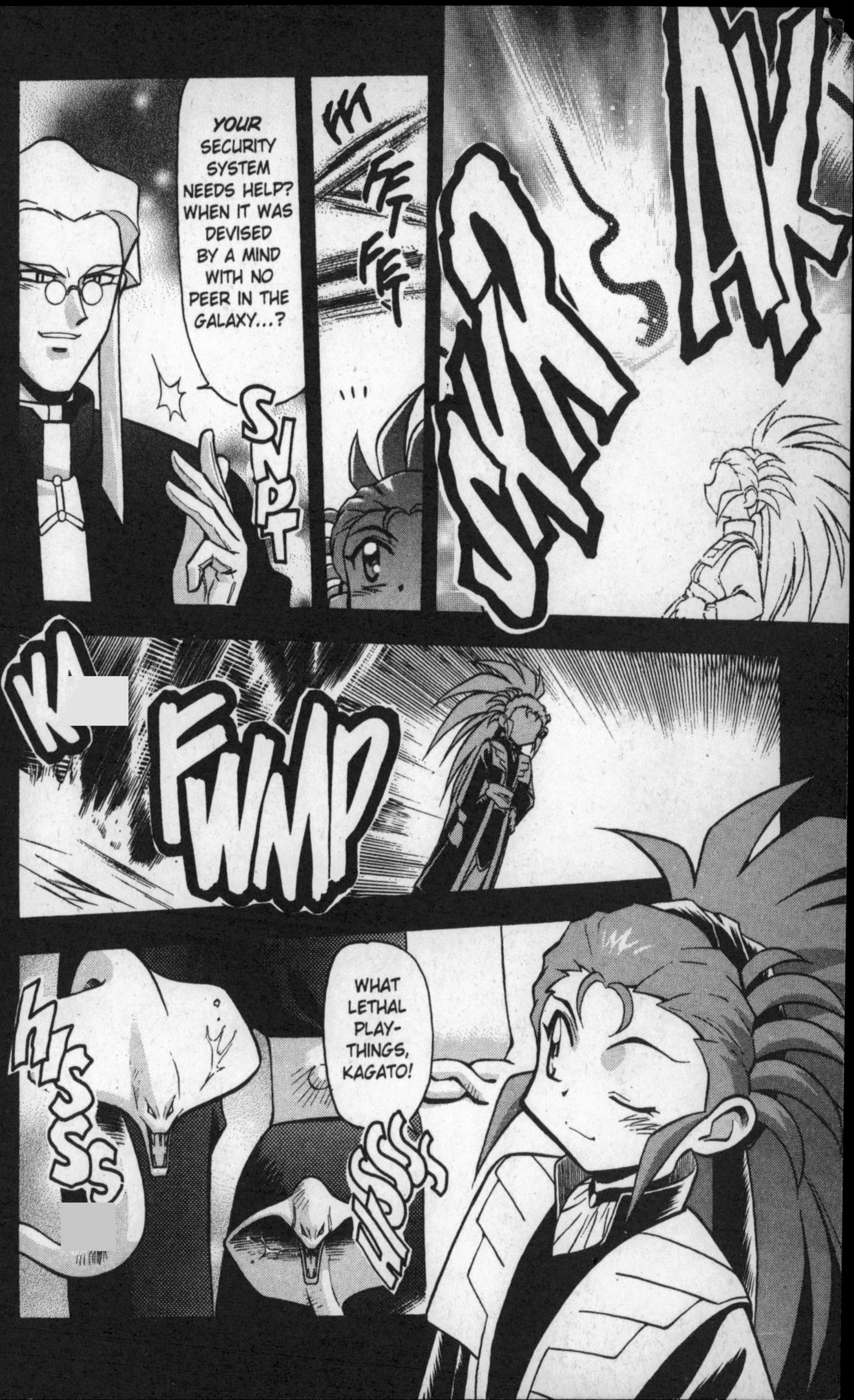
YOUR SECURITY SYSTEM NEEDS HELP? WHEN IT WAS DEVISED BY A MIND WITH NO PEER IN THE GALAXY...?
SNPT
FWMP
HISSS
WHAT LETHAL PLAY-THINGS, KAGATO!

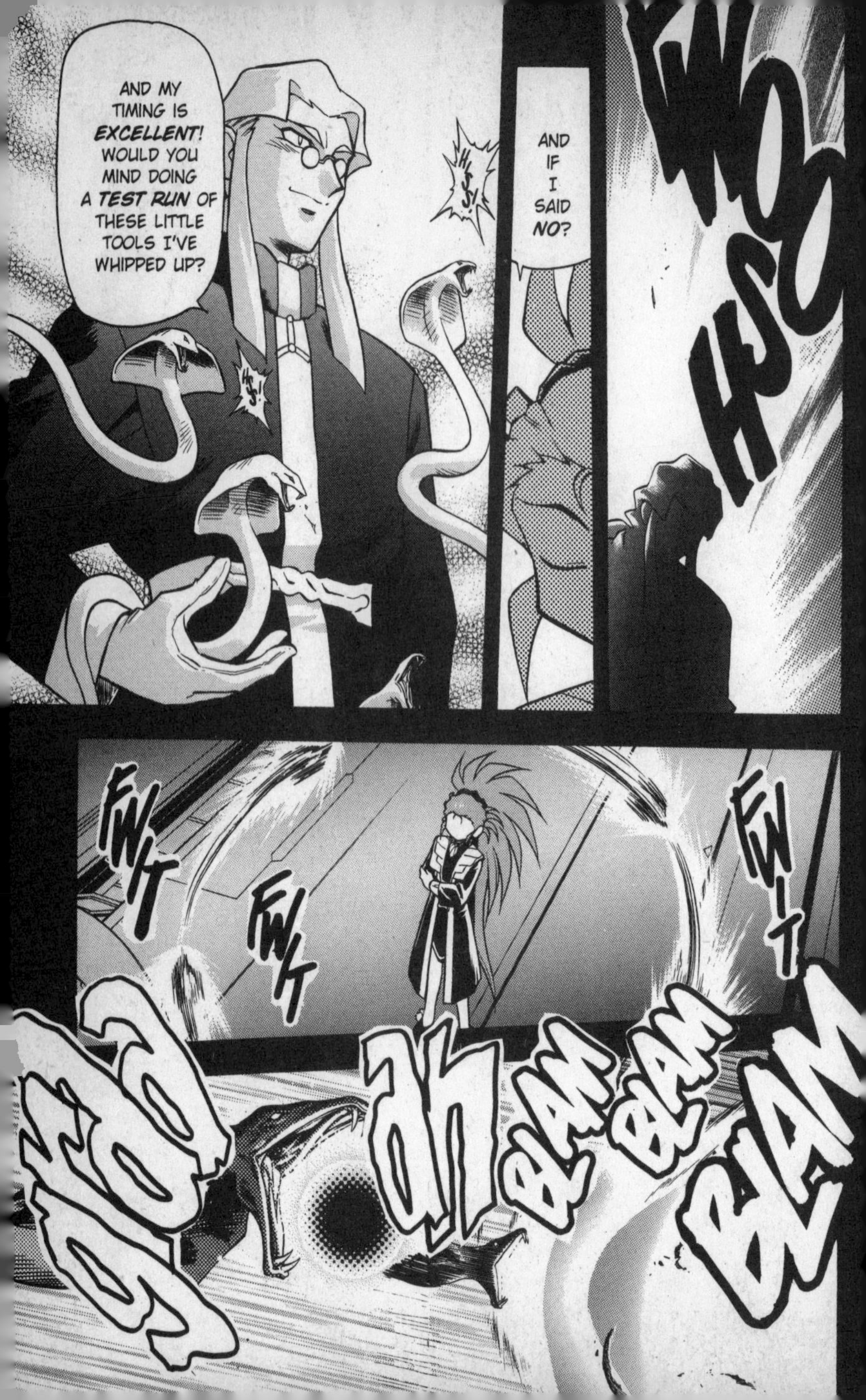
AND MY TIMING IS **EXCELLENT**! WOULD YOU MIND DOING A **TEST RUN** OF THESE LITTLE TOOLS I'VE WHIPPED UP?
HISS!
HISS!
AND IF I SAID **NO**?
FWIT
FWIT
FWIT
BLAM
BLAM
BLAM

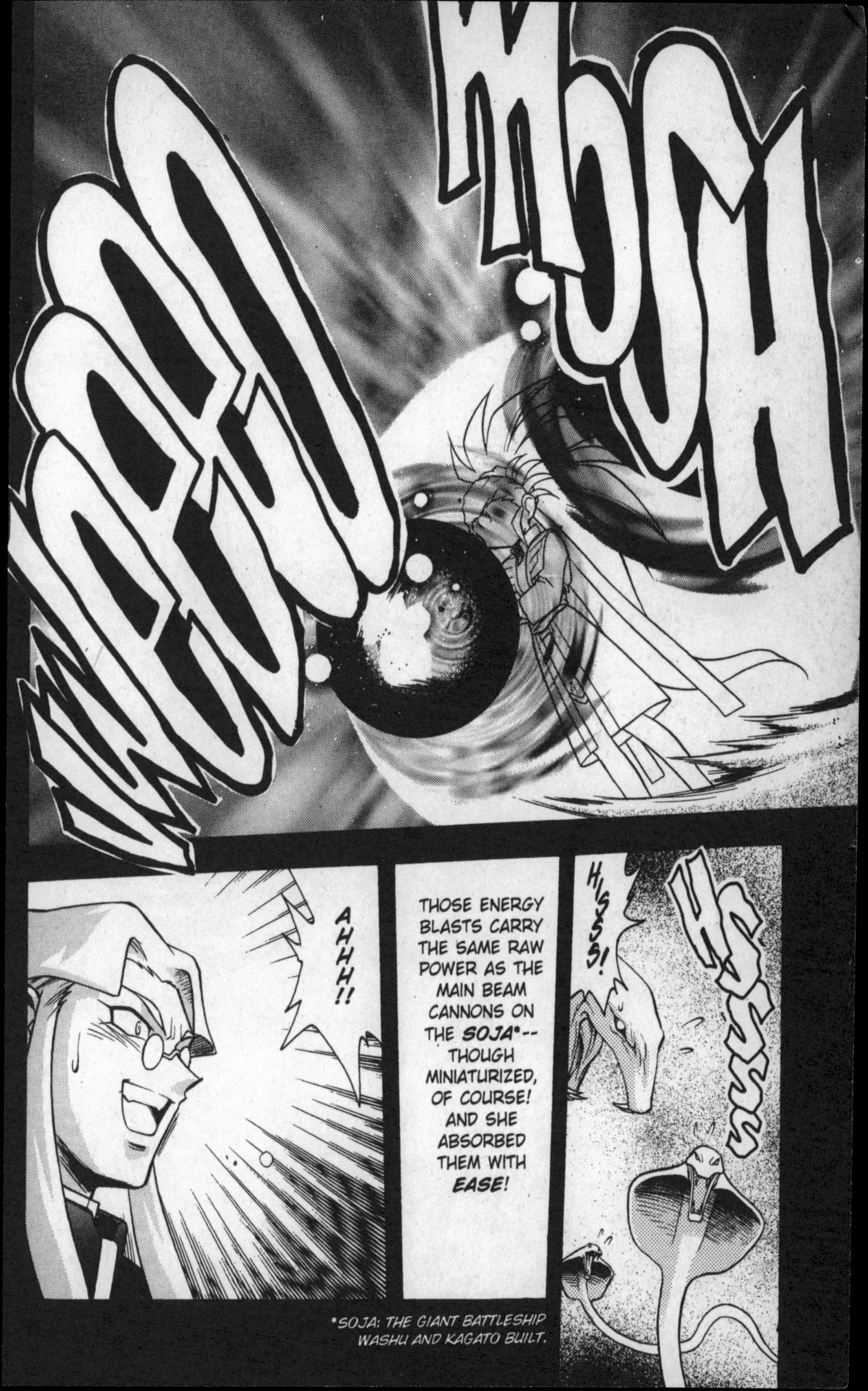
AHHH!!
THOSE ENERGY BLASTS CARRY THE SAME RAW POWER AS THE MAIN BEAM CANNONS ON THE ***SOJA****-- THOUGH MINIATURIZED, OF COURSE! AND SHE ABSORBED THEM WITH ***EASE***!
HISSS!

*SOJA: THE GIANT BATTLESHIP WASHU AND KAGATO BUILT.

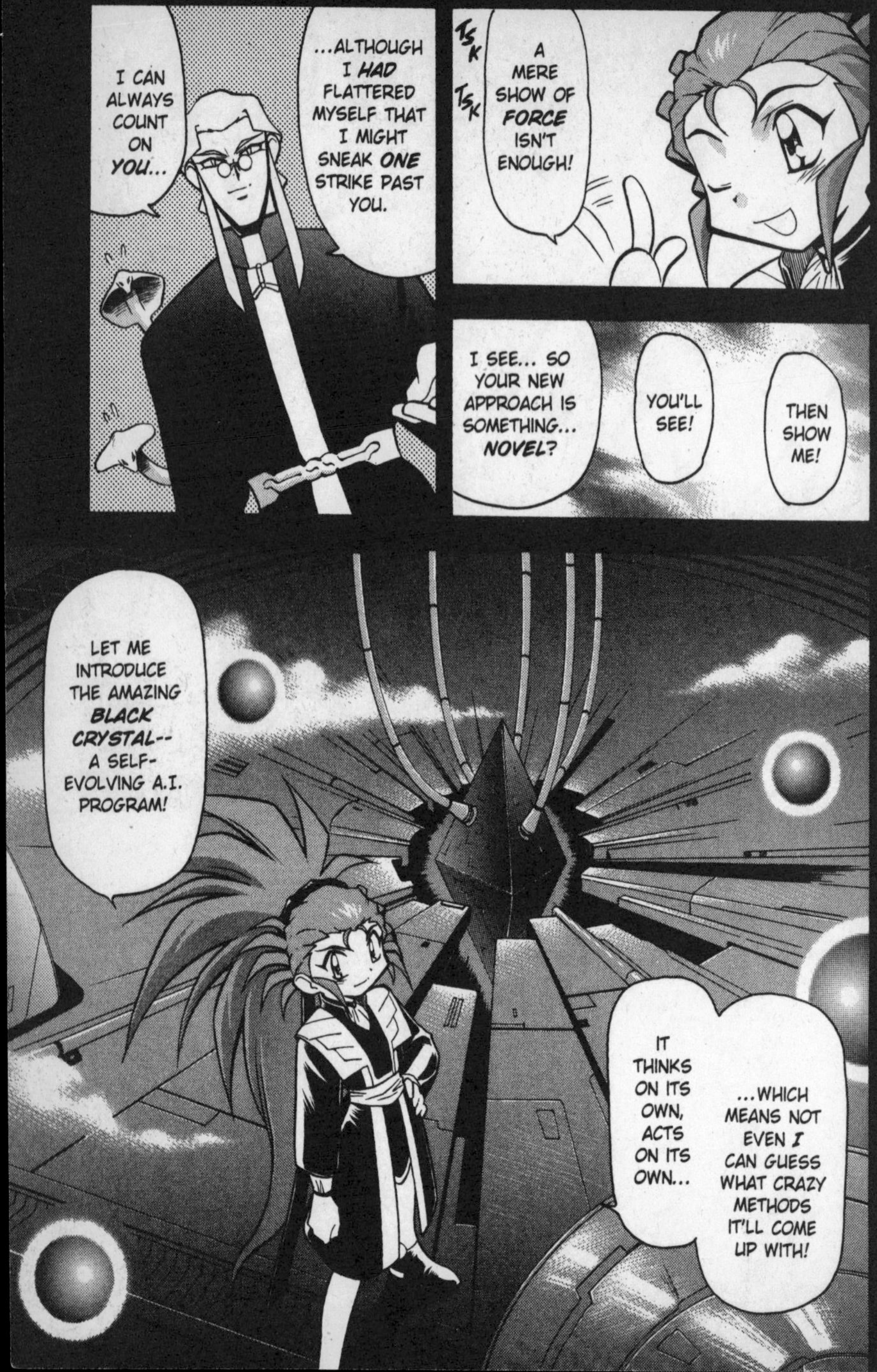
I CAN ALWAYS COUNT ON YOU...
...ALTHOUGH I HAD FLATTERED MYSELF THAT I MIGHT SNEAK ONE STRIKE PAST YOU.
TSK TSK
A MERE SHOW OF FORCE ISN'T ENOUGH!
I SEE... SO YOUR NEW APPROACH IS SOMETHING... NOVEL?
YOU'LL SEE!
THEN SHOW ME!
LET ME INTRODUCE THE AMAZING BLACK CRYSTAL-- A SELF-EVOLVING A.I. PROGRAM!
IT THINKS ON ITS OWN, ACTS ON ITS OWN...
...WHICH MEANS NOT EVEN I CAN GUESS WHAT CRAZY METHODS IT'LL COME UP WITH!

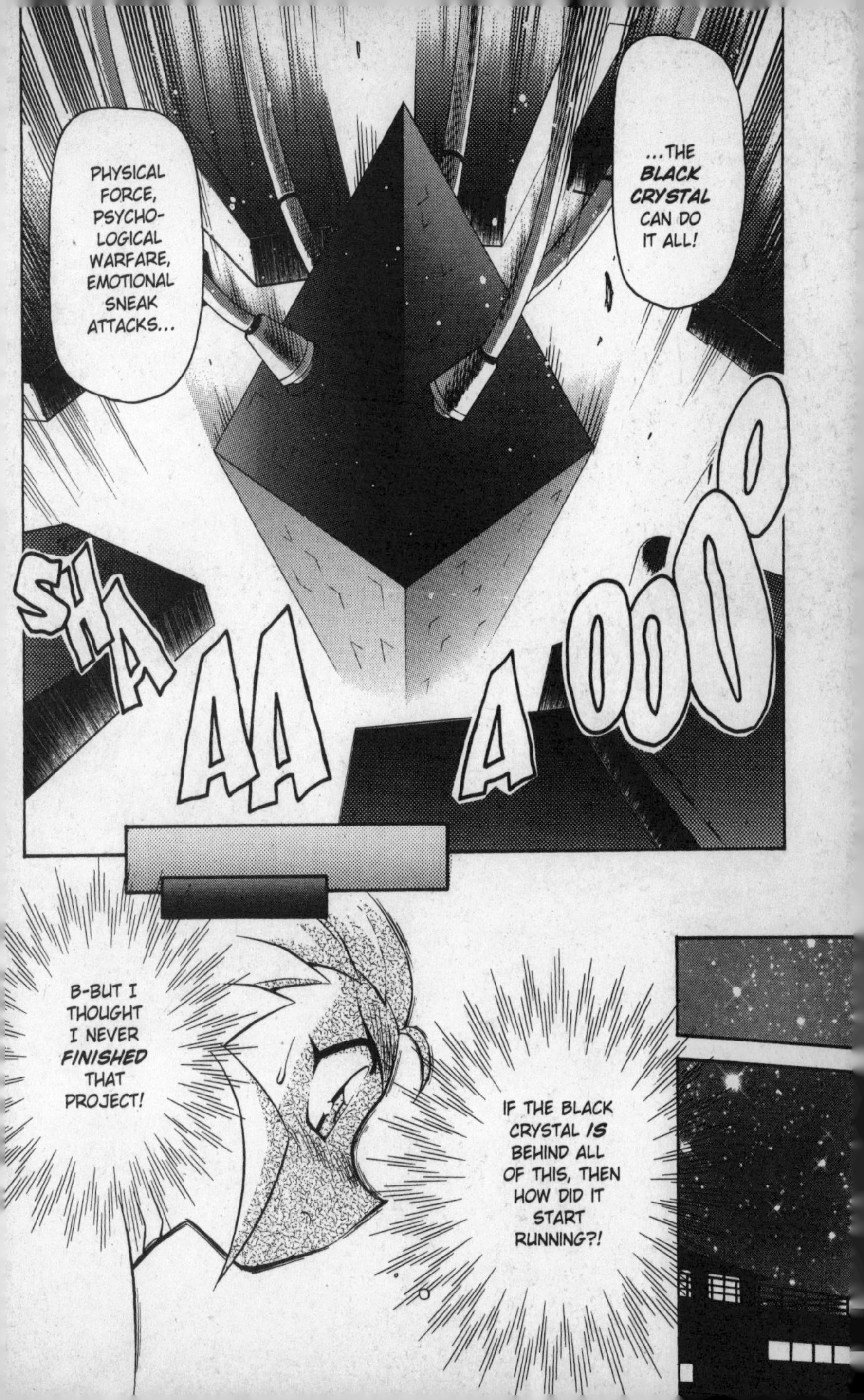
PHYSICAL FORCE, PSYCHO-LOGICAL WARFARE, EMOTIONAL SNEAK ATTACKS...
...THE BLACK CRYSTAL CAN DO IT ALL!
SHAAAAOOOO
B-BUT I THOUGHT I NEVER FINISHED THAT PROJECT!
IF THE BLACK CRYSTAL IS BEHIND ALL OF THIS, THEN HOW DID IT START RUNNING?!

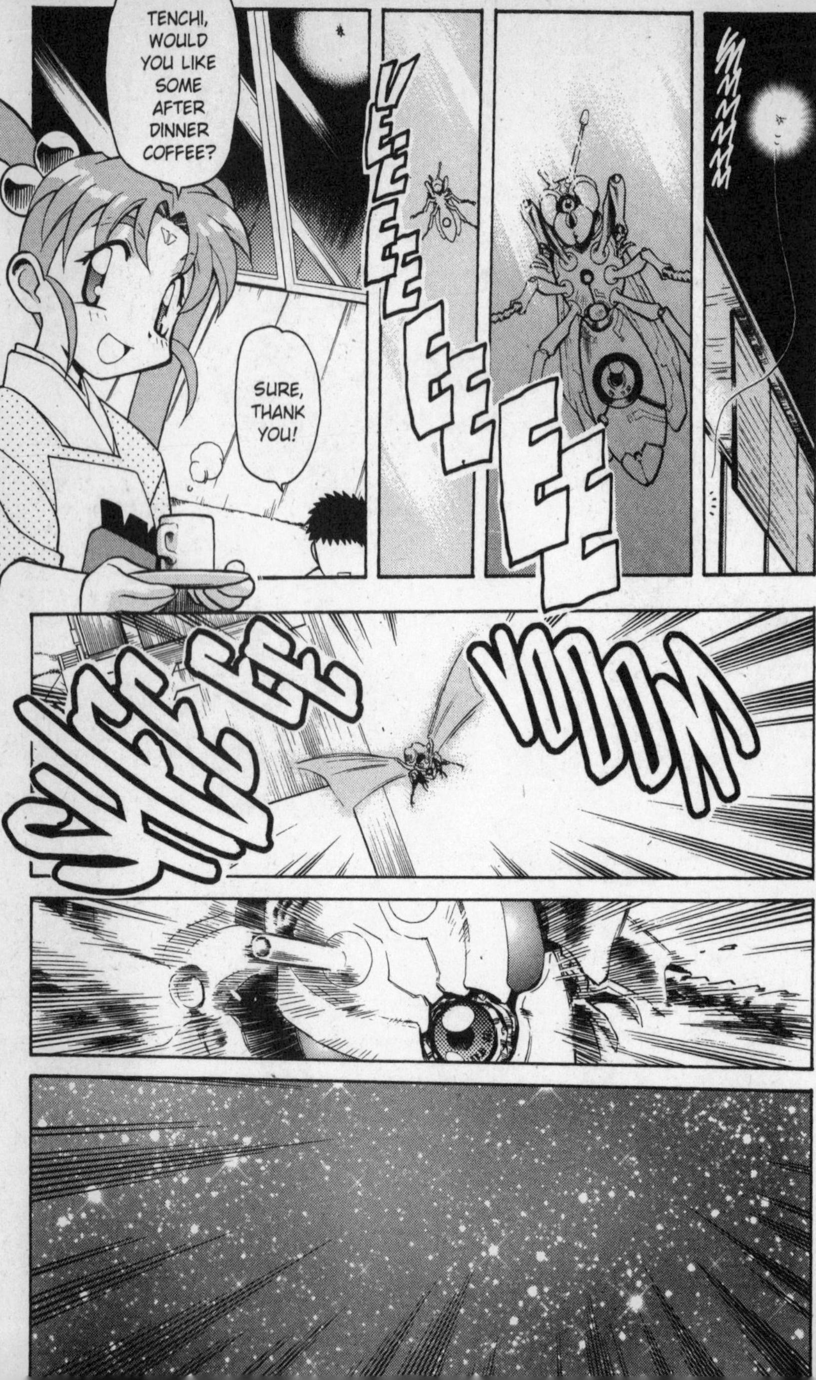
TENCHI, WOULD YOU LIKE SOME AFTER DINNER COFFEE?
SURE, THANK YOU!

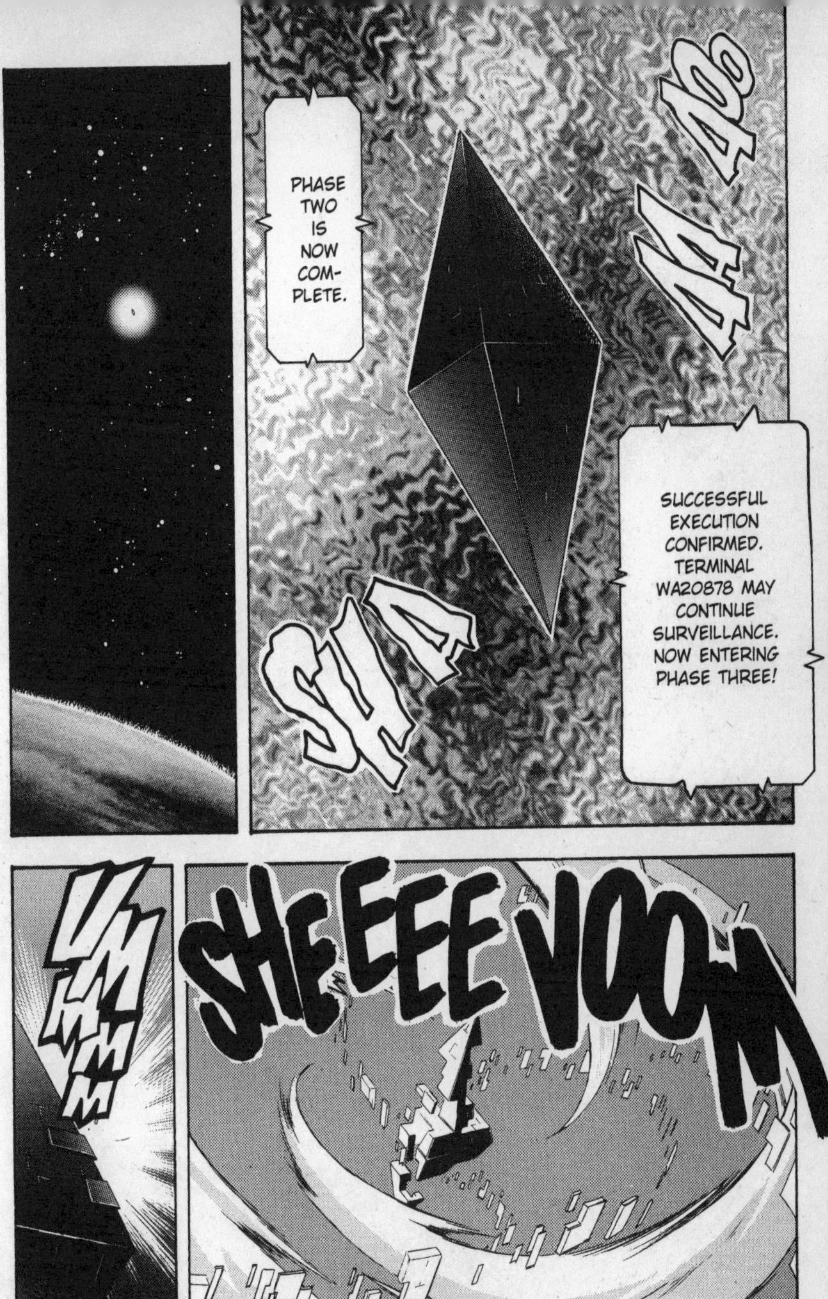
PHASE TWO IS NOW COMPLETE.
SHA
SUCCESSFUL EXECUTION CONFIRMED. TERMINAL WA20878 MAY CONTINUE SURVEILLANCE. NOW ENTERING PHASE THREE!
SHEEEE VOOM

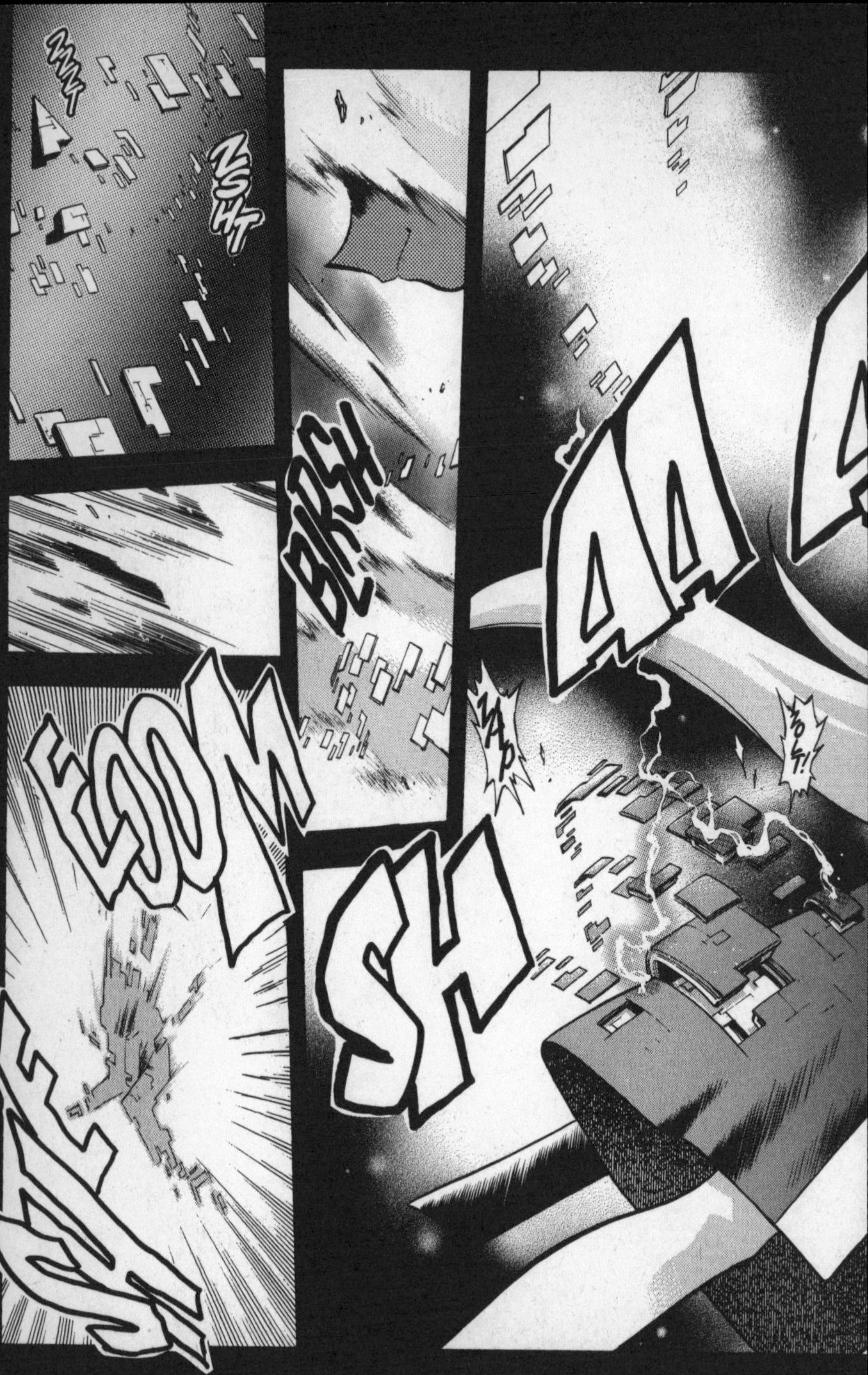
VOLT!
ZAP
SH
BRSH
NSHT
ZNNK
FOOOM

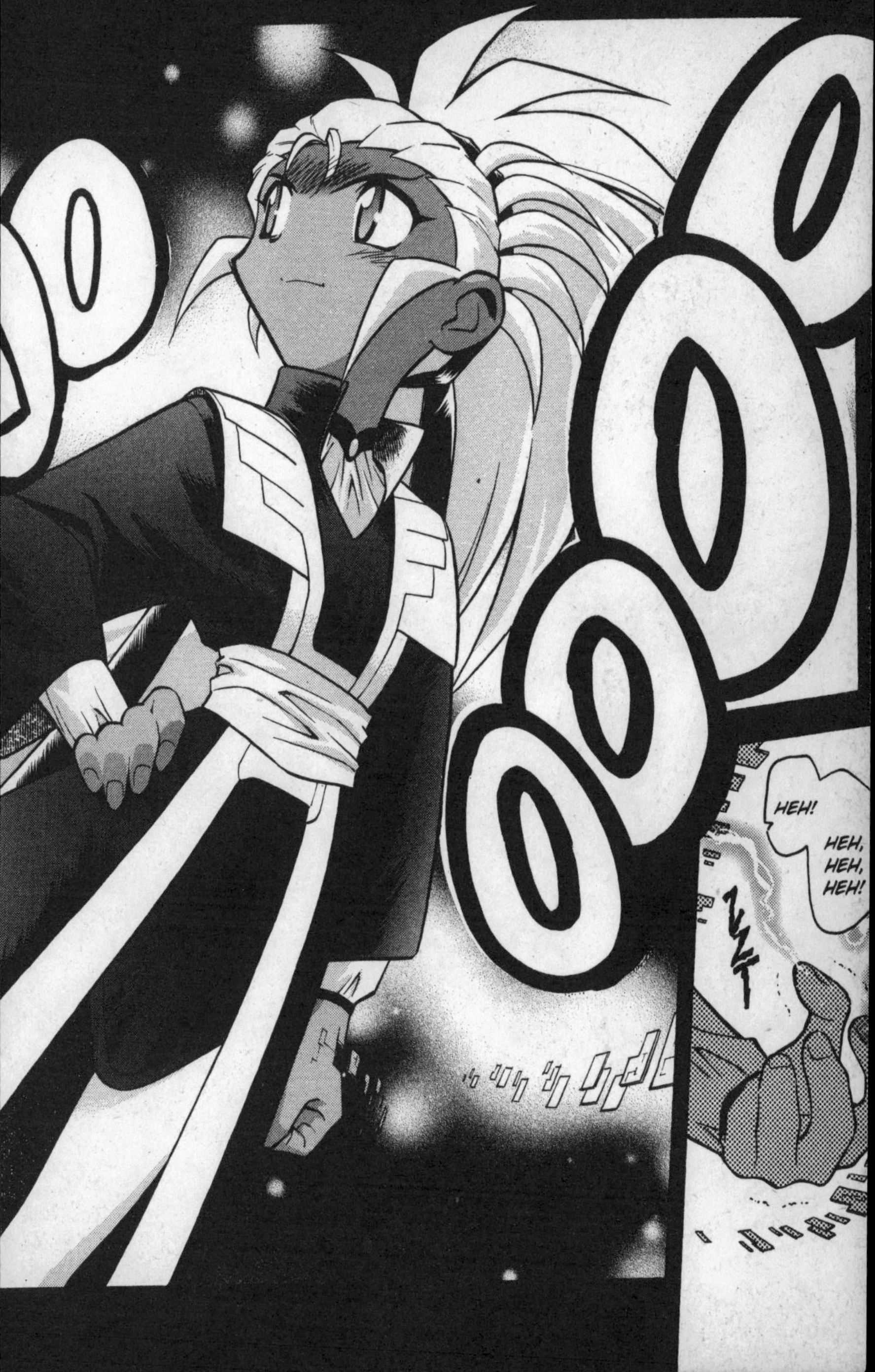
HEH!
HEH, HEH, HEH!

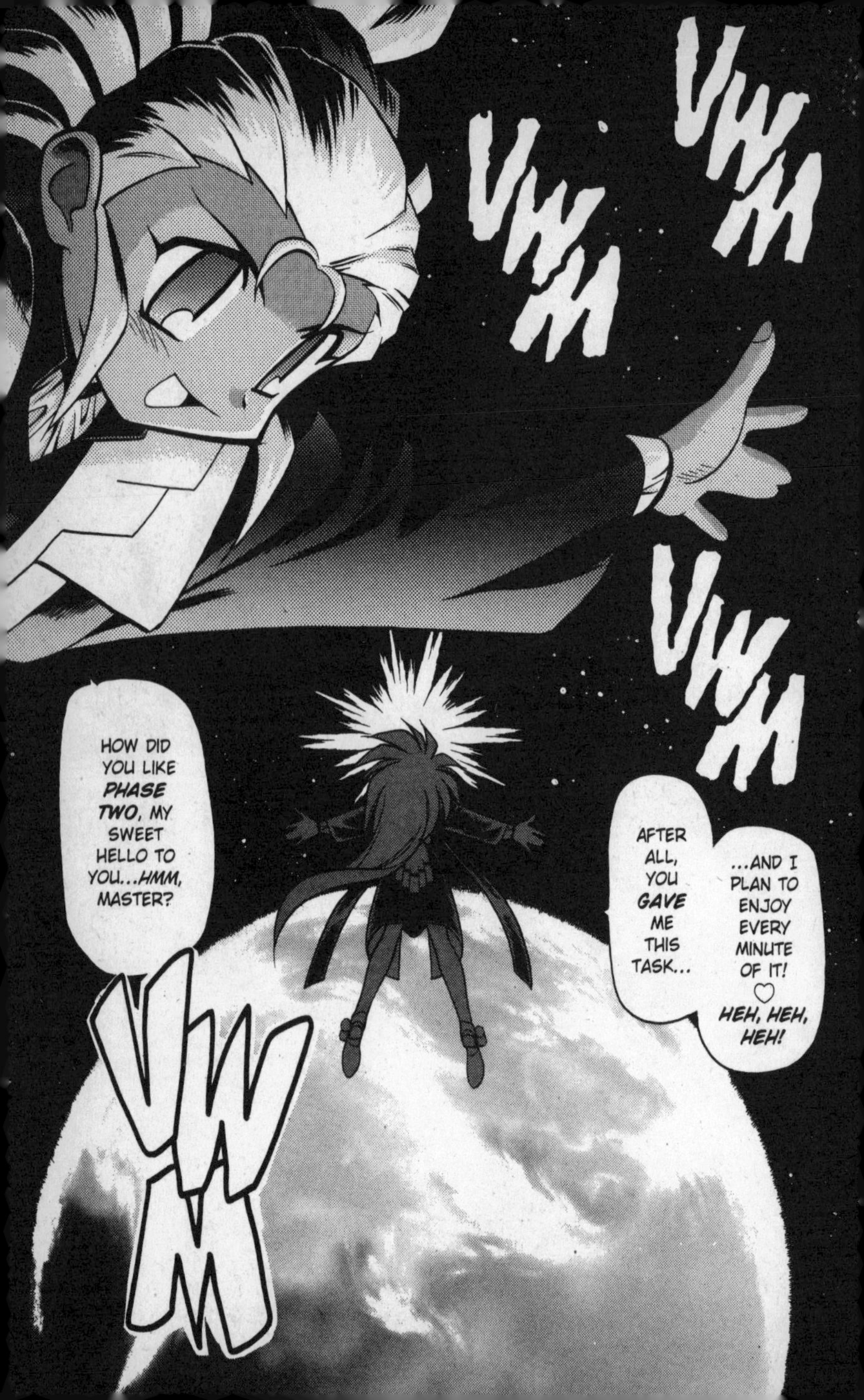

VWM
VWM
VWM
HOW DID YOU LIKE ***PHASE TWO***, MY SWEET HELLO TO YOU...*HMM*, MASTER?
AFTER ALL, YOU ***GAVE*** ME THIS TASK...
...AND I PLAN TO ENJOY EVERY MINUTE OF IT! ♡ ***HEH, HEH, HEH!***
VWM

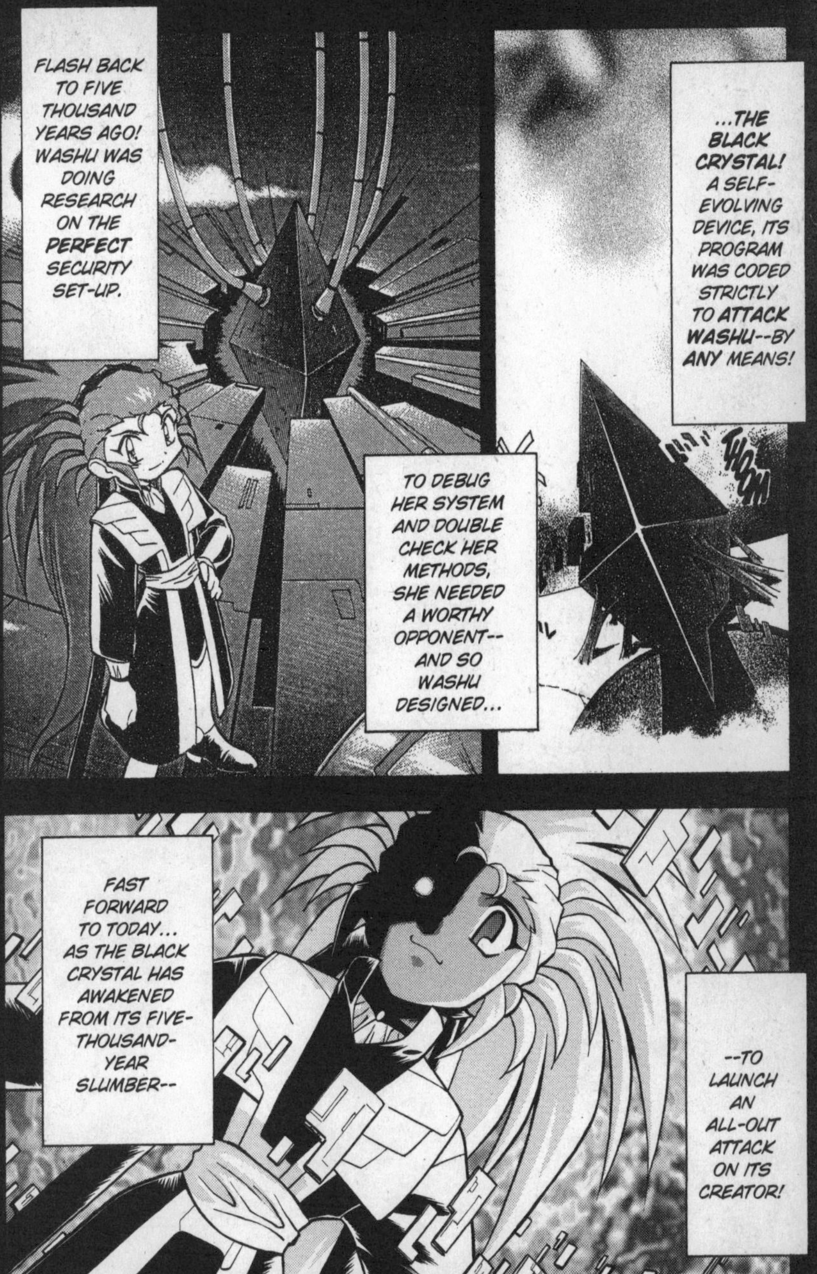
FLASH BACK TO FIVE THOUSAND YEARS AGO! WASHU WAS DOING RESEARCH ON THE PERFECT SECURITY SET-UP.
TO DEBUG HER SYSTEM AND DOUBLE CHECK HER METHODS, SHE NEEDED A WORTHY OPPONENT-- AND SO WASHU DESIGNED...
...THE BLACK CRYSTAL! A SELF-EVOLVING DEVICE, ITS PROGRAM WAS CODED STRICTLY TO ATTACK WASHU--BY ANY MEANS!
THOOM
FAST FORWARD TO TODAY... AS THE BLACK CRYSTAL HAS AWAKENED FROM ITS FIVE-THOUSAND-YEAR SLUMBER--
--TO LAUNCH AN ALL-OUT ATTACK ON ITS CREATOR!

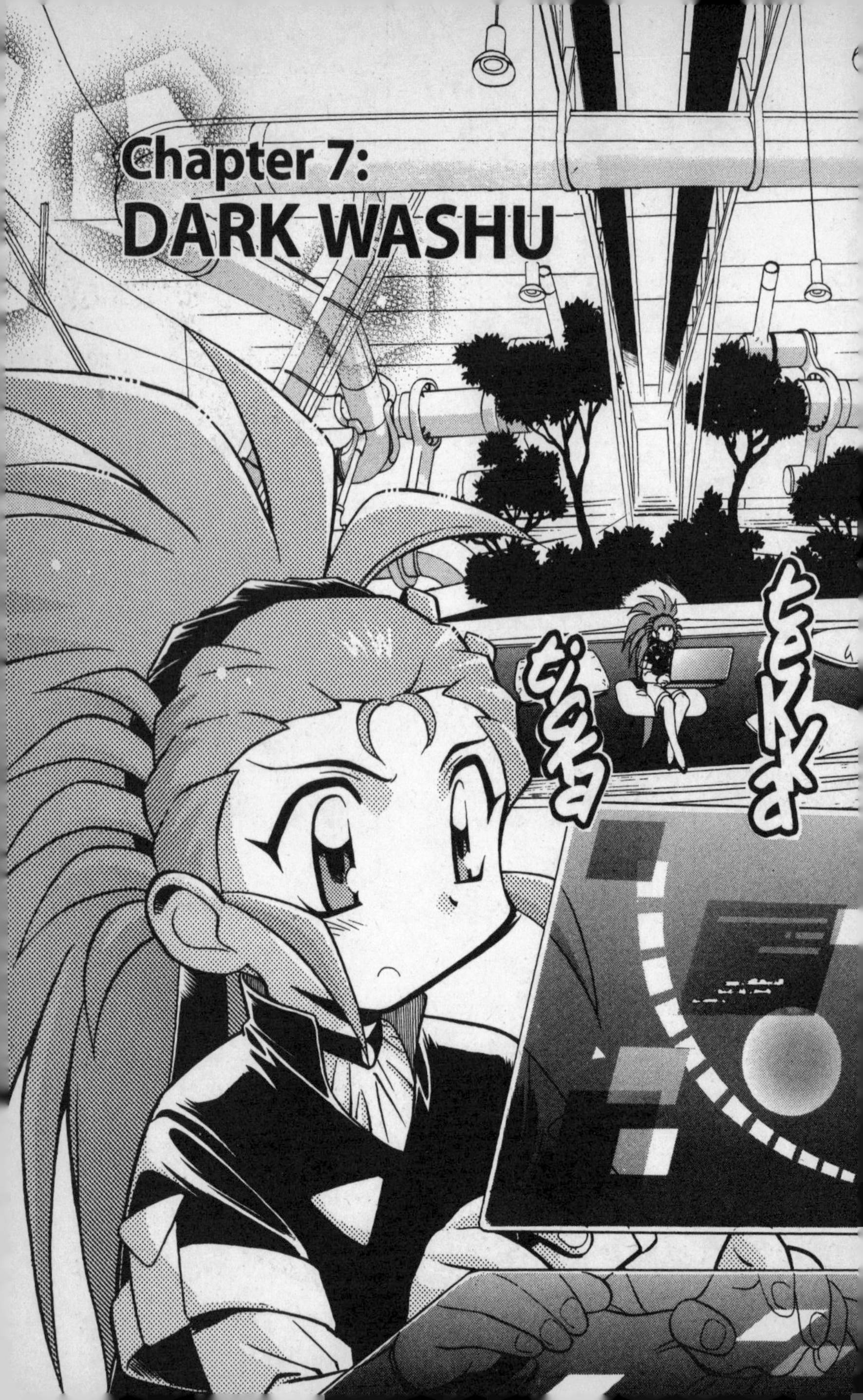
Chapter 7:
DARK WASHU

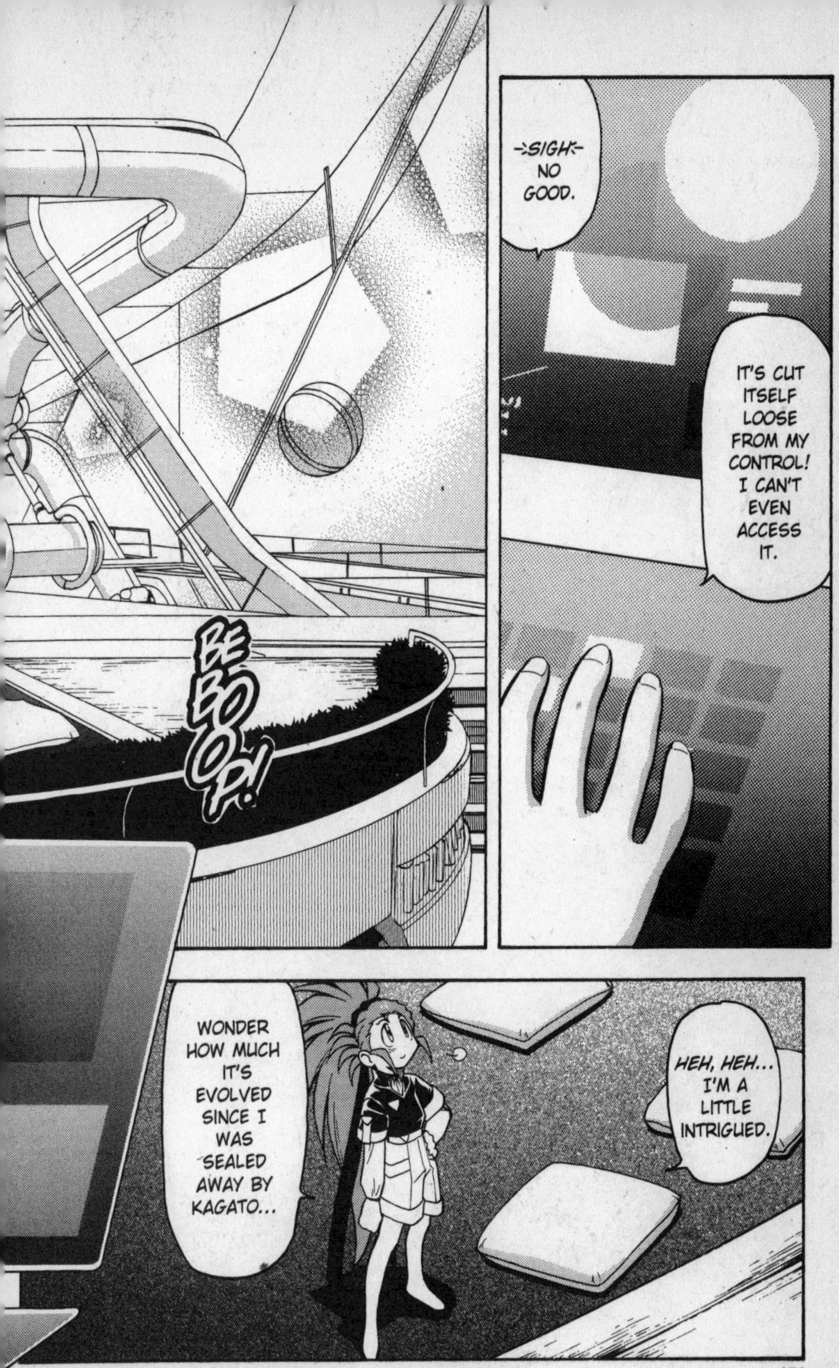
BEBOOP!
-SIGH- NO GOOD.
IT'S CUT ITSELF LOOSE FROM MY CONTROL! I CAN'T EVEN ACCESS IT.
WONDER HOW MUCH IT'S EVOLVED SINCE I WAS SEALED AWAY BY KAGATO...
HEH, HEH... I'M A LITTLE INTRIGUED.

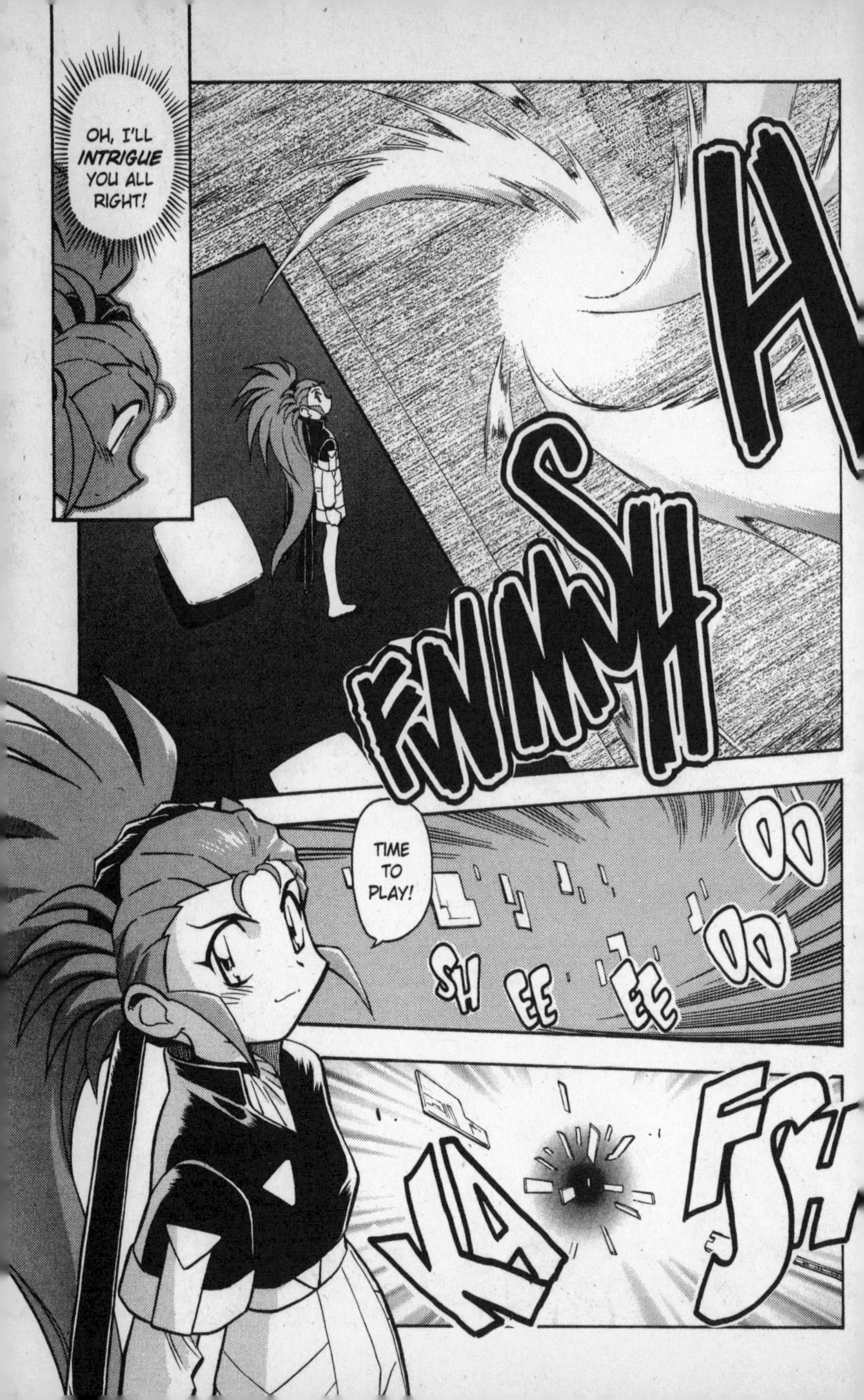
OH, I'LL INTRIGUE YOU ALL RIGHT!
FWMMSH
TIME TO PLAY!
SHEEEEOOOOOO
KA-FSH

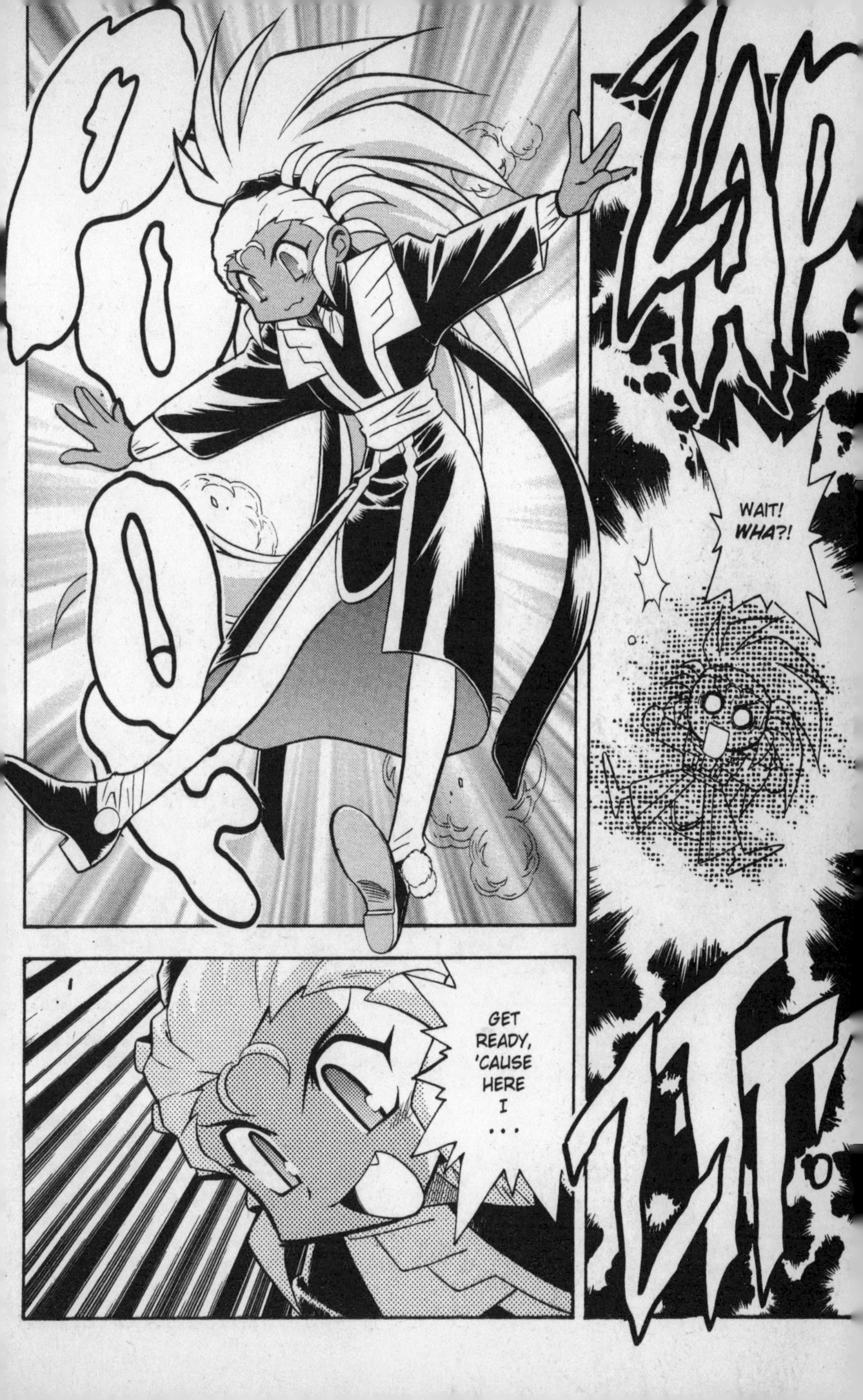
GET READY, 'CAUSE HERE I . . .
WAIT! WHA?!

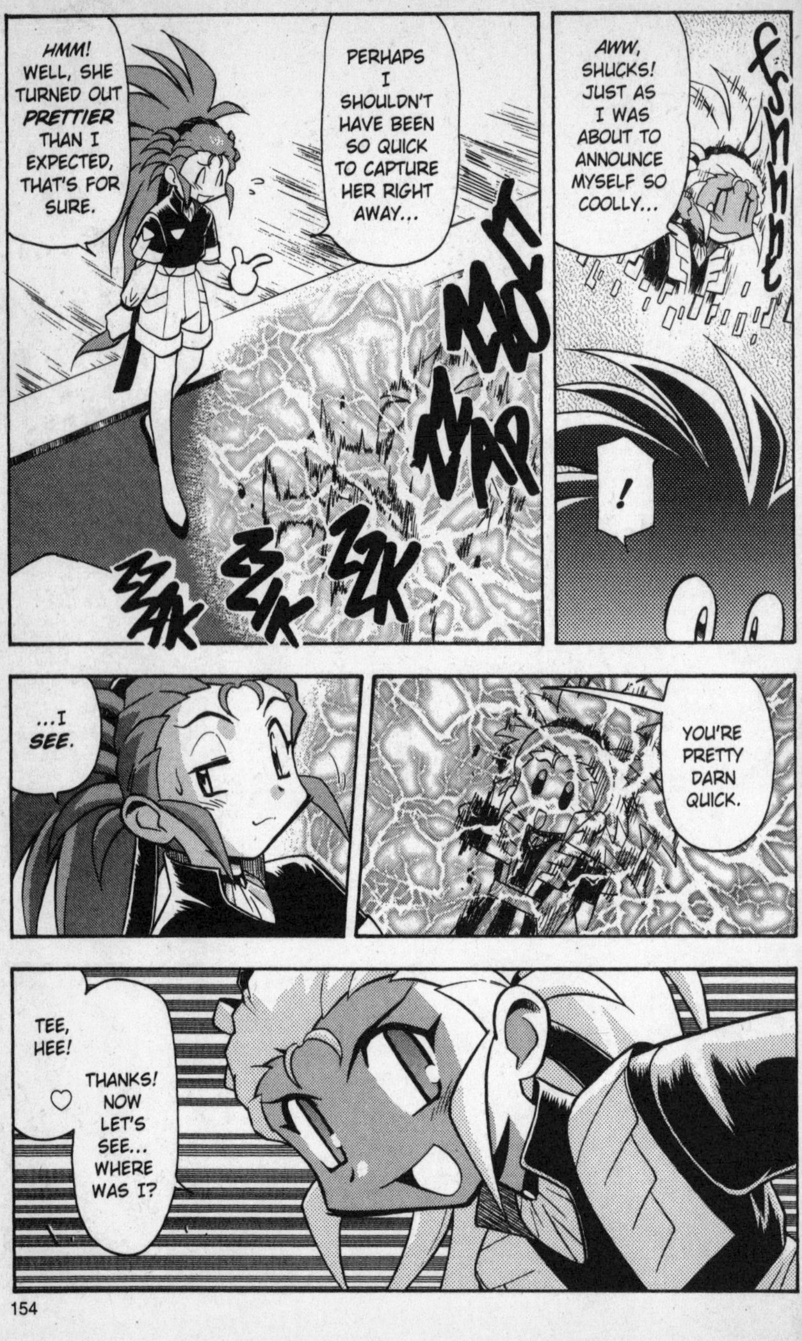
HMM! WELL, SHE TURNED OUT PRETTIER THAN I EXPECTED, THAT'S FOR SURE.
PERHAPS I SHOULDN'T HAVE BEEN SO QUICK TO CAPTURE HER RIGHT AWAY...
ZZAK
ZZIK
ZZK
AWW, SHUCKS! JUST AS I WAS ABOUT TO ANNOUNCE MYSELF SO COOLLY...
!
...I SEE.
YOU'RE PRETTY DARN QUICK.
TEE, HEE! ♡
THANKS! NOW LET'S SEE... WHERE WAS I?

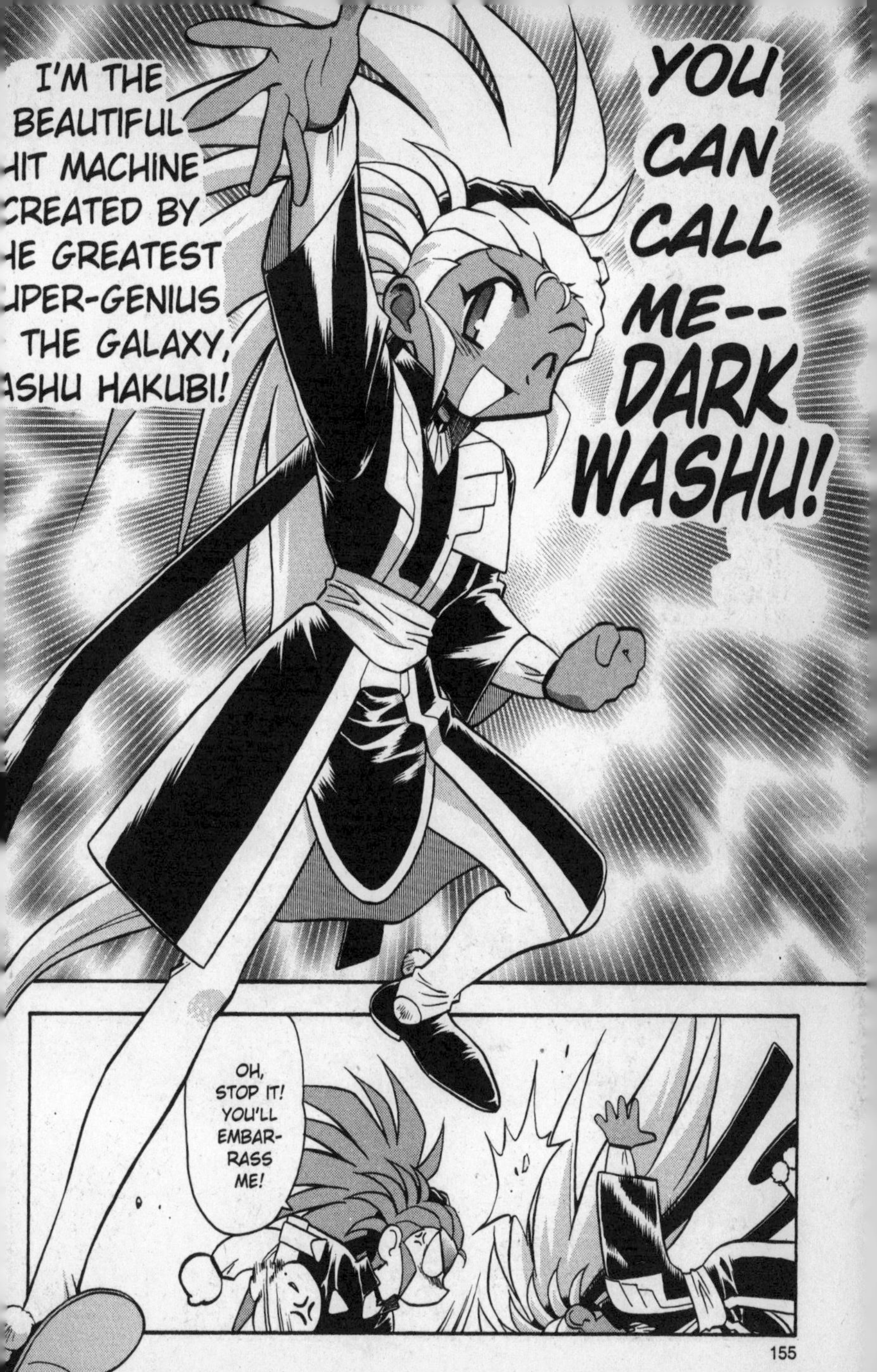
I'M THE BEAUTIFUL HIT MACHINE CREATED BY HE GREATEST UPER-GENIUS THE GALAXY, ASHU HAKUBI!
YOU CAN CALL ME-- DARK WASHU!
OH, STOP IT! YOU'LL EMBAR-RASS ME!

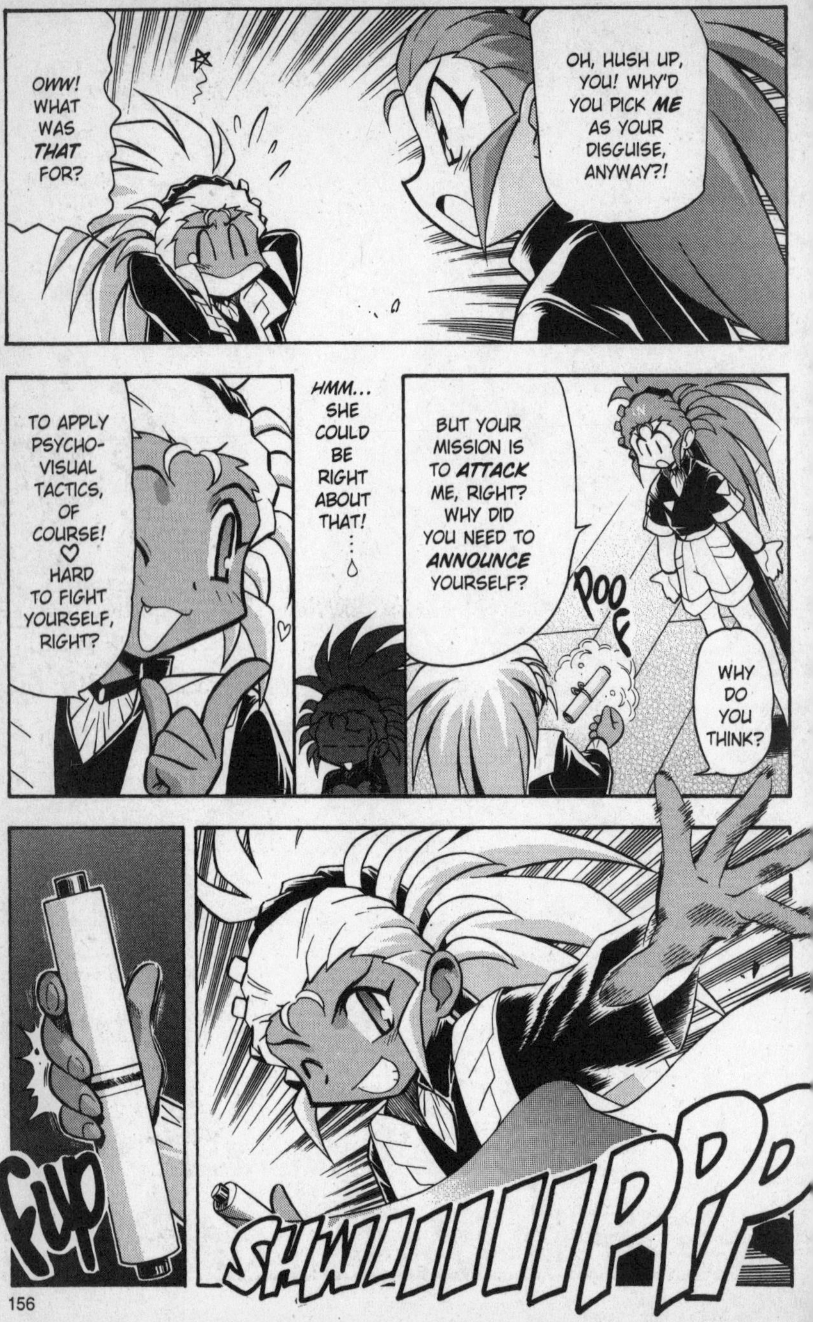
OWW! WHAT WAS THAT FOR?
OH, HUSH UP, YOU! WHY'D YOU PICK ME AS YOUR DISGUISE, ANYWAY?!
TO APPLY PSYCHO-VISUAL TACTICS, OF COURSE! ♡ HARD TO FIGHT YOURSELF, RIGHT?
HMM... SHE COULD BE RIGHT ABOUT THAT!
BUT YOUR MISSION IS TO ATTACK ME, RIGHT? WHY DID YOU NEED TO ANNOUNCE YOURSELF?
POOF
WHY DO YOU THINK?
FLIP
SHWIIIIIPP

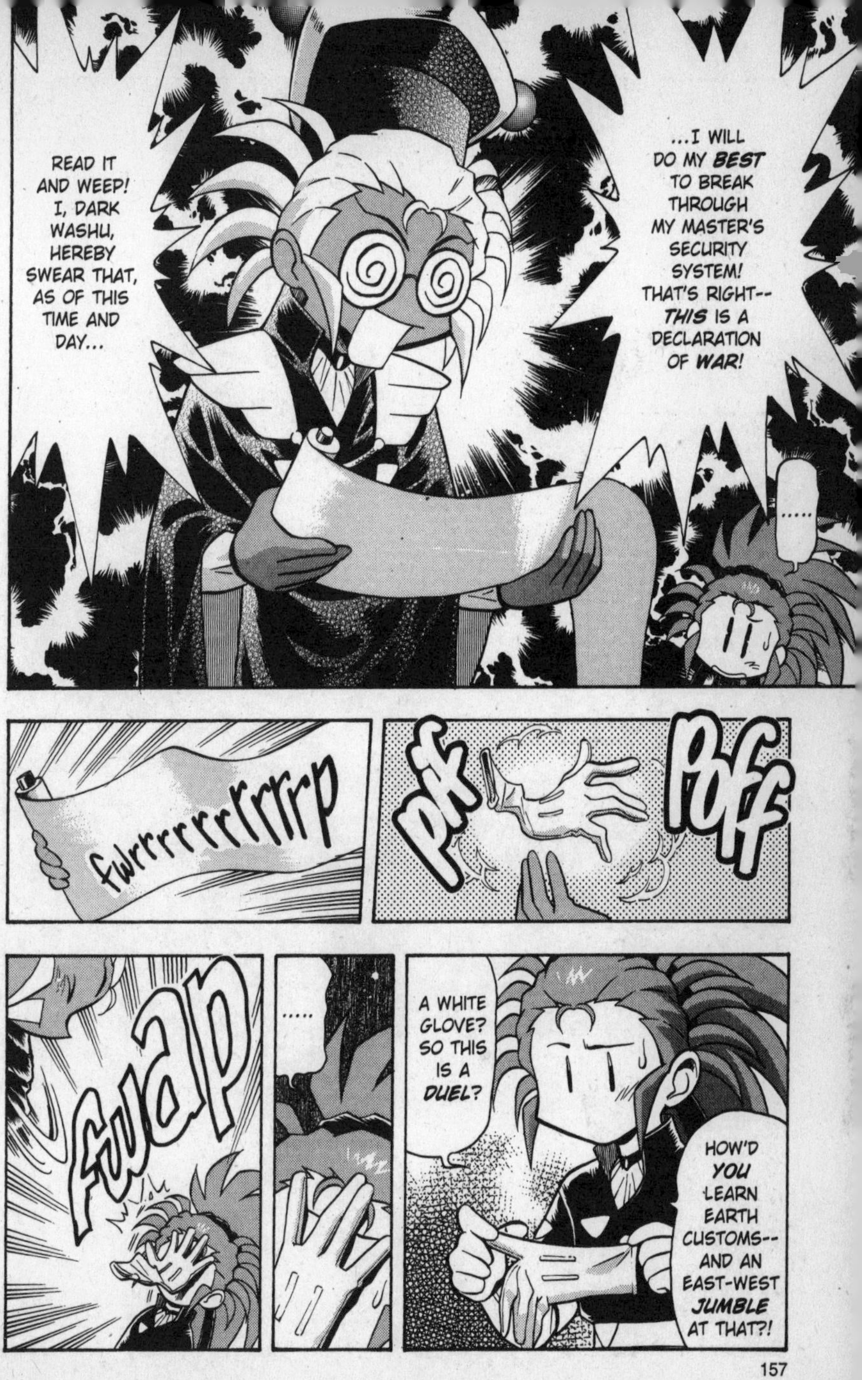
READ IT AND WEEP! I, DARK WASHU, HEREBY SWEAR THAT, AS OF THIS TIME AND DAY...
...I WILL DO MY BEST TO BREAK THROUGH MY MASTER'S SECURITY SYSTEM! THAT'S RIGHT-- THIS IS A DECLARATION OF WAR!
......
fwrrrrrrrrrp
pif
Poff
fwap
.....
A WHITE GLOVE? SO THIS IS A DUEL?
HOW'D YOU LEARN EARTH CUSTOMS-- AND AN EAST-WEST JUMBLE AT THAT?!

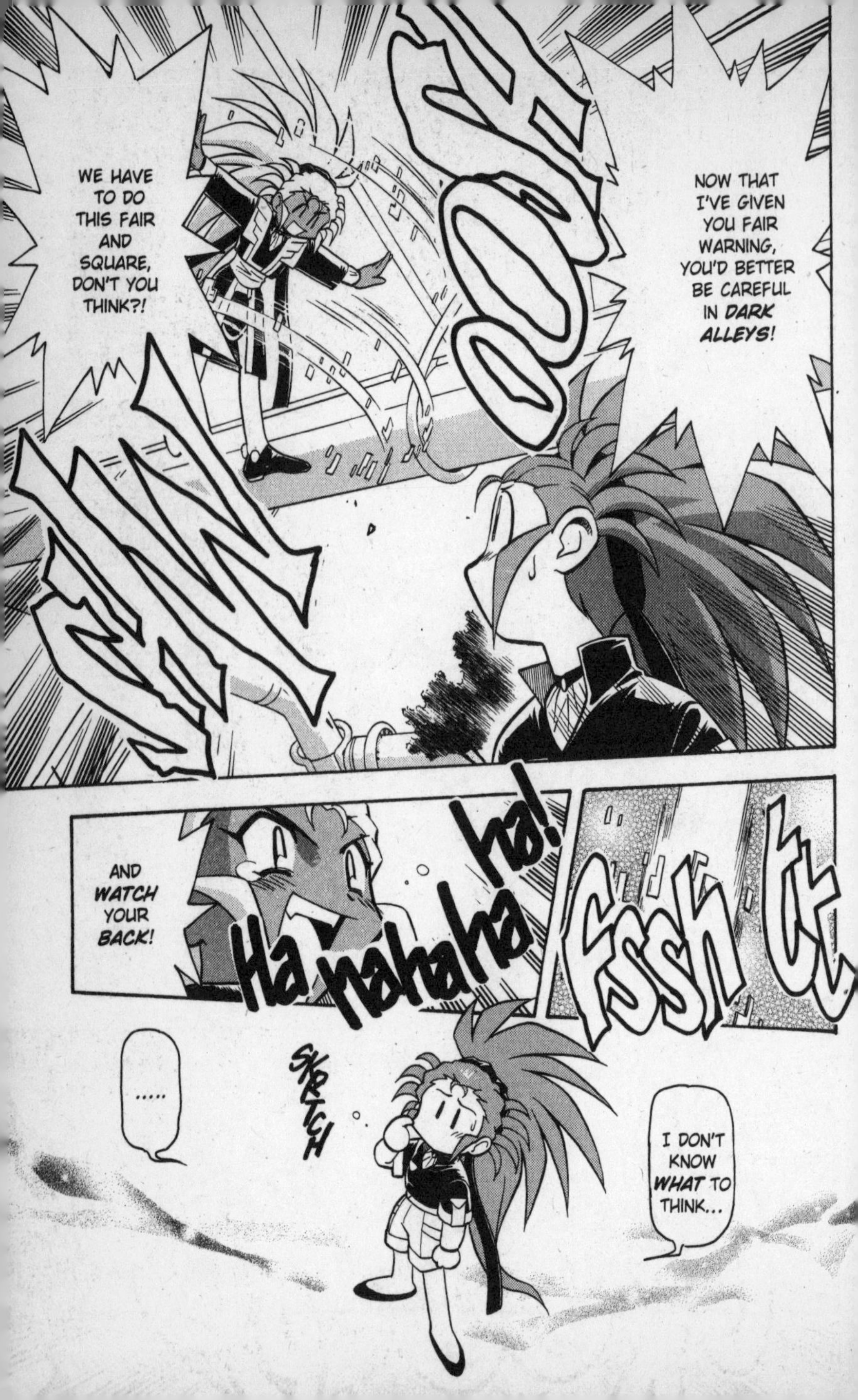
WE HAVE TO DO THIS FAIR AND SQUARE, DON'T YOU THINK?!
NOW THAT I'VE GIVEN YOU FAIR WARNING, YOU'D BETTER BE CAREFUL IN *DARK ALLEYS*!
AND *WATCH* YOUR *BACK*!
Ha hahaha ha!
fssh t
......
SKRTCH
I DON'T KNOW *WHAT* TO THINK...

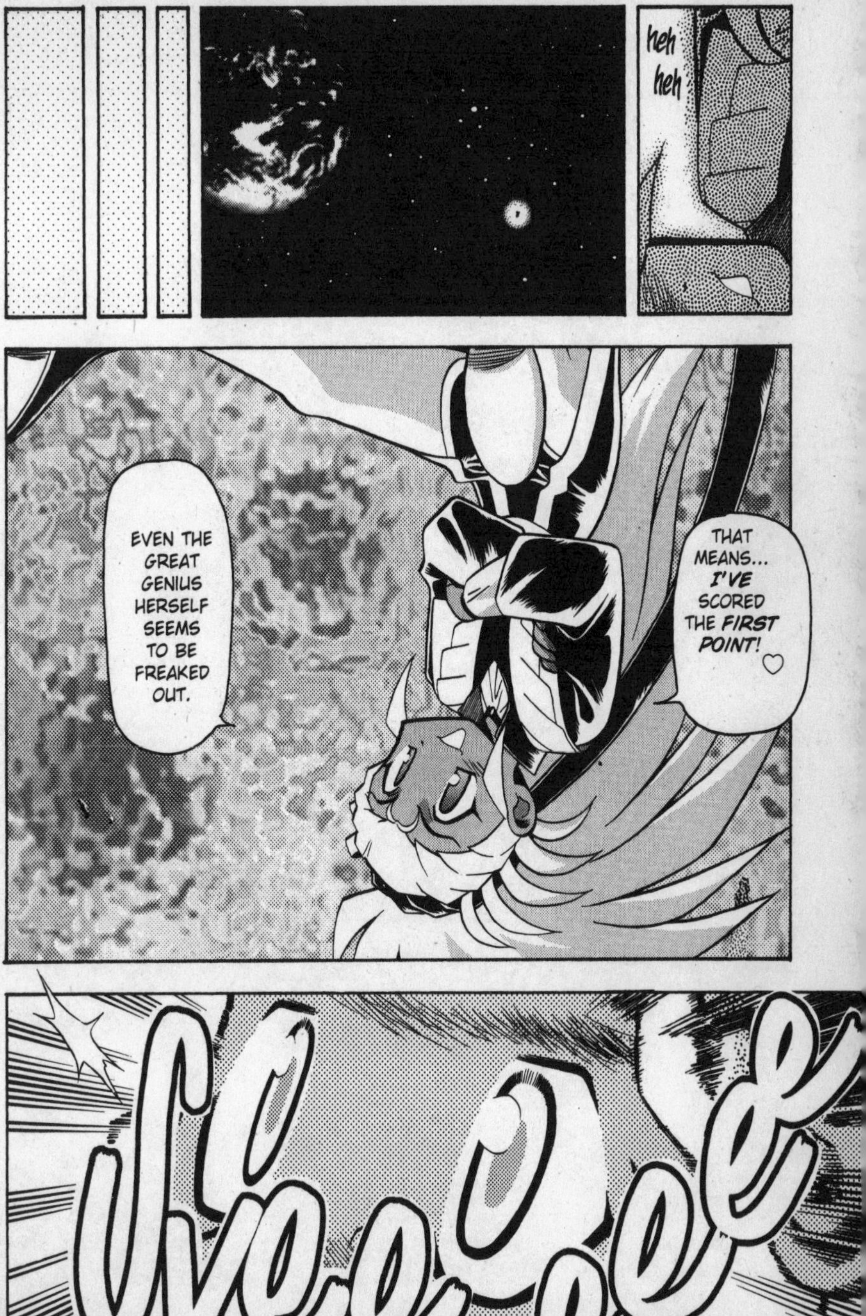
heh heh
EVEN THE GREAT GENIUS HERSELF SEEMS TO BE FREAKED OUT.
THAT MEANS... I'VE SCORED THE FIRST POINT! ♡
iKeeeeee

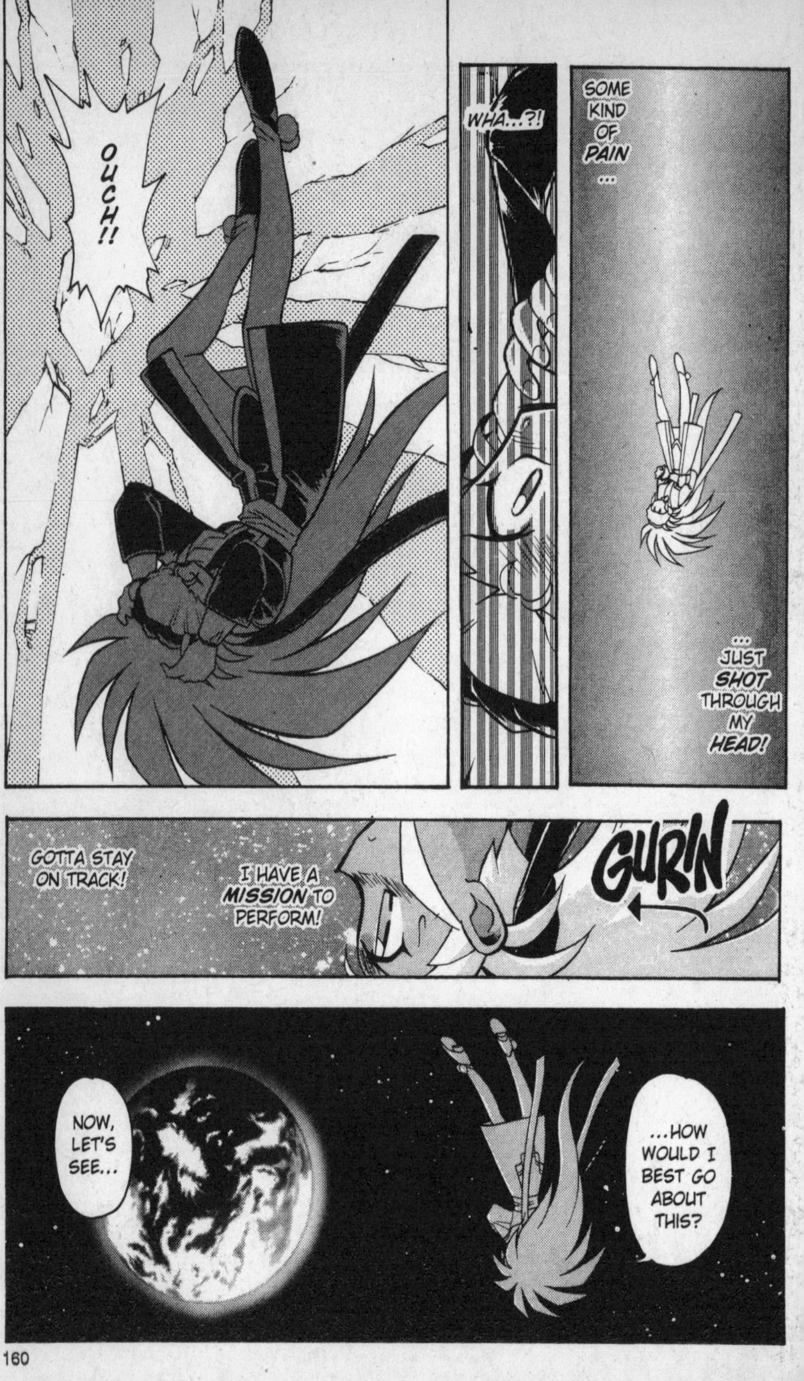
OUCH!!
WHA...?!
SOME KIND OF PAIN...
...JUST SHOT THROUGH MY HEAD!
GOTTA STAY ON TRACK!
I HAVE A MISSION TO PERFORM!
GURIN
NOW, LET'S SEE...
...HOW WOULD I BEST GO ABOUT THIS?

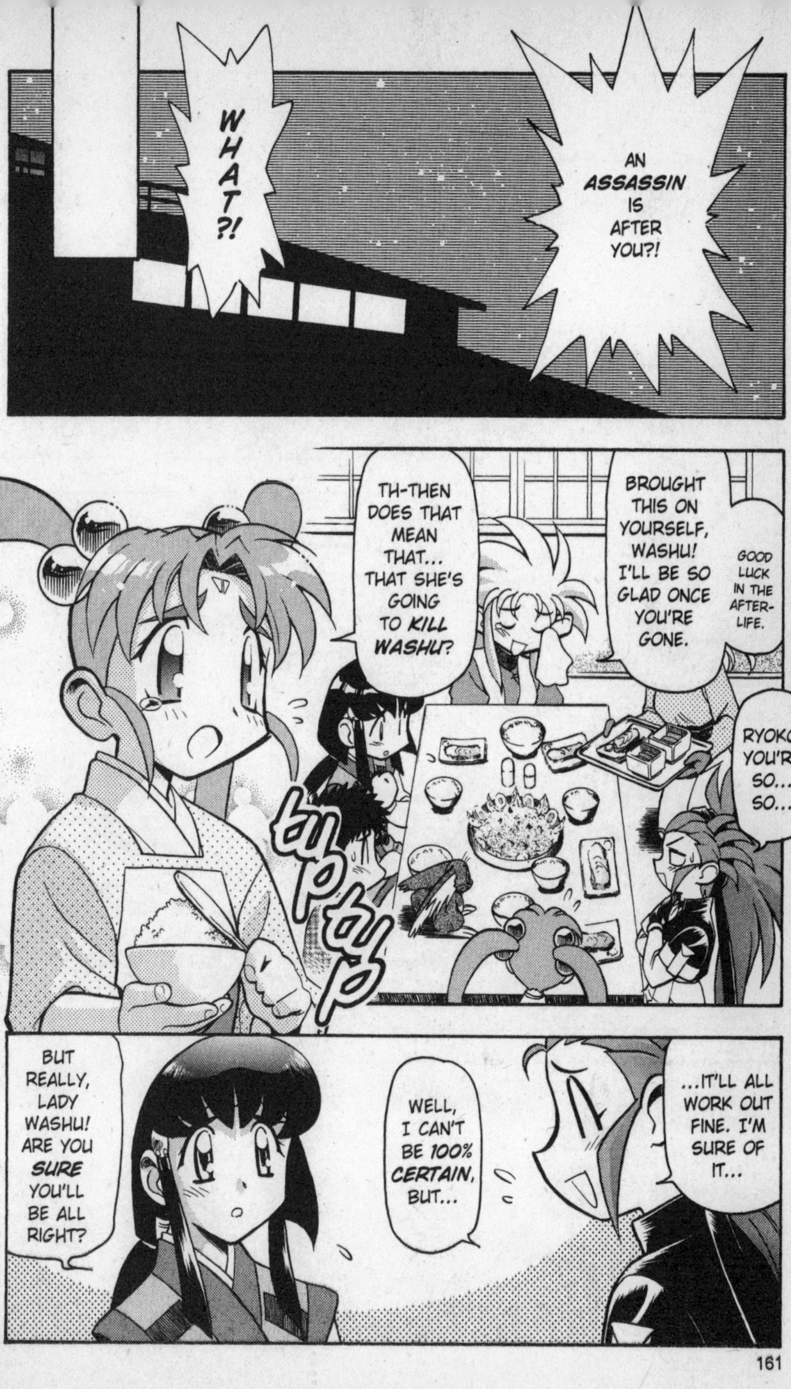
WHAT?!
AN ASSASSIN IS AFTER YOU?!
TH-THEN DOES THAT MEAN THAT... THAT SHE'S GOING TO KILL WASHU?
BROUGHT THIS ON YOURSELF, WASHU! I'LL BE SO GLAD ONCE YOU'RE GONE.
GOOD LUCK IN THE AFTER-LIFE.
RYOKO, YOU'RE SO... SO...
tup tup tup
BUT REALLY, LADY WASHU! ARE YOU SURE YOU'LL BE ALL RIGHT?
WELL, I CAN'T BE 100% CERTAIN, BUT...
...IT'LL ALL WORK OUT FINE. I'M SURE OF IT...

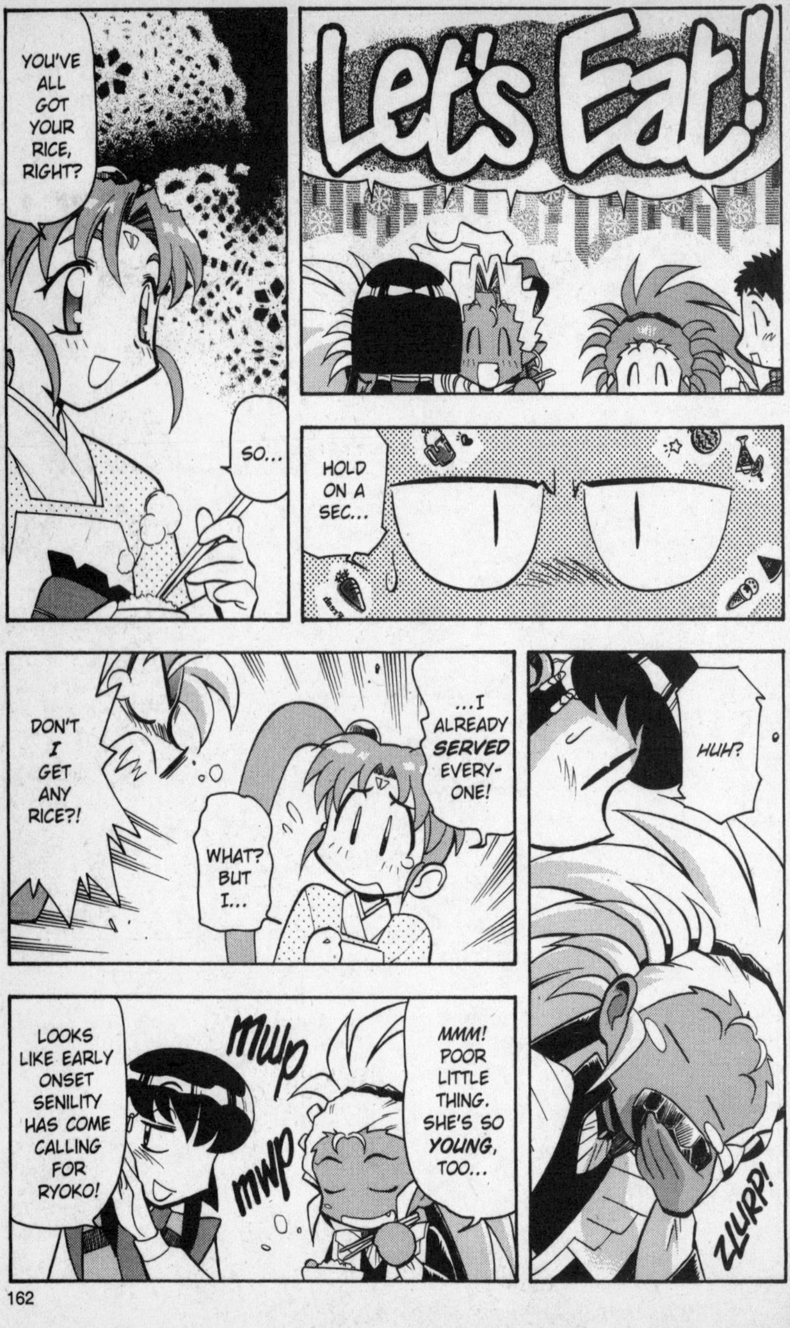

YOU'VE ALL GOT YOUR RICE, RIGHT?
Let's Eat!
SO...
HOLD ON A SEC...
DON'T I GET ANY RICE?!
WHAT? BUT I...
...I ALREADY SERVED EVERY-ONE!
HUH?
LOOKS LIKE EARLY ONSET SENILITY HAS COME CALLING FOR RYOKO!
MWP
MWP
MMM! POOR LITTLE THING. SHE'S SO YOUNG, TOO...
ZLURP!

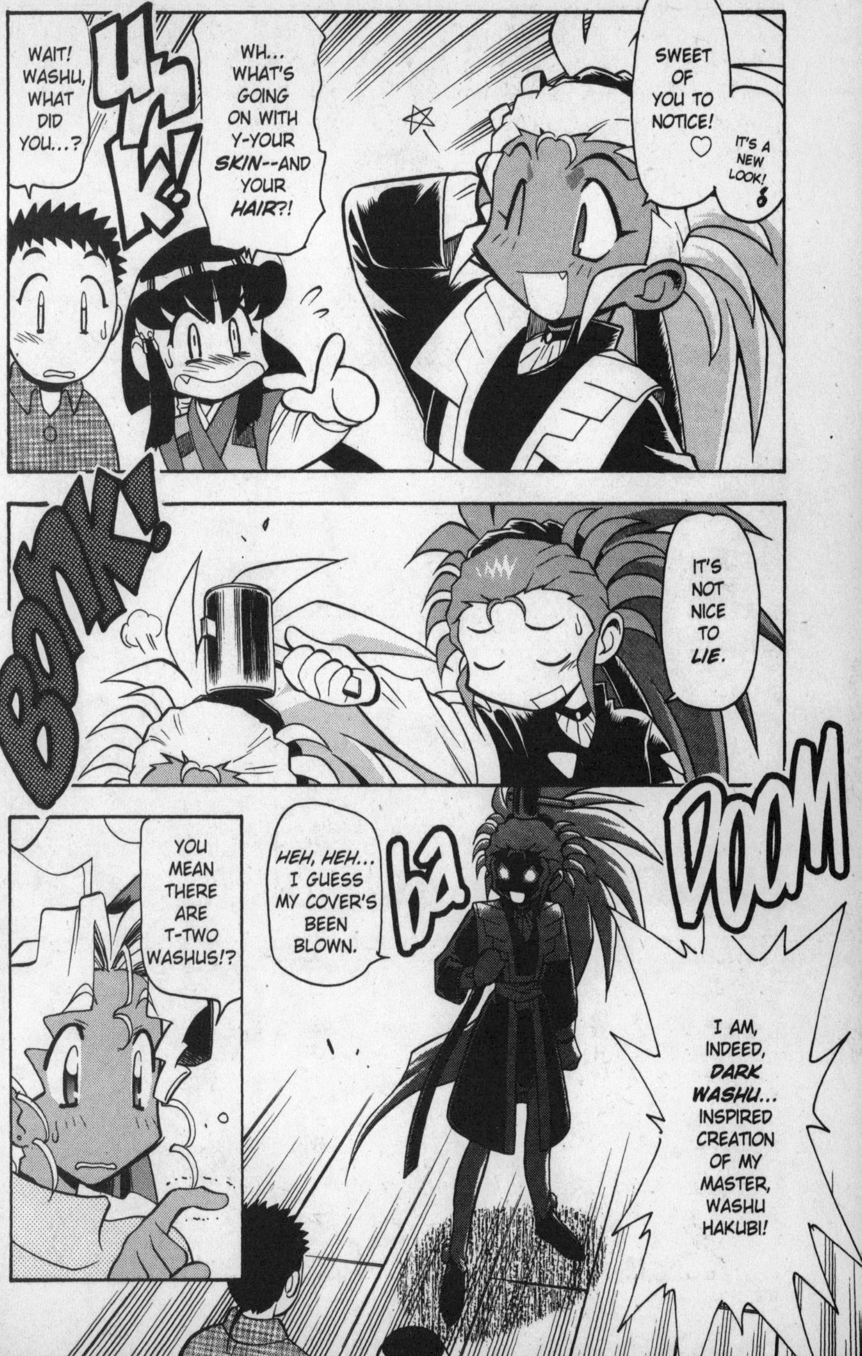
WAIT! WASHU, WHAT DID YOU...?
UNK!
WH... WHAT'S GOING ON WITH Y-YOUR SKIN--AND YOUR HAIR?!
SWEET OF YOU TO NOTICE! ♡
IT'S A NEW LOOK!
BONK!
IT'S NOT NICE TO LIE.
YOU MEAN THERE ARE T-TWO WASHUS!?
HEH, HEH... I GUESS MY COVER'S BEEN BLOWN.
BA
DOOM
I AM, INDEED, DARK WASHU... INSPIRED CREATION OF MY MASTER, WASHU HAKUBI!

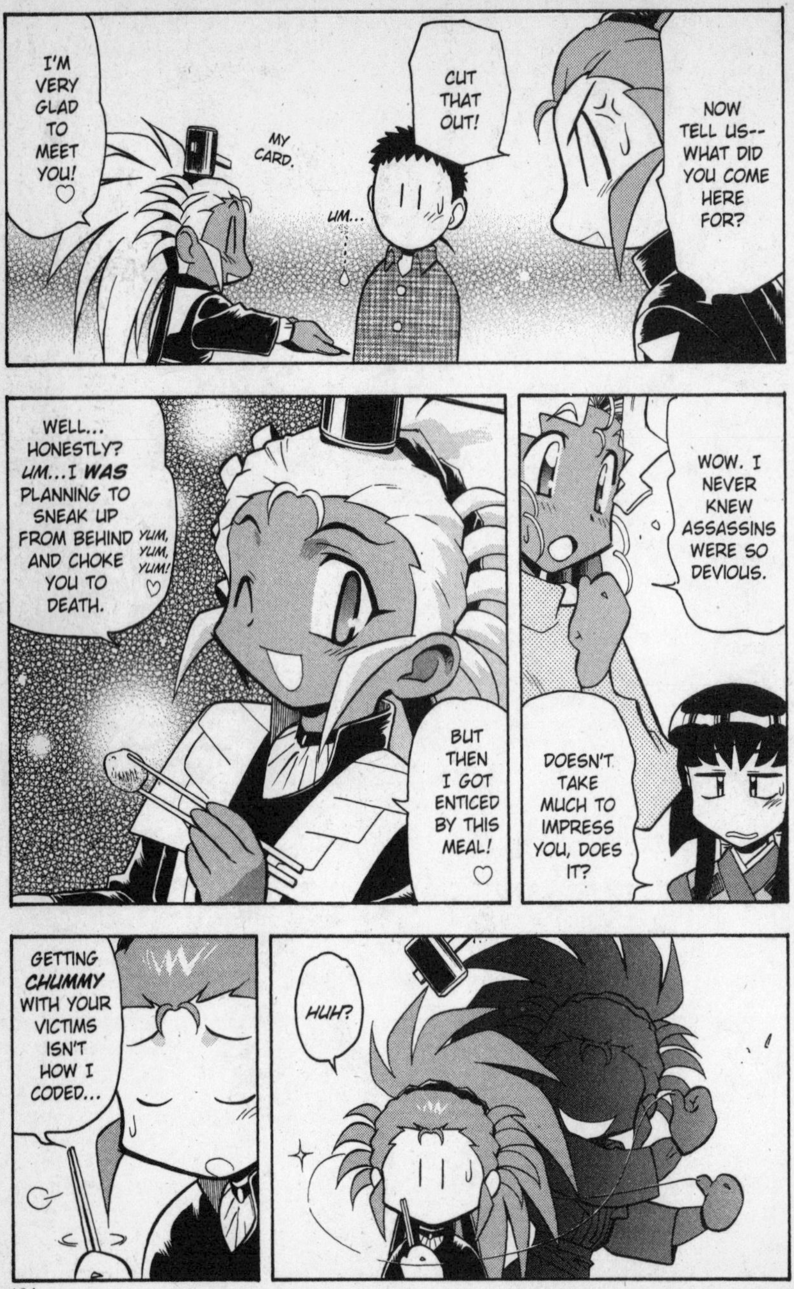
I'M VERY GLAD TO MEET YOU! ♡
MY CARD.
UM...
CUT THAT OUT!
NOW TELL US--WHAT DID YOU COME HERE FOR?
WELL... HONESTLY? UM...I WAS PLANNING TO SNEAK UP FROM BEHIND AND CHOKE YOU TO DEATH.
YUM, YUM, YUM! ♡
BUT THEN I GOT ENTICED BY THIS MEAL! ♡
WOW. I NEVER KNEW ASSASSINS WERE SO DEVIOUS.
DOESN'T TAKE MUCH TO IMPRESS YOU, DOES IT?
GETTING CHUMMY WITH YOUR VICTIMS ISN'T HOW I CODED...
HUH?

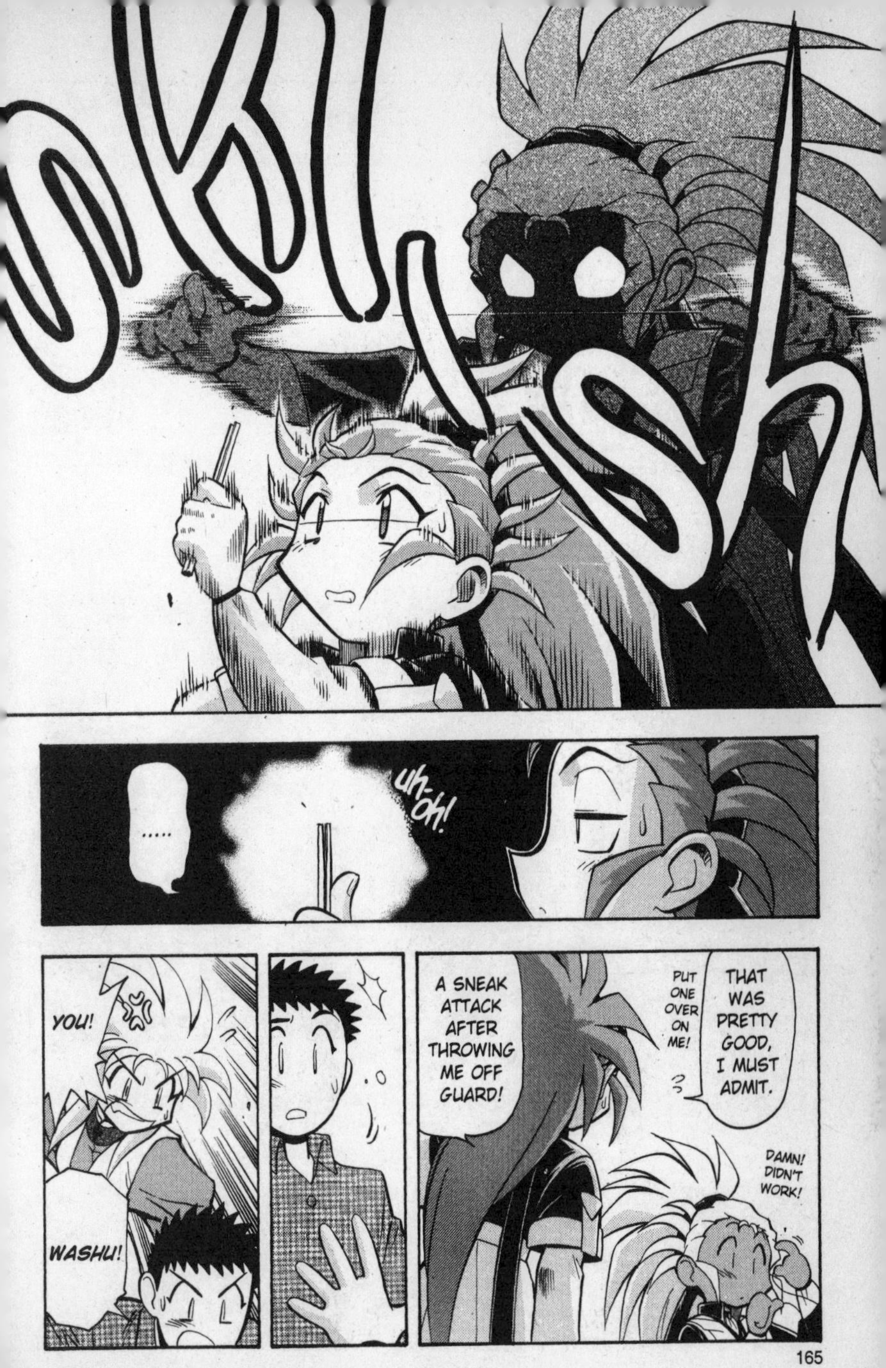
......
uh-oh!
YOU!
WASHU!
A SNEAK ATTACK AFTER THROWING ME OFF GUARD!
PUT ONE OVER ON ME!
THAT WAS PRETTY GOOD, I MUST ADMIT.
DAMN! DIDN'T WORK!

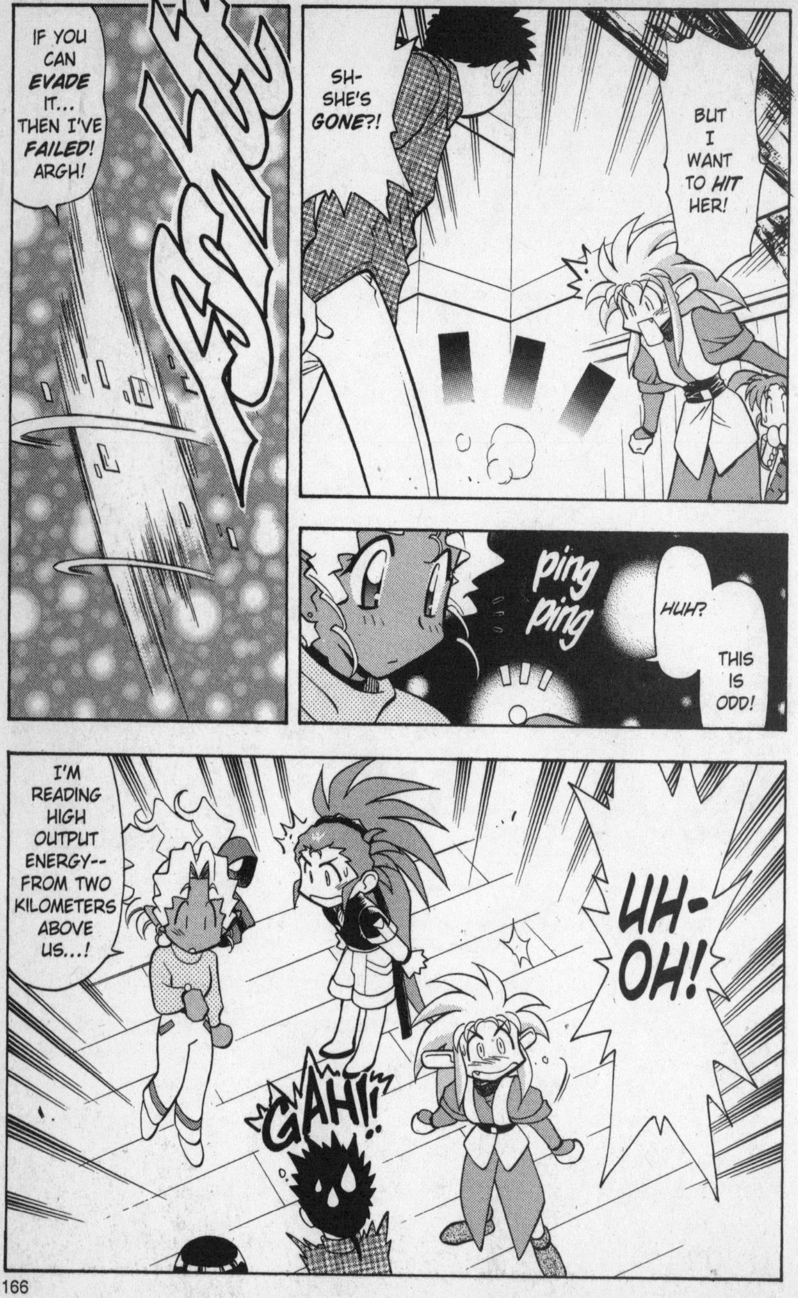
IF YOU CAN EVADE IT... THEN I'VE FAILED! ARGH!
SH-SHE'S GONE?!
BUT I WANT TO HIT HER!
ping ping
HUH?
THIS IS ODD!
I'M READING HIGH OUTPUT ENERGY-- FROM TWO KILOMETERS ABOVE US...!
UH-OH!
GAH!!

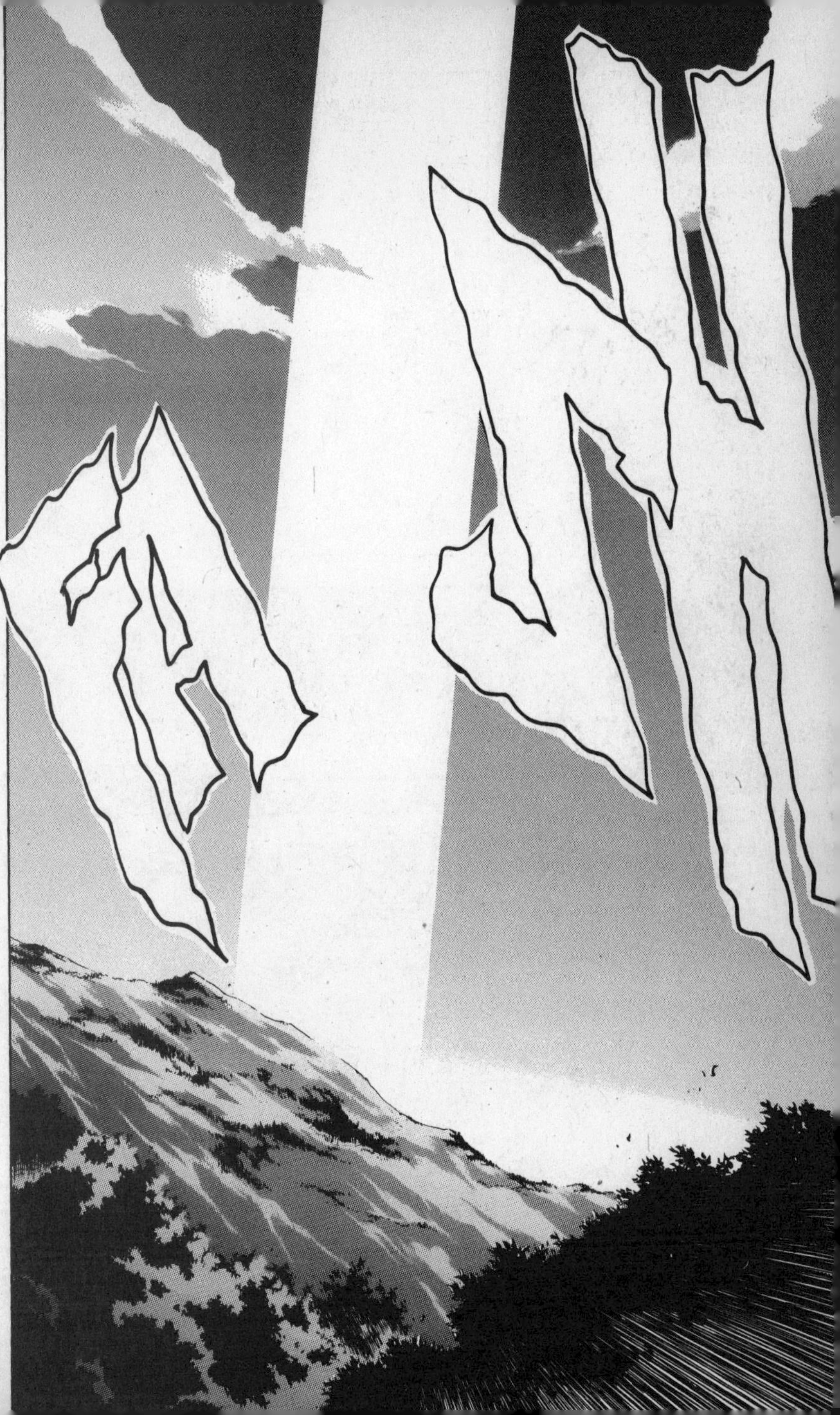

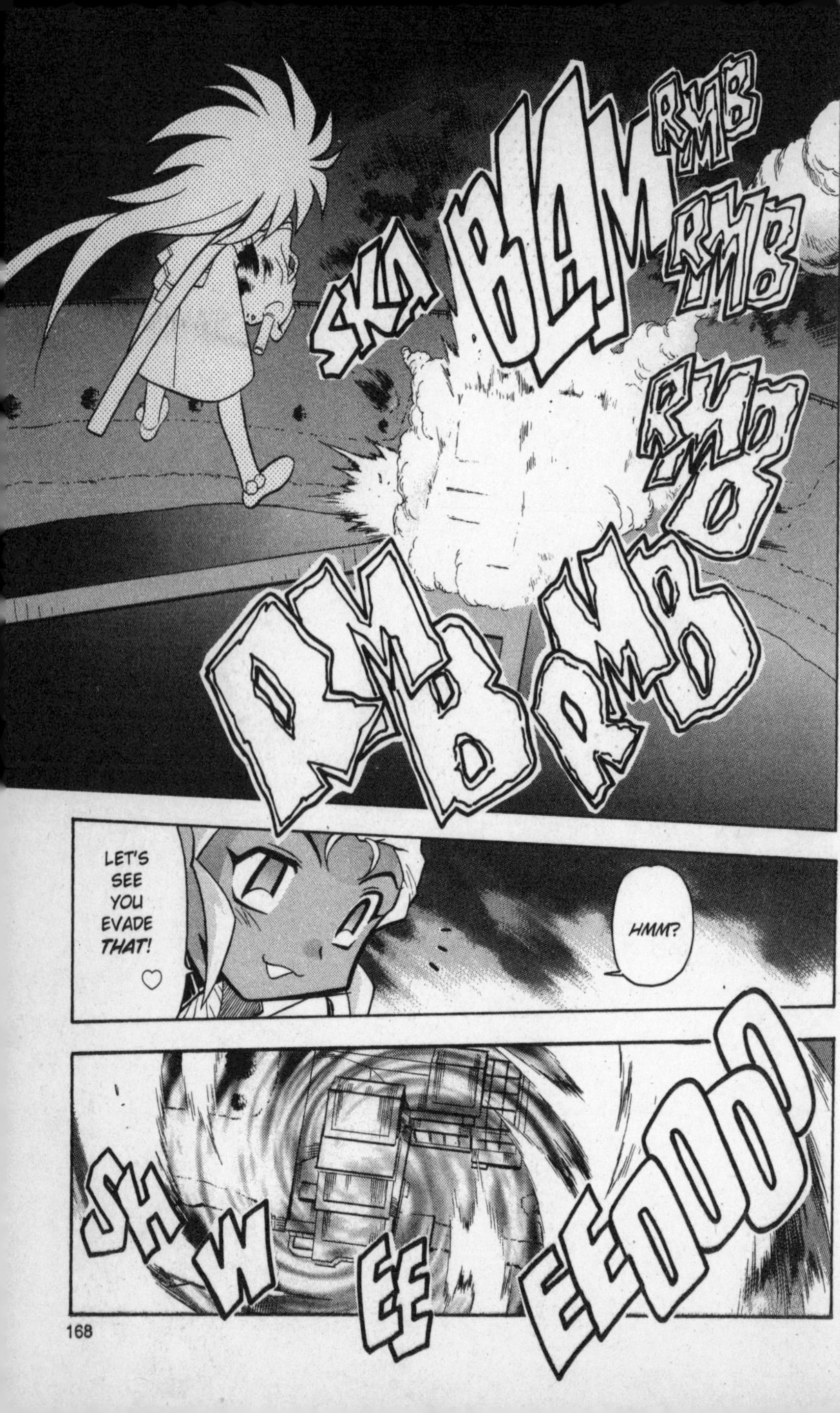
SKA BLAM
RMB RMB
RMB RMB
RMB
RMB RMB
RMB RMB
LET'S SEE YOU EVADE THAT! ♡
HMM?
SHWEE EEOOOO

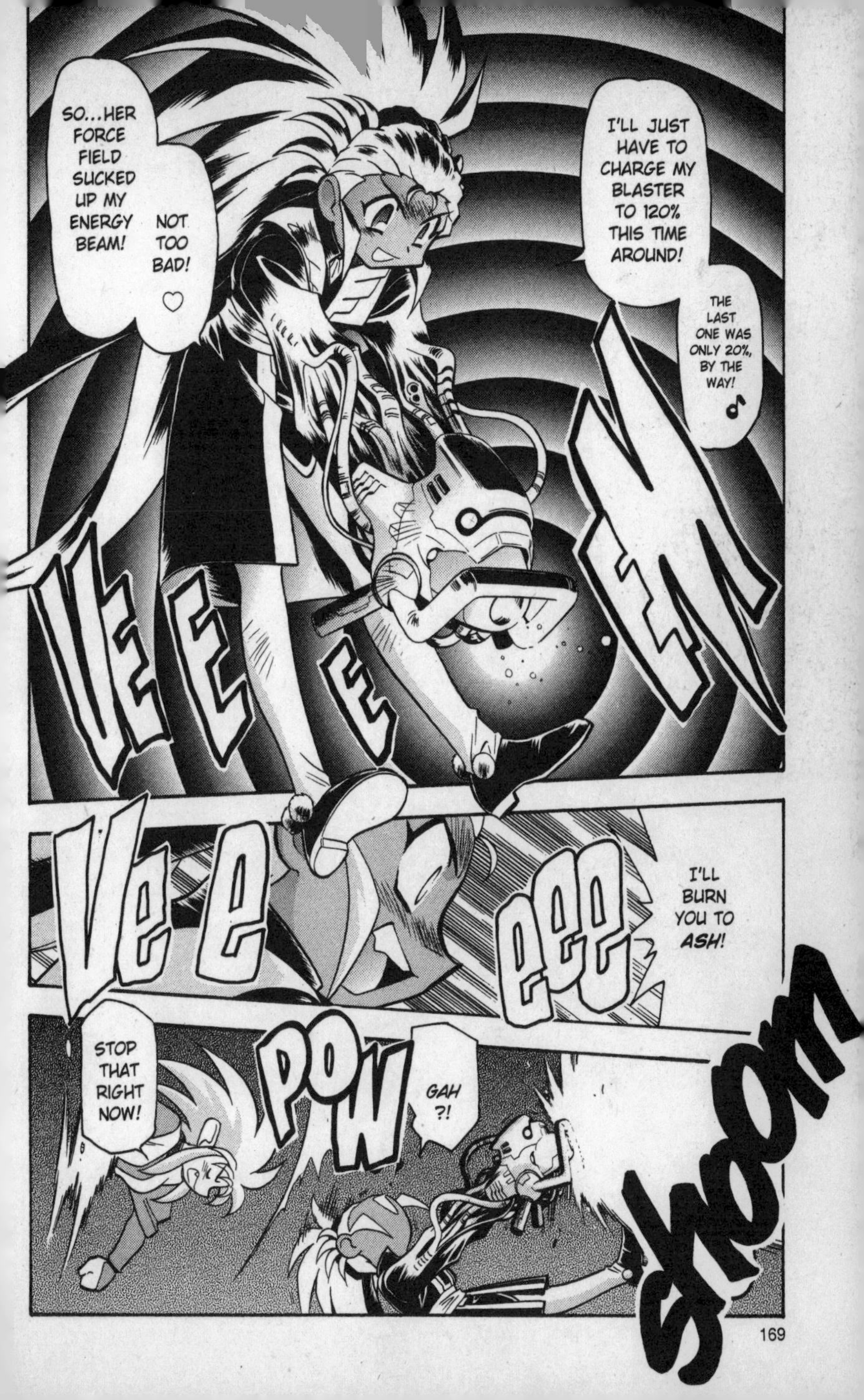
SO...HER FORCE FIELD SUCKED UP MY ENERGY BEAM!
NOT TOO BAD! ♡
I'LL JUST HAVE TO CHARGE MY BLASTER TO 120% THIS TIME AROUND!
THE LAST ONE WAS ONLY 20%, BY THE WAY! ♪
VEEEEM
VEEEEE
I'LL BURN YOU TO ASH!
STOP THAT RIGHT NOW!
POW
GAH ?!
SHOOM

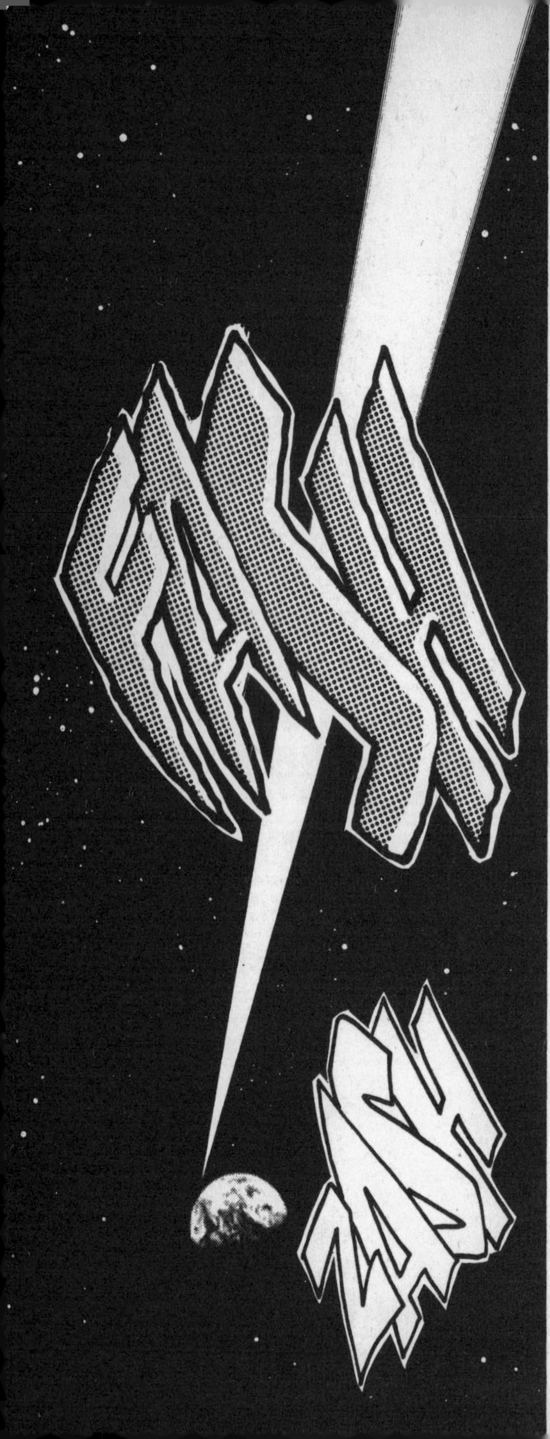

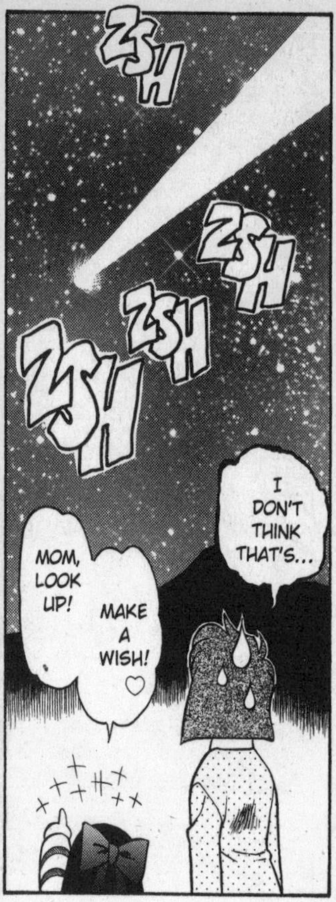
ZSH
ZSH
ZSH
ZSH
MOM, LOOK UP!
MAKE A WISH!
I DON'T THINK THAT'S...

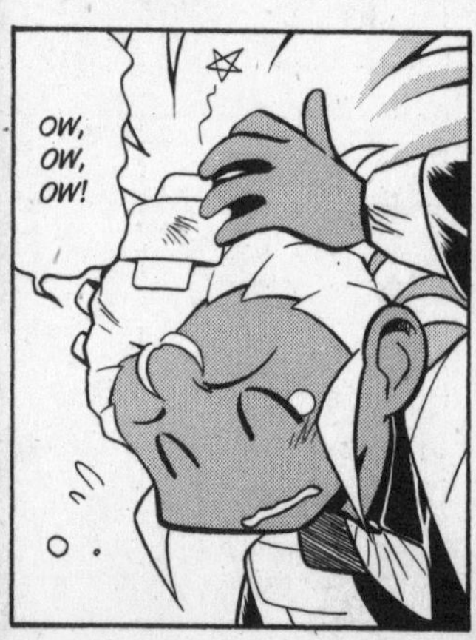
OW, OW, OW!

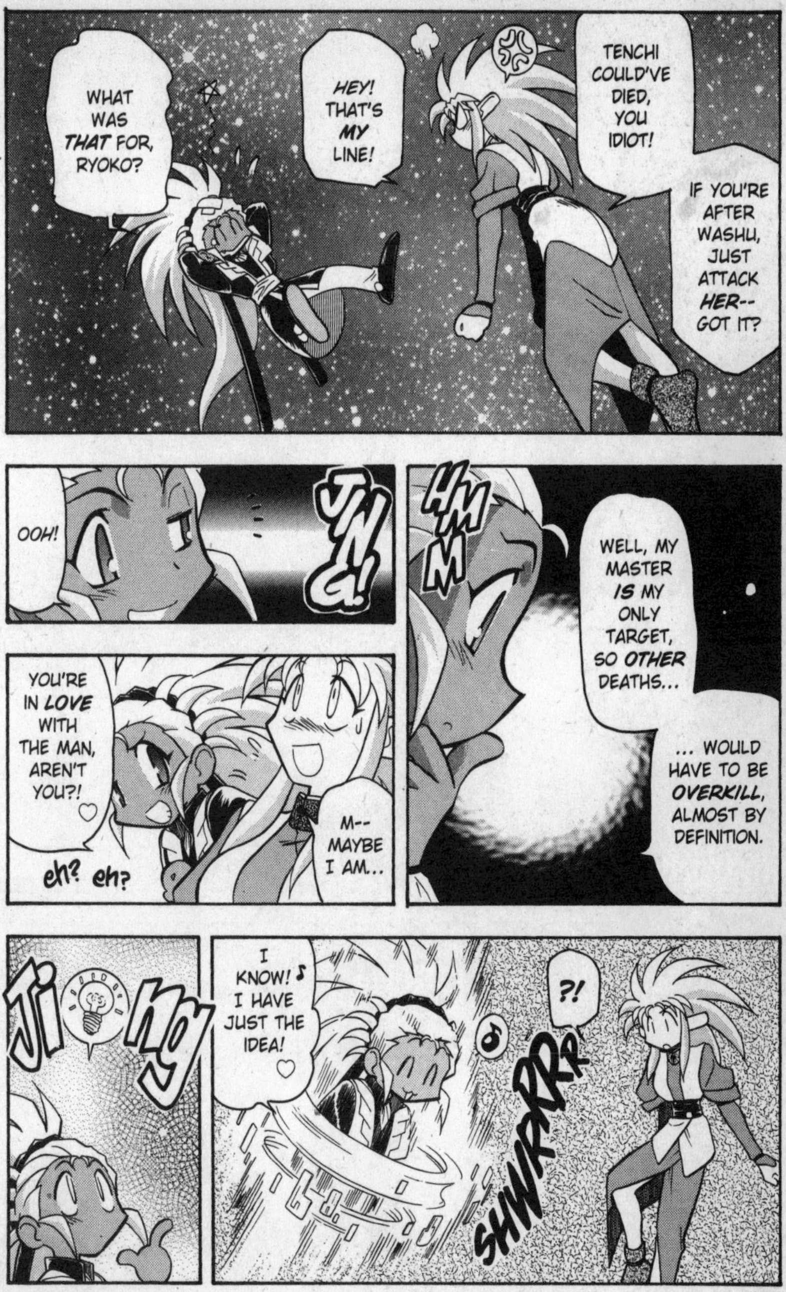
WHAT WAS THAT FOR, RYOKO?
HEY! THAT'S MY LINE!
TENCHI COULD'VE DIED, YOU IDIOT!
IF YOU'RE AFTER WASHU, JUST ATTACK HER-- GOT IT?
OOH!
JING!
HMMM
WELL, MY MASTER IS MY ONLY TARGET, SO OTHER DEATHS...
... WOULD HAVE TO BE OVERKILL, ALMOST BY DEFINITION.
YOU'RE IN LOVE WITH THE MAN, AREN'T YOU?! ♡
eh? eh?
M-- MAYBE I AM...
Jiong
I KNOW! ♪ I HAVE JUST THE IDEA! ♡
?!
SHWRRR

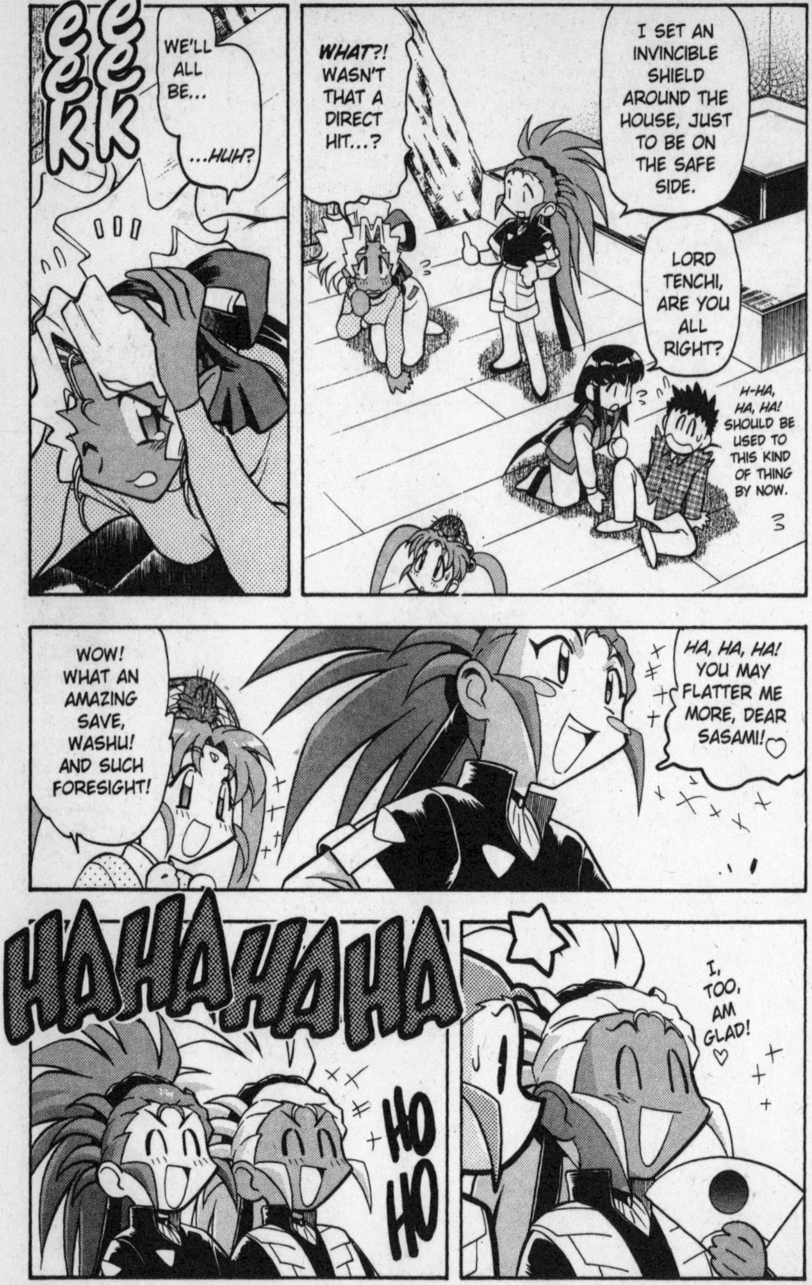
EEEK
WE'LL ALL BE...
...HUH?
WHAT?! WASN'T THAT A DIRECT HIT...?
I SET AN INVINCIBLE SHIELD AROUND THE HOUSE, JUST TO BE ON THE SAFE SIDE.
LORD TENCHI, ARE YOU ALL RIGHT?
H-HA, HA, HA! SHOULD BE USED TO THIS KIND OF THING BY NOW.
WOW! WHAT AN AMAZING SAVE, WASHU! AND SUCH FORESIGHT!
HA, HA, HA! YOU MAY FLATTER ME MORE, DEAR SASAMI! ♡
HAHAHAHAHA
HO HO
I, TOO, AM GLAD! ♡

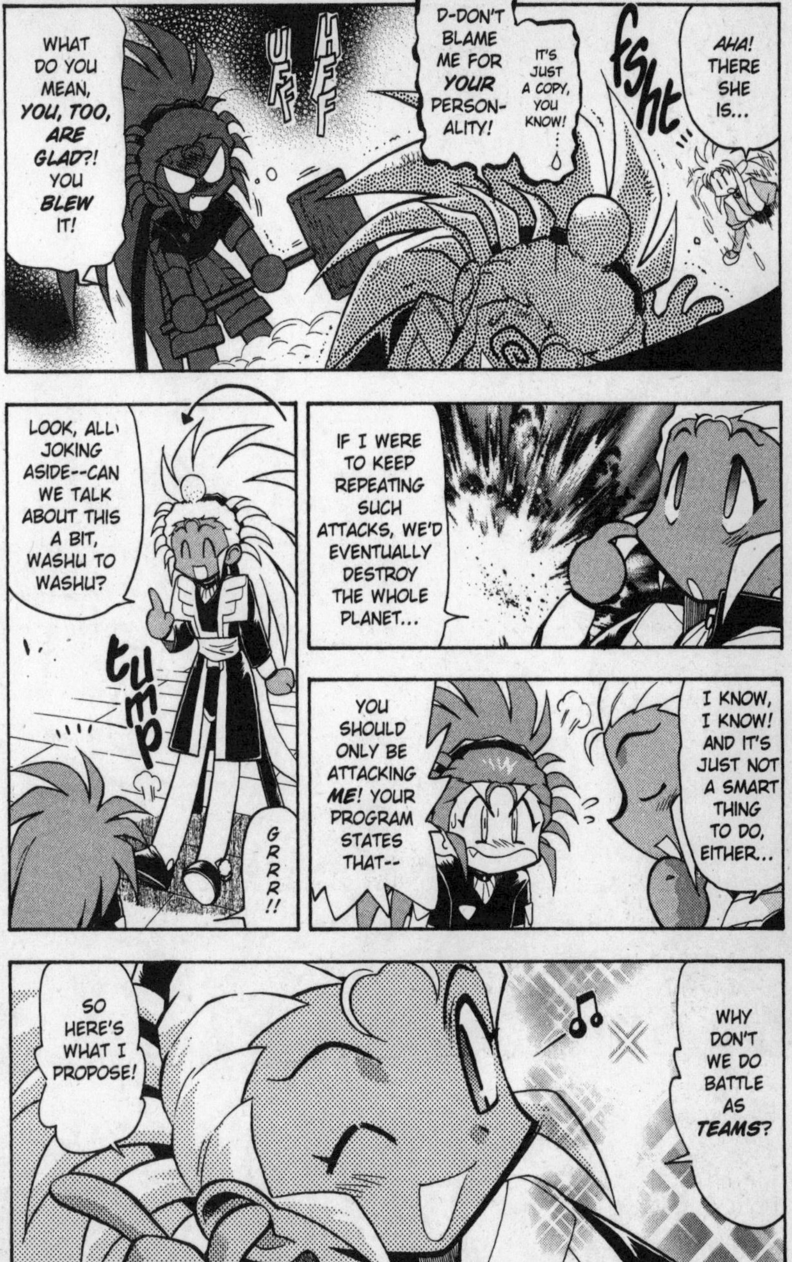
WHAT DO YOU MEAN, YOU, TOO, ARE GLAD?! YOU BLEW IT!
UFF
HFF
D-DON'T BLAME ME FOR YOUR PERSONALITY!
IT'S JUST A COPY, YOU KNOW!
fsht
AHA! THERE SHE IS...
LOOK, ALL JOKING ASIDE--CAN WE TALK ABOUT THIS A BIT, WASHU TO WASHU?
tump
GRRR!!
IF I WERE TO KEEP REPEATING SUCH ATTACKS, WE'D EVENTUALLY DESTROY THE WHOLE PLANET...
YOU SHOULD ONLY BE ATTACKING ME! YOUR PROGRAM STATES THAT--
I KNOW, I KNOW! AND IT'S JUST NOT A SMART THING TO DO, EITHER...
SO HERE'S WHAT I PROPOSE!
WHY DON'T WE DO BATTLE AS TEAMS?

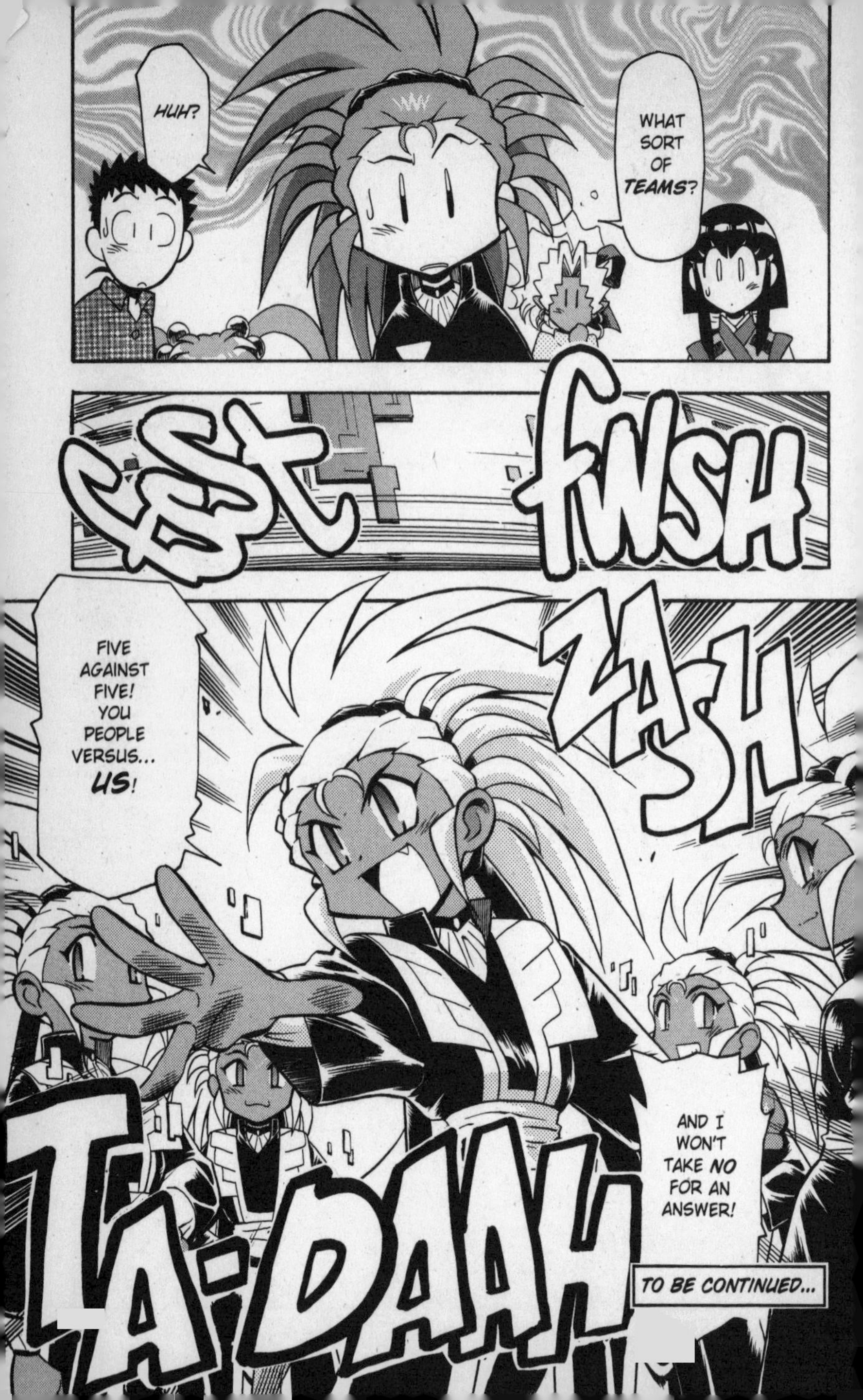
HUH?
WHAT SORT OF TEAMS?
FSST
FWSH
FIVE AGAINST FIVE! YOU PEOPLE VERSUS... US!
ZASH
AND I WON'T TAKE NO FOR AN ANSWER!
TA-DAAH
TO BE CONTINUED...

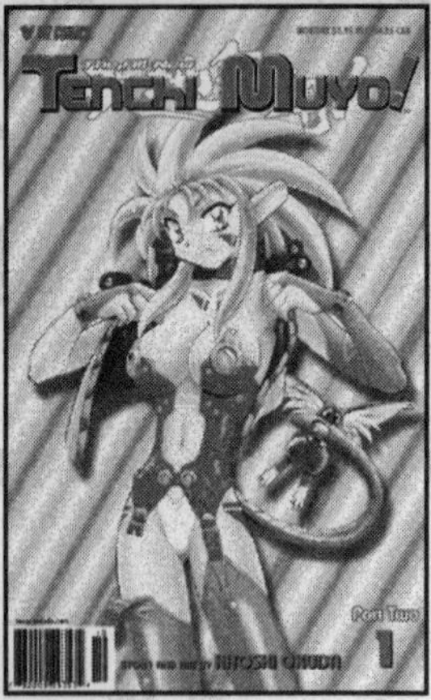
Tenchi Muyo!
Part Two
1
STORY AND ART BY HITOSHI OKUDA

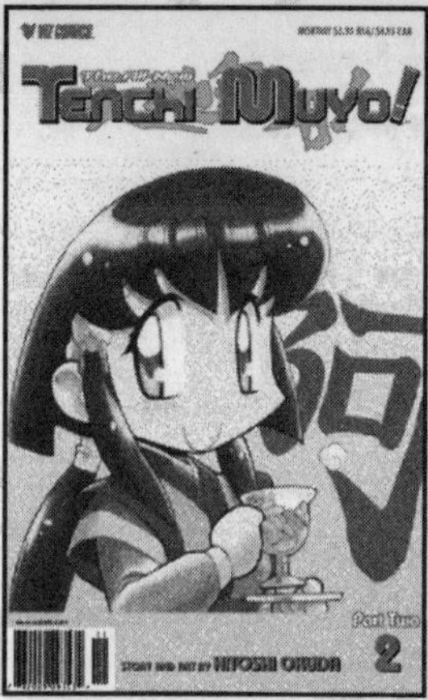
Tenchi Muyo!
Part Two
2
STORY AND ART BY HITOSHI OKUDA

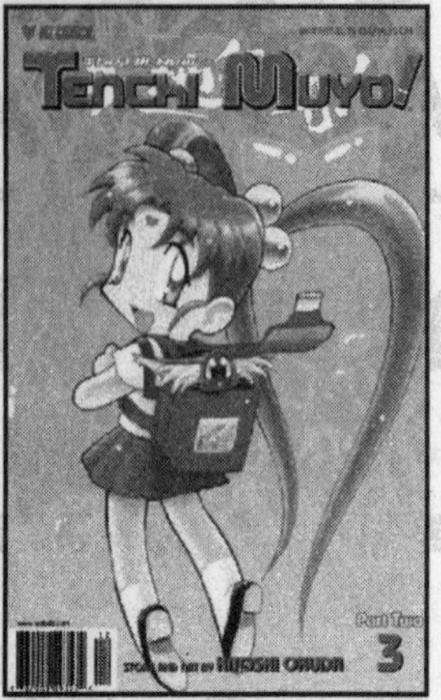
Tenchi Muyo!
Part Two
3
STORY AND ART BY HITOSHI OKUDA

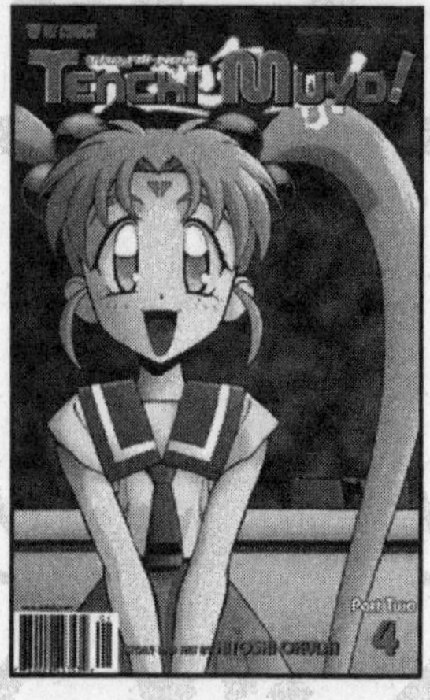
Tenchi Muyo!
Part Two
4

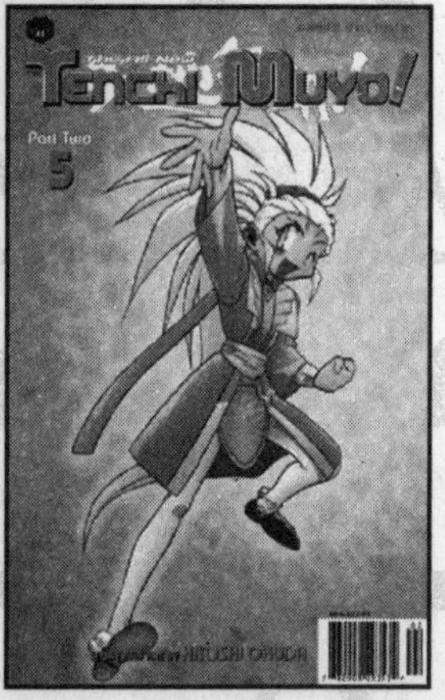
Tenchi Muyo!
Part Two
5
HITOSHI OKUDA

COVER GALLERY

The material in this volume was originally published by Kadokawa Shoten Publishing Co., LTD., Tokyo. The U.S. edition was first published by VIZ, LLC in monthly comics form as The All-New Tenchi Muyô! Part 2 #1 through #5. All covers were drawn by Hitoshi Okuda and all Viz covers were designed by Hidemi Sahara. The covers for Part 2 #4 and Part 2 #5 were colored by Paul Wilson.

In the beginning there was Tenchi...

Looking back, it all happened so fast. I saw the job posting on the Viz Web site, I applied for the job, I interviewed for the job and I was offered the job. Suddenly, I was an editor for the most revered publisher of manga in the U.S. My head was spinning.

Immediately, I was given a stack of **Tenchi** books, comics, DVDs, CDs and merch. My first assignment was simple: dive headfirst into the zany world of **Tenchi Muyô!**

As such, this volume contains my first tentative steps as a comic book editor. I took over for Jason Thompson, who, in turn, took over for Carl Gustav Horn and Annette Roman before him. In other words, I would be carrying the torch kept aflame by three of the best editors in the business.

No pressure, right?

Plus, over the years, the **Tenchi** books (along with a handful of other titles like **Ranma 1/2** and **InuYasha**) had firmly established themselves as the bedrock of the Viz empire. As a newbie, I didn't want to come in here and screw up a good thing. Thousands of **Tenchi Muyô!** fans were most assuredly counting on me.

I did the homework and hopefully I haven't disappointed anyone. I read the books, watched the videos, listened to the CDs and established a dialogue with all the readers who took the time to write letters. In the end, I'm happy to report the good ship **Tenchi Muyô!** remains afloat without a single leak.

But really, despite my initial worries, I was never totally without a safety net. Every single one of my coworkers came forth with help and advice when I needed it. Readers, too, chimed in with their comments and encouragements.

That, ultimately, was the most pleasant thing I discovered. The **Tenchi** universe is filled with thousands of friendly people. And believe me, I'm thankful for every single one.

Eric Searleman
Editor of **The All-New Tenchi Muyô!**

Do you *love* Tenchi Muyô!?

Here's some additional books the editor recommends:

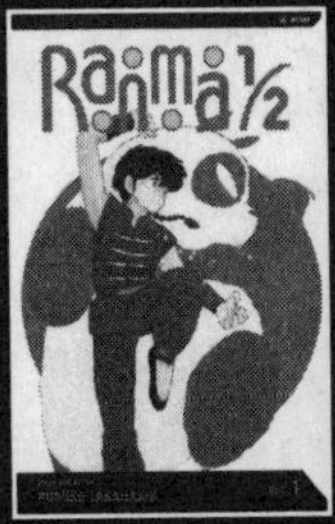
Ranma 1/2

• Ranma 1/2:
Gender mix-ups, martial arts shenanigans and regular bathing (?) power this well-loved comedy series from Rumiko Takahashi. The yin yang of sexual identity was never so much fun.

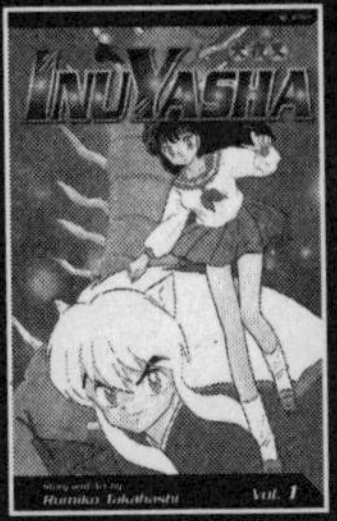
InuYasha
Rumiko Takahashi
vol. 1

• InuYasha:
Worlds collide when a teenager suddenly finds herself trapped in an ancient Japanese fairy tale. From the creator of **Ranma 1/2**, here's the historical fantasy adventure which proves sometimes a dog can be a girl's best friend.

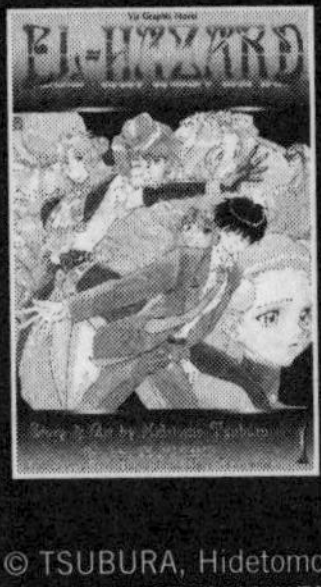
El-Hazard

• El-Hazard:
Screwball science fiction adventures don't get any more screwy than this. Can an average teenage boy defeat evil and fall in love at the same time? The answer is... maybe!

LOVE MANGA? LET US KNOW!

☐ Please do NOT send me information about VIZ products, news and events, special offers, or other information.

☐ Please do NOT send me information from VIZ' trusted business partners.

Name: _____

Address: _____

City: _____ **State:** _____ **Zip:** _____

E-mail: _____

☐ Male ☐ Female   Date of Birth (mm/dd/yyyy): ___ / ___ / _____   (Under 13? Parental consent required)

What race/ethnicity do you consider yourself? (check all that apply)

☐ White/Caucasian   ☐ Black/African American   ☐ Hispanic/Latino

☐ Asian/Pacific Islander   ☐ Native American/Alaskan Native   ☐ Other: _____

What VIZ shojo title(s) did you purchase? (indicate title(s) purchased)

_____

_____

What other VIZ shojo titles do you own? _____

_____

Reason for purchase: (check all that apply)

☐ Special offer   ☐ Favorite title / author / artist / genre

☐ Gift   ☐ Recommendation   ☐ Collection

☐ Read excerpt in VIZ manga sampler   ☐ Other _____

Where did you make your purchase? (please check one)

☐ Comic store   ☐ Bookstore   ☐ Grocery Store

☐ Convention   ☐ Newsstand   ☐ Video Game Store

☐ Online (site: _____)   ☐ Other _____

How many manga titles have you purchased in the last year? How many were VIZ titles?
(please check one from each column)

MANGA	VIZ
☐ None	☐ None
☐ 1 – 4	☐ 1 – 4
☐ 5 – 10	☐ 5 – 10
☐ 11+	☐ 11+

How much influence do special promotions and gifts-with-purchase have on the titles you buy?
(please circle, with 5 being great influence and 1 being none)

1 2 3 4 5

Do you purchase every volume of your favorite series?

☐ Yes! Gotta have 'em as my own ☐ No. Please explain: ______________________

What kind of manga storylines do you most enjoy? **(check all that apply)**

☐ Action / Adventure	☐ Science Fiction	☐ Horror
☐ Comedy	☐ Romance (shojo)	☐ Fantasy (shojo)
☐ Fighting	☐ Sports	☐ Historical
☐ Artistic / Alternative	☐ Other ______________________	

If you watch the anime or play a video or TCG game from a series, how likely are you to buy the manga? **(please circle, with 5 being very likely and 1 being unlikely)**

1 2 3 4 5

If unlikely, please explain: ______________________

Who are your favorite authors / artists? ______________________

____

What titles would like you translated and sold in English? ______________________

____

THANK YOU! Please send the completed form to:

VIZ media

NJW Research
42 Catharine Street
Poughkeepsie, NY 12601

Your privacy is very important to us. All information provided will be used for internal purposes only and will not be sold or otherwise divulged.